*West African Poetry*

# West African Poetry

## A CRITICAL HISTORY

*Robert Fraser*

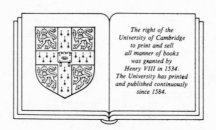

The right of the
University of Cambridge
to print and sell
all manner of books
was granted by
Henry VIII in 1534.
The University has printed
and published continuously
since 1584.

**Cambridge University Press**

CAMBRIDGE

LONDON   NEW YORK   NEW ROCHELLE

MELBOURNE   SYDNEY

Published by the Press Syndicate of the University of Cambridge
The Pitt Building, Trumpington Street, Cambridge CB2 1RP
32 East 57th Street, New York, NY 10022, USA
10 Stamford Road, Oakleigh, Melbourne 3166, Australia

First published 1986

Printed in Great Britain by
Redwood Burn Limited, Trowbridge, Wiltshire

*British Library cataloguing in publication data*
Fraser, Robert, 1947–
West African poetry: a critical history.
1. African literature – History and criticism
I. Title
809.1    PL8010

*Library of Congress cataloguing in publication data*
Fraser, Robert, 1947–
West African poetry.
Includes index.
1. West African poetry – History and criticism.
I. Title.
PL8014.W37F73 1986    809.1'00966    85–29976

ISBN 0 521 30993 X hard covers
ISBN 0 521 31223 X paperback

FOR
*Susheila Nasta*

AND FOR
*Stewart Brown*

# Contents

# Acknowledgements

The author and publisher would like to thank Heinemann Educational Books for permission to use translations of prose and poetry from Leopold Sédar Senghor, *Nocturnes*, trans. John Reed and Clive Wake, pp. 53–4 and Jean-Joseph Rabéarivelo, *Translations from the Night*, trans. John Reed and Clive Wake, p. 7; and also Oxford University Press for John Reed and Clive Wake (eds.), *Leopold Sédar Senghor: Prose and Poetry*, pp. 83, 103, 106–7, 109, 111–12, 150–1, 157.

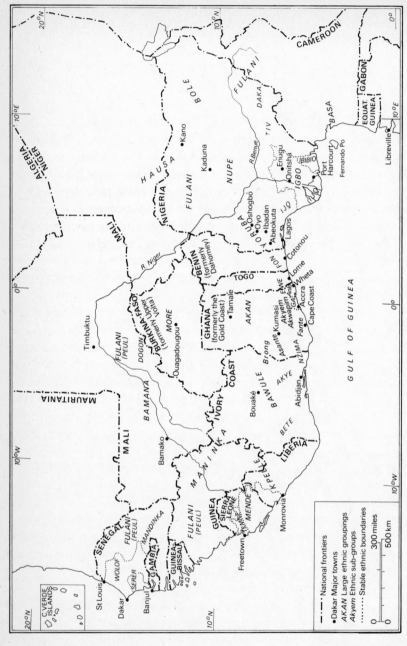

West Africa: State borders and principal ethnic groupings

# Introduction

When choosing a title for his book it pays an author to tread warily. Too small a scope may cramp his style, while wider prospects may raise expectations which he cannot fulfil. In approaching the seemingly infinite subject of West African poetry I have limited my sights in two important respects. I have not sought to cover fully the voluminous field of vernacular orature, a task for which I possess neither space nor competence. Nor have I provided an entirely representative survey of poetry written in Portuguese or French. A glance at the contents page will confirm that throughout my principal focus has been the procession of poets who have emerged in English-speaking Africa since the end of the Second World War.

To treat of this and only this, however, would have been to demonstrate a shortsightedness of which I hope not to be accused. No cultural phenomenon exists in isolation, and especially not the most fluid art of poetry. Therefore as fast as I have battened down the hatches I have opened up port-holes to the fresh sea breezes. Since written verse from this part of the world has always drawn much of its richness from its oral foundations, my opening and closing chapters propose tentative ideas as to the relationship between the two, ideas which also to a certain extent serve as guidelines for the remainder of the book. My second chapter examines the origins of written verse in the eighteenth, nineteenth and early twentieth centuries. And my third and eleventh chapters between them provide an accompanying account of developments in French-speaking West Africa, less as a token gesture toward francophone poetry than as a much needed insight into one significant element in the pervading cultural milieu over the period I have elected to discuss.

The justification for such a book at this time can only stem from its adoption of an historical perspective. Criticism of contemporary literature is notoriously prone to crippling impulses of advocacy or disparagement which result from the critic himself existing in the thick of battle. To the extent that such comment may lay claim to the term 'criticism' at all, it does so in the same sense as does the periodical review. Viewed from an historical standpoint it soon comes to appear almost as much a branch of literature as the writing which it surveys. When the dust of battle has settled and truces have been signed, a different kind of exercise becomes possible. Priorities become easier to establish, and something like a canon begins to emerge.

Very little criticism of modern African literature has allowed itself the luxury of such detachment. The political and social exigencies of societies undergoing rapid change have forced the critic into the rôle of watchdog while besetting the writer himself with restrictive demands. Since by common consent a poetic literature of great worth has now come to light, it may now at last be time to ask ourselves far-reaching questions as to what this literature consists of and by what stages it has evolved.

In the present study the primary emphasis is unashamedly on form. I have tried to broach tentative conclusions as to the fundamental nature of written African verse, conclusions as to what extent it is appropriate to consider it a cultural hybrid and to what extent a branch of the oral tree. My principal contention is that the inception of written verse initially marked a sharp break with the traditions of oral verse, after which occurred a slow flirtatious reconciliation. To a large extent this then is a history of a hasty, indignant divorce followed by a considered and fruitful remarriage.

The subject has as yet been cursorily served. No complete history of West African poetry in English or French exists, though two surveys touch upon it: Romanus Egudu's *Modern African Poetry and the African Predicament*[1] and Ken Goodwin's *Understanding African Poetry*.[2] Both possess distinct biases which conceal as much as they disclose. Egudu's book is a case study of the politically alert artist at odds with his society. He begins by citing Socrates' definition of the philosopher from Plato's *Apology* as a gadfly tormenting the body politic, and proceeds to apply this model *mutatis mutandis* to the poet. But, though Sir Philip Sidney considered philosophers a species of poet, not all poets are of a philosophical turn of mind, and Plato elsewhere banishes them from his Republic. Moreover Egudu's approach leads him to imply that the relationship between a poet and his subject is very

---

[1] Romanus Egudu, *Modern African Poetry and the African Predicament* (London: Macmillan, 1978).

[2] K. L. Goodwin, *Understanding African Poetry: A Study of Ten Poets* (London: Heinemann, 1982).

2

much the same as that enjoyed by the political commentator, the novelist or the dramatist. While directing an incisive beam at the poet in his discursive rôle he thus leaves in darkness all that pertains to him uniquely as the exponent of a particular genre. All poets are sculptors in sound; some are also social or political *vigilantes*, but by no means all consider themselves as such. To saddle the whole of a non-collegiate profession with the preferences of a few is tantamount to turning all actors into tragedians or all doctors into acupuncturists.

The direction of Goodwin's book is controlled by its author's earlier research interests. Goodwin has written on the poetry of Ezra Pound and remains convinced that for the contemporary poet of whatever nationality a mastery of the techniques of Modernism is the beginning of creative wisdom. Running through his study is the assumption that any poet who wishes to produce work relevant to our age must first prove his credentials by coming to terms with the school of verse associated with the names of Gerard Manley Hopkins, T. S. Eliot and Pound. The characteristics of this school he defines as

a movement towards 'verse as speech', dynamic rhythms growing organically from the material, the primacy of the line rather than the stanza, absolute precision of description, the use of clear, hard images either by themselves or in associated clusters to give the exact nuance intended, concentration rather than discursiveness ... and a belief that poetry was not confined to the beautiful but could deal equally well with anything, even the sordid.[3]

Though Goodwin's succinct resumé of the guiding tenets of European Modernism has some relevance to the school of poets who emerged from West African universities in the late fifties, it has to be asked whether it is strictly applicable to African writing of any period, and, to the extent that it is so, to what extent it represents a set of conditions sufficient for growth. Goodwin is guilty of assuming a little too glibly that the factors which set a certain generation of European writers free from earlier restraints they had come to resent necessarily worked an equivalent magic for African poets of a later period.

I deal with many of these questions at some length in chapter 4, where it will be seen that I have reason to challenge Goodwin's conclusions. There are, however, some preliminary observations which it may be helpful to make. African poets were never, I believe, held in a straightjacket of nineteenth-century verse for the perfectly good reason that, though they visited the appropriate tailoring establish-

---

[3] Goodwin, *Understanding African Poetry*, p. vii.

ment, they never enjoyed more than a half-hour fitting. As proof of a dependence on Victorian models Goodwin quotes a stanza from Dennis Osadebay's *Africa Sings* (1952) of which he comments its form is 'based on Tennyson's *In Memoriam* stanza with short prelude and postlude lines'.[4] There is, however, no evidence that Osadebay had ever read *In Memoriam*, or indeed any Tennyson at length. Had he done so, his own metrical procedures might have been a great deal more flexible than they were, since one of Tennyson's more remarkable qualities is his rhythmic inventiveness. Osadebay's practice on the other hand seems to be based on Wesleyan hymns loosened up with a little light Georgian verse. As might be expected of someone from his generation and background, Osadebay is far closer to Newbolt than to Tennyson, and closer to *Hymns Ancient and Modern* (Unrevised) than either. No bad thing it might be thought for a poet whose entire purpose was to march ahead of a column bound, bands playing, for Independence Square.

It is important that we do not despise the pioneers of West African poetry in English, and in the second chapter of this critical history, I have been careful not to do so. These were men and women who knew just what they wanted to achieve, and set their words to tunes reflective of passions which needed stirring. To see the movement which superceded them as an act of complete emancipation is another simplification I have avoided. The activities of the Ibadan school of the late fifties certainly marked a turning point, as a result of which English language poetry in Africa moved up-market, but did not in every instance improve. In many cases the Modernism of West African verse in the sixties was a worse affectation than the neo-Georgian effusiveness of what went before, since less certain in its control of the norms imitated. Whatever may be said of a poet such as Osadebay, his ear faithfully picked out the iambic trot of church hymnody and reproduced it with a fair amount of accuracy. The same fidelity of representation cannot unfortunately be ascribed to all of the university-trained poets of the sixties, many of whom limped after the effects of Sprung Rhythm with very little idea of what in fact constituted its guiding principles. The costume which they came to wear as a result was all too obviously borrowed. Goodwin may therefore be right in stating that the poets of the period sought to slough off the artificiality which they sensed in the verse which preceded theirs, but if the liberating panacea was, as he implies, 'verse as speech', the speech was from a

[4] Goodwin, *Understanding African Poetry*, p. vi.

different clime and couched in scarcely imitable accents. In order to strike out for a terrain more truly their own, the poets of more recent years have, as I hope to demonstrate in the last chapter of this work, been obliged to take a very different direction toward, not poetry as speech, but poetry as dance, poetry as drama, poetry as song.

Though Egudu's study approaches its material from a very different vantage point to Goodwin's, both books appear to this author to fail because, in their anxiety to persuade their readers of the salutary effect of certain influences, in one case political, in the other technical, they have neglected the property most integral to the African poet: the way in which his manner of hearing and speaking has been conditioned by an exposure to poetry in languages other than that in which he writes. Poets as poets are neither social commentators nor determined advocates of the modern, but they are cantors, whose primary activity is to sing. And since song, like every other avenue of human expression, is affected by the contours of a pre-existing tradition, so the manner in which the African poet sings will not be understood until some attempt is made to account for it in terms intrinsic to the aesthetic in which the poet was himself reared. If the following book has made some contribution, however inadequate, to such an understanding, it will have earned its author's gratitude.

*eh?*

This book has been too long in the making. During the period in which it has been in preparation, several portions of it have leaked out in the shape of conference or seminar papers. The essence of chapter 5 on the poetry of Christopher Okigbo was delivered as a contribution to the Conference on Commonwealth Language and Literature at the University of Gothenburg, Sweden in September 1982, and was subsequently written up under the title 'Christopher Okigbo and the Flutes of Tammuz' in *A Sense of Place*, ed. Britta Olinder, University of Gothenburg, 1984. A much abbreviated version of chapter 7 likewise made a live debut at the Sixth Conference on Commonwealth Literature and Language in West Germany held at the *Iwalewahaus*, Bayreuth in June, 1983. It was subsequently published under the somewhat cumbersome title 'The Resurrecting Back: Centripetal Forces in Ijaw Poetry: John Pepper Clark and Gabriel Okara' in the volume *Studies in Commonwealth Literature*, eds. Eckhardt Breitinger and Reinhardt Sander, Tübingen, Gunter Narr Verlag, 1985. None of the following chapters, however, has so far appeared in its entirety.

Over the same period I have benefited from dozens of conversations, some lengthy and fully documented, some snatched and half-forgotten, with a number of writers and scholars, any of whom might have written this book better than myself. I am consequently much indebted to more people than I have space to acknowledge. Though inclusive acknowledgement is an impossibility, I would like especially to thank several people who had been particularly generous with either their advice, their encouragement or practical assistance, namely: Martin Banham, Chinuezu, James Currey, Melanie Daiken, Robin Derricourt, James Gibbs, Liz Gunner, Geoffrey Hill, Tony Humphries, Jackie Hunt, Bernth Lindfors, Michael Mann, Gerald Moore, Alastair Niven, Ben Okri, Philip Spender, Loretta Todd, Ahmed Sheikh, Clive Wake and Adzo Zagbede-Thomas. Above all, my loving gratitude goes to Catherine Birkett for her help and constant support, without which this project would never have been brought to completion.

CHAPTER 1

# From oral to written verse: development or depletion?

Any critic embarking on a study of West African poetry ought perhaps to be accused of presumption. There are few histories of the poetry of Western Europe, and those that exist are prominent for their sketchiness. Africa is arguably a much more complicated case. To begin with, the number of potential literatures to be considered is daunting. It has been calculated that there exist between 700 and 1,250 distinct languages within sub-Saharan West Africa,[1] an area itself larger than Western Europe. Each of these possesses an oral literature, though our knowledge of them is as yet very incomplete. To do justice to this range of human expression would be too much at the present time to expect of any one scholar. Moreover, though oral and written verse from these areas demonstrate many interconnections, there are few students trained in such a way as to give a coherent account of the relation. As things stand, we have, on the one hand, folklorists reared in the techniques of field work and subsequent classification; on the other, critics cast in a literary mould who have been encouraged to read and then render an account of their subjective reactions. The two approaches do not often marry well.

There is a crying need for an integrated African poetic which would enable us to make sense of written literature in European languages within a context determined by oral performances in the vernacular. Until such a body of theory is supplied, however, the best for which the critic can hope is to establish for himself guidelines which will help him to account for the richness of the written material at his disposal as one product of a culture whose poetic experience stretches back many centuries before the introduction of printed books.

In the circumstances it has seemed wise to concentrate in this history on the written forms of verse practised in Anglophone and

---

[1] The higher figure is in accordance with the definition of language employed by David Dalby, *A Provisional Language Map of Africa and the Adjacent Islands* (London: International African Institute, 1977), from which some features of the map on p. x are also derived.

Francophone Africa, taking cognisance of oral poetry insofar as it has broken surface and declared its intentions in writing. The result is a study of the exposed tip of an impressively large iceberg. To the extent that this is so, it is to be hoped that its limitations will be ascribed to the difficulties attending an underwater survey rather than to the author's defective skill in swimming.

Even so, to treat of the oral foundations of written verse without at first addressing oneself to the essential characteristics of the two and the nature of their interrelation would be to deal in unhelpful and unwieldy abstractions. It is therefore wise at the outset to establish a way of talking about the properties of oral verse and to settle on a provisional language which will help cast its differences from written poetry in relief. To examine the range of oral expression throughout the area of sub-Saharan Africa is clearly beyond my brief, but it may prove instructive to begin by examining the relationship between oral poetry and connected written expression over a limited area. One of the most instructive ways of approaching this problem would seem to be to examine the process of transformation which has turned one local tradition of oral verse into a written poetry produced by writers from the region itself.

Several candidates recommend themselves for such an analysis, many of which are treated in some detail in the course of this book. It might for example be possible to consider the Wolof *poème gymnique* from Senegambia and its influence on the later writing of Léopold Sédar Senghor, poet–president of Senegal, a subject treated at some length in chapter 3. It would also be feasible to look at the influence of antiphonal Igbo songs on the sequence *Silences* by the Nigerian poet Christopher Okigbo (1933–67), the subject of chapter 5. Alternatively we could examine the Yoruba hunters' song or *ijala* and its effect on contemporary Yoruba poets such as Wole Soyinka, whose collection of verse *Idanre and Other Poems* is discussed in chapter 9.

At first setting out, however, it seems wisest to concentrate on a tradition which is both ample and continuous and which notably spans the generations. Among the traditions which qualify, few are more instructive or more fully documented than the variety of elegiac dirge performed on public occasions in the small coastal town of Wheta in the Volta Region of Ghana by the semi-professional oral Ewe (pron.: Eveh) poet or cantor known as the *heno*. The advantages of this as a provisional case study are manifold. The tradition has been investigated by folklorists and musicologists of three generations, including scholars from both the locality itself and beyond. The records thus assembled exist in the form both of musical score and of verbal transcript. Though the most distinguished exponent of the genre Vinoko Akpalu (1878–1974), is now dead, he has no shortage of successors. Moreover, though few Ewe poets would deny the effect of the work of Akpalu and his fellow cantors on their own verse, two English-language writers emanating from the area and nurtured in the heritage of Akpalu have attained special prominence. These are Kofi Awoonor, born in Wheta in 1935, whose first volume of poetry *Rediscovery and Other Poems* leans markedly towards the example of Akpalu, and Kofi Anyidoho also born in Wheta, in 1947, a poet who, in addition to undertaking academic research into the elegiac art of the *heno*,[2] has in his own English-language poetry extended the resources of the genre into a field of political commentary not previously undertaken. A comparison between in particular Awoonor's early poetry and the work of Vinoko Akpalu proves very illuminating to those interested in the contrastive aesthetics of written and oral verse.

Though Akpalu himself never moved far from Wheta, his work attracted the curiosity of scholars for many decades. In 1956, when Akpalu was seventy-eight years of age, the ethnomusicologist A. M. Jones spent several months recording and transcribing Ewe poetry and song with the help of the master drummer, Desmond Tay. One chapter of the resultant two-volume work *Studies in African Music*[3] is devoted to the activities of the Nyayito musicians' association and especially their rendition of various instances of Akpalu dirge. It is therefore a primary source for the understanding of Akpalu's work in its original, performed state.

Akpalu was orphaned at an early age, and himself died childless. A constant theme of his laments is thus his isolation within a community in which kinship ties are valued. The following represents, in Ewe and in English translation, the text of one of his songs, lines 6 and 7 of which are also given in full musical score in figure 1, where it will be seen that Akpalu is accompanied by an ensemble of drums and hand-gongs, together with the 'hand-claps' of the assembled multitude:

> I am an only child with no one to stand up for me
> (lit. I am a trapped bird)

---

[2] Kofi Anyidoho, *Oral Poetics and Traditions of Verbal Art in Africa* (Ph.D. Thesis, University of Texas, 1984). For Wheta, see map, p. x.
[3] A. M. Jones, *Studies in African Music*, 2 Vols. (London: Oxford University Press, 1959).

9

I will die alone in the crowd
Oh! This the song:
Our *tɔbaha* song is never ending –
It is just like unceasing rain falling in Nyima quarry,
The people of Anyako have gone to praise Akpalu,
I will sing unceasingly to you like the sparrow
I have told you I will sing to you
The song of this drumming, I will sing it to you.
My father died and I wandered distractedly
for a hunting-dog to come and snatch,
    or a leopard to devour.

Beble tsitsie menye
Nye la gɖeawo domee maku ɖo
Halé ya hee
Miawo tɔbaha zu make make
Ʋedzia ɖe dza ɖe 'nyi me ʋenu
Anyakoawo yi adza wu ge na akpalu-ee
Mado alɔewɔ gbe na mi dzro
Megblɔe na mi be medzi ge na mi
Ʋu yawo ha medzi ge na mi
Tɔnye ga ku(a) medze axɔ ɖo gbe loho
Adevu nava lé, medze axɔ ɖo gbe sati nava tsɔ.[4]

It will be seen that the text itself runs on several levels: it is a dirge
for the deceased, a lament on the human condition and a complaint by
a lonely childless man himself raised an orphan. From a comparison of
the sixth and seventh lines with the equivalent musical score provided
by Jones, it is also clear, however, that the words represent merely the
dry bones of the performance, the flesh of which dwells in the sur-
rounding penumbra of complex, interweaving sound. It is therefore
extremely doubtful whether attention to the words alone, however
rewarding, will help us to give an account of the form, the earmarks of
which lie elsewhere.

It is at this point that the literary critic's traditional equipment
breaks down, for to concentrate on the words to the exclusion of the
music is as harmful in this context as it would be, in another, to attend
to the printed ciphers on a page with no appreciation of the way in
which the eye interprets them. Nor can the critic escape by handing
over to the musicologist, for to do so would be to abrogate a re-
sponsibility integral to his attempt to describe the poem. Indeed the
very term 'poem', with its implication of armchair pleasures, sits very

[4] Jones, *African Music*, Vol. 1, p. 33.

Fig. 1

oddly on the subject matter, for the *akpalu* is at once poem and song, dance and percussive fantasia. As Kofi Anyidoho, speaking of the analogous *haikotu* song and dance form, has reason to state: 'Any text-orientated study of Ewe oral poetry is likely to lead to certain wrong conclusions about the composition and performance of this poetry', and consequently, it is essential to recognize that 'the very structure and utterance of such texts is governed by the larger musical framework since much of the poetry exists only as part of a complex art form involving drumming, singing and dancing'.[5] When examining an instance of *akpalu*, then, we are faced with a total subsidence, not merely in the received theory of genres, but in the division between the conventional disciplines as well.

Bearing these facts in mind, how can we best describe the poem's form? The performance begins with an introductory statement of the theme by the *heno*, in this case Akpalu, written out for our benefit by Jones as if in F Major, though in fact the musical scale employed comes nearest in Greek terms to the Mixolydian mode. One by one the percussion instruments enter in a compound rhythm regulated by hand-claps. The musical structure thus initiated is both polyrhythmic and polytonal, for, though the percussion parts are transcribed in 12/8, the cantor's declamation cannot be fitted easily into it, shifting as it does between bars of 6/8 and others of 2/4 or 3/4. Moreover, the only percussion instrument to agree modally with the singer is the small standing drum *kidi*, the others embracing a variety of subsidiary keys from the Lydian mode on E♭ of the master drum *atsimevu*, the Hypophrygian in G of *sogo* and the simple alternation between the pitches of A♭ and B♭ on the *kagan*. This classification is approximate, however, since, as Jones himself is careful to state 'the whole ethos of . . . African melodies is different'[6] from that suggested by the categories of European music, themselves founded on Greek example.

At first hearing it might appear to the untutored listener that the flexibility of melody and pulse thus achieved is the product of pure group improvization. In fact, the various elements of the performance, every one of which is overseen by the *heno*, combine to elicit something much nearer to the sort of controlled improvization that we meet in jazz. For example the rhythmic shapes enunciated by the

---

[5] *Cross Rhythms: Papers in African Folklore*, eds. Kofi Anyidoho, Daniel Avorgbedor, Susan Domowitz and Eren Giray-Saul (Bloomington Indiana: The Trickster Press, 1983), p. 173.
[6] Jones, *African Music*, Vol. 1, p. 33.

*kagan* are predisposed in such a way as to establish a continuous syn-
copation with the lead drummer on *atsimevu*, each phrase of the first
setting out one beat prior to those of the second. Moreover, though
*atsimevu* may appear constantly to change his rhythm, his drumming
unfailingly accords with one of six pre-determined patterns between
which he alternates, marking his gravitation from one to another by a
set of brief repeated phrases which act both as pauses in the structure
and as indications to his fellow musicians that another phase of the
composition is about to commence. By this method it is possible for
him to co-ordinate the rhythmic complexion of the whole, for as soon
as he leads into a fresh pattern, *kagan* and the other two accompanying
drums follow suit, both *sogo* and *kidi* having been provided with a set
of corresponding patterns to match those of the master drum. There
are therefore distinct points at which the entire composition sets off in
a new direction agreed between the *heno* and his colleagues. It is these
junctures which may be described as the points around which the
poem/song essentially turns.

At once an objection may be entered. It may be said that what Jones
is describing is a musical structure, and as such irrelevant to any con-
sideration of the poem as 'verse'. If this were a transcription of a Euro-
pean song the proviso would hold. But Ewe is a tonal language in
which pitch determines meaning. The singing of an *akpalu* dirge
cannot then be said to correspond to a 'setting' of the words in the
same way as a Schubert *Lied* based on a poem by Goethe. The music is
an integral part of the text: as Anyidoho, himself an interpreter of the
form, protests, any talk of the words as a separable element is mean-
ingless. There is a sense in which even Jones's transcriptions from his
recordings represents a reduction of the original. Jones entitles the
performance the 'Nyayito Dance', thus calling our attention to one im-
portant dimension which he was unable to reproduce. It is in reality,
much more than that; at once dance, song, poem and liturgy. To
decide which is the more accurate term would be to involve the reader
in a radical theory of genres for which there is here no space. It would
furthermore be to perplex the issue, since the *akpalu* belongs to none of
the classifications for which the critic has so far had room. This was a
problem which defeated Jones, who merely settled for the arbitrary
description 'dance' while leaving his readers, possessed of a text and
full score but no dance notation, to imagine the steps.

Thus a recognition of the mutual relatedness of different dimen-
sions in oral African verse has important theoretical implications.

13

While it is not suggested that the intensely local *akpalu* tradition equips us with anything like a universal set of poetic laws, the elements which go into its making are such as recur throughout much of the geographical area covered by this study. In every case one is moved to ask the same question: what, in this context, can we mean when we apply the term 'verse'? It is a word which many would abjure because of its literary associations; in doing so, however, they miss an important opportunity. The term 'verse' simply means turning. In the Occidental traditions, it refers to the instant around which classical and European verse turns, namely the end of the line, which thus retains a major strategic significance. In the *akpalu*, however, the turning occurs round a number of different axes. Jones's division into line lengths in his verbal transcription is very artificial, since, as he explains elsewhere, the cantor's words are more aptly divisible into a series of phrases, which can be distributed among the musical bars allotted to him in the proportions 4 + 4 + (1+4) + (1+4) + 4 + 4. Considered from the narrow perspective of the verbal text, therefore, there are, within each delivery of the lyric, four turning points, which do not, however, coincide with anything comparable in the musical surround. For its part, the musical accompaniment may be said to 'turn' at points marked by the master drummer whose 'turning' from one rhythmic figuration to the next brings in its train an automatic response from his fellow musicians. The musical and phrasal structure thus proceed in a state of tense agreement, of unity within diversity, for which the most appropriate technical term is 'counterpoint'.

Again, we need to pause to reconsider terms. The word 'counterpoint' which properly belongs in the domain of musical theory, was requisitioned towards the close of the nineteenth century by Gerard Manley Hopkins to describe a particular effect in poetic rhythm, when variations of pulse within any one line conflict with the poet's own chosen metre. The result is a playing of one rhythmic figuration against another, very similar to the jostling of divergent rhythms we meet in jazz or the fugues of Bach. It is, to quote Hopkins's exact words, an effect produced by 'the superinducing or *mounting* of a new rhythm upon the old; and since the new or mounted rhythm is actually heard and at the same time the mind naturally supplies the natural or standard foregoing rhythm, for we do not forget what the rhythm is that by rights we should be hearing, two rhythms are in some manner running at once and we have something answerable to counterpoint in music, which is two or more strains of tune going on

14

together, and this is Counterpoint Rhythm'.[7] Here, from Hopkins's sonnet 'God's Grandeur' of 1877, is a quatrain which clearly demonstrates what he had in mind:

> Gĕnĕrātiŏns hăve trōd, hăve trōd, hăve trōd;
> Aňd all iš sēared wĭth trāde; bleāred, smeāred wĭth tǫil;
> Aňd wears măn's smūdge aňd shāres măn's smēll: the sōil
> Iš bāre nŏw, nōr căn fŏot fēel, bēiňg shōd.[8]

The line here which defines the running or standard rhythm is the third, which is straight iambic throughout. Hopkins's idea is that we hear this regular pulse even when it is absent, so that other rhythmic formulations when they occur are stacked against it, producing the pleasing psychological tension we experience through musical syncopation. Thus at the beginning of the first line we read 'Gĕnĕrātiŏns' while with our inner ear we hear ˘—˘—and in the last read 'nōr căn fŏot fēel' while hearing at the same time ˘—˘—.

In order to see the relevance of this model to sung African verse, we only have to examine what is happening in figure 1 at the bar/line marked 'A'. It will be noted that the performance letter coincides only with the inception of phrases in the upper drums, both the handclaps and the voice part overlapping so that the cantor finishes his phrase 'Anyakoawo yi a-dza wu ge na akpa-lu-ee' a good two beats after *atsimevu* has embarked on his next phrase. At the same time the consort of lower drums is caught between two conflicting cross-rhythms of its own, the lead drum *atsimevu* coming down hard on a unison C with the double hand-bell (*gankogui*) while both *sogo* and *kidi* accompany *kagan* in a complex compound rhythm quite at variance to the master beat. Thus not two sets of accents coincide, as in the Hopkins poem, but four sets, each holding its own within the continuing texture. In relation to the whole ensemble the cantor himself has an important but by no means an overriding part, since if there is a running rhythm against which the other pulses are assessed, it is that given out by the master drum in its supervision of the main percussive group.

☽          ☽          ☽

[7] *The Poems of Gerard Manley Hopkins*, ed. Robert Bridges (London: Humphrey Milford, 1918), p. 3.
[8] *The Poetry of Gerard Manley Hopkins*, eds. W. H. Gardner and N. Mackenzie (London: Oxford University Press, 1967), p. 66.

How much of this cornucopia of aural sensation can be transferred to a text written in a European language and intended primarily for silent reading? The most effective way to answer this question is to compare the *akpalu* above with a poem in English by a contemporary Ewe poet working explicitly within the same elegiac idiom. Fortunately there is a suitable instance to hand. When Kofi Awoonor published his *Rediscovery and Other Poems* in 1964, Ewe readers were not slow to notice a strong affinity between various of the poems and *akpalu* dirges familiar to members of the Ewe language community. A notable case in point is the first of Awoonor's 'Songs of Sorrow', the opening lines of which read:

> Dzogbese Lisa has treated me thus
> It has led me among the sharps of the forest
> Returning is not possible
> And going forward is a great difficulty
> The affairs of this world are like the chameleon faeces
> Into which I have stepped
> When I clean it cannot go . . .
>
> My people, I have been somewhere
> If I turn here, the rain beats me
> If I turn there the sun burns me
> The firewood of this world
> Is for only those who can take heart
> That is why not all can gather it.[9]

Behind these lines, with their undeniably moving evocation of private tribulation, lies the shadow of another *akpalu* dirge, transcribed in 1950 by Sam Obianim:

> Xexemenyawo zu ganami mefa,
> Metutui hã mele vɔvɔm o.
> Dzɔgbese lisae wɔ num loo!
> Tsɔm ɖo ati glãmawo dome;
> Tɔtrɔ yi megbe megali o;
> Ŋgɔgbeyiyi hã zu dɔ nam loo!
> Xexemenyawo zu ganami mefa,
> Metutui hã mele vɔvɔm o.
> Lã manyεa ɖe meda,
> Vinɔkɔ, lã manyεa ɖe meda;
> Ku loo, agbe loo meda.
> Akpalu wu lã, hεsinɔviwo, wòzu adesimaɖu,

---

[9] Kofi Awoonor, *Rediscovery and Other Poems* (Ibadan: Mbari, 1964).

Adekplɔviwo ka le ye nu hã.
Xexemenyawo zu ganami mefa,
Metutui hã mele vɔvɔm o.
Dzɔgbese lisae wɔ num loo!
Tsɔm ɖo ati glãmawo dome;
Tɔtrɔ yi megbe megali o;
Ngɔgbeyiyi hã zu dɔ nam loo!
Kodzogbenyawo zu ganami mefa;
Metutui hã mele vɔvɔm o.[10]

A direct comparison of the two texts is complicated by the fact that these passages do not exactly overlap, since Awoonor's version is less a translation than an artful reworking of the original. Nevertheless, when Awoonor's poem is compared to the *akpalu* transcribed by Jones, one or two facts immediately become obvious. The first is the shrinking of the dimensions present in the composition: a polytonal, polyrhythmic structure reduced to thirteen lines of cold print. The second is a shift in rhythmic focus. Deprived of the support of musicians, Awoonor has had to look elsewhere for a method of rhythmic organization. His solution seems to have been to construct his poem around a series of balanced antithetical phrases, either within the line or strung between two ('If I turn here the rain beats me,/If I turn there the sun burns me.'). The concerted rise and fall of these phrases, admittedly effective in its own sphere, depends on the inflections of the speaking not of the singing voice. Moreover, Awoonor's ability to set rhythmic patterns against one another is relatively restricted. There is no possibility of strict musical counterpoint, since he has dispensed with an accompaniment. The line cannot therefore feasibly syncopate with a background pulse, since none is heard, nor, in Hopkins's sense, can it syncopate with itself, since, being in free verse, it lacks a 'running rhythm'. Awoonor has thus cut himself adrift both from the stimulus of participation within a larger group and the formal challenge of a conventional metrical scheme. His poem thus languishes in a structural limbo, beguilingly lit, but a limbo nonetheless.

Awoonor's transition to a specifically literary mode has also involved him in a corresponding thematic shift, the implications of which may easily be viewed by examining his use of the first person singular. Who is this 'I' that speaks, and what is its relationship to the community it appears to be addressing? In the dirge transcribed by

[12] Sam J. Obianim, *Evegbe Ɖuti Nunya: An Ewe Grammar* (London: Macmillan, 1950), p. 79.

Jones, Akpalu refers to himself by name. Awoonor prefers the neutrality of the personal pronoun. One reason that, having transferred to the techniques of written verse, Awoonor has entered a convention in which the decorum of self-disclosure is subtly different. A poet need only refer to himself by name if he is personally known to his audience, as did Akpalu, declaiming before a crowd most of whom he recognized, and all of whom certainly recognized him. As a literary artist, Awoonor has forgone these privileges. When speaking of his personal affliction, he elects then for the generalizing effect of an 'I' which embraces both himself and his readership, each one of whom exists in isolation. There is thus no possibility of collective response, nor, since each reader is invisible to the author, can there be any feedback from audience to poet. None of these restrictions applied to the original *akpalu*, where the concentration of the cantor's personal grief was pointedly offset by the collaboration of a large group consisting not merely of drummers and gong-players but of a much wider company including most of the listeners, who sang the refrains and underscored the rhythm with hand-claps. The chemistry of this communal involvement is very complicated. Few of those present would be themselves either orphaned or without children; yet the total feeling which they are expressing stretches out to involve the cantor in his personal deprivation. Little of this can be reproduced by Awoonor, who has to be content with a poignant evocation of personal frustration amplified by a rhetorical nod ('My people') in the direction of an implied community beyond.

Kofi Awoonor is a writer very aware both of what he has been able to glean from the oral tradition, and of what, as a published poet, he has been forced to leave behind.[11] In opting for the prerogative of publication at the expense of a more direct relationship with his public, he is far from alone. The history recounted in these pages is of a long alienation from the heritage of orature followed by a gradual reconciliation with it. The term 'reconciliation' is used advisedly since written poetry can never, as we have already demonstrated, act as a precise imitation of what is sung or danced, a fact which the former use of the term 'literature' to cover both has until recently tended to disguise.

---

[11] See Kofi Awoonor, *The Breast of the Earth: A Survey of the History, Culture and Literature of Africa South of the Sahara* (New York: Anchor Doubleday, 1975).

There is a strong sense in which the majority of the poets discussed in the following ten chapters of this study took their artistic cue primarily from a European culture whose own oral origins were so remote as to be almost inaudible. There is an equally strong sense in which the poetry of the last ten years has represented an attempt to recover some of the ground lost in the earlier effort to secure at all costs international respectability for the poetry of one of the more remote parts of the English/or French-speaking world.

In the 'development' from oral to written verse something was gained – the personal kudos of the writer, the added stability of his text, an enlarged potential audience – but, as we have seen, much had also to be foresworn. To a growing number of West African poets it is coming to appear that the glamour of publication is lean compensation for the immediacy of active performance. The resulting restoration of that which cold print had sheered away is currently a matter of experiment and of debate throughout much of Africa. It may possibly be that, as international publishing prospects decline, so live performance may once again come into its own as the prime means of the dissemination of African verse. If such be the case, then the act of publication will have resumed the significance which it has possessed for the classical poets of every culture – for Homer and the author of *Beowulf* as much as for Vinoko Akpalu – a fortunate accident, of much benefit to the hard of hearing, but of limited relevance to that in which all true poetry essentially consists: the quick of orality.

CHAPTER 2

# Ladies and gentlemen

In 1950 a slim, cyclostyled volume of lyrical verse appeared in London-derry, Northern Ireland under the name of a young research scientist of West African origin. It was prefaced by these remarks:

The African has an inborn sense of rhythm, a tolerably good ear for music, and a sense of colour harmony. He is spontaneous and frank when dealing with his own people.

How then is it that the Negro in West Africa has done so little creative writing with his incomparable gift of song?

I do not propose to give any answers to these questions, except to remark that the poverty of literary effort on the West coast induced me to write, after an absence of well nigh twenty years, about the haunts of my childhood and youth.

If in this attempt I should succeed in inducing one West African to burst into song and sing of the beauties of our motherland, and of our heroes, then I shall have exceeded my wildest ambitions.

It is remarkable how little poetical work was forthcoming in Ireland till the middle half of the eighteenth century. And yet how great now is their contri-bution to English letters.[1]

The book was called *Between the Forest and the Sea* and its author Dr Raphael Ernest Grail Armattoe, was until then known as a specialist in human ailments with a lively side-line in anthropology and history. It is difficult nowadays, after the flood of African literature in English over the last thirty years and the critical canon to which it has given rise, to think oneself back into a situation in which such a thing was a novelty. But in 1950 the amount of English language verse which could be ascribed to West Africans was not large. Though verse can be credited to West Africans writing in English as far back as the late eighteenth century, by far the greater bulk of it has occurred after the historical watershed of the Second World War.

The factors which had inhibited written self-expression before 1945 were many and diverse, but one is suggested by Armattoe's compari-

---

[1] Raphael Ernest Grail Armattoe, *Between the Forest and the Sea* reproduced from type-script in Londonderry, Northern Ireland (1950), p. 1.

son of African to Irish literature, a parallel which impinges on the very crisis of vocabulary at the heart of this study. At the time of Armattoe's comments Ireland had possessed a written and oral literature in Gaelic for well over a thousand years, a fact which he prefers not to mention. In Armattoe's eyes Ireland did not become creatively alive until the inception during the eighteenth century of the Anglo-Irish literature of Sheridan and Swift. Similarly, as a son, like Akpalu and Awoonor, of the Ewe-speaking region of Ghana, Armattoe was very conscious of its fine heritage of oral verse. Yet, so preoccupied was he with the dictates of 'literary effort' that this again scarcely seemed to count. It was 'song'; it was 'dance'. Genuine 'poetic work' by contrast, for men of Armattoe's generation and persuasion, could only properly occur in a metropolitan language, and must perforce take its bow as a 'contribution to English letters'.

The late arrival of a poetry of 'English letters' on the West African coast was principally to be explained by the driving objectives of imperial policy. Early British incursions along the Gulf of Guinea had been motivated almost exclusively by trade, political and administrative considerations taking second place until the full-scale imposition of colonial rule towards the close of the nineteenth century. Under these conditions, until late in the Victorian period British cultural influence was largely confined to a string of coastal trading posts felt to be of special strategic importance, and where as a consequence small expatriate communities were maintained to secure vested interests. By the final decades of the nineteenth century four of these had attracted a growing English-speaking African population. The first of these was Freetown, Sierra Leone with its large Krio-speaking community of repatriated slaves. The second was Monrovia, centre of another substantial society of emancipated slaves who had brought back over the Atlantic American conceptions of democracy and government, and who, though existing outside the sphere of British influence, maintained throughout this period lively social connections with neighbouring territories where British influence was active. The third was the tiny settlement of Cape Coast (Oguaa) which, clustering around its ancient castle, held its position as capital of the Gold Coast colony until late in the century. The fourth was Lagos, the 'Liverpool of West Africa', the nexus of a network of trading links which stretched beyond Abeokuta in Yorubaland way into the far interior.

Michael Echeruo's researches into the life of Victorian Lagos[2] have

---

[2] Michael Echeruo, *Victorian Lagos, Aspects of Nineteenth Century Lagos Life* (London: Macmillan, 1977).

acquainted us with a vigorous, upwardly-mobile African society which, confronted by the undeniable fact of British commercial power, saw its salvation in clear thinking, clean living and modest self-expression. Just as Macaulay's Minute had produced a *cadre* of English-speaking Civil Servants in India, so the opening up of commercial opportunities in Lagos after its capitulation to the British Crown in 1861 produced a class of middle-men only too anxious to use English in the service of self-advancement. The linguistic and stylistic requirements of this new class can be gauged by an editorial which appeared in the columns of the *Eagle* newspaper on 28 April 1883:

It is of vital importance, in writing, always to come straight to the point, that the reader may not dive as it were into the recesses of dense jungles, nor get hopelessly entangled in meshes of verbal embarrassment in endeavouring to discover the meaning of what is written. The facts should mark the basis of their information, the style should be perspicuous, and the form condensed.[3]

This was a society ruled by the directives of Mr Gradgrind, a society which, in the face of indomitable British self-assertion – 'telegrams and anger' – was obsessed by a desire to catch up, to prove itself the equal in every respect of the hundred or so British residents in its midst. Such aspirations gave encouragement to the evolution of two different, though related kinds of English usage: on the one hand the dusty aridities of bureaucratic red-tape, and, on the other, the polite frivolity of petit-bourgeois social intercourse. The result was the development within the English-speaking African community of two effective verbal registers: a virile and declamatory prose, of much use in the ensuing period of nationalist agitation, and the sort of conversational tittle-tattle associated with garden parties and musical-cum-social *soirées*.

The effects of the second were effectively lampooned in *The Blinkards*,[4] a social comedy performed at the 'Cosmopolitan Club', Cape Coast in 1915. Its author was Kobina Sekyi, a Cape Coaster in his twenties who had recently returned to the colony after studying Philosophy at the University of London, and who was later to return there to qualify as a lawyer, eventually emerging in the 1920s as a leading theorist of the fledgling nationalist movement. In his play of 1915 the absurdities of local petit-bourgeois social climbing are epitomized by Mrs Brofusem, wife of a Cape Coast merchant:

[3] Quoted in Echeruo, *Victorian Lagos*, p. 8.
[4] Kobina Sekyi (William Esuman-Gwira Sekyi), *The Blinkards: A Comedy* (London: Heinemann, 1974).

I'm glad I've been to England
  Behold me spick and span
In silk and patent shoes, and
  With parasol and fan.

I'm glad I've been to England
  And learned to rule my spouse
For there the wives are bold, and
  Command in every house.

I'm glad I've been to England
  Where I have learned to make
Sweet dainty things like tarts and
  Blanc-mange and fairy-cake.

Had I not been to England
  I'd be at home all day
House-keeping with my maids, and
  With little time to play.

But now I've been to England
  Where ladies oft are out,
I like to call on friends, and
  With them, to gad about.[5]

Mrs Brofusem's life is controlled by a fear of 'going Fantee', that is reverting to local life and custom. In her desire to contest the rot of native backwardness she has surrounded herself with a considerable personal following, consisting of all the young flappers of the town. When these are invited to a garden party beneath the statue of Queen Victoria in the park adjoining the castle, their enthusiasm for Mrs Brofusem's teachings is ridiculed by a young Fante lawyer called Mr Onyimdzi, a thinly disguised mouthpiece for Sekyi himself:

GIRLS ALL: We follow Mrs Brofusem
            Who is so nice, you know;
          We like her ways, we'll follow them –
MR ONY (*interrupting*): Because they're loud and low.
GIRLS ALL: Oh, don't do that!

          She dresses up so very well,
            And walks with such an air,
          And her 'at Homes' are very swell –

[5] *Ibid.*, pp. 51–2.

MR ONY (*interrupting*): And vulgar, I declare.
GIRLS ALL: Oh, don't do that!

> We want to be like her, and walk
> > Like English ladies do,
> And sing like her, and laugh, and talk –

MR ONY (*interrupting*): As if you had the 'flu.[6]

Similar aspirations are expressed by one of the town's more eligible bachelors, Mr Okadu, a 'young blood' whose declaration of cultural loyalties at the beginning of Act Two lifts a passage from Sekyi's own narrative poem *The Sojourner*:

> I speak English to soften my harsher native tongue:
> It matters not if often I speak the Fanti wrong.
>
> I'm learning to be British and treat with due contempt
> The worship of the fetish, from which I am exempt.
>
> I was baptized an infant – a Christian hedged around
> With prayer from the moment my being was unbound.
>
> I'm clad in coat and trousers, with boots upon my feet:
> And *tamfurafu*\* and Hausas I seldom deign to greet:
>
> For I despise the native that wears the native dress –
> The badge that marks the bushman, who never will progress.
>
> All native ways are silly, repulsive, unrefined.
> All customs superstitious, that rule the savage mind.
>
> I like Civilization, and I'd be glad to see
> All people that are pagan eschew idolatry.[7]
> \*Wearers of native dress.

The effete social circle encountered in Sekyi's pages possesses an undeniable sub-Wildean charm, and Sekyi's verse parody, an undeniable tart humour. Yet, though Sekyi is known to have composed a number of satirical and philosophical poems between 1918 and 1952,[8] his work in reality illustrates the very impossibility of true poetic achievement in a society thus enfeebled in its imitation of foreign norms and influences. What was needed for the stimulation of an

---

[6] *Ibid.*, pp. 53–5.   [7] *Ibid.*, pp. 46–7.
[8] Sekyi papers, National Archive, Cape Coast, Ghana.

authentic poetic literature in English was the emergence of a linguistic register of spiritual inwardness, such as came awkwardly to the British themselves, and which, in the drive towards economic efficiency, they were slow to encourage in others.

The one group of Europeans who, at an early stage, might be thought of as having a vested interest in the cultivation of an English responsive to the movings of the spirit, namely the missionaries, often preferred to operate through the vernacular, which unlike the business community they took some pains to learn. The largest single piece of evidence for this is the rate at which the Bible was translated into a range of local languages for the purpose of evangelization. By the middle of the nineteenth century St Matthew's Gospel, which was viewed as the crucial text, had been translated into both Ga (1843) and Yoruba (1853). A Hausa version soon followed in 1857, and by the mid-sixties the complete text of the Bible had been turned into Ga (1866) and Yoruba (from 1865).[9] The one surprising exception to this rule is the Fante language of Cape Coast and its environs, which did not obtain a version of the New Testament until almost the turn of the century (1896).[10] The reason for this can possibly be found in the exceptional exposure to European influence to which the people of this section of the coast had been subject since the late fifteenth century, and the corresponding early penetration of English as a medium of daily conversation. It is not without significance that much of the earliest English-language poetry emanated from this area.

The concentration of British activity on the rapid expansion of trade and ancillary activities thus to a large extent limited the number of linguistic registers which West African English could sustain, and hence inhibited the undergrowth of attendant associations on which poetry might feed. Until very late in the nineteenth century, the only men and women subjected to the full range of English expression in all its perverse contradictory richness were those who had been violently abstracted from the West African environment by the slave trade.

[9] The translations referred to are as follows:
   *The Gospels of St Matthew and St John, Translated Out of the Original Greek into the Accra Language* by Rev. A. W. Hanson (British and Foreign Bible Society, 1843).
   *The Gospel of St Matthew, translated into Yoruba* by Rev. Samuel Crowther (B and FBS, 1853).
   *St Matthew's Gospel, Translated into Hausa* by Rev. James Fred Schoen (B and FBS, 1857).
   *The Bible Translated into Ga* by J. Zimmerman (Stuttgart, 1866).
   *The Bible Translated into Yoruba* by Rev. Adjai Crowther (B and FBS, 1865).
[10] *The Four Gospels in Fanti*, translated by A. W. Parker (B and FBS, 1896).

Of these the most prolific was certainly Phillis Wheatley (c.1753–84), a young slave girl of West African origin living in Boston at the house of her New England master, John Wheatley. We have no exact evidence as to where Phillis Wheatley was born, especially as, like most slaves of the period, she took her owner's surname; indeed her biographer Frederick Heartman is forced to state simply that she originated from 'somewhere in Africa'.[11] Our knowledge of the topography of the slave trade, however, allows us to conclude that she was from West Africa. At the age of eight by her own account she was taken away from her homeland, of which afterwards she retained only the haziest memory, and transported to the docks of New England where she was bought by the wife of John Wheatley, the tailor, and brought to their Boston house. Luckily for her, the atmosphere here proved to be benign and scholarly, so that, in exchange for relatively light domestic duties, she was treated to a rigorous linguistic training, firstly in English, and then in Latin and Greek. By the age of thirteen, Phillis was already an aspiring poet.

Phillis Wheatley's life was a blend of distress and corresponding good fortune. Deprived through cruel circumstances of both her cultural inheritance and mother tongue, she nevertheless escaped the harsh fate which awaited most slaves on their arrival in the New World, and grew up in the refined and erudite ambience of Massachussetts, home of the emergent American intelligentsia and seat of Harvard College, to which she later inscribed a tribute. Wheatley clearly imbibed much of this arcadian atmosphere, and her poetic style is an example of New England elegance and delicacy of sentiment, rich in supporting classical allusions. She cannot be identified with any African tradition, but belongs instead to the tradition of eighteenth-century European letters of which American literature was at that date an offshoot. Historically one can place her as a product of that enlightened, immediately pre-Revolutionary ambience in which women for the first time claimed a place in New World literature. Her verse technique was derived from the neo-classical Augustans such as Pope and Johnson, but her emotional temper has much of the idealization one associates with later poets of sentiment such as Collins and Thomson. Here, in the opening piece of her *Poems on Various Subjects, Religious and Moral* (1773), is a concise state of her poetic creed:

---

[11] Chas. Fred. Heartman, *Phillis Wheatley, a Critical Attempt and a Bibliography of Her Writings* (New York, privately printed, 1915), p. 3.

Great *Maro*'s strain in heav'nly numbers flows,
The *Nine* inspire, and all the bosom glows.
O could I rival thine and *Virgil*'s page,
Or claim the *Muses* with the *Mantuan* sage;
Soon the same beauties should my mind adorn,
And the same ardors in my soul should burn:
Then should my song in bolder notes arise,
And all my numbers pleasingly surprize,
But here I sit, and mourn a grov'ling mind,
That fain would mount and ride upon the wind.[12]

Here she aspires to the glories of the golden age of Latin literature, graced by the group of poets who were attached to the court of the Roman emperor Augustus after whom the Augustan poets in England had styled themselves. It is interesting that Wheatley does not seem to feel that this is at all an inappropriate ambition for an African writer, and takes comfort from the fact that one of the greatest of all the Latin dramatists, Terence (186–161 BC) was himself 'an African by birth', and also a slave:

The happier *Terence* all the choir inspir'd,
His soul replenish'd, and his bosom fir'd.[13]

But if Wheatley was capable of a proper pride in her race and its literary history, she seems convinced of the advantages that have accrued to her through her conversion to Christianity and baptism in the church. Much of her verse contains references to the 'Pagan land' from which she saw herself as having been rescued by a divine providence, and she clearly possessed a very ambivalent attitude to the fact of her own blackness: shame of the 'diabolic die' permeating her skin, yet pride that someone like herself should have achieved a state of spiritual salvation:

Remember, *Christians*, *Negros*, black as *Cain*,
May be refin'd, and join th'angelic train.[14]

It is clearly inappropriate to judge Phillis Wheatley against the political aspirations of a much later period, or to castigate her with having sold out to alien masters. It is, however, worthwhile remembering that she was far from politically innocent, living as she did in one of the most turbulent and nationalistic phases of American history – the

[12] Phillis Wheatley, *Poems on Various Subjects, Religious and Moral* (London, A. Bell, Aldgate, 1773), pp. 10–11.
[13] *Ibid.*, p. 11.     [14] *Ibid.*, p. 18.

lead-up to, and culmination of the American War of Independence (1775–81). Her attitudes to the war were again ambivalent. Although she inscribed a tribute to George III on his repeal of the Stamp Act in 1768, she later wrote an even more glowing panegyric to George Washington:

> One century scarce perform'd its destined round,
> When Gallic powers Columbia's fury found;
> And so may you, whoever dares disgrace
> The land of freedom's heaven-defended race!
> Fix'd are the eyes of nations on the scales,
> For in their hopes Columbia's arm prevails.
> Anon Britannia droops the pensive head,
> While round increase the rising hills of dead.
> Ah! cruel blindness to Columbia's state!
> Lament thy thirst of boundless power too late.
> Proceed, great chief, with virtue on thy side,
> Thy ev'ry action let the goddess guide.
> A crowd, a mansion, and a throne that shine,
> With gold unfading, Washington! be thine. [15]

One of her most successful poems, 'Goliath of Gath', celebrates the tide of Hebrew nationalism which staunched the invading Philistines and swept the young poet David to power. Here she is clearly able to identify with the patriotic fervour which drove the child of a disadvantaged, suspect race to contest the mastery of the giant Goliath, her description of whom turns him into a symbol of tyranny and injustice:

> Now front to front the armies were display'd
> Here *Israel* rang'd, and here the foes array'd.
> The hosts on two opposing mountains stood,
> Thick as the foliage of the waving wood;
> Between them an extensive valley lay,
> O'er which the gleaming armour pour'd the day,
> When from the camp of the *Philistine* foes,
> Dreadful to view, a mighty warrior rose;
> In the dire deeds of bleeding battle skill'd,
> The monster stalks the terror of the field.
> From *Gath* he sprung, *Goliath* was his name,
> Of fierce deportment, and gigantic frame:
> A brazen helmet on his head was plac'd,
> A coat of mail his form terrific grac'd,
> The greaves his legs, the targe his shoulders prest:
> Dreadful in arms high-tow'ring o'er the rest.
> A spear he proudly wav'd, whose iron head,

[15] Heartman, *Phillis Wheatley*, p. 21. For Washington's letter in reply, see *ibid.*, p. 22.

## Ladies and gentlemen

> Strange to relate, six hundred shekels weigh'd;
> He strode along, and shook the ample field,
> While *Phoebus* blaz'd refulgent on his shield.[16]

The sheer size of Phillis Wheatley's poetic output was impressive considering the fact that, following an unhappy marriage, she died at the age of thirty-one. The checklist of her published work in Heartman's memorial runs to eight pages. Much of this was conventionally elegiac, but the best of it is distinguished by a sort of deflected nationalism which enabled her to channel much of her frustrated patriotic feeling through the aspirations of the insurgent Americans or ancient Jews.

There is a gap of one and a half centuries before the appearance of the next West African English-language poet, significantly another woman: Gladys Casely Hayford of Sierra Leone and the Gold Coast. Hayford was the product of an élite family. Her father, Joseph Casely Hayford, was an eminent lawyer and nationalist, who in addition to a number of tracts on political and legal subjects, also wrote a remarkable work, half-fictional half-discursive, called *Ethiopia Unbound* (1911),[17] the opening pages of which give us one of the vividest pictures we possess of the activity of African students in London before the First World War. Her mother, Adelaide Casely Hayford, was also an author, and it is to this early family atmosphere, soaked in literature and associated political aspirations, that Gladys owed her personal orientation. Born in 1904 at Axim in what is now the Western Region of Ghana, she was sent off at the age of fifteen to complete her studies in the United Kingdom before returning to teach with her mother at the Girls' Vocational School in Freetown, Sierra Leone. Being of mixed Gold Coast and Sierra Leonean parentage, she seems to have taken readily to her new setting, especially to the Krio language spoken by the creole population of Freetown. It is her achievement to have raised this language, then despised as a sort of debased patois, into a valid vehicle for literary expression, and thus to have paved the way for a line of later Krio authors. Her Krio poems, together with one or two standard English pieces, were published in a slender volume in 1948 by the New Era Press of Freetown under the

[16] Wheatley, *Poems on Various Subjects*, pp. 31–2.
[17] Joseph Casely Hayford, *Ethiopia Unbound* (London, C. M. Phillips, 1911).

title *Take 'Um So.*[18] The title poem gives us some indication of the controlling point of view:

> Na den take 'um so Bobo ken better
> Na den take 'um so Titi kin wise,
> Den take 'um so mamy, en take 'um so dady.
> Kin eat den fat foll bone, en win dem prize.
>
> If God gie you abulay, or bammbo 'ouse or pan,
> Or den stone an cement mansion, whey some get.
> If God gie you life of leisure, en concur all you plan –
> Or E' turn and gie you worry, you no fret –
> Take 'um so.
>
> If God full some 'ouse wid pickin, en e' no gree full you, youn.
> Or E' gie you; don E take de pickin back;
> Or E' show you road way tranga, en E' put you for climb hill.
> En guide some oder person pan broad
> track – take 'um so.[19]

It may be thought that this kind of homespun fatalism was no philosophy for a committed nationalist. One has, however, to bear in mind the kind of influences to which Hayford had been exposed. Her father, a man of decided and clear-cut opinions, had been a disciple of the political reformer Edward Wilmot Blyden (1832–1912) who preached a form of black participation in an international brotherhood, as opposed to the narrower ethnic loyalties of thinkers such as Booker T. Washington and W. E. DuBois. In his introduction to Blyden's *West Africa Before Europe* (1905), which is quoted verbatim in chapter 17 of *Ethiopia Unbound*, Casely Hayford has this to say:

The work of men like Booker T. Washington and W. E. DuBois is exclusive and provincial. The work of Edward Wilmot Blyden is universal, covering the entire race and the entire race problem. What do I mean? I mean this: that while Booker T. Washington seeks to promote the material advancement of the black man in the United States, and W. E. Burghard DuBois his social enfranchisement amid surroundings and in an atmosphere uncongenial to racial development, Edward Wilmot Blyden has sought for more than a quarter of a century to reveal everywhere the African unto himself ; to fix his attention upon original ideas and conceptions as to his place in the economy of the world; to point out to him his work as a race among the races of men; lastly and most important of all, to lead him back unto self-respect.[20]

'Self-respect' is the key word here, with all its bracing Edwardian associations, and it is to this clean-scrubbed, carbolic wisdom that

---

[18] Gladys Casely Hayford, *Take 'Um So* (Freetown, New Era Press, 1948).
[19] *Ibid.*, p. 1.     [20] Joseph Casely Hayford, *Ethiopia Unbound*, pp. 163–5.

Gladys Casely Hayford owes her principal moral tone: resignation is the door to self-acceptance and happiness, and through them a place in the completed community of mankind. This emphasis comes out again in her poem 'Wings, dedicated to the R.A.F. men', based on an earlier poem by W. B. Yeats:

> I who am black yearn too to near the stars,
> To beat my planes' smooth wings across sky bars;
> To see Aurora rise, and glide near Mars –
> I who am black.
>
> I who am black now face the belching fire
> Where bullets spurt, to quench another's ire,
> If I must die, it is always my desire
> I who am black,
>
> That after crawling deep in trenches stain,
> To suit another's purpose and his gain,
> Wearing my wings, I'll travel through the flame
> And re-ascend in glory – whence I came,
> I who am black.[21]

Though the brand of Christianity here possesses a sort of Sunday school mawkishness, the theme gives us a very sharp idea of the sort of international comradeship to which men and women of Hayford's generation felt that they properly belonged. It is the same kind of motivated vision as encouraged hundreds of young Africans of the period to join the Boy Scout and Girl Guide movements, and, though its optimism may now seem a little misplaced, it is important to recognize the sense of meaning that it gave to many at the time. The feeling behind such pieces has the unabrasive friendliness of a fighting unit, and any tinge of resentment that remains arises from the suspicion that, in the officers' mess, at least, a membership card may not be forthcoming for coloured gentlemen – without a delay, that is, and a few searching questions.

If Hayford's loyalties are regimental, so is much of her rhythm and technique. Her verse characteristically marches to a rousing beat, and in this she owes as much to the traditions of hymn-singing in the Christian church as she does to anything more explicitly military. This is clearly demonstrated in a poem such as 'Rejoice':

> Rejoice and shout with laughter
> Throw all your burdens down,

[21] Gladys Casely Hayford, *Take 'Um So*.

31

## West African Poetry

If God has been so gracious
As to make you black or brown.
For you are a great nation,
A people of great birth
For where would spring the flowers
If God took away the earth?
Rejoice and shout with laughter
Throw all your burdens down
Yours is a glorious heritage
If you are black, or brown. [22]

In order to appreciate the aptness of the imagery here, it is important to recognize that the comparison of the negro race to 'the earth' in line 8 need not have pejorative associations. Earth connotes fecundity and fruition as much as lowliness, and it is this meaning which is uppermost in the poet's mind. Gladys Casely Hayford came from a generation of West Africans that was strongly disposed to think of themselves as inferior: hence the urgency of the appeal to self-respect. One could extend this idea by suggesting that the comparison of white people to 'flowers' in the previous line carried implications of effeminacy, but exactly how deliberate such an overtone is it is hard to say. The salient message, however, is one of interdependence. Hayford does not belong strictly to the nationalist phase of West African history, which was in full swing a decade later, but rather to the earlier period of commitment to working constructively within that vanished entity, British West Africa. It is to this notion that she responds most deeply, and it is this which gave her vocation as a guide and teacher meaning and direction.

Hayford's professional teaching career perhaps afforded her insights into the needs of her society denied to those whose way of life is more narrowly dedicated to art. In this she was not untypical of her age. It was highly unusual for West Africa's first generation of English language poets to earn a living through literature. Raphael Armattoe, amongst the most versatile, was a doctor by profession. He was in his late thirties before he published any poetry, and then in a flimsy and limited edition. He had already passed through all the stages of medical apprenticeship, and after qualifying, settled down to work in Northern Ireland, where he rose to the directorship of a leading research institute. His research into the use of the *abochi* drug against human parasites earned him a nomination for the Nobel Prize for physiology

---

[22] *Ibid.*

in 1948. In addition speculations poured from his ardent pen on a
whole range of other subjects, giving proof of his exceptionally
omnivorous, if occasionally idiosyncratic discursive energy. *A Racial
Survey of the British People* (1944)[23] was closely followed by a tribute
to *The Swiss Contribution to Western Civilization*[24] of the same year and
then by *A Homage to Three Great Men: Schweitzer, Schroedinger,
De Gennaro*[25] of 1945. His abiding enthusiasm, however, was for
the cause of Togolese independence and unity, for born in Keta in
what is now the Volta Region of Ghana in 1913, he always retained
a fierce affection for the Ewe fatherland of his childhood, and a
determination that at independence it should not be swallowed up
in the larger unit of Ghana – as in fact transpired – but follow ethnic
logic by joining up with the mandated French territory of Togo to form
an Ewe nation–state. To this end, in 1946 he delivered in Dublin a
strongly worded and erudite lecture entitled *The Golden Age of West
African Civilization*,[26] at the heart of which is a passionate plea for a rec-
ognition of the Togolese place within the wider political geography of
the African continent. This was later published by the Lomeshie Re-
search Centre for Anthropology and Race Biology in Londonderry in a
lavish edition including photographs of the glories of West African
civilization from the museums of the world. Armattoe was killed in
1953 in a motor accident while returning from a delegation to the
United Nations to demand the unification of French and British Togo.
His poems were collected after his death, and, in 1954, under the title
*Deep Down the Blackman's Mind*[27] published in a more substantial
edition by Arthur Stockwell of Ilfracombe, a firm much associated
with the early West African literary pioneers.

Though a nationalist by conviction, Armattoe spent very little of his
life in Africa. He was thirteen when he left his native land and went to
pursue his secondary education in Britain. Despite regular visits back
home, and an intense reading of africana in the libraries of Europe,
Africa seems always to have remained an abstraction for him. We can

[23] Raphael Ernest Grail Armattoe, *A Racial Survey of the British People* (Londonderry; Sen-
tinel, 1944).
[24] Raphael Ernest Grail Armattoe, *The Swiss Contribution to Western Civilization* (Dun-
dalk: Dundalgan Press, 1944).
[25] Raphael Ernest Armattoe, *A Homage to Three Great Men: Schweitzer, Schroedinger and De
Gennaro* (Londonderry: Sentinel, 1945).
[26] Raphael Ernest Grail Armattoe, *The Golden Age of West African Civilization* (London-
derry: Lomeshie Research Centre and Sentinel, 1946).
[27] Raphael Ernest Grail Armattoe, *Deep Down the Blackman's Mind* (Ilfracombe: Arthur H.
Stockwell, 1954).

see this quite clearly in a piece like 'Nostalgia or Spring in Eweland':

> Just to see my father now
> That the mangoes are in bloom,
> And all o'er the pleasant vale
> Gay butterflies gad about;
> When the all-pervading air
> Sweetly through the garden steals,
> And tall palm trees gently wave
> To orange trees with golden fruits;
> To be there, though quite alone,
> Is truly to be alive!
>
> Ah to see my mother now,
> When the mangoes are in bloom,
> Brown, purple, yellow, green and gold;
> When lilacs and hibiscus,
> Eucalyptus and lemon,
> Cannabis and lavender,
> And geraniums vie with roses
> On slender stems in the air!
> Oh, to be in Lomé now,
> At Easter, the year's springtime
> And see my own youth again![28]

This is not one of the pieces singled out for showcase treatment in Donatus Nwoga's 1966 anthology of *West African Verse*,[29] and with good reason. But it is a very good demonstration of the difficulties under which Armattoe laboured. If you exclude the reference to mangoes (which are observed, somewhat contentiously as being 'in bloom'), and to Lomé (which itself is seen as featuring in some kind of pastoral idyll), the description might well be a conventional English May-time celebration. The location is clearly Togo, where Armattoe grew up, and about which he had a detailed objective knowledge, but the poet lacks any efficient mechanism for bringing the particularity of that environment to life, nor has he any sense of the heritage of oral Ewe verse, of which we spoke in the last chapter. Instead he reclines upon Rupert Brooke (of whose *Vicarage at Granchester* the second line is a clear echo), and even more heavily on Robert Browning; the entire lyric is clearly a re-working of the famous lament 'Oh to be in England now that April's here'. The tragedy is that though Armattoe's longing for Eweland is deeply felt, it is parading in such a wardrobe of boaters and Oxford flannels as to make the place all but unrecognizable.

[28] *Ibid.*, p. 61.     [29] Donatus Nwoga, *West African Verse* (London: Longman, 1966).

Armattoe's deficiency, then, is not one of commitment, but of poetic vocabulary, and the faculty of visualizing and evoking situations accurately. There is another, related failure: the tendency to rely on derived patterns of expression, or a tone of voice, borrowed from the Georgians. It has been suggested, by the South African writer Lewis Nkosi[30] among others, that this is largely a matter of the verse form, as if the deployment of regular rhythm and rhyme itself constituted a sort of artistic betrayal. While this claim may to a certain extent be justified, it is not simply a matter of the verse technique being European and therefore derivative. Armattoe's manner of writing is not simply unafrican: it was even in its own time decades behind contemporary mainstream English verse, let alone the innovations of the *avant-garde*. At the time these poems were published, Eliot's *The Waste Land* (1922) had been around for the best part of thirty years. 'Free verse' so called was already conventional in Europe; poetically Armattoe can be seen to be turning his back, not only on Africa, but also on the European literary scene of his own time. We have already paid tribute to the considerations that led Gladys Casely Hayford to avoid free verse in favour of the martial music of the Methodist hymn, but none of this applies to Armattoe, whose Georgian gorgeousness is just a sort of hand-me-down fustian.

For all this, Armattoe has stronger moments – for instance this:

*The White Man's Grave*
For Sir Francis Galton, F.R.S., founder of the Galton Laboratory, University College, London, who hoped that the yellow races of China might 'extrude hereafter the coarse and lazy Negro from at least the metaliferous regions of tropical Africa'.

> No longer do the brave
> Brave the white man's grave
> For science has changed its face,
> Making a garden space
> For God's chosen race,
> Since kids and women grace
> The now lovely place,
> The bastard negro race
> Must leave without a trace,
> Must find some other place.
> Why not underground,
> Or just out of bound

[30] cf. *West Africa*, No. 3201, November 1978, pp. 2289–90.

For the bastard hound?
Offer him a pound;
Dope him well and sound.
Let him hang around,
A dog lost and found,
Choking without a sound,
Dying without a sound,
The poor bastard hound![31]

Here the callous and supercilious remark of a medical colleague has stung Armattoe into such an indignant though controlled response, that he has abandoned his usual effeminate languishing for a virile torrent of rage, mastered by the use of a simple repetitive metre and rhyme scheme which fits his cajoling tone exactly. Despite patches of roughness and a slight element of self-pity near the end, the poem as a whole is distinguished by its directness and wholly justified rage. At moments such as this, Armattoe is close to the changing mood of the times, and, despite his long exile, proves himself in the forefront of those who were demanding a new deal on the West coast of Africa.

By far the most successful poem of Armattoe's, however, is his vision of the young airman foreseeing his death:

I would like to go while still young,
While the dew is wet on the grass;
To perish in a great air crash,
With a silver 'plane burning bright
Like a flashing star in the night;
While the huge wreckage all ablaze,
Shines brightly for my last embrace
I'd like to see the flames consume
Each nerve and bone and hair and nail,
Till of dust naught but ash remains.
Or as stone, swiftly sink unseen.
But if I should hear someone wail,
Because dust has gone back to dust,
Mad with fury, I shall return
To smite the poor wretch on the head.
So, let me go when I am young,
And the dew is still on the fern,
With a silver 'plane burning bright,
Like a flashing star in the night.[32]

The kind of passionate refusal to compromise that would prefer an

[31] Armattoe, *Deep Down the Black Man's Mind*, p. 26.
[32] Nwoga, *West African Verse*, pp. 13–14.

*Ladies and gentlemen*

early and sudden death to a gradual waning of the physical and emotional powers is given dignity here by the slow, balanced lines, capped with delicate, unobtrusive half-rhymes. As in Gladys Casely Hayford's poem 'Wings', the aircraft itself, though a thing of steel, is transmuted by a sort of metaphysical glamour that makes it a fit receptacle for the poet's soul, and the flames of its conflagration are described in terms which recall a religious experience, a sacrificial self-immolation. The whole structure is tempered by a becoming restraint, which avoids either sentimentality or hysteria.

Despite their varying degrees of commitment to the idea of the progress of the black races, neither Phillis Wheatley, Gladys Casely Hayford nor Raphael Armattoe could be called political poets in any strict sense. The same cannot be said of the generation of poets who lived in West Africa itself during the 1940s and 1950s and were hence intimately involved in the independence struggle. These were the nationalist poets proper for whom verse was principally seen as a tool of political agitation. Among them were several politicians such as Nnamdi Azikwe of Nigeria, who published poems in newspapers and periodicals in addition to his political speeches. Amidst the host of other comparatively minor figures, however – including Roland Tombekai Dempster of Liberia, Crispin George of Sierra Leone and Benibengor Blay of Ghana – two names stand out: Dennis Chukude Osadebay of Nigeria, and Michael Dei-Anang of Ghana.

Like many of those writing at the time, Dennis Osadebay was a man of public affairs: jurist, journalist, politician, former premier of the Mid-Western Region of the Federation of Nigeria. Osadebay was both a very private and a very public writer. His poetic output, collected in 1952 in the volume *Africa Sings*[33] constitutes almost an autobiography in verse. On the one hand, he was much given to private reflections and on his twenty-fifth birthday wrote a dour poem lamenting the onset of middle age. His best verse, however, certainly deals with public events and attitudes, especially with what seems to have been for him the crucial turning point, the Second World War. The irony that, between 1939 and 1945, Nigerian soldiers were enlisted into the British forces to help fight a war against the threat of Hitler's German Empire, while their own country was still a subject colony, lends

[33] Dennis Chukude Osadebay, *Africa Sings* (Ilfracombe: Arthur H. Stockwell, 1952).

much of his verse written at the time a cutting edge:

> 'Tis not the vain desire to rule
> O'er foreign lands and peoples new
> That led us to this clash of arms;
> 'Tis but the duty to pursue
> The holy path of truth and right
> And help destroy encroaching might.[34]

He was very conscious of the part that Nigeria had to play in the international arena, and his best-known poem, 'Africa's Plea', deals with the falseness of the exotic interest which foreigners often take in African art and culture, a reaction which is currently epitomized in the fashionable cant phrase 'naïve art':

> Don't preserve my customs
> As some fine curios
> To suit some white historian's tastes.
> There's nothing artificial
> That beats the natural way
> In culture and ideals of life.
> Let me play with the whiteman's ways
> Let me work with the blackman's brains
> Let my affairs themselves sort out.
> Then in sweet rebirth
> I'll rise a better man
> Not ashamed to face the world.[35]

Michael Dei-Anang was a diplomat by career, and much of his poetic writing reads like a public relations exercise on behalf of 'Ghana Resurgent' (the title of a prose portrait of the country which he published in 1964).[36] Born in 1909 at Mampong Akwapim on the ridge above the Accra plains, he attended Achimota College in the early days before proceeding to London University. He was much interested in the history of his people, and published a couple of plays on incidents in Akan history: *Okomfo Anokye's Golden Stool* (1959) and the delightfully named *Cocoa to Mampong* (1949).[37] The latter deals with the heroic feat of Tettey Quarshiie in bringing the cocoa bean from Fernando Po to the Akwapim Ridge where it flourished to form the basis of Ghana's future wealth.

---

[34] *Ibid.*, p. 49.    [35] Nwoga, *West African Verse*, p. 17.
[36] Michael Dei-Anang, *Ghana Resurgent* (Accra: Waterville Publishing House, 1964).
[37] Michael Dei-Anang, *Cocoa to Mampong* (Cape Coast: Methodist Book Depot, 1949); *Okomfo Anokye's Golden Stool* (Ilfracombe: Arthur H. Stockwell Ltd, 1959).

Indeed, it is to the period of Ghana's short-lived prosperity in the 1950s and 1960s, when the country was in the forefront of Africa's advance, that Dei-Anang really seems to belong. His work is one long paean in praise of a nation whose birthpangs he had an excellent chance to observe and which, as a career diplomat, he was officially engaged in explaining to a wider world:

> Awake, ye Gold Coast sons
> And daughters of a reckless age!
> Awake, and scan with me,
> From page to page,
> The pregnant paragraphs
> Of our country's past;
> For history is God's traffic light  !!
> That beckons on the nations all,
> Or warns them to wait
> Their appropriate moments of advance.[38]

*this is awful!*

We are reminded of how much of a novelty traffic lights were in Accra in the fifties, and it is along the newly renamed Independence Avenue that Dei-Anang's poetry seems always to be sailing in a chauffeur-driven car, pointing out the sights and the spanking new buildings to some prestigious foreign visitor. Yet Dei-Anang was no naïve meliorist. He liked to set his views of modern Ghana against a backdrop of the country's past, and it is to this marked sense of history that we owe some of his strongest moments. One of his poems, from *Ghana Glory* is officially a celebration of the new Akosombo Dam, but the kernel of the poem arises not from the diplomat's need to justify, but from the poetic historian's sense of the majesty of ancestral inheritance:

> Akosombo, Nkosonkonsombo,
> Symbol of a people's hopes and faith;
> Akosombo Nkosonkonsombo,
> Chain of a host of cloistered hills,
> Refuge for brave Akwamu's fighting forces.
>
> As of old, the Akwamus of this land
> Seeking succour from the miseries of war,
> Found happiness and sustenance from these parts
> So, in our time, let the technicalities of science
> And the restless skill of the builder's mind,

[38] Michael Dei-Anang, *Wayward Lines from Africa* (London: United Society for Christian Literature, 1946), p. 31.

Conspiring to subdue and dominate these pristine waters,
Bring ample power and faith to this land of Gold.[39]

So also, at the heart of 'Awake ye Gold Coast Sons!' we have an evoca-
tion of the wanderings of the Akan people from the desert wastes to
the forest in search of a permanent home, a poetic chronicle which
recalls some of the longer Psalms of David concerning the tribulations
of the Israelites in the desert:

> They moved:
> Huts, children, wives and all,
> Undazzled by the glare of gold,
> Nor grace of royal rule.
>
> They trekked for months;
> No fears of hunger and of thirst,
> Nor e'en of desert heat,
> Desiccating the skin,
> Withstood their iron will:
> So strong in the strength
> Of a mind
> To some deed inclined.[40]

It is difficult to make great critical claims for West Africa's first gen-
eration of English language poets. Too often their technique was slack
or borrowed, or suffered from patches of clumsiness in which the
passion of political conviction failed to find any meaningful verbal
correlative in the verse. Their importance lies less in the poetic merit of
their work than in the fact that they opened up new terrain and, by
convincing reluctant publishers that West Africa had something
worthwhile to say, prepared a way along which the later generation of
more innovative writers could follow. Their work appears outdated
and faded now, like the strains of a Salvation Army Band retreating
out of earshot caught on the wind. Nevertheless, much of what they
said about the need for racial self-respect has not diminished in rel-
evance or urgency. The breadth of their appeal, the fact that they
addressed themselves to the problems that mattered in language
which a large public could understand, might very well have served as
a salutary lesson to a later generation of anglophone poets whose
work, through its very sophistication, excluded part of the potential

---

[39] Michael Dei-Anang, *Ghana Glory* (London: Nelson, 1965).
[40] Dei-Anang, *Wayward Lines from Africa*, p. 13.

readership. The extent to which their own work borrowed from debased antique models was a reflection of their intellectual isolation, not merely from the European *avant-garde*, but from a school of writers in neighbouring francophone Africa whose work we must now consider.

# CHAPTER 3

# *The* négritude *movement*

In 1927 by a riverside in Madagascar a twenty-six-year-old Malagasy poet composed a sonnet comparing the water's course to his own growing skill in the language of his French masters. If only, he wrote, his lines might aspire to the grace and undulating curve of the river bank itself:

> . . . que sa courbe épouse encore plus ta rive
> beau fleuve auquel l'azur éternel se fiance
> et sa souplesse aura la suprême élégance
> de tes bords ténébreux que le soleil ravive,
>
> afin d'honorer mieux cette langue étrangère
> qui sait tant à mon âme intuitive plaire
> et que j'adopte sans éprouver nul remords[1]

[. . . I would have my song's course wedded quite / to thine, fair river, sky-betrothed, that thence / its suppleness attain the elegance / of thy dim margins which the sun makes bright, / and I may honour more that foreign speech / which with delight my instinctive soul can reach, / which I adopt, nor grieve upon that head]

The island of Madagascar had been a French possession since 1896. Already by the 1920s its educational and social policies were dominated by the policy of Assimilation which was to have so far-reaching an effect on the intelligentsia of francophone Central and West Africa in the years before and immediately following the Second World War. As a lowly paid drudge in a printing works in Antananarivo, Jean-Joseph Rabéarivelo can be said to have escaped the full alienating force of that policy, but his mind and art were nonetheless captive, not simply to *cette langue étrangère*, but to an infatuation with the finest of French poetry and culture and to a tragic unrequited longing for a French *patrie* he was never to see.

Twenty years later, and a decade after Rabéarivelo's suicide, his work featured in two anthologies collated by poets from elsewhere in

---

[1] Jean-Joseph Rabéarivelo, *Sylves* (Nobles dédains; Fleurs mêlées: Destinées Dixains, Sonnets et poèmes d'Iarive) (Antananarivo: Imprimerie de l'Imerina, 1927).

the French Empire. The first was *Poètes d'expression française*, compiled by Léon Damas of French Guiana.[2] The second and more influential, *Anthologie de la nouvelle poésie nègre et malgache*[3] was edited by a brilliant young poet from Senegal, *agrégé de lettres* and *deputé* in the French Assembleé Nationale, called Léopold Sédar Senghor. Rabéarivelo's appearance alongside his fellow Malagasy Flavien Ranaivo[4] in an anthology largely devoted to verse from West Africa and the French West Indies is not difficult to understand. In Senghor's eyes Rabéarivelo was significant both as precursor and as emblem, since, though from the other side of the continent and exempt from the more drastic excesses of the French educational system, his life bore witness to two essential elements in the black francophone predicament: a liege-bond to French literature and a countervailing desire to assert his local uniqueness through an imitation of indigenous forms. Like so many of the writers of French expression who were to follow in his stead, Rabéarivelo had been torn between two impulses. He wrote some early verse in *hova* and later, in his last published collection[5] followed the structures of the local Madagascan *hain-teny* or proverb-poem. But at its most delicate and evocative his poetry reminds us most strongly of Baudelaire, of his beloved Rimbaud, and of the voluptuary lusciousness of Mallarmé.

It has become customary to bewail Rabéarivelo's physical and cultural isolation, and also his lack of any clear commitment to a truly national identity. In practice both forms of commiseration are misplaced. When compared with the anglophone poets discussed in the last chapter, Rabéarivelo enjoyed two supreme advantages. In the first place, though he never reached Paris, his acceptance amongst a small group of expatriate French writers resident in Madagascar had exposed him to recent developments in French literature. In the second, he possessed immediate access to an indigenous tradition which in his later French verse he learned to reproduce with a certain fidelity. All that he lacked compared with a later generation of more committed francophone writers was a cause, something which before

---

[2] Léon Damas, *Poètes d'expression française* (Paris: Editions du Seuil, 1947).

[3] Léopold Sédar Senghor (ed.), *Anthologie de la nouvelle poésie nègre et malgache de langue française* (Paris: Presses Universitaires de France, 1948).

[4] Author of *L'Ombre et le vent* (Tananarive: Imp. Officielle, 1947); *Mes Chansons de toujours* (Paris: author, 1955), and *Le Retour au bercail* (Tananarive: Imp. Nationale, 1962). See also *The Poetic Works of Flavien Ranaivo* (Nendeln, Liechtenstein: Kraus Reprint, 1970).

[5] Jean-Joseph Rabéarivelo, *Vieilles chansons de pays d'Imerina, précédeés d'une biographie du poète Malgache par Robert Boudry* (Antananarivo: Imp. Officielle, 1939), published after the author's death.

the ideologically inflamed years of the late thirties was not as manda-
tory a requirement for a self-respecting *indigène* as might now perhaps
appear. When in the forties the banner of *négritude* was raised aloft,
Rabéarivelo was dead and the poetry of French-speaking Africa had
changed decisively.

The term *négritude* was first coined by the Martinican poet Aimé
Césaire in his long confessional poem *Cahier d'un retour au pays natal*,
much fêted by André Breton on its first appearance in book form in
1947 and subsequently re-issued by Présence Africaine, the publish-
ing concern established in Paris by Alioune Diop in 1948 as a platform
for black writing.[6] Senghor's *Anthologie* included a lengthy extract
from the *Cahier*, and it was also due to Senghor's inspired advocacy
that *négritude* entered the arteries of francophone literature. Literally
construed, the word means the inherent attributes, traits and outlook
of the black peoples. In the context of a world dominated by imperia-
lism this was itself a sufficiently radical idea in the 1940s. Though
clearly intended by Césaire to carry a succinct political edge, the word
originally bore no precise philosophical connotation. Indeed, without
Senghor's aptitude for abstraction, sharpened by years at the Lycée
Louis-le-Grand and the Sorbonne, it is possible that *négritude* might
have continued to float in the air for years, an hibiscus fragrance never
to be distilled. In Senghor's incisive mind, however, it soon took
shape as a system, something which in itself was not calculated to rec-
ommend it to the intellectuals of English-speaking Africa.

*Anthologie de la nouvelle poésie* had carried a defiant preface by Jean-
Paul Sartre,[7] and something of Sartre's passionate logic entered too
into the formulation of *négritude*. Its method of deduction was Car-
tesian. To the monumental intellectual certainty of Descartes' classic
statement *je pense donc je suis* it returned a reply couched in terms
equally absolute: *je suis nègre donc je suis*. It was thus a theory very
amenable to the Existentialism fashionable in the Quartier Latin at the
time, since it represented both an act of choice and a definition of es-
sence. Regarded in another light it can be seen as having its origins in
the colonial Assimilation policy which attempted to transform all
*evolué* Africans into honorary Frenchmen, a violation of identity which

---

[6] Aimé Césaire's *Cahier d'un retour au pays natal* was originally published in the review
*Volontés* No. 20, Paris, August 1939, pp. 23–51, and first appeared in book form, with
an introduction by André Breton, in an edition by Bordas (Paris, 1947). An Edition Dé-
finitive was published by Présence Africaine (Paris, 1956) with a new introduction by
Petar Guberina.

[7] Jean-Paul Sartre, 'Orphée noir' in *Anthologie de la nouvelle poésie*, pp. ix–xliv.

it countered with a statement of intent conceived in exactly contrary terms.

In Senghor's mind *négritude* went further and became an entire critique of civilization. Educated to regard reason as all important, he soon proceeded to turn the armoury of reason against reason itself in the interests of a distinctive black aesthetic:

although with the African as well as the European the great rule is to please, they do not each find pleasure in the same things. In Greco-Latin esthetics, which survived in the West until the end of the nineteenth century, art is 'imitation of nature', or rather, a rectified imitation. In Africa, it is an explanation and understanding of the world, *a sensitive participation in the reality which underlies the world*, that is, in a *surreality*, or rather, in the vital forces which animate the world. The European finds pleasure in recognizing the world through the reproduction of the object, which is designated under the name of the 'subject'; the African, in becoming vitally acquainted with the world through image and rhythm. With the European, the line of sensation leads to the heart and the head. With the African, it leads to the heart and the belly, to the root of life.[8]

So in 1956 wrote the newly appointed Senegalese Secretary of State in the pages of *Présence Africaine*, the cultural review established by Alioune Diop at his Paris publishing house in 1948. The programme envisaged in such a passage is clearly designed as a defence of an authentically African way of apprehending reality. Yet it is arguable that, in attempting to transcend the teaching of both Voltaire and Rousseau towards a new synthesis, a fresh nexus of sensation located in the abdomen, Senghor is less obviously reflecting his own Senegalese, Serer inheritance, than perpetuating a rejection of the rational, ordering intelligence epitomized, in Senghor's student years, by the acolytes of the Surrealist movement.

In fact, though the poetry of Senghor's friend Aimé Césaire was much influenced by the Surrealists, Senghor's own early verse manifested a debt to a rather more conservative strand in contemporary French literature: the tradition represented by the *Grandes Odes* of Paul Claudel and by Saint-John Perse's *Anabase*. In *Hosties noires*, Senghor's second volume of 1948, most of which was conceived in a prisoner-of-war camp, and in which he celebrates the contribution of Senegalese troops to the liberation of Mother France, the influence of Claudel is

---

[8] Léopold Sédar Senghor, 'L'Esprit de la civilisation ou les lois de la culture négro-africaine, *Présence africaine*, Juin–Novembre, 1956.

particularly marked.[9] The tell-tale signs are easy to find: a swelling, free-wheeling line with flexible deployment of the caesura; elliptical syntax; stylized repetition and a preference for the metaphor over the simile. It is there, for example, throughout the poem 'Luxembourg 1939'[10] in the multiple repetitions and staggered syntax of line two, the inversions of line seven (*vaincus mes rêves, désespérément mes camarades*), and in the accumulated repetitions of the very next line. It is there even more spectacularly in the long, ceremonial pieces such as 'Prière de Paix'.[11]

At its most successful, this fusion of French verse technique and African sensibility achieves a strange, compelling alchemy. The earliest poems collected in *Chants d'ombre*, Senghor's first volume of 1945, are among the most effective Senghor ever wrote. Their impressiveness is partly a matter of their generosity of spirit, a sort of tragic optimism which suffuses the frictions and disappointments of the moment with a rejuvenating vision of hope, and partly of their deliberate exploitation of ambiguities of time and place, a Modernist technique which yields considerable dividends. In 'In Memoriam', for instance, we are treated to a fitful evocation of sleep in which the poet, tossing on his pillow in a rain-shrouded Paris attic, passes and repasses from the stark waking reality of exile to the soothing assurance of ancestral presences:

C'est Dimanche.
J'ai peur de la foule de mes semblables au visage de pierre.
De ma tour de verre qu'habitent les migraines, les Ancêtres impatients
Je contemple toits et collines dans la brume
Dans la paix – les cheminées sont graves et nues.
A leurs pieds dorment mes morts, tous mes rêves faits poussière
Tous mes rêves, le sang gratuit répandu le long des rues, mêlé au sang des
   boucheries.
Et maintenant, de cet observatoire comme de banlieue
Je contemple mes rêves distraits le long des rues, couchés au pied des collines
Comme les conducteurs de ma race sur les rives de la Gambie et du Saloum
De la Seine maintenant, au pied des collines.[12]

[Sunday / The crowding stony faces of my fellows make me afraid / Out of my tower of glass haunted by headaches and my restless Ancestors / I watch the rooves and hills wrapped in mist / Wrapped in peace ... the chimneys are

---

[9] Léopold Sédar Senghor, *Chants d'ombre, suivi de Hosties noires* (Paris: Editions du Seuil, 1948).
[10] *Ibid.*, pp. 101–2.    [11] *Ibid.*, pp. 145–53.    [12] *Ibid.*, p. 9

heavy and stark. / At their feet my dead are sleeping, all my dreams made dust / All my dreams, blood freely spilt along the streets, mingled with blood from butcheries. / And now, from this observatory, as if from the outskirts of the town / I watch my dreams listless along the streets, sleeping at the foot of the hills / Like the forerunners of my race on the banks of the Gambia and Salum / Now of the Seine, at the foot of the hills.]

As the poet surveys the cloudy contours of the city through a misty window, the blood of his own Serer people, poured out for strangers' gain, mingles with the effluent from the *abattoirs* while, nestling beneath the *butte Montmartre*, his ancestors like him stir on their bed of pain. Along with the confluence of place there is an accompanying conflation of rituals, the Catholic Feast of All Souls blending with a Senegambian reverence for the immanent arrival of the dead in the world of nahwal objects. It is the animist vision which prevails, supporting the poet in his isolation with its warm reassurance of fellowship. The poem maintains a fine balance between this firm, compensatory recognition of kinship and a humanism wide enough to embrace even the disdainful French. For, though *hauteur* of his hosts will not abate, nor the sterility of their religious observances quicken, the Parisians are still 'mes semblables' and the seclusion of the poet's garret perverse in its separateness. Finally he must descend to the *boulevards* and greet not only the victims of his own race, but even those stern unyielding Frenchmen with their averted gazes, their hands withdrawn from greeting.

If Senegalese presences haunt the streets of Senghor's Paris, Senegal itself is frequently viewed in these early pieces through French eyes. Much of *Chants d'ombre* is devoted to a series of reminiscences of the poet's homeland, written while Senghor was slowly making his way up the lower rungs of the educational and political establishment in Paris. In recalling the savannahs of his youth Senghor constantly takes refuge in the refined exoticism of the poet–diplomat Saint-John Perse, extracts from whose poem *Anabase* had made such an impact on French literary circles when published shortly after the First World War.[13] The tendency is present even when Senghor is evoking evening as it falls over Joal, his village of birth:

[13] In his essay 'Comme les Lamantins vont boire a la source' in *Ethiopiques* (Paris: Editions du Seuil, 1956) Senghor states that he first read Perse 'after the liberation'. However, portions of *Anabase* were published in the *Nouvelle revue française*, Tom. 22, as far back as 1919 and can scarcely have evaded his attention. The entire text was translated by T. S. Eliot under the title *Anabasis* and published in London by Faber and Faber in 1930.

Je me rappelle les signares à l'ombre verte des vérandas
Les signares aux yeux surréels comme un clair de lune sur la grève.

Je me rappelle les fastes du Couchant
Ou Koumba N'Dofène voulait faire tailler son manteau royal.

. . .

Je me rappelle les voix païennes rythmant le *Tantum Ergo*,
Et les processions et les palmes et les arcs de triomphe.

. . .

Je me rappelle, je me rappelle . . .
Ma tête rythmant
Quelle marche lasse le long des jours d'Europe où parfois
Apparaît un jazz orphelin qui sanglote sanglote sanglote.[14]

[I remember the *signares* in the green shadow of the verandas / *Signares* with eyes surreal as moonlight on the beach. / I remember the pomps of sunset / that Kumba N'Dofene wanted to cut to make his royal cloak. / . . . / I remember pagan rhythmic singing of the *Tantum Ergo* / And processions and palms and triumphal arches. / . . . / I remember, I remember. . . / In my head the rhythm of the tramp tramp / So wearily down the days of Europe where there comes, / Now and then a little orphaned jazz that goes sobbing, sobbing, sobbing.]

The use of the reiterated definite article to conjure up particularities of place and time; the unexplained proper name; the pervasive sense of an inimicable, obliquely sensuous life: all are strongly aromatic of *Anabase*. And, though Senghor's tone of nostalgic melancholy is undeniable, France is never very far away. The Gregorian setting of the *Tantum Ergo* sung by the Christianized Serer has a 'pagan' lilt, but the rite is Catholic nonetheless; and, though the mulatto *signares* (from the Portuguese *senhora*) hold themselves with native grace and dignity, their eyes are still 'surreal', their bodies fetchingly copper-coloured. In the closing lines Senghor gives us a glimpse of his work-weary self slumped over a drink in some dimly lit Parisian *boîte de nuit*, held by the sobbing strains of a jazz band. Yet, though the music lures him toward his *négritude*, the resulting poem appears to purvey a Senegal of the picture postcards, shot in soft focus and peddled by some *bouquiniste* of the *rive gauche*.

The closing allusion to jazz possessed some pertinence in the period in which Senghor wrote these early pieces. The perception of African culture by bohemian circles in the Quartier Latin in the 1940s was

---

[14] Senghor, *Chants d'ombre*, pp. 19–20.

largely channelled through music. The nightclubs portrayed in the novels of Sartre's *Chemins de la liberté* sequence abound with negro musicians hunched over their instruments on stage while, cast in an unreal light, white customers sit at the tables discoursing of being and nothingness. A 1944 painting by the French artist Jean Dubuffet perfectly captures the ambience of the period. Called 'Jazz Band: Dirty Style Blues'[15] it depicts six musicians, one hugging a saxophone, another a clarinet, a third plucking at a bass, a fourth groping at the keys of a Steinway grand. Unheard harmonies drift in the air while, sepia-tinted, the players stand mesmerized in a line, their eyes fixed in a drugged coma. It is just such ambivalent perceptions, such alien relishing of an 'orphaned' music, which Senghor is concerned to counter in the music of his early poetry, culled, however remotely, from his memories of far-away Joal.

Much of Senghor's poetry is implicitly built around a contrast in musical styles. 'I must confess, my preference falls on the ear,' he wrote in 1962. 'The elements that first enchant me in a poem are its sensual qualities: its rhythms of line and stanza; above all, its *music*.'[16] This verbal euphony has its equivalent in an implied instrumental accompaniment. From his very first collection Senghor adopted Paul Claudel's practice of stipulating precisely the instrumentation to which he envisaged his text being recited. The instrumentation may be largely notional, and performances precisely as he would have wished comparatively rare, but there is little doubt that the tonal colour of the text reflects Senghor's own inner experience of instrumental *timbre*. If we wish to hear his poetry as its author intended it then, it is as well to bear in mind the distinctive qualities of the accompaniment he has specified. Paul Claudel had inscribed several of his odes 'Pour grande orgue', as does Senghor himself in 'Prière de paix'.[17] In Senghor's own repertory of instruments the most commonly requested are three: the *kora* or Mandinka lute; the *balafong* or pentatonic African xylophone, and the *khalam*, a four-stringed plucked instrument believed by many scholars to be the precursor of the guitar. Of these, the most significant in its influence on the tonal quality of Senghor's own writing is the *kora*.

The *kora*, which may be played either as a solo instrument, as a member of an *ensemble* or as an accompaniment to a recited genealogy

[15] Private collection, Paris.
[16] Léopold Sédar Senghor, 'Saint-John Perse ou la poésie du royaume d'enfance', *Table Rond*, Mai, 1962.
[17] Senghor, *Chants d'ombre*, p. 145.

or chiefly panegyric, is constructed from a half calabash,[18] originally covered with antelope skin, now more usually with cowhide. On either side of a raised bridge run twenty-one strings in two parallel ranks, eleven on one side, ten on the other. The player or *jali* sits with the instrument facing him and resonates the strings with the thumbs and index fingers of both hands,[19] leaving the other fingers free to glide over the surface of the strings to determine volume and *allure*. The resulting tone quality is muted and astringent, at once thinner than the occidental harp and more mellow. Although the tuning of the strings most usually approximates to F Major, alternative tunings produce a range of possible modes, some of which are associated with solo performance, others with the accompaniment of a spoken or sung text. The *kora* tuning *saouta*, for example, corresponds to the Gregorian Lydian mode, while *toomara* is close to the Dorian mode.[20] The mode which Senghor would appear to have in mind for his poems is that which Anthony King calls the 'song mode',[21] the melodic shapes connected with which normally correspond to a short decorated scalic motif as in figure 2(a), followed by a set of more or less constant reiterated phrases, as in figure 2(b).

Fig. 2

[18] *La Kôra de keur moussa* (Senegal: Monastère de Keur Moussa, no date given), p. 1.

[19] Francis Bebey, *Musique de l'Afrique* (Paris: Horizons de France, 1971), p. 70

[20] *La Kôra de keur moussa*, p. 1.

[21] Anthony King, article on the *Kara* in *The New Grove Dictionary of Music and Musicians*, ed. Stanley Sadie 20 Vols. (London: Macmillan, 1980), Vol. 10, p. 190.

The poem in which the plangent strains of the *kora* may most clearly be heard is 'Que m'accompagnent kôras et balafong: Woi pour trois kôras et un balafong' from *Chants d'Ombre*. Composed late in 1939, it is headed by two lines from the Wolof poem from which its title was adapted:

> Eléyây bisimlây! mangi dêti woy Yâram bi.
> Biram Degen-ô! ndendâ'k tamâ'k sabar-ê![22]

[Eléyây bisimlây! Once more I sing the praise of the Noble one/ Biram Degeuen! Let *ndeundeus*, *tamaset* and *sabars* accompany me!]

The *woi* is a solemn choric lament often heard at Senegalese funerals. Indeed the whole poem may be read as an elegy for a communal way of life whose understanding of the meaning of mortality is seen as far surpassing the 'innocent' materialism of Europe. It is with a description of traditional Serer funeral rites that the poem's first section ends:

> La flûte du pâtre modulait la lenteur des troupeaux
> Et quand sur son ombre elle se taisait, résonnait le tam-tam des tanns obsédés
> Qui rhythmait la théorie en fête des Morts.
> Des tirailleurs jetaient leurs chéchias dans le cercle avec des cris aphones, et
>   dansaient en flammes hautes mes soeurs
> Téning-Ndyaré et Tyagoum-Ndyaré, plus claires maintenant que le cuivre
>   d'outre-mer.[23]

[The herdsman's flute piped to the slow movements of the cattle / And when in its shadow it fell silent, the drums sounded from the insistent *tanns* / Beating a rhythm for the line of dancers at the feast of the Dead. / The *tirailleurs* threw down their caps in the circle with aphonic shouts and my sisters danced like leaping flames / Tening-Ndyaré and Tyagum-Ndyaré, brighter now than copper from across the sea.]

The *tirailleurs* here are members of the élite corps of Senegalese infantrymen founded in 1857 by governor Faidherbe; they also, however, stand for the Senegalese soldiers recruited into the imperial army at the onset of the Second World War. The 'dead' represent both the deceased for whom the mourners are gathered and, prospectively, the casualties of the holocaust which is about to engulf Europe. 'Que m'accompagnent kôras et balafong' was written at Chateau-Gontier in the months from October to December, 1939. Like 'Neige sur Paris'

---

[22] Senghor, *Chants d'ombre*, p. 40      [23] *Ibid.*, pp. 41–2.

and 'Luxembourg, 1939', then, it is a product of the ominous period which intervened between the declaration of hostilities with Germany and the capitulation of Paris in June, 1940. All of this is very much in Senghor's mind as once more he recalls the blessed seclusion of Joal:

Quels mois? quelle année?
Koumba Ndofène Dyouf régnait à Dyakhâw, superbe vassal
Et gouvernait l'Administrateur de Sine-Saloum.
Le bruit de ses aïeux et des dyoungs-dyoungs le précédait.
Le pèlerin royal parcourait ses provinces, écoutant dans les bois la complainte
      murmurée.
Et les oiseaux qui babillaient, et le soleil sur leurs plumes était prodigue
Ecoutant la conque éloquente parmi les tombes sages.
Il appelait mon père 'Tokor'; ils échangeaient des énigmes que portaient des
      lévriers à grelots d'or
Pacifiques cousins, ils échangeaient des cadeaux sur les bords du Saloum
Des peaux précieuses des barres de sel, de l'or du Bouré et d'or du Boundou
Et de hauts conseils comme des chevaux du Fleuve.
L'Homme pleurait au soir, et dans l'ombre violette se lamentaient les
      khalams.[24]

[What were the months? What was the year? / Kumba N'Dofene Dyouf reigned at Dyakhaw, a proud vassal / And governed the administrator of Sine-Salum. / The noise of his forefathers and of the *dyoung-dyoungs* went before him. / The royal pilgrim went about his provinces, gave ear in the wood to murmured grievance / To the prattle of birds; the sun was magnificent upon their plumage / Gave ear to the conch eloquent among the prophetic tombs. / He called my father 'Tokor'. They exchanged riddles carried by greyhounds with golden bells, / Cousins in peace, they exchanged gifts on the banks of the Salum / Precious pelts bars of salt and of gold from Bouré, of gold from Boundou / And high council like horses of the River. / The man wept at evening, and in the violet shadow there was lamentation of the *khalams*.]

The *dyoung-dyoung* is the ceremonial drum of the nobility of Sine, the Serer chiefdom situated between the rivers Sine and Salum of which Senghor's family were subjects. Senghor is conveying a half-remembered incident from his childhood ('Quels mois? quelle année?') which led the last reigning monarch of Sine to Joal. Meeting Senghor's father, a cattle-trader of noble blood, Koumba Dyouf addresses him quite naturally as 'Uncle'. The episode is described in some detail in Senghor's later essay 'Saint-John Perse et la royaume d'enfance' (see note 16). Its significance here in the context of a poem

---

[24] *Ibid.*, pp. 45–6.

written under the shadow of war is evident: it is a poignant reminder of the sort of gentle, unforced authority which, under the relaxed régime of Sine, enabled a king equipped in full regalia to address a lowly kinsman with great respect without incurring any loss of face, a memory which puts to shame both the arrogance of imperial France and the egomania of the German Reich.

The theme of authority was increasingly to preoccupy Senghor in the late fifties and early sixties as his career advanced through successive phases as *deputé*, secretary of state, head of government and finally, when the fragile Fédération du Mali broke down late in 1960, president of the fully autonomous sovereign territory of Senegal. The poetry written by Senghor from the mid-fifties onwards was thus increasingly concerned with the meaning of leadership. In forsaking the privilege and privacy of academia for the maelstrom of active politics, Senghor had faced himself with a dilemma: how to remain true to the integrity of the visionary and poet while retaining a firm grip on a country rent by factional and party disagreements. In actuality Senghor proved something of a pragmatist, even, his critics would claim, a self-glorifying opportunist. The poetry of the period however, tells a different story. It gives us access to the precincts of a troubled conscience where the writer of *Chants d'ombre* and *Hosties noires*, the philosopher of *négritude*, strives to reconcile his new responsibilities with older loyalties not easily discarded, and to fashion a genuinely African conception of leadership at one with the harsh necessities of the unrelenting world of *realpolitik*.

*Chaka*, the dramatic poem for several voices from *Éthiopiques* published in 1956, four years before Senghor assumed the presidency, gives us a stark glimpse at the destiny he then predicted for all who attempt to combine the claims of spirituality with the demands of power. In it the great nineteenth-century Zulu emperor is revealed on his death-bed, harrowed by doubt and self-recrimination and hounded by the clamouring protestations of onlookers. Among the more insistent of the accusers is a White Voice, mouthpiece perhaps of liberal opinion, which presses the claims of Chaka's victims and demands reparation. In wresting the nation to his will, Chaka has forfeited not only the respect of the enlightened intelligentsia, but also, more tragically, his own inner creativity and peace of mind. This has been no Faustian gamble, but a decision taken in full knowledge of the consequences. There are certain qualities the true leader cannot afford, the poet implies, and among them are pity and sensitivity. 'Let the politician die and the poet live', cry the Chorus, but as the light fades on an empty stage, Chaka's life is extinguished and with it the frailty of human concern that once flickered within him.

The argument of the play rewards study not only for observers of Senghor's subsequent political career, but for all cynics inclined to deal harshly with leaders whose pursuit of supreme responsibility entails necessary moral compromise. For the critic of Senghor's poetry the structure of the poem proves equally rewarding. If Senghor's vision of the realities of power harks back to early African example, so here does his poetic and dramatic method. It is one of the greatest of the ironies that dogged Senghor's career that, as his allegiance to the purity of *négritude* seemed to grow slacker, and his autocratic style of government alienated more and more liberal opinion both at home and abroad, so his command of indigenous form of expression deepened and strengthened. Despite the lavish instrumentation of his early work, despite his championing of the relevance of vernacular literature to the work of contemporary poets, in his own writing the theory refused at that stage to cohere fully. When the exigencies of power forced him to reassess both his personal loyal ties and his relationship to his society, the result on the other hand was to throw him back on one particular strain of heroic verse which until that moment he had tended to neglect.

Immediately after the end of the Second World War, while working as a member of the research staff at the College Nationale d'Outre-Mer in Paris, Senghor had undertaken a systematic investigation of the aesthetics of Serer and Wolof oral verse, and in particular of the *poèmes gymniques* recited in honour of the contestants at athletic bouts through much of Senegal. His researches involved him in the patient transcription of a great many individual texts, as, over thirty years later, he was to recall:

I took the first steps in my own career under the poetic guidance of the women poets of my own native region, the Kingdom of Sine. Later I transcribed the better part of a hundred songs composed by those women I had come to style my 'three muses': Mariam Ndiayé, Koumba Ndaiasse and Siga Diouf, whose honey-golden voices caused me to tremble with feeling[25]

The *poème gymnique* is in essence a form of choric exhortation. Throughout, the ritual self-advertisement of the contestants is punc-

---

[25] 'Allocution de son excellence Monsieur Léopold Sédar Senghor', address to Pre-Colloque sur le Gabou, Dakar, Senegal, 19 May 1980, p. 6

tuated by the poet's praise and encouragement, her interventions themselves being underscored by the approving comments of the crowd. One such instance of choral participation is quoted at length by Senghor in *La Parole chez Paul Claudel et chez les négro-africaines*, his essay of 1977. A comparison of the text there cited with certain passages in *Chaka* proves helpful to all those interested in Senghor's artistic development:

> Yâga-nâ yâga-nâ yâga-nâ — *Dëgë la* !
> Yâga-nâ dâu rèn sóg a nyëu — *Dëgë la* !
> Wio ! bissimlâi ! dyâma ndôrân di dör — *Dëgë la* !
> Láula tyat láuta xel láula bët ! *Dëgë la* !
> Láula Lâmèny y dôm Ádama ! — *Dëgë la* !
> Kúluxum lú dyigèn súkë dyur ! *Dëgë la* !
> Woi ! dýanxa ndau tâtuy-lên gôr a yiu — *Dëgë la* !
> Gôr a yiu tyámèny al Dyógoma — *Dëgë la* !
> Wur ! gëwël-ô rëkël sâ ndâré li — *Dëgë la* !
> Ai bány a bon bány a bon bány a bon — *Dëgë la* !
>
> Bála ngâ xám né ai bány a bon — *Dëgë la* !
> Ndënde dyib ndâré dyib táma dyib — *Dëgë la* !
> Bé sábar nêká tya bôr bái mbalax — *Dëgë la* !
> Tayá lâ ngâ xám né ai bány a bon — *Dëgë la* !²⁶

> Long ago, long ago, too long — It is true,
> Too long since we met last year — It is true!
> Thanks be to God! Peace! And may the first commence — It is true!
> God protect me from the malice and barb of tongues — It is true!
> From the tongues of all the children of Adam — It is true!
> From all that are born of woman — It is true!
> Young girls, acclaim this lithe young man — It is true!
> This lithe young man, brother of Diogoma — It is true!
> Griot, now strike your drum — It is true!
> Dreadful is the contestant, dreadful, truly dreadful — It is true!
> Before you taste the might of his arm — It is true!
> Strike the *ndeudeu* drum, strike the *ndaré*, strike the *tama* — It is true!
> Let the *sabar* drum prance by the ringside — It is true!
> Then will you taste the might of his arm — It is true!

The *tama* is a small drum much like the Yoruba *dundun* carried under the shoulder by Senegalese *griots*. To the pulse of the *tama* and an accompanying orchestra of percussion instruments, the woman poet sings the praises of the young male contestants who are about to leap into the arena and commence the bout. Around her, a chorus of sup-

---

²⁶ Léopold Sédar Senghor, *La Parole chez Paul Claudel et chez les négro africains* (Dakar: Les Nouvelles Editions Africaines, 1973), pp. 51–2

porters add their refrains. The poem then is a variety of antiphonal panegyric. Senghor makes ironic use of this form at the beginning of the second act of *Chaka*:

LE CORYPHÉE

O Zoulou ô Chaka! Tu n'es plus le Lion rouge dont les yeux incendient les villages au loin.

LE CHOEUR

*Bayêté Bâba! Bayêté ô Bayêté!*

LE CORYPHÉE

Tu n'es plus l'Eléphant qui piétine patates douces, qui arrache palmes d'orgueil.

LE CHOEUR

*Bayêté Bâba! Bayêté ô Bayêté!*

LE CORYPHÉE

Tu n'es plus le Buffle terrible plus que Lion et plus qu'Eléphant
Le Buffle qui brise tout bouclier des braves.
'O mon père' dit 'o ma mère' le dos de la déroute.

LE CHOEUR

*Bayêté Bâba! Bayêté Ô Bayêté!*[27]

[LEADER OF THE CHORUS

O Chaka Zulu, you are no longer the fiery Lion whose eyes burn villages from afar.

CHORUS

*Bayete Baba! Bayete O Bayete!*

LEADER OF THE CHORUS

You are no longer the Elephant trampling the sweet-potatoes, uprooting the palm trees of pride.

CHORUS

*Bayete Baba! Bayete O Bayete!*

[27] Léopold Sédar Senghor, *Ethiopiques*, pp. 45–6.

LEADER OF THE CHORUS

You are no longer the terrible Buffalo, more terrible than Lion or Elephant
The Buffalo who breaks the shield of the brave.
'O my father' says 'O my mother' the back of the rout.


CHORUS

*Bayete Baba! Bayete O Bayete!*]

In *Nocturnes*, the volume of verse Senghor published in 1961 shortly after assuming the presidency, he returned to the *poème gymnique* to help structure a tribute to the trade union leader Anyina Fall. For Senghor Fall had been the very model of modern African leadership: strong, unbending yet responsive to traditional African concepts of collectivity. He was also the victim of unscrupulous elements within his own organization. In paying homage to a dead friend and colleague, Senghor employs the *poème gymnique* in a rather more straightforward, literal manner to salute all men of affairs who are forced to sacrifice privacy and peace of mind for an embattled cause:


LE CORYPHÉE

Les Cynocéphales se jettent sur lui, lui plantent leurs crocs dans le dos. Les Chacals aboient. Le sang ruisselle de ses blessures profondes, qui arrosent la terre d'Afrique. Comme Lion du Ferlo, d'un bond il est hors d'atteinte et, de ses yeux de foudre, tient l'Adversaire à distance.

Mais son coeur sans haine avait été touché – pas son bras.

[The Baboons flung themselves on him, they sank their fangs into his back. The Jackals barked. The blood ran from his deep wounds, watering the soil of Africa. Like the Lion of the Ferlo, with one leap he escaped and held the enemy at bay with his lightning eyes.

But his heart without hate had been touched – not his arm.]


CHOEUR DE JEUNES FILLES

Nina! Nina! Niiiii iiii iiii iiii na!
woi Nina!


CHOEUR DE JEUNES HOMMES

FALL![28]


[28] Léopold Sédar Senghor, *Nocturnes* (Paris: Editions du Seuil, 1961), pp. 79–80.

For a recent generation of critics it has become increasingly difficult to reconcile the poetry of Senghor's middle age, the verse of the states-man, with the earlier mood of tender regret and existential uncer-tainty. The truth is that Senghor's achievement, both as man and as poet, contains more consistency than his less sympathetic observers have been prepared to allow. The uncertainty is still there in the later verse, raised to an even more urgent pitch by the politician's dawning recognition of the ruthlessness which necessarily accompanies all de-cisive action. The grain of hardness some detected in the man's makeup during the years of his presidency was something nurtured with care, and the cost of its cultivation is written all too large over the poetic work of the period. Nor did the president's commitment to *négritude* dim in any real sense. It is important that we recognize what *négritude* was *not*. The strictures levelled at Senghor throughout the sixties were too often a result of a befuddled conflation of *négritude* with the separatist tendencies of the time, tendencies which, in the terms of the Black Power movement of the moment, Senghor might be seen as having betrayed. In contrast with more recent ideologies, *négritude*, however, was always conceived of as a form of black hu-manism, an account of the contribution which it was felt Africa could make to the totality of world civilization. In an essay written shortly after he became President, 'Pierre Teilhard de Chardin et la Politique Africaine', Senghor returned to this theme:

*Négritude* transforms itself from an act of negation to one of assertion. It remains the totality of the values – political, social and moral – of the black world. But henceforth it reposes not simply on the foundation of one unique race, but also on the facts of geography and history. Political and social history. These then are the values – no more or less than the cultural values implicit in the human heart – which constitute the distinctive offering of the black race at the crossroads of giving and receiving.[29]

The sort of cultural contribution to a reinvigorated humanity Sen-ghor has here most keenly in mind can be observed in one of his most justly celebrated poems, written during a visit to New York during the early fifties, a period when the flags of the nations first flew outside the new United Nations Building on Manhattan's East Side, signal of the hopes of all countries, new and old, for post-war reconstruction.

[29] 'Pierre Teilhard de Chardin et la politique négro-africaine', *Cahiers Pierre Teilhard de Chardin*, No.3, 1962, reprinted in Léopold Sédar Senghor, *Pierre Teilhard de Chardin et la politique africaine* (Paris: Editions du Seuil, 1962), p. 63

To the daunting façades of Fifth Avenue and the ostentatious wealth of Wall Street, Senghor replies with his own small plea for compassion, and the sort of immediacy of human warmth to be found uptown among the decaying tenements of Harlem. And as Senghor strains his ear 'autitif' to the music of the New World, it is not the angular certainties of Charles Ives or Elliott Carter to which he responds, but to a lonely horn resounding from the precincts of Harlem's Apollo Theatre, no less American, no less a pledge of vitality in this, the melting pot of nations:

New-York! Je dis New-York, laisse affluer le sang noir dans ton sang
Qu'il dérouille tes articulations d'acier, comme une huile de vie
Qu'il donne à tes ponts la courbe des croupes et la souplesse des lianes.
Voici revenir les temps très anciens, l'unité retrouvée la réconciliation du Lion
    du Taureau et de l'Arbre
L'idée liée a l'acte l'oréille au coeur le signe au sens.
Voilà tes fleuves bruissants des caïmans musqués et de lamantins aux yeux de
    mirages et nul besoin d'inventer les Sirènes.
Mais il suffit d'ouvrir les yeux a l'arc-en-ciel d'Avril
Et les oreilles, surtout les oreilles à Dieu qui d'un rire du saxophone créa le ciel
    et la terre en six jours.
Et le septième jour, il dormit du grand sommeil nègre.[30]

[New York! I say to New York, let the black blood flow into your blood / Cleaning the rust from your steel articulations, like an oil of life / Giving your bridges the curve of the hills, the liana's suppleness. / See, the ancient times come again, unity is rediscovered the reconciliation of the Lion the Bull and the Tree / The idea is linked to the act the ear to the heart the sign to the sense. / See your rivers murmuring with musky caymans, manatees with eyes of mirage. There is no need to invent the Mermaids. / It is enough to open your eyes to the April rainbow / And the ears, above all the ears to God who with a burst of saxophone laughter created the heavens and the earth in six days. / And on the seventh day, he slept his great negro sleep.]

Apart from Senghor himself *Anthologie de la nouvelle poésie nègre et malgache* included only two other poets in its section 'Afrique Noire'. It was a paucity for which its editor felt a need to apologize. Yet, as Sartre intimated in his introduction, apology was scarcely necessary. David Diop and Birago Diop were sufficiently different in talent and tone to suggest a range well beyond what is normally implied by the term 'a school'.

[30] *Ethiopiques*, pp. 56–7

On his appearance in the anthology David Diop, born in Bordeaux of mixed Senegalese and Cameroonian parentage, was only twenty-one. The three poems included – all very early work – were already sufficiently distinctive for Sartre to single them out for their phosphorescent anger, and for Senghor himself to speak of their 'sombre vigeur du vers'.

The difficulty for the modern reader in appreciating these early poems is that their imagery has since become so much the common coin of racial protest as to deprive them of the freshness and violence with which they must once have broken on their audience:

> Tu n'es qu'un nègre!
> Un nègre!
> Un sale nègre!
> Ton coeur est une éponge qui boit
> Qui boit avec frénésie le liquide empoisonné du Vice
> Et ta couleur emprisonne ton sang
> Dans l'éternité de l'esclavage.[31]

[You're only a nigger! / A nigger! / A dirty nigger! / Your heart is a sponge that drinks / Frantically drinks the poisoned liquid of Vice / And your colour imprisons your blood / In an eternity of slavery.]

The technique here is of a sort of sadistic repetition which finally bestows on the words a kind of negative brilliance, like lampblack or polished ebony. Diop converts the very substance of distaste into a sort of black diamond. These poems are short, but always on the move. There is a rapid transition between different voices so as to produce a diversity of perspective and response. 'Un blanc me dit' for example begins by mimicking the contempt of the racially bigoted and then, in the next instant, reverses the tone of voice to that of the poet's own incandescent self-acceptance:

> Donne-moi ce dos qui ruisselle
> Et ruisselle de la sueur fétide de tes fautes.[32]

[Give me the back that streams / And streams with the rank sweat of your offenses.]

And in 'Le temps du martyre' Diop starts with a litany of cherished resentments ('Le Blanc a tué mon pere / Mon père était fier') and then, with a whisk of a napkin, transports us to a wayside *bistro* where the

---

[31] *Anthologie de la Nouvelle Poésie*, pp. 175–6.  [32] *Ibid.*, p. 175.

object of the poet's loathing becomes a tetchy customer and himself the *garçon* hovering in the corner: 'Hé boy, un berger, une serviette, de l'eau.' In 'Celui qui a tout perdu' his voice becomes the voice of Africa itself, dispossessed and deprived, seemingly in an instant, of all that once gave it charm and fecundity:

> Puis un jour, le Silence. . .
> Les rayons du soleil semblèrent s'éteindre
> Dans ma case vide de sens.
> Mes femmes écrasèrent leurs bouches rougies
> Sur les lèvres minces et dures des conquérants aux yeux d'acier[33]

[Then one day, Silence . . . / It seemed the rays of the sun went out / In my hut empty of meaning. / My women crushed their painted mouths / On the thin hard lips of steel-eyed conquerers]

The poems collected in Diop's volume *Coups de pilon* (1956) demonstrate some concentration of theme and a vast access of technique. Their strength, unsuspected from the earlier verse, is a mastery of the long line. Diop had publicly stated his conviction that the day of the alexandrine was over: he went on to say that for him each poem, each germ of inspiration, must now find its own appropriate form irrespective of norms or constraints. Yet the poetry of *Coups de pilon* shows him gravitating with a seriousness of temper quite natural to him towards measured units of verse distinguished by their suppleness and grace. Even in the book's dedicatory poem, an almost classical gravity of line is apparent:

> Quand autour de moi surgissent les souvenirs
> Souvenirs d'escales anxieuses au bord du gouffre
> De mers glacées où se noient les moissons
> Quand revivent en moi les jours à la dérive
> Les jours en lambeaux à goût narcotique[34]

[When memories rise around me / Memories of anxious halts on the edge of the abyss / Of icy seas where harvests drown / When days of drifting live in me again / Days in rags with a narcotic flavor]

The whole of this poem, addressed to Mandessi, the poet's Cameroonian mother, is one sentence, evincing a slow steady accretion of syntax quite alien to the early poems. Gone is the boisterous humour, gone are the quick hot jabs of resentment: the pestle blows of

---

[33] *Ibid.*, p. 174.
[34] David Diop, *Coups de pilon* (Paris: Présence Africaine, Edition Définitive, 1973), p. 19.

which the volume's title misleadingly speaks. Instead there is a gradual seeping anger and a well of frustrated love.

The other technical achievement of *Coups de pilon* is its grasp of cadence. If in individual lines the control occasionally falters, where these later poems gain is in their ineluctable advance towards a conclusion which always appears perfectly judged. Diop has more good last lines than practically any other francophone African poet:

> Malgré vos chants d'orgueil au milieu des charniers
> Les villages désolés l'Afrique écartelée
> L'espoir vivait en nous comme une citadelle
> Et des mines du Souaziland à la sueur lourde des usines d'Europe
> Le printemps prendra chair sous nos pas de clarté.[35]

[Despite your hymns of pride among boneyards / Villages laid waste and Africa dismembered / Hope lived in us like a citadel / And from the mines of Swaziland to the heavy sweat of Europe's factories / Spring will put on flesh under our steps of light.]

These closing lines have all the graphic tenacity of the best of Soviet realist art: at the same time the notion of spring taking flesh while a strange luminosity bursts forth from beneath the heels of the advancing proletariat holds a world of suggestiveness. The English translation 'steps of light' does insufficient justice to the French: what is implied is both an unreal beatitude and a clarity of seeing. It is a line perfectly prepared by the shorter measure which precedes it, a line which crowns the great swoop of the poem with a finely timed moment of uplift.

Diop works a similar miracle at the end of 'L'Agonie des chaînes' where he assembles an extraordinary collage of suffering interspersed with repeated lines ('Dimbokro Poulo Condor'), building up the sense of limitless oppression until in the very last line he suddenly releases us blinking into an incongruous Paradise:

> Et des savanes aux jungles
> Nos mains crispées dans l'étreinte du combat
> Montrent á ceux qui pleurent des éclats d'avenir
> Dimbokro Poulo Condor
> Entendez-vous bruire la sève souterraine
> C'est la chanson des morts
> La chanson qui nous porte au jardins de la vie.[36]

[35] *Ibid.*, p. 20.      [36] *Ibid.*, p. 23.

[And from savannas to jungles / Our fists clenched in the grip of battle / Show flashes of future to those who weep / Dimbokro Poulo Condor / Do you hear the sap rumble underground / It is the song of the dead / The song that carries us to the gardens of life.]

It is not surprising that Diop's poems often remind us of canvases, or rather of broad pan-global *tableaux*. He himself held the image in very high regard, seeing it as the point of flame at which the spirituality of the poet and the tactility of reality are bonded. It is this bonding process which he saw as the very essence of the poetic art:

it is the harmonious fusion of the sensuous with the cognitive, the faculty by means of which, through sound and sense, through image and rhythm, an intimate union is effected between the poet and the world which surrounds him. Poetry, life's spontaneous language, may neither spring forth nor renew itself except through contact with the real.[37]

It is this commitment to tangible experience, insufficiently grounded as it was in any sustained exposure to the continent about which he desired most to write, which constituted Diop's limitation. Despite infrequent trips to Senegal and Cameroon, Diop was brought up for the most part in metropolitan France – latterly in Paris, where his mother took a flat opposite the offices of *Présence Africaine*. In one of his most frequently anthologized poems, Diop worships the body of Africa, but has finally to admit his innocence:

> Afrique mon Afrique
> Afrique des fiers guerriers dans les savanes ancestrales
> Afrique que chante ma grand-Mère
> Au bord de son fleuve lointain
> Je ne t'ai jamais connue[38]

[Africa my Africa / Africa of proud warriors in ancestral savannas / Africa of which my grandmother sings / Beside her faraway river / I never knew you]

In the absence of an intimate acquaintance with his geographical subject matter, too many of Diop's later poems seem to possess a specifically literary source. At least two pieces in *Coups de pilon* refer back to sacred texts of *négritude*: 'Nègre clochard' to the episode in *Cahier d'un retour au pays natal* in which Césaire encounters an African tramp on the *métro*, and 'A une danseuse noire' to Senghor's Africanized Hymn to the Virgin 'Femme nue, femme noire'. Whereas Senghor's madonna manages to represent both the savannahland of

---

[37] *Ibid.*, p. 23.　　[38] *Ibid.*, p. 33.

Senegal and the prostrate body of his wife, Diop's vigour is crippled by abstraction. But if the theme flounders, the technique as ever triumphs, the fluctuation of long and very short lines shivering with all the pent-up sensuality of the dancer's hips. Once again, *malgré lui*, Diop proves himself a poet of form.

Despite the desire for return which pervades his poems, Diop did not settle back in Africa until 1958, the year in which he married Alioune Diop's sister and took up a teaching post in Dakar. By this time, however, virtually all of his surviving verse had been written. There was, moreover, something about his childhood and youth in far-away France and the fact of his exogamous parentage which enabled Diop to see Africa as few others have seen it: as something whole and pure, like a single bead of jet. Unlike Senghor he had little feeling for landscape or even sense of place: his *milieu* is the brutal no-man's land of shuffled identities and brittle international contact. By virtue of his passport he is normally classified as Senegalese, but in reality he speaks with a voice which transcends regional frontiers, addressing itself to the central aboriginal hurt. It is for this reason that, a quarter of a century after his death in a plane crash in 1960 at the age of 33, he still retains his appeal. His work is not limited by ethnic divides but offers instead a permanent expression, enraged but sensitive, of the disappointments and frustrations which many feel in a world where dispossession is still the lot of many on the earth. There are not many poets of whom one may say so much.

Birago Diop's reputation was and is as a short story writer and purveyor of indigenous *contes*. In *Anthologie de la nouvelle poésie* he was represented by a couple of short poems and a longish piece of prose. It was not until 1960, with the publication of *Leurres et lueurs* that the reading public came to realize that he had been writing verse prolifically long before the appearance of the anthology, long even before he and Senghor jointly edited the single influential issue of the magazine *L'Etudiant noir* in 1939.[39] His collected verse shows him to have been working in a number of parallel, though fairly conventional veins since 1925, when the slender vignette 'Vision' finds him playing with

[39] For a rewarding account of Birago Diop's collaboration with Senghor see his autobiography, *La Plume raboutée mémoires* I (Paris: Présence Africaine, 1978).

*imagiste* intimations of a fugitive beauty:

> Une forme vague s'enfuit
> Dans le clair-obscur du lourd soir,
> Et lentement descend la nuit
> Qui enveloppe tout de noir.[40]

[A misty form takes flight / Through evening's twilit shades, / And falls across the night / as daylight slowly fades.]

Diop's early control of patterned modes was usually convincing, though occasionally his structures seem to fit just a little too snugly. His earliest work suffers from a defective capacity for surprise. The poet presses his passions like petals between the pages, but on opening his book, the reader cannot quite believe in the authenticity of the perfume. In 'Les Yeux Secs', for example, the suppressed distress is so effectively distanced as to fade away completely, leaving only a faint impression of prettiness:

> Hélas les larmes non tombées
> Peu à peu corrodent le coeur
> Comme une pierre imbibée
>     D'infernales liqueurs.[41]

[Alas! The heart is choked / By tears that lie unshed, / And rots like brimstone soaked / In potions from the dead.]

From this point on Birago Diop's habit of dating his poems enables us to chart his progress with some certainty. Born in Dakar, where his parents' residence in one of the four privileged *communes* of colonial Senegal bequeathed him a French citizenship initially denied to Senghor, Diop was by profession a veterinary surgeon, and the forty years covered by *Leurres et lueurs* take him through studenthood in St Louis and subsequently Toulouse to postgraduate studies in Paris, where he met Senghor, and then successive tours in the Sudan, the Ivory Coast, Upper Volta and Mauritania. Throughout, his spiritual mainstay seems to have been a profound sense of continuity, of the abiding validity of tradition and the regenerative force of nature, beliefs which place him beyond the passing fads of the *écoles* and the squabbling of the *literati*. In 'Souffles' he speaks plainly out of his deepest convictions:

---

[40] Birago Diop. *Leurres et lueurs; poèmes* (Paris: Présence Africaine, 1967), p. 11
[41] *Ibid.*, p. 31.

Ceux qui sont morts ne sont jamais partis:
Ils sont dans l'Ombre qui s'éclaire
Et dans l'Ombre qui s'épaissit.
Les Morts ne sont pas sous la Terre:
Ils sont dans l'Arbre qui frémit,
Ils sont dans le Bois qui gémit,
Ils sont dans l'Eau qui coule,
Ils sont dans l'Eau qui dort,
Ils sont dans la Case, ils sont dans la Foule:
Les Morts ne sont pas morts.[42]

[The dead have not departed. / They are in the dusk which glows / And in the dusk which thickens. / The dead ones do not dwell beneath the Earth: / They are in the shivering tree, / And in the whimpering wood, / They are in the water as it courses / And in the water as it slumbers, / They are in the hut or in the multitude: / The dead ones do not die.]

This certainty of knowledge gives Diop's mature work a calm independence. Unlike other poets he seeks to identify himself through neither inclusion nor exclusion but through complete individual fidelity to a stable, healing vision. The best of his work springs from this confidence, this ability to see beyond the fractious and the commonplace to presences which linger through history, never to be dismissed if never quite comprehended. It is this subtle grasp of the ineffable which grants Diop his rare moments of undisputed magic, as in 'Viatique':

Dans un de trois canaris
des trois canaris où reviennent certains soirs
les âmes satisfaites et sereines,
les souffles des ancêtres,
des ancêtres qui furent des hommes
des aïeux qui furent des sages,
Mère a trempé trois doigts,
trois doigts de sa main gauche:
le pouce, l'index et la majeur;
Moi, j'ai trempé trois doigts:
trois doigts de la main droite:
le pouce, l'index et le majeur.[43]

[In one of three urns / where on certain evenings / the souls of our ancestors return / bloated and serene, / the sighs of our ancestors are heard / that once were men, / our elders who were wise, / Mother dipped three fingers / of her left hand: / middle, index and thumb: / Then I dipped three fingers / of my right hand: / middle, index and thumb.]

[42] *Ibid.*, p. 64.     [43] *Ibid.*, p. 71.

Canaris are tall lipped jars used in many Senegambian households for the storage of water or grain. The poem succeeds supremely because it relays age-old certainties through the medium of tactile detail: the shape of the jars, the wetting of fingers, the serene, almost eerie authority of the mother as she tempts the child into the rite and, in so doing, lures the reader into his own kind of vicarious acquiescence. There is no elaboration, no extrapolation, no fuss: simply the huddled figure of the mother in the semi-darkness, the jars and the boy, agog with wonder. It is a poem which many lesser craftsmen might learn from: a poem which in its unflustered, uninsistent way digs deeper into the sub-soil of *négritude* than a thousand tracts or *thèses*.

Bernard Dadié, from the Ivory Coast, is another poet whose reputation has lain principally in other spheres: as novelist (most famously of *Climbié*, 1953); as playwright (of, among other pieces and *tableaux*, *Monsieur Thôgô-Gnini*, 1970 and *Iles de tempête*, 1973) and lastly as government official and minister of culture. It was as a writer of verse, however, that he first established himself with *Afrique debout!* published in 1950 shortly after Dadié's release from a sixteen-month prison sentence for his involvement in the anti-colonial activities of the Parti Democratique de Côte d'Ivoire. Of all the poets who flourished in francophone Africa during the late forties and early fifties he has most in common with the pioneers of English-language verse discussed in the last chapter. His poetry is fuelled by rejection: rejection first of the squalor of colonial Africa with its inadequate facilities and demeaning priorities:

> Les maternités sans lits,
> Les hôpitaux sans médicaments
> Les ides de Mars sur la Paix déchaînées,
> Et la petite colombe blanche qui ne sait où se poser,
> Et tant d'autres, tants d'autres sujets[44]

[Maternity wards without beds, / Hospitals devoid of drugs, / The Ides of March let loose on the paths of Peace, / And the little white dove who knows not where to perch; / And so much else, so, so much else]

Rejection of Western technological sophistication, a reaction shared by both Léopold Sédar Senghor and Aimé Césaire; rejection too of

[44] Bernard B. Dadié, *Légendes et pòemes* (Paris: Editions Sénghers, 1966), p. 12.

the cult of acquisition and petit-bourgeois emulation of the glories of Touraine:

> Parce que je n'ai pas une auto,
> Je ne suis pas un homme pour eux!
> Parce que je n'ai pas un château,
> Je ne suis pas un homme pour eux![45]

[Because I have no car, / To them I am not a man! / Because I have no château, / To them I am not a man!]

Rejection of the petty brutality of colonial officialdom:

> La vie n'est pas un rêve, mon frère,
> Tout te le dit à chaque coin de rue:
> La houle de cimes qui obstrue ton horizon.
> Le bâton du policier sur ton échine,
> Et le stick du 'Commandant' pendu aux basques
> Du Gouverneur qui veut faire de l'Afrique une prison,
> Une immense ossuaire où viendront jouer
> Les corbeaux et les renards;
> La femme du ravitaillement qui vous rit au nez,
> Toi et ta faim, en rangeant ses laisses de tickets,
> Et le commerçant qui refuse de te servir, sans raison[46]

[Life is no dream, my friend, / Every street corner proclaims it: / The surging peaks that shuts out the sky, / The truncheon at your spine, / The swagger-stick swinging at the hips of, / The Governor who'd turn this Africa into one prison, / One great charnel house where / Crows and foxes come to play; / The lady at the packet store who laughs right in your face, / You and your hunger, while stacking lottery tickets, / The trader who, giving no reason, will not serve you]

In response to such assaults on basic human dignity the poet sounds the authentic groundswell of *négritude*, a gathering crescendo of fury whose *élan* is familiar from *Cahier d'un retour au pays natal* and *Coups de pilon*:

> Mais voici venir la nuit, la grande nuit des métamorphoses,
> Et les immortelles nimbées d'ombre s'estompent, s'évanouissent.
> Demain donc sera la résurrection,
> La résurrection d'un peuple
> La résurrection d'un monde enchaîné,
> L'allégresse des hommes unis,
> Le concert émouvent des coeurs accordés . . .[47]

---

[45] *Ibid.*, p. 14.    [46] *Ibid.*, p. 27.    [47] *Ibid.*, p. 14.

[But here comes the night, the great metamorphosis of night, / As the undying haloes of night soften and vanish. / For tomorrow will see the resurrection, / The resurrection of a people, / The resurrection of a world enchained / The ecstasy of men at one, / A concert of harmonious hearts.]

The 'coeurs accordés' of French West Africa did not, however, always strike a sympathetic note with their neighbours in the English-speaking territories of Sierra Leone, Ghana and Nigeria. The response to *négritude* in anglophone Africa followed a fairly straightforward pattern: initial indifference, then a brief flicker of interest in the late fifties, soon followed in its turn by a growing mood of resistance. The reasons are not difficult to fathom. Historically viewed, *négritude* was a direct reaction to the Assimilation policy, which, ignoring native traditions and systems of government, had imposed a French blueprint on African life irrespective of regional and ethnic alignments. For the whole period of colonial control Senegal, Ivory Coast, Upper Volta, Mali and Guinea had been administered as *départements* of mainland France. Meanwhile in British West Africa, Lord Lugard had devolved an alternative policy of Indirect Rule, the effect of which had been to bolster up local chiefdoms and reinforce regional differences. Though repressive in intention, this policy had produced in the subject population no equivalent to the existential *angst* which rent the new élites of francophone Africa. To the extent that Nigerian and Ghanaian intellectuals felt inclined to explore the African personality, their *credo* was less likely to be phrased in terms such as *je suis nègre donc je suis* than 'I am Yoruba, therefore I am'; I am Ewe, therefore I am'. As a result, the formulations of *négritude*, devised as they were by men for whom philosophy had been a compulsory *lycée* subject, seemed to anglophone writers overblown, even racialist in their ramifications.

For a short period in the late fifties *négritude*, representing as it did any undeniable manifestation of energy within the African mind, was nevertheless hotly debated in anglophone circles, especially in Nigeria. The main forum for this discussion, the journal *Black Orpheus* was itself named after 'Orphée noir', Sartre's Preface to Senghor's 1948 *Anthologie*. A principal motive for the foundation of this magazine was the need to create an *entente cordiale* between two linguistic camps and hence to provide a platform for mutual exchange of views.

To facilitate this, *Black Orpheus*, as we shall see in the next chapter, instigated from its very first issue a policy of printing, side by side, work by anglophone intellectuals and contributions from francophone Africa in translation. In so doing, it was responding to the initiative of the Paris-based journal, *Présence Africaine*, which, from its inception in 1948, had published items in both languages.

The honeymoon did not last long. The decline in *négritude*'s fortunes can be charted with a fair amount of accuracy through the cyclostyled pages of *The Horn*, the undergraduate literary magazine founded in 1957 by students of the University College of Ibadan, a year when, in the aftermath of the First Congress of Black Writers held in Paris in 1956, *négritude* was very much in the air. The first number of the magazine carried a gesture of editorial fraternity from a twenty-two-year-old student called John Pepper Clark:

We venture to submit Négritude as a most compendious word! ... it stands for ... that new burning consciousness of a common race and culture which black men in Africa, the West Indies and America are beginning to feel towards one another... It is to arrest ... imperialism that we join those already fighting to preserve our heritage by launching this magazine.[48]

By issue three, however, warning shots were already audible from the trenches behind. A visiting Trinidadian lecturer, John Ramsaran, was brave enough to declare *négritude* to be 'a negative view of things, a passive acceptance without that inner conviction which comes from the glimmering of truth'.[49] *Négritude* still had its supporters among the contributors to *The Horn*, notably Abiola Irele, a student of French, but with limited exceptions 'passive acceptance' soon turned to outright hostility, so that two issues later John Pepper Clark as editor-in-chief was forced formally to concede defeat.

It is against this background that we must view the intervention three years later in the pages of the same periodical of a postgraduate fellow newly arrived from England bearing a clutch of play-scripts and a burgeoning reputation as dramatist and controversialist. Wole Soyinka's article 'The Future of West African Writing', which appeared in *The Horn*, in 1960, established what was to become the main line of anglophone defence against the incursions of *négritude*. The article begins with an attack on the notion of 'authenticity', by which its author means an abject reverence for static customs and forms, a

---

[48] John Pepper Clark, Editorial, *The Horn*, 1, 1, 1958, p. 11.
[49] John Ramsaran, 'New Voices', *The Horn*, 1, 3, 1958, p. 7.

'mummification' of traditional life of the kind so amenable to senti-
mental liberals. As both antidote and augury of a more confident atti-
tude, Soyinka then recommends Chinua Achebe's *Things Fall Apart*,
published two years previously, a novel which contradicts patroniz-
ing notions by portraying one localized African culture as subject to
continuous and rapid change. He then addresses himself directly to
*négritude*:

if we would speak of 'negritude' in a more acceptable broader sense Chinua
Achebe is a more 'African' writer than Senghor. The duiker will not paint
'duiker' on his beautiful back to proclaim his duikeride; you'll know him by
his elegant leap. The less self-conscious the African is, and the more innately
his individual qualities appear in his writing, the more seriously he will be
taken as an artist of exciting dignity. But Senghor seems to be so artistically
expatriate that his romanticism of the negro becomes suspect... One has
heard it all among the Chelsea artifarts, not to mention the New Venetian
beatniks of America. I would say that poets like Leopold Senghor ... are a
definite retrogressive pseudo-romantic influence on a healthy development
of West African writing. The African Renaissance is not the easy refuge in lit-
erary nationalism, which anyway is self-indulgence and no substitute for
art.[50]

Two years later the analogy to the duiker was restated by Soyinka at
a much publicized Swedish conference, where, however, the animal
became a tiger.[51] It is a remark which has since been criticized by a sub-
sequent generation of Nigerian intellectuals as a wilful misconstruc-
tion of the essence of *négritude*.[52] Seen in the context of the article
where it first appeared, however, the statement is clearly an attempt
not so much to counter *négritude* as to redefine it. Soyinka opposes
neither the energy nor the commitment of Senghor's programme,
merely its 'self-consciousness', that is, the narrowness of its self-
definition. His reservations imply a mistrust neither of nationalism *per
se* nor of racial assertiveness. What they do amount to is a deep-seated
distrust of the speculative intelligence. The advance represented by
Achebe is seen as being due neither to his anglicization nor even his
regional rootedness, but rather to his pragmatism, itself a legacy of the
English empirical tradition. Achebe describes; he does not conjecture.

---

[50] Wole Soyinka, 'The Future of West African Writing', *The Horn* 4, 1, 1960, pp. 14–15.
[51] Cf. 'The Writer in a Modern African State' in *The Writer in Modern Africa*, ed. Per Wast-
berg (Uppsala: The Scandinavian Institute of African Studies, 1968), pp. 14–21.
[52] See especially Chinuezu, Onwuchetwa Jemie and Itechuchukwu Madubuike, 'The
Leeds–Ibadan Connection: the Scandal of Modern African Literature', *Okike* 13,
January, 1979.

Commencing as tributaries of the same broad river, anglophone and francophone literature had by the early sixties drifted so far apart as to be considered parallel streams. At the dividing point stood the generation of English-speaking undergraduates who passed through West African colleges in the years between 1956 and 1965. Before returning to chart the progress of francophone poetry, it is thus essential that we travel a little upstream toward the common source to consider the patterns of turbulence which hit African poetry of English expression in the late 1950s, patterns which were to have as much of an influence on the parting of the ways as *négritude* itself.

# CHAPTER 4

# Poetry and the university, 1957–63

The turning point for the future of English language verse in West Africa came in the late 1940s with the setting up in various British colonial territories in university colleges initially affiliated to the University of London. Previously those who wished to embark upon a course of higher education had either to set sail for Europe or America, or wend their way to Fourah Bay College in Freetown, Sierra Leone, established in 1827 but still in 1945 primarily geared to the training of aspirants to the Christian ministry. The forces of history in the 1930s and 1940s had ensured that such poetry as had been written was subjected to the needs of pressing political objectives. The establishment of university communities, however, provided a zone free from public pressure where younger writers could find their feet, experiment and test themselves against the example of literature which, in the syllabuses pertaining in those years, came exclusively from abroad.

From 1948 until at least 1962, when it achieved autonomous status as an independent university institution, the University College of Ibadan drew its staff largely from among the younger graduates of British colleges, themselves trained in the traditional disciplines. The same was true of the University College of the Gold Coast, initially set up in Achimota as a training ground for teachers. Though the calibre of the teaching staff was high, the curricula of all departments, including English, were determined less by the men and women engaged to teach them and thus aware, however fleetingly, of local needs, than by the authorities of the University of London who were responsible for devising courses for all external students, whether registered at affiliated institutions within the United Kingdom or abroad. As a result scant regard was paid to the special needs of African undergraduates. It was assumed somewhat benignly that a grounding in the great classics of English Literature was as suitable to the intellectual requirements of a young person from Brong-Ahafo as to those of a student from Kuala Lumpur or Cambridge. A look at the syllabuses operative in Ibadan in the late fifties is sufficient to make the point.

Students in the English Department had a choice of two syllabuses, each consisting of nine papers. The first embraced the Development of the English Language; Old and Middle English Texts and Unseens; the History of English Literature to 1500; equivalent period papers for 1550–1660, 1660–1790 and 1790–1880; the History and Principles of Literary Criticism, and a special subject which might consist of work in the modern field. The second syllabus provided for more extensive work in the Middle Ages and in Anglo-Saxon, together with a Shakespeare paper. The only provision for study of Twentieth Century texts was within the option 'English Literature from 1800 to the Present Day' which stipulated a survey of 'the most important developments in poetry and prose, including the literary drama', and a concentration on certain specified authors who, from 1958 to 1961 consisted of Thomas Hardy, Henry James, Joseph Conrad, Oscar Wilde, W. B. Yeats, Bernard Shaw, E. M. Forster, D. H. Lawrence, Virginia Woolf and T. S. Eliot. Other enthusiasms had to be indulged in a student's spare time. Whether such a concentrated exposure to a bracing but alien tradition was more productive of the sort of creative tension which sets imaginations aflame than the current compulsory fare of African and assorted international literatures stipulated in many present-day departments remains an open question.

As a result of the official neglect of local creative aspirations, initiatives in that direction were left either to students themselves or to motivated members of the academic staff working in an unofficial capacity. These efforts were not always encouraged: it is notable for instance that of the younger expatriates instrumental in stimulating creative work amongst students in Ibadan in the 1950s several, such as Gerald Moore and Ulli Beier, functioned not from the English Department but from the Department of Extra-Mural Studies where, released from the narrow demands of the BA (External) London degree, they were free to commit themselves to a task in which their hearts lay, the monitoring of cultural change amongst a generation of students who were among the first to emerge from a rural background to receive the uncertain benefits of a university education. Whatever may now be said about the patronizing attitudes bred of such interaction, there were several men who did sterling work at a crucial period to which several eminent writers have since borne witness.

In Ibadan, the student poetry magazine *The Horn* owed its inception to collaboration between students and staff. Within the English Department Geoffrey Axworthy was laying the foundations of what eventually became the Department of Theatre Arts, aided on his return from Britain in 1959 by Wole Soyinka. Meanwhile, through his Mbari Press, Ulli Beier provided an avenue by which many of the writers discussed later in this book found their way through to the light of recognition. At nearby Oshogbo, Susanne Wenger, Beier's Austrian wife, set up a craft workshop which inspired many of Nigeria's painters and sculptors, stimulating amongst other techniques the art of copper-relief. These were heady days, and literature was only one branch of cultural activity to benefit, taking its place alongside politics, graphics, music, dance and theatre as an outlet of the burgeoning national spirit.

It is to poetry, however, that we must here confine ourselves. The late fifties saw the inception in Ibadan literary circles of two publishing ventures which, between them, helped to see most young African poets of the date on their way: the journal *Black Orpheus* and the student-edited magazine *The Horn*. Of these, though skimpy in presentation, *The Horn* was perhaps the more remarkable. Issued between 1958 and 1962, it supplied an invaluable enclave, protected but not unstringent, where undergraduate poets from the English Department of the University College of Ibadan and beyond could try their strength. Its disadvantage was that, unlike *Black Orpheus*, it addressed itself purely to a university audience and could hence fight shy of exposure to the national scene. Had it cast itself into the market place, however, it is doubtful if it would have survived. Besides it is arguable that at this stage of its development African poetry in English was served best less by prestige publication, than by the stimulus of a magazine with a limited circulation but welcoming editorial policy. For any poetic school in its earliest years, the ephemeral plateau of periodical publications is essential. Poetry has seldom been a commercially profitable art form. The work of poets, unless they happen to hit an especially receptive market, sells for the most part in tiny numbers, and most publishers are for this reason careful before accepting it. Before the eighteenth century publication of poetry, where it existed at all, was a rare privilege, and many is the practitioner, including men such as Andrew Marvell, who have gone down to the fine and private place of the grave without a book to their name. In the nineteenth century publication of a poet's first verses at his own expense was common: A. E. Housman was driven to this extremity before in 1896 the new firm of Grant Richards offered to bring out *A Shropshire Lad*. In this century, and more especially from the thirties to the pres-

ent day, the scene has been transformed by a flurry of small maga-
zines catering for every taste and enabling young poets to soldier on to
the point at which a publishing house is prepared to take a risk on
them.

The facts of publishing life were spelled out in no uncertain terms in
the introduction to an anthology recommended at the time to students
of the Ibadan English Department. Robert Conquest's *New Lines*
(1956), heralded the arrival on the British scene of a group of writers
who have come subsequently to be known as the Movement. In his
introductory remarks Conquest was anxious to make precisely this
point about small beginnings: 'It is remarkable how many of the poets
in this book owe their first publication in book or pamphlet form to
small presses running off limited editions – Fantasy Press and the Uni-
versity of Reading School of Art – or to the new Marvell Press, and
how many of them have still not had larger volumes published.'[1]
Nigeria was no exception to this rule. In fact, since African Poetry was
at that time an almost unknown quantity in publishing circles, the
situation was arguably worse until in the late sixties one or two of the
larger London houses woke up to the potential of the African market.
At first there was nothing but to foot it alone, and where better to start
a small magazine but at a new and growing university?

In October 1956 Martin Banham was a young lecturer fresh from the
University of Leeds. There he had encountered *Poetry and Audience*, a
student-run magazine founded in 1953 during the Professorship of
Bonamy Dobrée, and published with dogged (and sometimes dog-
eared) persistence to this day. Though administered on a shoe-string,
*Poetry and Audience* had enjoyed a distinguished history and a list of its
editors or contributors read like a roll-call of recent British poetry:
Geoffrey Hill, George Barker, Philip Larkin, David Wright, Ted
Hughes.[2] By the time the present author came to edit the magazine be-
tween 1974 and 1977 it had turned into a monthly periodical issued in
photolithographic form with the aid of a grant from the Yorkshire Arts
Association and selling for the price of a packet of cigarettes. As
Banham knew it in the early fifties it was a stapled pamphlet of five or
six cyclostyled pages run off weekly on a wheezy superannuated
duplicating machine and flogged around the new brick-built Union at
lunchtime for the price of a box of matches. The flame thus lit was,
however, considerable.

[1] *New Lines*, ed. Robert Conquest (London: Macmillan, 1956), p. xiii.
[2] For a few sample growls from this plucky little monster, see *21 Years of 'Poetry and Audi-
ence'*, eds. Tom Wharton and Wayne Brown (Breakish: Aquila, 1976).

Shortly after his arrival at Ibadan, Banham saw the need for a similar magazine and the following year, in W. H. Stevenson's words, 'persuaded one of his students, J. P. Clark, to start one'. Stevenson continues:

Clark gathered a committee of three – Bridget Akwada, Aigboje Higo and John Ekwere – and so in January 1958 the first issue of *The Horn* appeared. There were no official funds available for such a venture. Martin Banham himself provided enough cash to start it; the English Department's typewriter was borrowed, and in later years the Department provided paper also (see Vol. 3, No. 3, p. 2). But funds had to be raised, and so *The Horn* was sold at twopence a copy (raised after the third issue to three pence, a price maintained until the end). It could never afford to appear in any but the most modest form – which was probably just as well if it were to remain a genuine student magazine. There was a printed heading on the first page, giving title, price, issue number, and names of the editors and committee. Beneath the heading was the first poem, typewritten as was the rest of the copy. The first issue was broader than it was high, but after that every issue was made up of foolscap sheets folded in two and stapled together, book-fashion. The page size was therefore 8 inches high × 6½ inches wide.[3]

Copies of *The Horn* are now extremely rare, and efforts to secure a reprint have not been successful. Thus, though the more successful contributors later published volumes which drew on their early contributions to the magazine, *The Horn* itself has no permanent showcase. One limited gesture towards comparative permanence, however, was the publication in 1960 by the University of Ibadan Press of an anthology of verse by *The Horn* contributors called *Nigerian Student Verse (1959)*. Few of the items from this book have found their way into the literary canon, and John Pepper Clark, the chief mover of the magazine who might have been expected to supply much of quality, preferred to bide his time. Nevertheless the anthology is interesting in that it highlights the problems which preoccupied Nigerian poets and critics at the time. The volume was edited by Martin Banham and set in elegant 12-point bembo by Doig Simmonds (a medical illustrator by trade, then employed at the University Museum). In his Preface, Banham put his finger on the principal question hanging over most of the content, the problem of influence:

I believe that it is of far more value to Nigerian school children to read this small selection of unpretentious Nigerian verse than to immerse themselves in the *Golden Treasury*. Some of the verse presented here shows only too clearly how deep is the influence of the alien verse of English romanticism

---

[3] W. H. Stevenson, '*The Horn*: What it Was and What it Did,' *Research in African Literatures* 6 (1975), pp. 5–31.

upon aspiring Nigerian writers. The more Nigerians can be encouraged to write as Nigerians, about Nigerian themes for Nigerian audiences, the better for the development of a healthy national literature. This is not, of course, to say that they should ignore the great literatures of other parts of the world – but one must not be enslaved by them.[4]

These were brave remarks, but the alternatives, it may be thought, a little too sharply drawn. Nigerians had been making literature about Nigerian themes for Nigerian audiences for centuries: the dilemma was how to channel this activity into the English language. At this date the major models of English literary usage available were parochial English ones; it may be asked how students who were required to immerse themselves in 'English Literature from 1790 to 1880' were expected to escape the language of Romanticism. Moreover, the choice did not only lie between Palgrave and Frank Aig-Imoukhuede;[5] there were the classics of European modernism to be taken into account, as Clark for one had already discovered.

Fundamentally, the issue resolved itself into a problem of employing the language and the way 'influences' were conveyed through it, as Abiola Irele, a frequent contributor both as poet and as literary and music critic, was quick to point out when reviewing the anthology in the very next issue:

the main interest of the anthology centres mostly upon Banham's remarks in the introduction, especially with regard to a national literature. Few writers have been able to create lasting work in any alien language, and however conversant we have been with English, it still remains for us something of a second language, if not less. The difficulties of expressing our own national sentiment and our own native sensibility in a language radically different from ours are not less for our constantly hearing the language and using it in academic work, not even for those of us who have devoted ourselves to the study of English literature. The truth is that we not only study in English, we study it – we do not, like an English raised undergraduate, come up and *read* it.[6]

---

[4] *Nigerian Student Verse 1959*. A selection of verse written by students of the University College, Ibadan and first published in *The Horn*, ed. Martin Banham (Ibadan: Ibadan University Press, 1960), p. 7. The model for this publication was probably the annual volumes of *Oxford Verse* published regularly since before the war.

[5] Frank Aig-Imoukhuede's celebrated pidgin poem 'One Wife for One Man', one of his seven contributions to *The Horn*, appeared for the first time in Vol. 3, No. 2, p. 5, and was reprinted in *Nigerian Student Verse*, p. 29. It subsequently made return appearances in *Ibadan* 8, 1960, p. 11 as well as *Exiit* 5, 1964, p. 14. For this and other relevant bibliographical detail in this chapter I am naturally indebted to Bernth Lindfors's indispensable *Bibliography of Literary Contributions to Nigerian Periodicals 1946–72* (Ibadan: Ibadan University Press, 1975).    [6] *The Horn* 4, 1, pp. 6–9.

There are several problems here which only a linguist could perhaps properly answer. Irele is unnecessarily depressing about the defective control of nuance by second-language users, a charge which his own fluency seems to deny, and absurdly idealistic about English undergraduates. The problems which younger poets have in expressing themselves in authentic terms are common to all cultures. For all it is a problem of superseding or integrating the influence of writers who may for a time beckon a little too brightly in the poetical sky. Irele goes on to say 'the result is that we are unable to avoid influences; we cannot do more than imitate the poets and writers we have read'. That 'cannot' was a little too dour. The difficulties outlined were not necessarily the 'result' of working through a borrowed linguistic medium so much as a reflection of the intellectual subservience common to undergraduates.

We can test the strength of Irele's assertions against his own practice by looking at his poem 'Giulia (An attempt to imitate an Elizabethan sonnet)' published in Vol. II, No. 3 of *The Horn*:

> What is a star's light when your eyes are near?
> If man could but the heav'nly music hear,
> How rude and harsh would your sweet voice make it.
> A fairer throne could not be found so fit
> As that from which, by the sun's side, you reign
> And make men's hearts obey, and men's loves train
> To suit your will.[7]

This piece of very competent pastiche cannot be said to be a product of the inability to do 'more than imitate' Irele highlights in his review. It represents rather a deliberate decision to imitate, and a fair one at that. There are hiccups and anachronisms of course; the rhyming of the stressed 'fit' with the unstressed 'it' in lines three to four is early twentieth-, not sixteenth-century practice. However, the stresses themselves are credibly disposed, and Irele, whose music criticism elsewhere in *The Horn* shows him to advantage,[8] is evidently endowed

---

[7] Abiola Irele, 'Giulia (An attempt to imitate an Elizabethan sonnet)', *The Horn* 2, 3, p. 9. It was not only sixteenth-century English verse which attracted the imitator in Irele, 'Once upon a Time' (*The Horn* 1, 5) represents a rare instance of adaptation from the Italian, in this case 'C'era una volta' by Arturo Graf, *Nigerian Student Verse*, p. 33

[8] Cf. 'Baptism of Fire', *The Horn* 2, 3, 1958, p. 12; 'Soprano Recital', *The Horn* 2, 4, 1959, pp. 8–9; 'The Beggar's Opera', *The Horn* 3, 1, 1959, pp. 8–11 (a review of a musical play which later, in *Opera Wonyosi*, inspired Wole Soyinka to his own kind of emulation); 'New Directions in Music', *The Horn* 3, 9, 1959, pp. 8–11; and 'Froth Opera', *The Horn* 3, 3, 1960, pp. 11–12.

with a sensitive ear. What he had given us is a moderately good sonnet in the Shakespearean rhyme scheme, with a basic iambic line relieved by variations only slightly outside the Elizabethan norm ('Whāt iš ă | stār's līght' is a dactyl followed by a spondee, which <u>only</u> the Victorians would have allowed). The end result is to suggest that, though Irele had read sixteenth-century lyrics (presumably in 'English Literature 1550 to 1660'), his ear was more accustomed to nineteenth-century prosody which he may well, as Banham was to suggest, have got from Palgrave's *The Golden Treasury*. The subservience to the Victorians and Georgians, however, is less one of attitude than of metrical emulation, and the criss-crossing of British influences from different periods serves to raise a basic point which neither Banham nor Irele himself mention, namely that whereas traditional African verse is tonally organized, European poetry is predominantly accentual. With this factor working in the background it is not surprising that apprentice African poets imitating English models had a tendency, like Irele, to mishear patterns. It is also hardly surprising that within a very few years poets of the Nigerian school transferred their allegiance to 'free verse' which gave them ample scope for the indulgence of syllabic pitch without encumbering them with accentual requirements which were, in these terms, decidedly 'alien'.

The classics of the English tradition confronted student poets of the time with a challenge that was both linguistic and formal. Linguistic because, as Irele implied, the mastery of a language encountered during the procedures of academic discourse is a mere preliminary to the sort of instinctive effortless familiarity required for the writing of verse; formal because the received discipline of classical English prosody, itself based obscurely on the rhythms of Greek music, provided a model which could not at first be ignored. The staple diet of poetry courses in West African universities in the late fifties consisted largely of a procession from the Renaissance to the late nineteenth century. By singling out for attention 'the alien verse of English Romanticism' Banham had highlighted but one phase of this. The Romantic attitude is one which is easily aped and easily discarded. More tenacious was the temptation to beat the English masters at their own game, and by a sufficient use of the techniques of rhyme, metre, assonance and stanzaic structure to demonstrate a complete competence in the niceties of versification. Free verse is an alluring prospect, but its practitioners open themselves to the charge that fluency in the procedures of classical discipline is beyond them.

It was not therefore merely inevitable but perhaps also salutary that the pioneers who filled the pages of student periodicals in the late fifties should have at first tried their hands at a variety of patterned modes from the quatrain to the ballad. The sort of indebtedness suggested by these exercises was of a different kind than that which afflicted the poets treated in chapter 2 who possessed for the most part a very fleeting acquaintance with the varieties of English verse, and whose practice was therefore purloined either from hymn books or from anthologies which came easily to hand.

Though the poetry which resulted was seldom distinguished, the technical exercise was for the most part successful. The very first issue of *The Horn*, for instance, carried Pious Oleghe's 'A Sudden Storm' which, if less impressive than the Malawian poet David Rubadiri's later 'African Thunderstorm',[9] does demonstrate, within the permutations of a four-line alternately rhymed stanza, a nice sense of elastic rhythm, of the tension and release that accompanies most natural events:

> The wind howls, the trees sway,
> The loose house-top sheets clatter and clang,
> The open window shuts with a bang,
>     And the sky makes night of day . . .
>
> A bright flash! – a lighted plain;
> Then, from the once-black heavens,
> Accompanied by noise that deafens,
>     Steadily pours the rain.[10]

The hard dactylic beginning of the very last line here distils that moment when the sudden insistence of the downpour releases the pent-up energy of the storm, and the whole has an immediacy of descriptive vividness which recalls Browning's 'Meeting at Night'.[11] Oleghe's philosophical poetry may also have had an aphoristic Polonius-like heaviness, but its message was conveyed with a dexterity of metrical variation which is sometimes in line with Kipling:

> There is a calm born of inaction:
> Safe, you watch the storm rage,

[9] Cf. *The Penguin Book of Modern African Poetry*, eds. Gerald Moore and Ulli Beier (London: Penguin, 1984), p. 137.
[10] *The Horn* 1, 1, 1958, p. 9, reprinted in *Nigerian Student Verse*, p. 20.
[11] 'Meeting at Night', *Browning, Poetical Works, 1833–1864*, ed. Ian Jack (London: Oxford University Press, 1970), p. 472.

Safe, see it subside. But a cage
Might suit you best, for that.
Act, man, act . . .[12]

In the first number of the next volume U. I. Ukwu takes over from the Augustans a habit of allowing bustling physical movement to jostle with the formal patternizing of the heroic couplet in his description of a 'Bus Ride'. At one point he goes in for a touch of Popean bathos:

On every side there's animated talk
on the state, on love – down to the price of pork.[13]

*The Rape of the Lock* was clearly on the syllabus, though Pope himself would have used an unemphatic conjunction rather than the phrase 'down to', which protests too much. In this justly anthologized poem Ukwu demonstrates not merely a sufficient control of the eighteenth century convention but a refined sense of the uses to which it may be put, the more so since he knows when to abandon the effect, as in the second verse paragraph in which a call at one of the many lorry parks *en route* causes a break in the convention just as it breaks the onward momentum of the journey.

Even more effectively, R. Opara had apparently learned from W. H. Auden a satirical deployment of the ballad form which in 'The Ballad of Sputnik' provides one of the most diverting moments in *Nigerian Student Verse*:

Prof Shinsky was a scientist
    Of Bolshevik renown;
He strewed his genius all about
    The great Siberian town.

Karl Marx he loved, and Lenin too,
    Krushchev and Bulganin;
Above all these he loved his wife
    (Un-Soviet bargainin').[14]

This is a *jeu d'esprit* which many a craftsman might envy, and in it we have a glimpse of one direction which Nigerian verse never took.

[12] Pious Oleghe, 'Calm', *The Horn* 1, 5, 1958, p. 6, reprinted in *Nigerian Student Verse*, p. 22.
[13] *The Horn* 2, 1, 1958, p. 3, reprinted in *Nigerian Student Verse*, p. 27.
[14] *The Horn* 1, 2, 1958, pp. 1–2, reprinted in *Nigerian Student Verse*, p. 28.

The confident use, nay positive subversion of the ballad metre here not merely heightens the effect of the satire: it also perfectly fulfils Martin Banham's prescription in his Introduction that 'one should not ignore the literature of other parts of the world, but one must not be enslaved by it'. A poem like Opara's denies its enslavement by staging a deck mutiny, and then taking over control of the ship. Satire was to become one of the dominant modes in African verse throughout the sixties, but the increased popularity of free verse caused writers to neglect the possibilities of the formal broadside.

It was not to purloined convention that *The Horn* owed its strongest moments, however, but to a quite specific emotional reflex: the discovery, among the clamour of everyday life, of the awe and mystery of the commonplace. There are several factors which may have contributed to this: the relief of undergraduates force-fed on elevated thought and then released for the vacation back into the consoling stabilities of rural life; the desire to make atonement for an exploitative sophistication; and, more discernibly, a reading of certain of the English poets. A sense of the inexplicable wonder of the ordinary is very much part of the Wordsworthean and Blakean inheritance, and it was therefore hardly surprising, if, let loose on the raptures of *The Prelude* over the hidden power within common surroundings, African poets should have turned to discover something of the same power in the sounds and sights of the village. Here is Minji Karibo extolling a sudden encounter with a ferryman:

> Twinkles from the dim shore beckoned us home,
> And our smoke-seasoned buckets full of fish
> Heaved sighs of relief when we at last sought
> Our faithful dugout, patient in bondage.
> Eager feet humping over white sands.
> Dusk was our escort.
> And suddenly He was there – the Waterman.
> Like a lone palm in an enchanted lake;
> White as the sand, long hair his only wear. [15]

Here the lone figure of the waterman looms with something of the ominous presence of Wordsworth's Leechgatherer and, if the pathetic fallacy in line four sits awkwardly, the rest is firmly installed in a received, if redirected tradition. To speak, with Martin Banham, of

---

[15] *The Horn* 1, 5, 1958, p. 7, reprinted in *Nigerian Student Verse*, p. 17.

'the alien verse of English romanticism' here would be to miss an important point. As W. H. Stevenson implies, the Romantic attitude in such poetry reinforces rather than detracts from the authentic emotional response.

There are many influences at work in such poetry, not least that of the new English poets of the late 1950s – known familiarly as the Movement. In the introduction to his anthology of their work Robert Conquest had pointed to one characteristic which he believed separated the writing of the Movement from the generation which had immediately preceded it:

If one had briefly to distinguish this poetry of the fifties from its predecessors, I believe that the most important general point would be that it submits to no great system of theoretical constructs nor agglomerations of unconscious commands. It is free from both mystical and logical compulsions and – like modern philosophy – is empirical in its attitude to all that comes. This reverence for the real person or event is, indeed, a part of the general intellectual ambience (insofar as that is not blind or retrogressive) of our time.[16]

It may be objected that Conquest's remarks applied primarily to the British scene – by 'modern philosophy' he quite clearly meant Anglo-Saxon Logical Positivism – but the attitudes were capable of transference. The pragmatism outlined here had been a recurrent feature of British society at different periods, and one means by which the British people have fended off any claim to continental inclusion. For the Nigerian poets of the 1950s attempting to cope with, and in some cases discourage the equivalent claims of *négritude* and other ideologies, empiricism was also a valuable standby and a means of self-definition. In 1960, Vol. 4, No. 1 of *The Horn*[17] already saw Wole Soyinka attacking *négritude* in terms which anticipate his famous remarks on the subject a few years later, and the general intellectual ambience of the magazine, while initially sympathetic to the ideological platforms of fellow writers from the francophone region, soon turned against it. There was in fact, surprisingly little political verse in *The Horn*. In general the student writers of this generation were too busy finding their feet both as Nigerians and as poets to bother about noises resounding from the Quartier Latin.

Among the writers who expressed the prevailing attitude most

---

[16] *New Lines*, pp. xiv–xv.
[17] Wole Soyinka's 'The Future of West African Writing' was scheduled for *The Horn* 3, 4 in March, 1960 but 'due to unforeseen circumstances' had to be held over the Easter vacation to appear in May in Vol. 4, No. 1, pp. 10–16.

memorably was John Pepper Clark, co-founder and editor of *The Horn*, the name of which was his inspiration, and to which between 1958 and 1961 he contributed no fewer than fourteen poems, continuing to send pieces in the academic year following his own graduation. Among these are several included either in his Mbari Press booklet of 1962 or in *A Reed in the Tide* of four years later. It is noticeable that, with the exception of the lengthy *Ivbie*,[18] by far the more successful of these are poems which turn on the rediscovery of rural *moeurs* and customs by one temporarily removed from them. Such are 'The Fulani Cattle' (*sic*), so entitled in Vol. 3, No. 2 (1959, p. 12); 'Agbor Dancer' (Vol. 3, No. 1, 1959, p. 6) and 'Return of the Fishermen' (Vol. 4, No. 3, 1961, p. 10), all products of the securely earthed phase in Clark's writing which also produced the admirable 'Night Rain' (*Nigeria Magazine*, Vol. 74, 1962, pp. 87–8). *The Horn* was in a very real sense Clark's nursery. It was here that he learned both the respect for the nuances of intimately felt life which later stood him in such good stead, and the stylistic vices which have marred his less confident work. Vol. 2, No. 6 saw the entry of one of his more spectacular affectations with 'Variations on Hopkins on theme of Child Wonder'. The piece is of interest in a number of respects. Firstly, 'child wonder' was to be the theme of many of Clark's most convincing pieces, including 'Night Rain'. The attractive encapsulation of a similar response in Gerard Manley Hopkins, one of the formative influences on twentieth-century English verse, would seem to have tempted Clark into an ill-advised emulation. Hopkins was studied in the moderns option at Ibadan and had featured in lectures by Martin Banham which Clark had attended, but the resulting imitation does justice neither to the original nor to the shared theme:

> Amá, are you gall bitter pent?
> Have paltry pittance spent?
> Is not the world so small pity plenished,
> So dry cut úp, self-finished
> 5 Fást, that all her men,
> Though unseeming, should out of ken
> Paupers be over bald bones?
> Therefore wíll you haul on them stones,
> This horde of hogs upon dung,
> 10 So sparing of tongue
> And not yourself surcease greed

[18] *Ivbie*, Clark's undergraduate *magnum opus*, first appeared in *The Horn* 2, 2, 1958, pp. 2–15, taking up most of that issue. For a full discussion, see chapter 7.

To increase another's need?
Of course, yóu are sick, soulful sick
Of stench carrion thick;
15  Worse, would worse live on loan
As were best off left alone . . .[19]

One would like to feel that this is parody. Unfortunately it appears to be a serious attempt to imitate Hopkins's poem 'Márgarét, áre you gríeving / Over Goldengrove unleaving?'[20] As such it is an experiment in Sprung Rhythm, and Clark has gone as far as to mark instances of rhythmical counterpoint with stress-marks, thus demonstrating his awareness that, although Hopkins's system stipulated the number of stresses in a line, it was flexible about their displacement. The trouble is that, even reckoned thus, line three has five feet and line four only three. There is a possibility that 'plenished' is an 'outride' or hanging foot permitted at the end of a line, but, if such, it should be marked with a loop. Lines thirteen and fourteen exemplify a similar inconsistency. In neither case is there any real fidelity to Hopkins's convention, since the 'running' or basic rhythm is evidently four sprung feet, and the departures cannot be reconciled with the ideas outlined either in Hopkins's journals or in his letter to Dixon. The truth seems to be that, lured by the apparent freedom of Hopkins's rhythmical processes, Clark has attempted to follow suit, and in so doing has been led into the mazes of a system whose accentual requirements are in their way as exacting as those of the Elizabethans, if more varied. The result is a metrical hotchpotch which, far from liberating Clark's voice, asphyxiates it.

The poem also serves to raise a fundamental point of relevance not merely to the student poets here discussed, but to the whole future of English-language verse in West Africa. It is often asserted that the influence which set the generation of the late fifties and early sixties free of the dead weight of Victorian practice was the delighted discovery of a school of poets active in England, Ireland and America earlier in the century: the 'Modernist' camp of Hopkins, Yeats, Eliot, Pound and Whitman – men who, though often politically reactionary, possessed a versatility of metrical technique and a range of cultural

[19] *The Horn* 2, 6, 1959, p. 3. For a further imitation of the modern school, see Clark's 'To a Prodigal', *The Horn* 3, 4, 1960, footnote 'On reading W. B. Yeats's twin poems "To a child dancing in the wind" and "Two Years Later"'. The theme of childhood preoccupied Clark throughout much of his early twenties.
[20] 'Spring and Fall', *The Poems of Gerard Manley Hopkins*, eds. W. H. Gardner and N. H. Mackenzie (London: Oxford University Press, 4th edition, 1967).

allusion profoundly inviting to young Africans trying to break away from provincial English models. A detailed examination of the contributions to *The Horn*, however, suggests that something like the opposite was the case. Exposure to the great experiments of Hopkins, who, though a Victorian, belongs in spirit to the 'Modernist' movement in Literature, tempted men like Clark into stylistic indulgences which choked their expressive urge with sorts of redundant ornament which made it immensely more difficult for them to speak with lucidity about experiences unique and important to them. What was needed then, as in many instances is needed now, was a model of expression which might enable the poet to talk directly and naturally of intuitions instinctual to him. Within the English tradition the fittest source of such an example was not the worldly wise, ostentatiously erudite writers influential in the twenties and thirties, but, on the one hand, the first generation of Romantic Revival poets – and more especially Wordsworth – and, on the other, certain contemporary writers of the post-war period, who, reacting against the cultivated sophistication of their elders, were pioneering a new ease and a new clarity of style. This is no place to discuss Clark's more successful poems, which are the subject of chapter 7. Suffice it to say that, when Clark is writing most naturally of the things he loves, it is not of Hopkins, Eliot or Yeats that he reminds us, but, on the one hand, of the Wordsworth of *The Lyrical Ballads*, and, on the other, of contemporary writers such as Philip Larkin.

If as a rule the experimental poetry of the Modernist source had a deleterious effect upon early West African poetry in English, this rule possessed one exception, but it was such as pertains only to talents of the first order. Christopher Ifekandu Okigbo had come down from Ibadan with an Honours Degree in Classics eighteen months before *The Horn*'s inception and was, for most of the period of its publication, a master of Fiditi Grammar School. While still at Ibadan he had been introduced to the refinements of Modernist poetics by Clark, who, though academically two years his junior, was registered in the English Department and thus had access to the moderns course. Okigbo's writing was at the time more deeply influenced by the Latin lyricists whom he had studied in the original than by anything which English literature had to offer, but when under Clark's influence he looked into Eliot and Pound, he discovered much that he liked. The crucial difference between Clark and Okigbo was this: that the allusions and echoes Okigbo found in these poets were to literatures which he had already encountered in their own language. He was thus not dependent on the kind of second-hand acquaintance with the international classics to which lesser talents fell foul. The result was a kind of unforced cosmopolitanism suggested by the poem 'On the New Year' published in *The Horn* in 1960:

> Now it is over, the midnight funeral that parts
> The old year from the new;
> And now beneath each pew
> The warden dives to find forgotten missals
> Scraps of resolutions and medals;
> And over lost souls in the graves
> Amid the tangled leaves
> The Wagtail is singing:
> Cheep cheep cheep the new year is coming;
> Christ will come again, the churchbell is ringing
> Christ will come again after the argument in heaven
> Christ . . . Nicodemus . . . Magdalen . . .
> Ding dong ding. . . .
>
> And the age rolls on like a wind glassed flood,
> And the pilgrimage to the cross is the void . . .
>
> And into time time slips with a lazy pace
> And time into time
> And need we wait while time and the hour
> Roll, waiting for power?
>
>
> II
>
> To wait is to linger
> With the hope that the flood will flow dry;
> To hope is to point an expectant finger
> At fate, fate that has long left us to lie
> Marooned on the sands
> Left with dry glands
> To suckle as die.
>
> Wait indeed, wait with grief laden
> Hearts that throb like a diesel engine.
> Throbbing with hopes:
> Those hopes of men those hopes that are nowhere,
> Those nebulous hopes, sand castles in the air –
> Wait and hope?
> The way is weary and long and time is
> Fast on our heels;
> Or forces life to a headlong conclusion

Nor yet like crafty Heracles
Devolve on someone else
The bulk of the globe?

### III

Where then are the roots, where the solution
To life's equation?

The roots are nowhere
There are no roots here
Probe if you may
From now until doomsday.

We have to think of ourselves as forever
Soaring and sinking like dead leaves blown by a gust
Floating choicelessly to the place where
Old desires and new born hopes like bubbles burst
Into nothing – blown to the place of fear
To the cross in the void;
Or else forever playing this zero-sum game
With fate as mate, and forever
Slaying and mating as one by one
Our tombstones rise in the void.[21]

There are Modernist echoes here, but they are remarkably well absorbed. 'Hearts that throb like a diesel engine' is just the sort of technological image in which the Audenesque poets of the thirties revelled, but probably owes more to the human engine 'like a taxi throbbing waiting' in line 217 of Eliot's *The Waste Land*. The beginning of section III also alludes unmistakably to the second verse paragraph of 'The Burial of the Dead' from *The Waste Land*. What is remarkable, however, is not the occasional tendency to half-quotation, but the aural techniques which a reading of a twentieth-century verse has clearly made possible: the facility with half-rhyme (usually well judged), with pari-rhyme, internal rhyme, the fluctuation between strict *vers libre* and symmetrically stressed measures which recall both Christmas carols and the rugged shapes of folk literature. Thematically the poem owes far less to Eliot's Anglo-Catholicism than to the way in which Okigbo's own youthful Roman Catholicism has enabled him to see the destiny of present-day Nigeria as part of an age-old rhythm of decay and renewal. It was a theme that was to preoccupy him for many years to come.

[21] *The Horn* 3, 4, 1960, p. 4, cont. on p. 9. Not listed in Lindfors.

'On the New Year' was one of only two pieces which Okigbo sub-
mitted to *The Horn*, the remainder of his juvenilia appearing in the
pages of *Black Orpheus*. This is scarcely surprising: Okigbo detested
parochialism of all sorts, seeing himself as heir to a wider, older tra-
dition than that suggested by the fleeting influences active among his
slightly younger contemporaries. To appear to advantage he needed
the sort of international forum that *The Horn*, student-run and
campus-based, could not provide. He was not the only one to feel this
need. At about the time *The Horn* was getting on its feet, there was a
strong sense among the faculty and beyond that Africa deserved a
serious-minded review of letters which would accommodate the very
best of contemporary writing while serving as a platform for those
who wished to air their views as to the direction which African culture
was taking. In 1957 the appropriate initiative was taken by Ulli Beier of
the Department of Extra-Mural Studies at Ibadan and Jahnheinz Jahn,
Arabic scholar, freelance translator and critic, who, though resident in
Germany, passed frequently through Nigeria. In naming the journal
*Black Orpheus* the editors were implicitly acknowledging two sources
of influence. The title itself derives from 'Orphée noir', Jean-Paul
Sartre's Introduction to Senghor's anthology *Anthologie de la nouvelle
poésie nègre et malgache* of 1948.[22] Secondly, the format, designed as it
was to invite contributions from both French-speaking and English-
speaking Africa, owed much to the initiative of Alioune Diop's Paris
based journal *Présence africaine*. Since 1955 this had appeared in bi-
lingual editions and already possessed a distinguished record as a
showcase for writers from every part of Africa. In deciding to publish
in both English and French, Diop had been hoping to attract an audi-
ence in anglophone Africa, but by 1957 he had experienced little suc-
cess, with the result that Nigerian intellectuals of the time remained
strangely resistant to the achievements of their brothers not only in
neighbouring francophone countries, but also in the French, Hispanic
and even English islands of the Caribbean. By choosing a name so
closely associated with francophone letters the committee of *Black Or-
pheus* were attempting to support the bridge with pylons from the
other side. As well as a cultural bridgehead, however, *Black Orpheus*
fulfilled another function. Its name calls attention to the high regard in

---

[22] *Anthologie de la nouvelle poésie nègre et malgache de langue française* (Paris: Presses Univer-
sitaires de France, 1948). See chapter 3.

which the editors held the art of poetry, to the extent of seeing it as the nodal point of the cultural matrix. This, on the face of it, highly eccentric view was one associated with a number of leading British periodicals in the thirties and forties, notably Edgell Rickword's *Calendar of Modern Letters* (1925–7) and T. S. Eliot's *Criterion* (1922–39). The ambitions of the *Black Orpheus* committee can thus be seen as extending both to the establishment of a leading journal open to the whole black world, and to the inauguration of a new school of Nigerian poetry which might be viewed critically in an international context.

At first new poetry came in slowly, so that the pages of the first six issues, which Beier and Jahn edited jointly, were filled for the most part with translations out of the French and Spanish, critical articles and reviews. The intentions of the editors were substantially suggested by the spread of interest in the very first issue: three poems by a poet in his thirties called Gabriel Okara,[23] translations from the poetry of Senghor, and an introduction to the work of Amos Tutuola by Gerald Moore (then resident in Hong Kong), an article entitled 'The Conflict of Cultures in West African Poetry' by Beier himself,[24] and a report by Jahn on the First World Congress of Black Writers held in Paris the previous September. In the absence of recent innovative work, the examples in Beier's article were drawn from the pioneering poets discussed in our first chapter, and the francophone writers discussed in our second. Drawing on such writing, within which he assumed more homogeneity than his quotations justified, his conclusions were a little naïve. Beier was hamstrung by a simple dualistic model of cultural differentiation: poets were either seen as belonging to 'our' culture (by which he meant the culture of the West) or their own local cultures. By seemingly crossing over to the other side, Senghor was seen as having compromised his *Africanité* which he then converted into a sort of compensatory banner. The tone of the essay draws our attention to liabilities under which *Black Orpheus* laboured but *The Horn* did not: though addressed ostensibly to an international black audience, it could not resist the temptation in the early numbers to talk over their shoulders to a metropolitan community beyond. The position improved after issue seven, when Ezekiel Mphalele and Wole Soyinka joined the editorial team, but in the meantime there was

---

[23] These were 'Spirit of the Wind', p. 36, 'The Call of the River Nun', p. 37 and 'Were I to Choose', p. 38, in *Black Orpheus* 1, 1957.
[24] Ulli Beier, 'The Conflict of Cultures in West African Poetry', *Black Orpheus* 1, 1957, pp. 17–21.

no sense in Beier's article of a common world culture to which authors from a variety of different backgrounds might contribute. In the late fifties critics still lived in an historical milieu in which liberal accommodation of extraneous manners and norms tended to be based on a frank recognition of differences. Beier's 'our' which persisted throughout his essay, betrayed a weakness in the magazine's editorial stance. In his understandable desire to place his observations in a proper international context, Beier fell foul of a double tendency to situate himself as a European onlooker on the changing African scene and to assume that his readers, including his African colleagues, necessarily shared the same perspective. It is to the credit of *Black Orpheus* that it gradually shed the protective umbrella of such attitudes.

The tendency repeated itself in the very first paragraph of Miriam Koshland's analysis of 'Six Chants from the Congo' in issue two: 'The African manner of self expression is different from our own and the social background of the poetry is different from ours.'[25] Despite this Koshland's contribution built on what had already become one of the journal's cornerstones: a serious and sympathetic consideration of oral literature. If initially the translators were for the most part European and the method of commentary anthropological rather than critical, the sections of the magazine devoted to this area served both as a training-ground for younger indigenous scholars of oral poetry such as Adeboye Babalola, whose essay on Yoruba *ijala* in the first issue laid the foundations of a life's work,[26] and as a gesture of recognition toward the vernacular tradition as one foundation on which future writers must construct. Already, by issue two, the results of this emphasis were making themselves felt. Under the collective title 'African Genesis' Beier introduced a couple of local creation myths, the second of which was a scintillating reworking of an Ijọ legend by Okara, some of whose poetry had already appeared in the first issue of *Black Orpheus*. Its inclusion was significant for two reasons: firstly in that it showed a marked similarity to the Yoruba myth in which Beier was himself much interested, and secondly, in that it demonstrated the way in which at least one contemporary Nigerian writer, as yet not widely known, was prepared to learn from the spoken traditions of his own people.

In the first five years of *Black Orpheus*'s existence, Okara contributed

[25] *Black Orpheus* 2, 1958, p. 18.
[26] S. A. Babalola, 'Ijala: the Poetry of Yoruba Hunters', *Black Orpheus* 1, 1957, pp. 5–16. Cf. also his *The Content and Form of Yoruba Ijala* (Oxford: The Clarendon Press, 1966).

six poems to the magazine. This was not a large total, but then Okara was always a sparing writer. These pieces included some of the very best later collected together in his volume *The Fisherman's Invocation and Other Poems*,[27] including 'The Call of the River Nun', 'Were I to Choose', 'Piano and Drums'[28] and 'The Fisherman's Invocation' itself. If *The Horn* was Pepper Clark's cradle, then *Black Orpheus* was Okara's nursery. He was never, as was Clark later, one of the editorial panel; yet his contributions lend stature and weight to a journal to whose liberal, concerned, locally responsible ethos they seemed peculiarly to belong. At times their inclusion seemed almost calculated to endorse actively the editorial stance. 'Piano and Drums', for instance, was a piece which perfectly illustrated Beier's thesis in the first issue concerning the cultural dilemma facing modern Africans, while 'The Call of the River Nun' and 'The Fisherman's Invocation' relied heavily on strands in Ijǫ folklore and hence served as a neat complement to the magazine's ethnographic items.

Okara was several years older than the poets who appeared alongside him and, as such, was unusual in offering up seasoned work which has since stood the test of time. For the most part, however, *Black Orpheus* provided a period of apprenticeship for promising writers who, their induction complete, then passed on to distinction elsewhere. Prominent among these were Wole Soyinka (seven contributions); Christopher Okigbo (eleven contributions) and Lenrie Peters (sixteen contributions). Issue five already saw Soyinka entering the lists with 'Three Poems', posted from England where, on the completion of his studies at the University of Leeds, he was surviving in London as a secondary school teacher and later the reader for the Royal Court Theatre. The 'Three Poems' from *Black Orpheus*, as Gerald Moore admits, are not Soyinka's best work and hence do not belong in a discussion of his maturity. All three display a vein of racial self-consciousness later skilfully disguised by irony and oblique satire. While 'Telephone Conversation',[29] published for the first time in the journal *Ibadan* the following year, later earned itself a revered place in Soyinka's *oeuvre*, these earlier efforts have usually been judged as of no more than historical interest. The reason is not difficult to discover. All display their author's vulnerability naked of artful disguise.

---

[27] Gabriel Okara, *The Fisherman's Invocation and Other Poems* (London: Heinemann, 1978).
[28] *Black Orpheus* 1, p. 38.     [29] *Ibadan*, 10, 1960, p. 34.

If 'Telephone Conversation' may be read as witty anecdote recounted at an Old Boys' Dinner by a young professional who hides his personal disquiet beneath an ample cummerbund, the 'Three Poems' are cries from the centre of an infected wound. It is a wound which supplies the dominant image in 'The Immigrant', where the black protagonist, rejected by a wall-flower at a dance at the Hammersmith Palais, eases his sense of private humiliation by a quick stab of phantasy.

> He felt the wound grow septic
> (Hard though he tried to close it)
> His fingers twitched
> And toyed with the idea,
> The knife that waited on the slight,
> On the sudden nerve that would join her face
> to scars identical
> With what he felt inside.
> The blade remained
> In the sweat filled pocket.[30]

The phallic thrust, held in a scabbard of conventional reserve, later releases itself in the arms of a prostitute picked up beside a lamp post. 'The Immigrant' was written in 1959, the year of the Street Offences Act which temporarily drove prostitutes off the London streets, and there is something about the slightly awkwardly swashbuckling defiance of the piece that dates it as surely as its social milieu. Though it would be fatal to mistake the protagonist for the author, the text reels in half-suppressed feeling which suggests an involvement barely resolved. The other two pieces are more evidently character portraits. 'The Other Immigrant' is an early portrayal of the neo-colonial middle class at play abroad. It displays with stark humour but little sympathy the dilemma of an earlier generation of immigrants from the New Commonwealth which had sought to solve the dilemma of racial disparity by sinking its identity in what they perceived as the more exclusive reserves of the host culture. The results of such an attempt as portrayed by Soyinka are at best uncomfortable to witness, and at worst ludicrous in their self-deception:

> My dignity I rescue
> From the shop assistant's levity
> From the raucous laugh
> Of the unmannered station guard

[30] *Black Orpheus* 5, p. 10.

> (Who hasn't learnt his place)
> From the familiarity
> Of the Cockney taxi man
> Who thinks I'll bandy jokes with him,
> A mere
> Public servant –
> One and all,
> They wilt at the touch of ice.
> My mouth is showed perpetually
> Upon the word 'riff-raff'.[31]

It is not the ear of the poet but the eye of the dramatist that is here engaged. 'The Other Immigrant' comes from the same drawer as the opening scene of Soyinka's play *The Lion and the Jewel*, first produced the very same year,[32] where the anglophile affectations of the schoolmaster Lakunle are pilloried with a similar severity. The third of the poems, 'My Next Door Neighbour', smacks less of London than of the backstreets of Leeds, where among the crowded tenements of Woodhouse, Hunslett or the Brudenells, students and working people then as now lived cheek by jowl. It is the weakest of the pieces, a back-number describing the antics of the neighbourhood tart, lip-sticked and predictably drawn to the allurements of the new Juke Boxes:

> My next door neighbour
> Times her men
> With music.
> A disc, or two or three
> Vending same apathy
> Of love
> (The lyrics' one and every word)
> And an extra charge for the extra disc
> Falling
> In quick succession.[33]

Where the immigrant poems portray defence mechanisms adopted by two bashful intruders, 'My Next Door Neighbour' constitutes an observation on the behaviour of the native species, drawn by an amused, sardonically tolerant naturalist. Seen another way, the poem is a leaf from a playwright's notebook.

Soyinka's later contributions to the magazine were confined to number 10, and date from two years later. In these poems, by

---

[31] *Ibid.*, p. 11.
[32] Produced in a double bill with Soyinka's play *The Swamp Dwellers*, directors Geoffrey Axworthy and Ken Post, Ibadan, February, 1959.
[33] *Black Orpheus*, 5, p. 12.

contrast, Soyinka's style is practiced and confident, producing fully achieved work which, as such, is dealt with in a later chapter. Read within the context of the journal, however, these now celebrated poems yield additional riches. 'Abiku', 'Death in the Dawn', 'Season' and 'Night', all later collected in *Idanre and Other Poems* (1967) occur as part of a medley of 'New Nigerian Poetry' which also featured Frank Aig-Imoukhuede, Dorothy Obi and John Pepper Clark. Some of the editorial juxtapositions seemed especially piquant. There could, for instance, be no more incisive insight into the differing temperaments of Soyinka and Clark than that afforded by the printing, a mere two pages apart, of their two poems both entitled 'Abiku'. An *abiku* is a wandering spirit which continually re-enters a mother's womb only to arrive still-born or die in infancy. To encourage it to stay more permanently or else desist, certain rites must be performed: the skin of the corpse must be serrated, and offerings made of 'goats and cowries / palm oil and sprinkled ash'. The pieces by Clark and Soyinka approach the same situation from opposing but complementary viewpoints. Clark's is a heart-felt cry from the bosom of the family beseeching the fleeting brother to stay in the compound 'where many more mouths gladden the heart'. Soyinka's is a defiant declamation from the innermost recesses of the mystery. It is an incantation or curse delivered by a lofty presence disdaining to encumber itself with the demands of mere mortals.

> In vain your bangles cast
> Charmed circles at my feet;
> I am Abiku, calling for the first
> And the repeated time.[34]

What in Clark arouses tenderness and domestic yearning inspires in Soyinka's half-child nothing but supernatural disgust: 'Where I crept, the warmth was cloying'. Though the juxtaposition of these two poems is no more than happy coincidence compounded by editorial cunning, Soyinka's piece, if read immediately after Clark's, resounds like a deliberate answer delivered in a dark sonorous undertone. Moreover, by 1961 Soyinka was one of the journal's editors and might expect a say in the arrangement of items.

The very next issue early in 1962 saw the seductive entry of a still, small voice: Christopher Okigbo, librarian and classicist. Though the *Four Canzones*, as his friend the critic Sunday Anozie acknowledges,

---

[34] *Black Orpheus* 11, 1962, p. 7.

are properly juvenilia, they mark a decided advance on the New Year poem published two years earlier, and to read them is to watch a luminous talent finally emerging like a full moon from behind clouds. Typically Okigbo makes his initial mark as a translator out of the Latin. 'Song of the Forest', written a year after Okigbo's graduation from Ibadan, is a rendition of the opening of Vergil's First Eclogue which adapts the plaintive song of the Roman groves to the more familiar forests of the Igbo countryside:

SONG OF THE FOREST
(with *ubo*)

YOU LOAF, child of the forest,
beneath a village umbrella,
plucking from tender string a
    Song of the forest.
Me, away from home, run-
away, must leave the borders of our
land, fruitful fields,
    must leave our homeland.[35]

The second word 'LOAF' seems inexplicable until you consult the original Latin:

Tityre, tu, patulae recubans sub tegmine fagi,
Silvestrem tenui Musam meditaris avena:
Nos patriae finis, et dulcia linquimus arva
Nos patriam fugimus: tu, Tityre, lentus in umbra,
Formosam resonare doces Amaryllida silvas.[36]

The music of these lines derives partly from alliteration and partly from the assonantal long vowels 'u' and 'o' contrasted with the tighter 'i' and 'e'. Line one combines both elements: alliteration on the initial letters of 'Tityre' and 'tu', and the long 'u' cooing through 'tu', 'patulae' 'recubans' and 'sub'. Okigbo has disposed of the alliteration, so it is essential that he retain Vergil's open vowels: hence 'YOU LOAF'. 'Song of the Forest' is an experiment in vowel contrast. Throughout it the poet places his fingers on open and stopped holes as if on the stops of the Igbo flute which he requests to accompany him. Ten minutes' study of this piece are sufficient to raise inconvenient questions for those who condemn classical studies as 'irrelevant' to the needs of African students. Quantitative Latin metre, based as it is upon the length of individual vowels, is a great deal

[35] *Black Orpheus* 11, 1962, p. 5.
[36] *P. Vergilii Maronis Opera* (Venice: Giunta, 1544), Vol. 1, p. 1.

closer to tonal African systems than is conventional English prosody with its alien insistence on stress. Okigbo learned as much from the mellifluousness of the Latin poets as he did from the pitch formations of his Igbo forebears, and in his finest verse these two influences combine to stunning effect. 'Song of the Forest' is a minor tribute to two great civilizations: an act, not of imitation, but of its opposite, re-creation, the practice piece of a master.

The second *Canzone*, originally published in *The Horn*, takes us forward two years to 1959 when Okigbo was working as a classics master at Fiditi Grammar School. It is dominated by one influence: T. S. Eliot's choral monologue *The Hollow Men* of 1925. Eliot had been a joint discovery of Okigbo and Clark while at Ibadan, where Clark was at the time of the poem's composition still in his final year. *The Hollow Men* is set in a 'twilight kingdom', an arid desert terrain signifying a state of moral neutrality stranded between Good and Evil. Okigbo's 'Debtor's Lane', by contrast, is less a religious statement than a sober assessment of personal prospects after the 'blast and buffets' of the undergraduate years. Like the American novelist Scott Fitzgerald, Okigbo is engaged in documenting the fall of a brilliant but doomed generation. It is an early instance of his uncanny gift for prophecy:

> A. NO heavenly transports now
>    of youthful passion
> and the endless succession
> of tempers and moods
> in high societies;
> no blasts no buffets
> of a mad generation
> nor the sonorous arguments
> of the hollow brass
> and the copious cups
> of fraudulent misses
> in brothels
> of a mad generation.[37]

'Buffets' could refer either to the jolts of adolescent competition or to cold cuts after a May Ball, while the 'fraudulent misses' are both the shadow play, parry and thrust, of eager young men and the low-born women with whom they delight sometimes to consort.

The reference to the underworld of the stews alerts us to another Eliotic influence on this *Canzone*: the Aristophanic Melodrama *Sweeney*

[37] *Black Orpheus* 11, 1962, p. 6.

*Agonistes* of 1932 set in a London brothel frequented by American visitors. The influence, however, is one of situation rather than sound: throughout the aural effect is that of the dry monotone of *The Hollow Men*, the syncopated jazz rhythms of *Sweeney* nowhere intruding. There are other allusions also, line 4 being identical with line 376 of *The Waste Land*:

> B. THERE was a tenement
> in hangman's lane
> where repose was a dream
> unreal
> and a knock on the door
> at dawn
> hushed the tenant humped
> beneath the bed:
> was it the postman
> or the bailiff with a writ?
> And if the telephone rang –
> alas, if the telephone rang . . .
> Was he to hang up his life
> on a rack
> and answer the final call?[38]

Okigbo's *oeuvre* which proceeds from this moment with an almost remorseless logic towards a fated conclusion, developed gradually through a systematic assimilation and refining of influences. To some readers it has seemed that, in the early work at least, the allusions lie so deeply encrusted that the voice of the poet lies several feet beneath the surface vainly struggling to get out. A look at the second *Canzone* refutes this. There is more Eliot lying around these lines than in any of Okigbo's later work, even *Heavensgate* where the echoes are fairly thickly amassed. Yet two things are noticeable: Okigbo never simply takes over his mentor's voice; he always subverts it to his own ends, which are sometimes far removed from Eliot's. And secondly, the processes of assimilation go beyond intellectual ingestion to achieve a softly tuned aural finesse: finally it is the ear which domesticates the echoes and makes them its own.

One can see this operation at work perfectly in the third *Canzone* where Okigbo moves away from middle Eliot to an expansion of the refrain from François Villon's 'Ballade des Dames Temps Jadis' the nostalgic strains of which yield this:

[38] *Ibid.*

Where are the Maytime flowers,
Where the roses? What will the
Watermaid bring at sundown,
a garland? A handful of tears?
Sing to the rustic flute:
Sing a new note. . . .[39]

In the Ballade which lies behind these lines, Villon, mediaeval vaga-
bond, ruffian and versifier was indulging in feelings which owed
more to the artful sentiments of the troubadours than to a yearning for
any real state intuitively perceived. Okigbo's watermaid and rustic
flute, on the other hand, are not simple figments, but emerge from a
rural background with which the poet is still in touch. The watermaid
is Idoto, the river goddess of Okigbo's birthplace, whom his grand-
father served as priest, and to whom it was intended that Okigbo him-
self should eventually minister.[40] The flute is the *ubo* to whose music
the first *Canzone* was sung: still clammy with the player's breath. Far
from serenading some never-neverland of the remote past the flute
expresses a 'new note' and hence encourages the poet to interpret the
future. The poem's sub-title 'Lament of the Flutes' is shared by the
later sequence *Distances*, where a point of transition to the future is
similarly envisaged.

Lastly, 'Lament of the Lavender Mist' finds Okigbo struggling
towards Idoto, his mistress and muse, through enveloping shrouds of
mistrust and guilt. We are now in the world of 'Heavensgate', the first
mature sequence, where the poet is forced into a cat-and-mouse game
with a goddess who finally eludes him. We are still also in the com-
pany of Eliot, who shadows the poet's every step, and whose imagery
of the spiral stair-well from *Ash Wednesday* (1930) mediates between
Okigbo's subjective longing and his own image of a circuitous path-
way:

AT THE FIRST fork of the road
Saint Vitus' dancer,
At the fork of the lightning
Lady of the lavender –
    mist, scattering
Lightning shafts without rain,
    came forging
Thunder with no smell of water –

[39] *Ibid.*, p. 7.
[40] Sunday O. Anozie, *Christopher Okigbo: Creative Rhetoric* (London: Evans, 1972), pp.
    43–4.

Abyss of wonders
Of masks, black masks, idols,
From whose pest of fireflies,
    Phosphorescence
Over me at sundown
In an empty garden
Wounded by the wind lie dead leaves.[41]

The appearance of the *Four Canzones* in the pages of *Black Orpheus* reminds us of their provenance: this is university poetry at its best. Still arrested at the student stage, still smelling rankly of the lecture hall, it projects nevertheless a poetic personality which is both attractive and unmistakable. The *Canzones* are a double tribute to the Ibadan academic system and to the undoubted talent of one individual who, during the course of a short life, was able gradually to transmute the base metal of scholarship into the gold of imaginative work which in the history here recounted has no parallel. The course of that transforming alchemy is the subject of our next chapter. Meanwhile, the *Canzones* serve both as foretaste and as a testament to the ambience, both academic and journalistic, which helped foster them.

Of all the issues of *Black Orpheus* produced between 1957 and 1963, number eleven was poetically the most distinguished. As well as Okigbo's *Canzones* it also witnessed the arrival, from Sierra Leone via the United Kingdom of one 'L. Peters', then of University College Hospital, London. Unlike the younger Soyinka and Okigbo, Peters, then twenty-nine, had not sent his talent out to dine until the wine was mature. Hence all four of the pieces printed in *Black Orpheus* 11, together with five poems from number 14, were taken with complete confidence into Peters's first collection, *Poems* (Mbari, 1964). Already the poet's chief concerns are apparent: a mistrust of lavish gestures, whether personal or political; a feeling of being earthed in the natural world; a fascination with the processes of scientific evolution; a slight clinical distaste for the grossly physical; a compulsive search for a private myth of return. All of these themes are treated in chapter 8, which takes Peters through from the publication in 1966 of his second volume *Satellites*. Yet already his distinctive atmosphere is observable in pieces which, though included in *Poems*, were not to be reprinted in the later book. 'Wild Excursions', for instance, is very much a poem of its time, evincing precisely that wariness of ideological assertion

---

[41] *Black Orpheus* 11, 1962, p. 9.

which Robert Conquest had already diagnosed as symptomatic of the philosophical and artistic temper of the poets of the Movement, whose work Peters had encountered while working in England:

> If I was asked
>   How I would face the task
> Of camping out in space,
>   I would reply
> With infinite distaste
>   That I had rather die.
> Because to meddle
>   In this confounded puzzle
> Would only represent
>   My innate discontent.
> That if it was my face
>   Men seemed to hate
> Then it would be in place
>   To offer an estate.
> On some detested piece of earth
>   Where suited to my girth
> And my most earthy temperament
>   I would be proud to represent
> The Non-progressive element.[42]

Here is Peters's voice already formed: informal, confidential, modest, urbanely reflective, sad. There is nothing in it of Okigbo's erudition or Soyinka's snarling satire, both of which required the sort of personal projection which Peters disliked. If in Soyinka we are always aware of the grease-paint and the brittle humour of the theatrical review, and in Okigbo of flowers pressed between yellowing pages, in Peters we seem always to sense a tired figure hunched in a dimly lit surgery at sunset after a hard day's work and reflecting over a smouldering cigarette on the contradictory nature of a fraught, unsatisfactory existence. The unambitious pragmatism of Peters's themes is matched by a self-deflating tone very much of its period. This too is a legacy of the intellectual ethos, in many ways common to both London and Ibadan, of the late fifties and early sixties.

◉      ◉      ◉

By the time that Peters's poems appeared in the pages of *Black Orpheus*, John Pepper Clark, soon to join the editorial board, already

---

[42] *Ibid.*, p. 61.

had a book in print. In the face of continuing indifference from the metropolis, *Poems* (1962) was produced locally in Ibadan by an imprint which was also the product of local enterprise. By the early sixties it was already becoming increasingly clear that such was the talent on offer locally in Nigeria that some sort of provision for more permanent publication had to be made. It was thus that Beier came to set up, in Ibadan, a small concern known as Mbari, a writers' club accommodating a press capable of running off limited editions tastefully designed. Of the six poets principally discussed in this chapter four first came to a wider public attention by this means. In 1962 Clark's *Poems* were published with illustrations by Susanne Wenger. In the same year Okigbo's first mature sequence *Heavensgate* saw the light of day, to be followed two years later by *Distances*. Two new names entered the list in 1964: Lenrie Peters whose first book was also entitled, with an austerity typical of first titles, *Poems*, and George Awoonor Williams, now Kofi Awoonor, whose *Rediscovery and Other Poems* is discussed in chapter 6. The poets thus made available to a wider reading public were all taken onto the lists of major London publishing houses within a few years, though Okigbo was not thus to appear until after his death. The importance of Mbari, however, lay less in the slender bridgehead which it afforded to international exposure than its solitary championing of the publication of African poetry on African soil. *South Africa?*

The combined achievement of *The Horn*, *Black Orpheus* and Mbari are strong testimony to the fact that the finest art often has very humble beginnings. Of that fact nothing provides a more cheering example than the short brilliant career of Christopher Okigbo, which we must now examine.

CHAPTER 5

# The achievement of Christopher Okigbo

When in 1967 the young Igbo poet Christopher Okigbo met his un-
timely death at the age of thirty-five on the battlefield of Nsukka
during the Nigerian Civil War, he left behind him enough poetry to fill
one slender volume.[1] Yet this tiny offering, a mere seventy-two pages
in length, arguably represents the most revered trophy in the gallery
of English-language verse in Africa, and Okigbo himself the most
talented of modern African poets. The verse of *Labyrinths*, as his collec-
ted works have come to be known, has a strange haunting quality, dif-
ficult to account for in orthodox critical language. It also triumphs over
petty historical distinctions by refusing to lend itself to any one tra-
dition, making a mockery of our painful efforts to allot it to any defin-
able school or recognizable manner. It is the product of a deeply
sophisticated mind, as steeped in the mythologies of Europe, Asia,
and the ancient world as in the folklore of the rural Igbo amongst
whom Okigbo grew up. Okigbo was a man of wide and voracious
reading in the literatures of Greece and Rome which he read while a
student of classics at the University College of Ibadan, in the poetry
and legends of ancient Babylon, which he encountered in translation,
and in the literatures of Europe and America, in which he retained a
lively interest throughout his life. For him, to be a writer was to par-
take in an international community of letters. He disdained any sug-
gestion of literary nationalism, going as far as to turn down a prize at
the first festival of black arts held in Dakar, Senegal, on the grounds
that he could not consider himself an exclusively African writer.[2] Yet
all of his poetry is deeply indebted to the beliefs and traditional poetic
practice of the Igbo people with which he never lost touch. In his deli-
cate cadences the music of oral Igbo poetry blends with echoes from

---

[1] Christopher Okigbo, *Labyrinths with Path of Thunder* (London: Heinemann, 1971). All
subsequent page references are to this edition. For convenience the name *Labyrinths*,
though strictly confined to the first four sequences only, has been used throughout to
signify the volume as a whole.

[2] *A Reader's Guide to African Literature*, eds. Hans Zell and Helene Silver (London: Heine-
mann, 1st edition, 1972), p. 168.

the modern English poets and with the strains of American jazz, which he loved to play on the clarinet while still an undergraduate. Thematically too his work may be viewed as an attempt to reconcile these various traditions and, above all, to come to terms with the tension between residual Christian promptings and the claims of indigenous Igbo theology.

One persistent problem in attempting to discuss Okigbo's work meaningfully is that, patient reviser as he was, most of his works have appeared in different versions under different imprints. The better part of the sequence known as *Limits* and *Silences* for instance appeared in the pages of the influential East African journal *Transition*, which, under Rajat Neogy's editorship, did so much to advance the cause of African letters in the early and mid-sixties.[3] Mbari of Ibadan, the Nigerian publishing house responsible for bringing out first volumes by a number of promising poets of the period, also issued the whole of *Heavensgate* (1962), *Limits* (1964) and *Silences* (1965), before, in 1965, Okigbo decided to sit down to revise all of the earlier poetry, which he proposed to reissue, with the new sequence *Distances* (already published in *Transition* Vol. 4 No. 16, 1964) under the joint title *Labyrinths*. He wrote an introduction for this project, which, however, never came to fruition before his death. Meanwhile, under the impact of the Nigerian *coup d'état* of January 1966, he wrote a fresh sequence called *Path of Thunder* which was performed in his lifetime but not published. As a result, a lengthy correspondence ensued between Okigbo's literary executors, Heinemann in London and his lifetime friend Sunday Anozie, who had been close to the poet during the composition of the early work, and who could hence be expected to know something of his intentions.[4] Anozie argued against the joint publication of *Labyrinths* and *Path of Thunder* but eventually the practicalities of publishing won the day, and the printed version of Okigbo's work now most widely available contains both works, in revised versions, dubbed by Okigbo himself as 'final' together with the 1965 introduction which, however, only applies to *Labyrinths*. A strong case can be made for reprinting the Mbari booklets in an accessible form, but, meanwhile, it seems best to confine oneself to an analysis of the later, Heinemann version, while bearing in mind that the differences

---

[3] For individual sequences, cf. 'Lament of the Silent Sisters' in *Transition* 8, 1963; 'Distances' in No. 16, 1964.

[4] Sunday O. Anozie, *Christopher Okigbo: Creative Rhetoric* (London: Evans, 1972), cf. especially pp. 171–3.

*colection*

between this and the first editions sometimes vary enormously, the differences in the text of *Silences*, for example, being especially marked.

In his preface Okigbo clearly states that he regards the trilogy of *Limits*, *Silences* and *Distances* as an interconnected sequence, and *Heavensgate* as an anticipatory sequence which is 'organically related' to it. In his monograph Sunday Anozie endorses this arrangement, and also sees *Heavensgate* as apprentice work.[5] It will be instructive, therefore, to deal with *Heavensgate*, the trilogy, and *Path of Thunder* in turn as statements belonging to successive phases of the poet's career, and then to turn to the question of their mutual relatedness.

Okigbo states that *Heavensgate* was 'originally conceived as an Easter sequence'.[6] There is much evidence in the text of Christian antecedents: references to the Biblical version of Creation, to ecclesiastical processions, to John the Baptist. One has therefore to treat with extreme caution Romanus Egudu's view of Okigbo as an anti-ecclesiastical, anti-clerical poet,[7] since these insignia are not here treated as icons to be destroyed but as facets of the poet's inner experience. The most one can concede is that these Christian images do tend to recede towards the end of the sequence, 'Lustra' and 'Newcomer' in particular drawing on predominantly pagan sources. Indeed the reference to the initiate as 'prodigal' in the very first lyric suggests an at least partial regret at personal infidelity to the traditional gods, one catalyst of which may be seen as Christian conversion. The posture *vis-à-vis* the Christian faith is thus strongly ambivalent. Though, conceived of in Christian terms they almost seem at points to be desiring a reconversion to a state of apostacy, even if the phrases in which this intention is expressed often bear strong Christian overtones, and the orthodox Christian terms of reference also come back in full force in later sequences, albeit suffused with exotic references.

We know from Anozie's account that Okigbo wrote *Heavensgate* shortly after a brief return visit to his home village of Ojoto, where he re-encountered the traditional mysteries and in particular the cult associated with the riverain goddess Idoto.[8] We learn further from Okigbo's own testimony that as a young boy he was expected to shoulder the burden of the priesthood of this cult when he grew up,

[5] *Ibid.*, pp. 41–2.    [6] *Labyrinths*, p. xi.

[7] Romanus Egudu, 'Defence of Culture in the Poetry of Christopher Okigbo' in *African Literature Today*, Vol. 6: *Poetry in Africa* (London: Heinemann, 1973), pp. 26–46.

[8] Anozie, *Christopher Okigbo*, pp. 42–3.

but later found it impossible to reconcile this with his professional career as librarian and publisher. The opening section of 'The Passage' recounts his feelings of guilt. As he stands before the neglected shrine he is seized with a feeling of regret and reclines symbolically on the totems of 'the oilbeam, the tortoise and the python' which he would have employed in his capacity as priest. Yet at the very moment of his greatest yearning he gives expression to this feeling in a précis of the opening sentence of Psalm 130, one of the greatest penitential supplications of the ancient church:

> Out of the depths my cry:
> give ear and hearken . . .                    (*Labyrinths*, p. 3)

This leads him straight into an evocation, at the beginning of the next lyric, of the Biblical vision of Genesis, the first act of a God who is Alpha and Omega, whose physical intervention begins with the creation of tiny wavelets of ultra-violet light and culminates with the holocaust of Armageddon, 'the fire that is dreamt of'. This reference, however, is only one strand in the texture of a lyric that is compounded of many echoes, from the evident allusion to the Eliot of *Burnt Norton* in the third stanza to the side-glance at the mediaeval carol 'I sing of a maiden' in the last line. The rainbow in stanza three is elusive, but its occurrence in a context so rich in Biblical echoes seems to justify Paul Theroux's connection of it with the Covenant of the Old Testament,[9] even though his additional interpretation of it as a 'snake capable of both leading and devouring the poet' is over complex and confused. Okigbo at this stage is merely embarking on his religious journey, and is concerned typically with false beacons, one of which may well be the all-embracing Christian view of history as God-directed. Anozie sees the boa-constrictor as a powerful emblem of religious intuition,[10] but we must note that it is 'bent to kill' and thus Theroux's suggestion of sinister intent cannot entirely be dismissed. At this point Okigbo almost seems to anticipate the thematic concerns of 'Fragments out of the Deluge' from *Limits* where Christianity is viewed simply as a destructive agent. In any case, at this stage, the poet's search for authentic visionary inspiration seems to be captive to Christian trappings to the extent that the mother-goddess Idoto comes to be viewed in the guise of a Madonna ('a mother on the spray'). Only

---

[9] Paul Theroux, 'A Study of Six Poets: Voices out of the Skull', *An Introduction to African Literature*, ed. Ulli Beier (London: Longman, 1972), p. 125.
[10] Anozie, *Christopher Okigbo*, p. 45.

at the very end with 'the young bird at the passage' does an indigenous note intrude.

The last segment of 'Passage' is among the most beautiful moments of the whole sequence. The 'silent faces at crossroads / festivity in black' may, as Anozie suggests, be implicitly satirical,[11] but the satire appears, to the present reader, to be muted beneath a dominant strain of ambivalent reverence. Okigbo would have seen plenty of such processions in the rural Igboland of his youth, and the slight reek of cassocked stuffiness in 'the hot garden' cannot overlay the devotional atmosphere of the first three stanzas, the last of which leans heavily on Eliot's *East Coker*. The 'Anna at the knobs of the panel oblongs' may indeed be Okigbo's mother, but she is also St Anne. Furthermore, the 'old lovely fragments' practised on the consoles of provincial organs in the Eastern Nigerian countryside are in no sense set up in contrast to the spontaneous music of the wind 'leaning over / its loveliest fragment' in the last line, but is on the contrary seen as complementary to it. Hence, at this juncture, which corresponds to the first station of the poet's cross, Christian and African religious intimations are made to fuse, to haunting effect.

It is only with 'Initiations' that a divisive note begins to emerge. The plural of the title is meticulous, since the poet is recalling his three-fold initiation into three distinct and potentially conflicting schools of thought: the Christian / individualistic, the professionally artistic and the ancestral and folkloric. The first of these has obviously been the most insistent, coercive and puzzling, and to it Okigbo devotes forty-three lines. In the first stanza, the sign of the cross inscribed in water on the initiate's forehead is compared horrifyingly to the branding of a slave with 'red-hot blade'. The comparison seems extreme, but seen from the vantage point of one newly seized with a desire for spiritual emancipation, is naturally and historically fitting. Kepkanly, as we know from the author's footnote, was the village schoolmaster who initiated Okigbo himself into the mysteries of the Catechism, and, therefore, as a locally recruited employee of the colonial educational system, both the instrument of missionary instruction and its victim. The result of the education he offered is induction into the safe port of Christian commitment, where the agonizing complexity of moral responsibility disappears in a reassuring 'confluence of planes' corresponding to the 'orthocentre' of a triangle. An orthocentre is the point at which the perpendicular from the vertices of a triangle meet.

[11] *Ibid.*, p. 48.

'Ortho-', however, also suggests 'orthodoxy', and hence a completely water-tight creed, such as the church supplies for weaker brethren, those who do not share the poet's compulsion to forge a personal spiritual vision. The symbolism of geometric figures seems to distil the angularity of attitude characteristic of those with blinkered minds, constricted either by the simplifications of Christian doctrine, by the petty bureaucracy of 'fanatics and priests and popes / organizing secretaries and party managers', or, worse still, by the sheer rapacity of the social parasites: 'brothers and deacons / liberal politicians / selfish self-seekers' (*Labyrinths*, p. 7).

It may be instructive here to dwell on the note of social criticism present in these lines. Most commentators on Okigbo's work have tended to interpret his development in the light of an evolution from private to public concerns, and yet here, close to the beginning of his first sequence, we have an unmistakable suggestion of disaffection with the status quo of the Federation of Nigeria which was, at the time of Okigbo's writing, little more than two years old. Its starting point is a recognition of the gap between the morality of the new political élite and the controlling moral vision of the old lore, represented in the two ensuing sections by Jadum the village minstrel and Upandru the 'explainer' who were jointly responsible for introducing the young Okigbo into the subtleties of Igbo belief and custom. Both of them, we notice, possess characteristics of the poet, Jadum his visionary madness and Upandru his deliberate tactical manipulation of meaning; yet these sources of traditional poetic energy will never be released until the poet learns to tear out his limiting inhibitions by the root, a process violently suggested by a quotation from the incantation recited by the rural Igbo on the occasion of a ram's castration:

> And he said to the ram: Disarm.
> And I said;
> Except by rooting,
> Who could pluck yam tubers from their base?

> (*Labyrinths*, p. 9)

When this process is metaphorically complete, the poet is free to renew his quest unencumbered by alien restraints.

'Watermaid' issues in a new mood. Abhorring false gods, the poet is observed in quest of a presiding lady or muse. The identity of this female figure, who crops up at regular intervals throughout the rest of *Labyrinths*, and who in *Distances* reveals herself as the focal point of the poet's search, takes us into a web of connected mythologies. Though clearly reminiscent of the Mother Idoto of 'The Passage' (with whom at the culmination of *Distances* she also seems to fuse), she is at once a 'lioness', a 'watermaid' and a 'white queen'. These titles seem to connect her with a whole series of divinities which derive from both African and exotic religious traditions. West African readers will automatically think of the 'Mammywata' common in local folklore. More specifically, Yoruba readers are likely to remember Lemanja, goddess of the sea, that ubiquitous figure worshipped throughout the area of the black diaspora, from Oyo to Haiti to Brazil; while European readers are more likely to think of Isis or Diana, Egyptian and Graeco-Roman goddesses who are both identifiable with the White Goddess whom the British poet Robert Graves regards as the chief source of authentic poetic inspiration.[12] Indeed the constant references to white as the colour of her adornment, and a reiterated link with the moon, lead one straight to Graves's theory with which Okigbo was clearly familiar and which will henceforth provide a useful analytical tool in discussing the intellectual scheme of *Labyrinths*, in the Introduction to which the 'White Goddess' features as an organizing idea (*Labyrinths*, p. xiv). Graves's theory will be discussed in greater detail at a more appropriate point, but suffice it here to say that the White Goddess is regarded, both by Graves and Okigbo, as at once the guide and tormentor of the dedicated artist, with whom she is intermittently obsessed but whom she is constantly in danger of destroying. She therefore serves as an apt symbol for the beguiling risks of the poetic vocation which offers fugitive glimpses of ultimate truth while constantly harassing the unfortunate victim with threats to his sanity and self-respect.

The essence of the goddess consists in her elusiveness. Thus in the three sections of 'Watermaid' we are granted three transient visions of this female persona taken from three different perspectives. 'Watermaid' as a whole is in fact largely concerned with various ways of seeing, the open eye of the observer being compared with a number of heavenly bodies. In the first section the eye of the prodigal poet surveys the barren landscape of a sandy beach for evidence of a secret which he has earlier buried. Exactly what this secret is does not emerge until the later section 'And I am here abandoned' where we learn that the poet is languishing for loss of his 'white queen' without whom he has no access to wisdom or knowledge. Meanwhile he is teased by maddening memories of her longed-for presence, 'maid of

[12] Cf. Robert Graves, *The White Goddess* (London: Faber, 1948).

salt-emptiness, / sophisticreamy'. Indeed the second section can be read as a hymn of praise to the goddess, here viewed with the flattering eye of a worshipper. The hymn has much of the intensity of a Catholic paean to the Madonna, a *Salve Regina*, but also recalls instances throughout world literature of mystical encounters with the muse, a fine instance of which occurs at the culmination point of Apuleius' fable *The Golden Ass*, Graves's translation of which Okigbo may also have read.[13] After this moment of possibly illusory enlightenment, a mirage thrown up in the fevered mind's eye, the poet is left with a feeling of anti-climax and abandonment. In the very last section he regards his goddess, here unequivocally identified with the moon, not with the passionate eye of one possessed, but with the bleak objectivity of one who knows that his attentions are rejected, his goal as far off as ever:

> THE STARS have departed,
> The sky in monocle
> surveys the worldunder
>
> The stars have departed,
> and I – where am I?              (*Labyrinths*, p. 13)

One of the most impressive qualities of *Heavensgate* is its versatility of mood, recalling at times the change of tempo associated with the structures of classical music. Here, at the end of 'Watermaid' with its listless adagio, we bound straight into the opening lines of 'Lustra' with their bucolic recollections of Housman and early Yeats. The return to the countryside, which in 'The Passage' was a matter of solemn dedication, here achieves all the lightheartedness of a vacation spree. Likewise, the search for the moon goddess, which in 'Watermaid' was conducted in an atmosphere of nervous exhaustion and strain, is rendered here in language which recalls a holiday expedition. Whether the 'mid-term' of the last line of the first section is a literal reference to the academic or legal recess matters little; the fundamental fact is that the poet has taken a momentary break from high seriousness before plunging into the deliberate self-impalement of 'The flower weeps, unbruised'. It is a lull before the storm, since the *Lacrimae Christi* mood of the next poem represents the low point of the poet's quest, a dark night of the soul relieved only by a faint hope of a Second Coming: 'Messiah will come again'. If, as Okigbo suggests in

[13] Cf. Lucius Apuleius, *The Transformation of Lucius or The Golden Ass*, trans. Robert Graves (London: Penguin, 1950).

his Preface, the various sections of *Heavensgate* represent the stations of the poet–celebrant's cross, this section is the last obstacle before enlightenment can be reached. The return to a Christian language here and in the sections immediately following reflects a sense of remoteness from a homogenous, authentically traditional truth. On visiting the village palm-grove, where the spirits of the ancestors reside, however, the poet is released from his burden of doubt by a customary inscription of five parallel lines of chalk, the customary manner of greeting between man and ancestor, man and man, familiar in all Igbo households. With that a fanfare of 'drums and cannons' announces the triumphal return to a confident mastery of knowledge. The prodigal has paid his respects and his offering is finally accepted; and with that the quest embarked on in 'The Passage' is almost complete.

There remains, however, a coda, 'Newcomer', evidently intended as a postscript to the main sequence, but considered by many commentators as unsatisfactory. There are several reasons for this. First, whereas the sequence proper has been dominated by two figures, the poetic persona who recounts his own spiritual adventure in the first person singular, and the mother–mistress–muse to whom he addresses his attentions, 'Newcomer' introduces a male personality who is described in the third person. This is clearly the 'Newcomer' of the title, but who is he? The reference in the second strophe to the Angelus, the thrice-daily prayer in which Catholics reiterate the angels' greeting at the Nativity, would seem to connect him with Christ. Yet in the last stanza of the same lyric we have a note of ardent rejection aimed at the heavenly host:

> *Anna of the panel oblongs*
> *Protect me*
> *from them fucking angels;* (Labyrinths, p. 17)

The ambivalent attitude towards Christianity noted in the earlier sections has here reached extremes. The fragmented syntax of the fourth strophe merely reinforces the impression, not merely of ambivalence, but of thematic muddle. It is with relief that we turn to the limpid clarity of 'For Georgette', which reads as a wedding anthem or song to the spring, very reminiscent in atmosphere to the *Song of Solomon*, in which a bridegroom is addressed in similar terms. However, this has hardly solved the problem, since, though in mediaeval theology Christ was often seen as the bridegroom of the church, the link with the thematic concerns of the rest of *Heavensgate* still seems slender. The sense of dissatisfaction we feel was clearly shared by Okigbo himself, since this section was subjected to drastic alteration, one whole poem (addressed to the Welsh poet Peter Thomas) having been excised, and the very last lyric (which in some versions is entitled 'Bridge'), having moved position from the beginning to the end. The probable truth is that, as the scattered sub-titles suggest, these are occasional pieces which the young poet attempted to bring within the frame of a culminating movement, but which failed ultimately to cohere.

There is just one element in 'Newcomer' which proves of importance, as it enables us to make sense of an insistent strand that runs through the whole of *Labyrinths*. This is the description of the poet in the very first line of 'Bridge' as 'standing above the noontide'. Here the poet clearly envisages himself as the sun, a possible rival to the lunar presence of the muse who right at the end of *Heavensgate* he would seem to have supplanted. A look at the mythological antecedents of *Heavensgate* places this in context. In his Introduction Okigbo refers to the poet–celebrant as 'a personage like Orpheus' (*Labyrinths*, p. xi). The fact that he later comes to be associated with the sun refers us straight to a common version of the Orpheus myth, quoted here by Eratosthenes of Alexandria: 'Orpheus believed the sun, who he named Apollo, to be the greatest of the gods. Rising up in the night he ascended before dawn to the mountain called Pangaeum that he might see the sun first. At which Dionysus, being enraged, sent against him the Bassarids who tore him in pieces.'[14]

The Bassarids were the Maenads whose possession by the god Dionysus caused so much trouble in Euripides' *The Bacchae*, and their fatal rage against Orpheus was caused by the fact that his new-found devotion to the sun was an act of disloyalty to the moon goddess whom he had previously worshipped. Thus here, right at the heart of *Heavensgate*, we have a reference to the supplanting of a moon by a sun cult, a theme which proves to be of fundamental relevance to Okigbo's three following sequences. It is thus not for nothing that Okigbo called this last poem a 'bridge', though Theroux's comparison of it to a solo bridge passage in jazz is also germane.[15]

It would be an error to see the opening of *Limits* as in any way continuous with *Heavensgate*, yet there are many factors which connect

---

[14] *The White Goddess*, p. 92.    [15] Theroux, 'Six Poets', p. 127.

them. Indeed much of the thematic structure of *Limits*, which has never been satisfactorily construed, concerns preoccupations which run through from *Heavensgate* and, above all, the central trio of poet / protagonist, mistress / muse, and a third masculine figure who is only, however, properly identified in the new sequence. Again, the ascription in the very opening lines to the hero of *Limits* of a prattling loquaciousness, 'suddenly become talkative / like weaverbird', would seem to connect him sardonically with Orpheus, drunk with song. The mistress / muse appears in the last strophe of the same lyric, and *Limits* II sees the entrance of a male rival who is once again identified with Christ in a passage which recalls the Messianic prophecy of Isaiah 53:

> For he was a shrub among the poplars,
> Needing more roots
> More sap to grow to sunlight,
> Thirsting for sunlight.                    (*Labyrinths*, p. 24)

The consistency of this triple scenario both in *Limits* and in the remaining portions of *Labyrinths* is too remarkable to be merely coincidental, and demands explanation in terms which will satisfy our sense of Okigbo's stability of vision, grounded as it was in a firm grasp of classical and African mythology.

As previously mentioned, there is a clear parity between the triumvirate of *Labyrinths* and the trio of personages which occur in Robert Graves's theory of poetic ancestry articulated in *The White Goddess*. All true poetry, claims Graves, is written in a state of trance induced by the poet's recollection, conscious or unconscious, of an ancient mythological theme, which is to be found in various forms in Celtic, Babylonian, Greek and African folklore:

The theme, briefly, is the antique story . . . of the birth, life, death and resurrection of the god of the waxing year; the central chapter concerns the god's losing battle with the god of the waning year for love of the capricious and all-powerful Threefold Goddess, their mother, bride and layer-out. The poet identifies himself with the god of the waxing year and his Muse with the Goddess; the rival is his blood-brother, his other self, his weird. All true poetry . . . celebrates some incident or scene in this very ancient story.[16]

The mythological scheme here suggested enables us to make sense of a number of facets of *Limits* that otherwise might perplex the reader: the intrusion of a third party with whom the poet both does and does

---

[16] *The White Goddess*, p. 24.

not identify, the nameless threat under which the poet seems to be languishing, and the ambiguous place of the triple queen in his affections. Taken together with the theme of the obliteration of the moon by a sun cult already proposed, this helps us to tie together many of the loose ends in *Limits*. If the poet–protagonist, who is in love with the moon goddess, is identified with the waxing year, then his destruction at the hands of a rival associated with the rising sun comes to seem a fitting conclusion to a projected tussle between two religious systems. Moreover, if the rival, who is related to Christ, is seen as the agent or accomplice of the sun cult, then we add a significant dimension: the ascendancy of a male-orientated, sun-inspired religion coincides with the usurpation of the ancient shrines by Christianity. This is precisely the theme explicitly spelled out in 'Fragments out of the Deluge', the second half of *Limits*.

Armed with this scheme we can begin to make sense of the various sections of the sequence. *Limits* I expresses the gratitude of the poet–protagonist to Idoto, his muse and queen, to whom as 'he-goat-on-heat' he is sexually bonded, for her progressive enlightenment of his condition. In *Limits* II his attention is distracted by the appearance of his *alter persona*, a Christ-like figure whose evident isolation and need to communicate attract him. This person is, however, literally his weird or fate. Despite a superficial appearance of weakness (shared incidentally by the missionaries on their first appearance), his sun is potentially in the ascendant, and the lyric which introduces him ends on a note of menace, an acrid smell of Armageddon:

> Horsemen of the apocalypse;
>
> And crowned with one self
> The name displays its foliage,
> Hanging low
>
> A green cloud above the forest.     (*Labyrinths*, p. 24)

*Limits* III corresponds to a moment of confusion, a mingling of dissonant voices, as the insistent claims of the poet and rival clash:

> And this is the crisis point
> The twilight moment between
> Sleep and waking     (*Labyrinths*, p. 25)

The stealthy advance of the rival cult is as muted as a cat's paw, and, in the 'dust of combat' the poet mistakes the rival's voice for his own, so that their voices appear stifled by a similar constraint:

> Then we must sing, tongue-tied,
> Without name or audience,
> Making harmony among the branches. (*Labyrinths*, p. 25)

In a desperate attempt at rededication to the traditional gods, the poet undertakes a pilgrimage to the Sacred Cable Point at Asaba, but 'the dream wakes / the voice fades,' and the protagonist is finally left with a lucid sense of his own downfall.

Though this scheme may seem over-tidy, there is no doubt that, at the end of 'Siren Limits', the sense of personal eclipse is complete. The 'image' of the loved Goddess in the first strophe of *Limits* II is evidently a memory, and much of the poignancy of that lyric comes from a strong sense of loss and failure. The closing lines find the poet, like the evening sky of Eliot's *Prufrock*, etherized upon a table, stunned it would appear by a recollection of his mistress's fragrance. As he metaphorically loses consciousness, he brings the lid down on his own creative effort, thus signalling in the reign of the predators in 'Fragments Out of the Deluge', whose sacrificial victim he has become:

> When you have finished
> & done up my stitches,
> Wake me near the altar,
> & this poem will be finished . . . (*Labyrinths*, p. 27)

The morbidity of the close here is given graphic shape by the use of one stark visual image, a hideous embodiment of the act of self-immolation. Indeed, if the poetry of *Limits* marks an advance on that of *Heavensgate* it is by reason of the superior potency of its visual appeal, and much of it can be absorbed on first reading at the level of a series of vivid tableaux. At the beginning of 'Fragments out of the Deluge', for instance, we are transported to the exotic surroundings of an Egyptian tomb where a 'beast' is still licking its chops after making a meal of the poet's corpse. The horror of this image is heightened when we appreciate that the sarcophagus stone was originally selected as a coffin-making material by the Greeks in the belief that it had the power to devour the flesh deposited within it. Okigbo's own footnotes to this section direct our attention to its underlying mythological significance. The poet–hero here is depicted as Gilgamesh 'legendary king of Uruk in Mesopotamia' and the beast is promptly identified as 'the lioness of *Limits* IV who destroyed the hero's second self' (*Labyrinths*, p. 28). We further learn that this second-self is none other than Enkidu, who in the ancient Babylonian *Epic of Gilgamesh* features as the king–hero's companion and shadow-self who, after his downfall and death at the hands of the revengeful goddess Ishtar, becomes the object of Gilgamesh's frenetic, bereaved search.

There are obviously a whole host of implications to be picked up here. If we are right in connecting the lioness with Ishtar, the goddess's slightly ghoulish carnality represents one aspect of her personality since it was commonly held that Ishtar had two principal characteristics: she was both the compassionate mother goddess and the lustful goddess of sex and war. Identified in the ancient world with Isis, the Egyptian moon-goddess, and, by extension, with the Graeco-Roman figures of Artemis, Aphrodite and Hera, she has already appeared in *Heavensgate* in her alternative rôle as the nurse of the poet's nascent talent. It is on her ruthless destructiveness, how-ever, that the *Epic of Gilgamesh* itself concentrates. Here, for instance, is the complaint of Gilgamesh, as, disturbed by the goddess's atten-tions, he catalogues the long list of her amorous victims:

> For Tammuz, thy youthful husband,
> Thou has decreed wailing year after year.
> The variegated roller thou didst love
> Yet thou didst smite him and break his wing.
> Now he stands in the graves, crying 'Kappi!'
> Thou didst love the lion perfect in strength
> But thou didst dig for him seven and yet seven pits.[17]

The love of Ishtar for her ill-fated young consort Tammuz represents, as we shall see, one major strand running through *Silences*, yet suffice it to note here that, in the context of *Limits*, Ishtar supplies the female component of the human-cum-comic triangle already mentioned as a structural element in the total sequence. The two male protagonists coincide, in this case, with Gilgamesh and Enkidu, the blood brothers depicted in the *Epic of Gilgamesh*. Thus at this point Okigbo would seem to have conflated two myths, the legend of a love triangle sur-rounding the fickle affections of a goddess who destroys one lover that she may enjoy a second, and the saga of Gilgamesh with its portrayal of two male friends locked in eternal bonds of loyalty. The second of the friends then comes to stand for none other than the rival who re-enters in *Limits* VI and appears in the guise of both Christ and Enkidu. There is a strong flavour once again of Isaiah's prophecy, already echoed in *Limits* II, and the italicized refrain which serves for

[17] Alexander Heidel, *The Gilgamesh Epic and Old Testament Parallels* (Chicago: Illinois: University of Chicago Press, 1946), p. 51.

the second verse paragraph is also redolent of Matthew 6:27 and Luke 4:24. Yet Enkidu is clearly intended in the references to the forced training which the hero undergoes, since the domestication of Enkidu, originally a wild man of the plains, is a dominant theme of the second tablet of *Gilgamesh*. With his acceptance into the royal household of Uruk, Enkidu enjoyed a brief period of ascendancy, evoked in *Limits* VII, where the rising star of a male rival is associated with the spread of alien belief associated in Africa with the arrival of Christian, and, in the case of Igboland, more specifically Catholic, missionaries. The section then ends appropriately with the vision of an Igbo village in flames, introducing a suggestion of violence taken up in the next lyric where colonial intervention is described in terms of a military attack or – prophetically as it happens – of an air raid. To view this episode objectively and dispassionately is clearly impossible and hence it is rendered in the form of a lament delivered by Nwanza the sunbird who is, as Anozie reminds us, among the most powerful of Igbo religious symbols, and hence a likely focus for proselytizing attack. The inevitable terror of her attitude is distanced in *Limits* X, where the same incident is described retrospectively in the past tense. The continuity here, however, is broken by a short interlude at *Limits* IX where the cries of a blind dog, known for its prophetic skill, take us at once forward to a vision of menacing desolation and backward to a dimly recalled memory of Okigbo's childhood nurse who herself seems to merge imaginatively both with the threatened sunbird and with the softer aspects of the goddess's personality. Does this composite female persona here fear the possibility of her own destruction? The penultimate stanza of *Limits* X, where the devastation of the traditional shrines is related to the dwindling of Irkalla, Sumerian goddess of the underworld, would seem to give substance to such an interpretation. Moreover, there is a clear reference throughout these closing sections to the growth of a male-orientated sun cult at odds with the lunar influence of the goddess, who, through Eunice her mouthpiece, gives a clear indication of her personal anxiety at the spreading of solar supremacy:

> Give him no chair, they say,
> The dawn's charioteer,
> Riding with the angry stars
> Toward the great sunshine.     (*Labyrinths*, p. 32)

By *Limits* XI the sacred shrines lie deserted, bereft both of official praise and the dignity of office, honoured only by the muffled strains of the poet and the chirping memory of the sunbird who, as the sequence draws to a close, calls our attention to the humiliation of another great people, the Spanish insurgents of Guernica who suffered a similar baptism of fire in the Civil War. Here allusion and prognosis fuse, for the reference to Picasso's canvas of 1937 brings us up against the perennial violence of every age at the very moment at which it highlights the plight of the Igbo, poised, as Okigbo wrote, a mere three years away from the first bombing raids on Enugu.

Okigbo clearly regarded the double sequence *Silences* as transitional between *Limits* and *Distances*. There are several clear senses in which this is the case. First, it marks a temporary recession from the first person singular, consisting as it does of a couple of highly ritualized lamentations in choric style. Secondly, whereas the programme of *Limits* delineates a downward curve, ending at a point of bleak self-annihilation, and that of *Distances* an upward curve towards self-restoration, *Silences*, which occupies the lowest point, respresents an attempt to come to terms with the tragic condition. It is best considered in the light of two tragic odes, of the kind which the Athenian dramatists employed to comment on the action of their tragedies, and with which Okigbo, as a student of the classics would have been familiar. Each sub-sequence is scored for a distinctive ensemble which plays the part of a choric commentator on a central tragic incident. The 'Silent Sisters', as Okigbo reminds us, recall both the Sirènes, of Debussy's third Nocturne and the drowning Franciscan nuns in Hopkins's *Wreck of the Deutschland*. They also function, however, as a chorus of village women whose rôle as observers and sufferers recall the choruses of Attic tragedy. The drums endorse their incantation with reverberations which resound with the accents of the long dead: they are the ancestors commenting on the world of the living. In both cases, however, the archetypal tragic event is classical and the same: the decease of Tammuz, lover of the goddess Ishtar, god of the waxing and of the waning year. Like Adonis, Tammuz was said to die each winter and to be reborn with the spring: he thus represents both rivals portrayed in the *Limits* sequence, both the discarded lover and the one who will supplant him. It is thus in a very direct sense that *Silences* comments on the aftermath of *Limits* to which, in one sense, it may be regarded as an epilogue. The climax of the sequence, to which both phases of it ascend, occurs in the closing section of 'Lament of the Drums', where the quotations in italics consist, in slightly reworded form, of extracts from the 'Lament of the Flutes of Tammuz' quoted by Sir James Frazer near the beginning of his volume on *Adonis, Attis and Osiris* from *The Golden Bough*.[18] Frazer's commentary provides us with a vivid account of the original context:

His death appears to have been annually mourned, to the shrill music of flutes, by men and women about midsummer in the month named after him, the month of Tammuz. The dirges were seemingly chanted over an effigy of the dead god, which they washed with pure water, anointed with oil, and clad in a red robe, while the fumes of incense rose into the air, as if to stir the dormant senses by their pungent fragrance and wake him from the sleep of death.[19]

Extending the argument, it is possible to infer that, since Tammuz's death is associated with the transition between the phases of the waning and waxing year central to the mythology of *Limits* where it is associated with the supplanting of a sun for a moon cult, and hence with the usurpation by militant Catholic Christianity of the sanctity of the old shrines, then the pivotal calamity of *Silences* can be identified with the historical hiatus featured in 'Fragments out of the Deluge'. This, however, is to take its political dimensions as all embracing. In fact, the true theme of *Silences* runs far deeper than any such précis might suggest.

The real theme of *Silences*, succinctly stated, is the triumph of the authentic tragic consciousness over the demeaning facts of decay and death. 'Tragic' here must be taken to mean 'congruent with the spirit of Greek tragedy', yet, in order to explain to himself the mode of its operation, Okigbo has drawn wider in his understanding of the tragic condition. His main source, apart from the Greeks, is a set of remarks on tragic awareness contained in a letter from Herman Melville to Nathaniel Hawthorne (written when they were close neighbours in New England), a line of which Okigbo quotes as two strategically important points. Melville's letter, a fulsome and rather ingratiating one, written in acknowledgement of a gift to him of Hawthorne's *House of the Seven Gables*, ends by ascribing to the elder author a special kind of

---

[18] Sir James Frazer, *The Golden Bough: A Study in Magic and Religion* (London: Macmillan, 3rd edition, 1935–6) V. *Adonis, Attis and Osiris: Studies in the History of Oriental Religion* Vol. 1, pp. 9–11.

[19] *Ibid*. I have quoted the extract at length in 'Christopher Okigbo and the Flutes of Tammuz' in *A Sense of Place*, ed. Britta Olinder (University of Gothenburg, 1984), pp. 191–2. Another version of the Lament, in some respects closer to Okigbo's may be found in Jessie Weston, *From Ritual to Romance* (Cambridge: Cambridge University Press, 1920), p. 37. Okigbo may well have been familiar with Weston's book as a major source for Eliot's *The Waste Land*.

authorial courage, the sort which, refusing the blandishments and easy comforts of political or religious ideology, manages to stare the tragic facts of human existence straight in the face and to exult in the very teeth of their negativism. It is this ability to transcend superficial and assertive palliatives for human suffering by the power of the undiluted creative will which Okigbo sees as the mainstay of the tragic sense, and which simultaneously appealed to that side of his nature which, at least in 1964, was so deeply suspicious of the ideological stances associated with cultural nationalism, *négritude*, and opportunistic Marxism. The last paragraph of Melville's letter is worth quoting in full:

There is the grand truth about Nathaniel Hawthorne. He says NO! in thunder; but the Devil himself cannot make him say *yes*. For all men who say *yes*, lie; and all men who say *no* – why, they are in the happy condition of judicious, unencumbered travellers in Europe; they cross the frontiers into Eternity with nothing but a carpet-bag – that is to say, the Ego. Whereas those *yes*-gentry, they travel with heaps of baggage, and, damn them! they will never get through the Custom House. What's the reason, Mr Hawthorne, that in the last stages of metaphysics a fellow always falls to *swearing* so? I could rip an hour. You see, I began with a little criticism extracted for your benefit from the *Pittsfield Secret Review*, and here I have landed in Africa.[22]

Melville's distrust of yes-saying ideologues, and his preference for those who are able to thrive on the bleakness of the philosophical 'no' is central to Okigbo's vision in *Silences*. In his Introduction he states that the 'Lament of the Silent Sisters' was partly inspired by the death of Patrice Lumumba, first prime minister of Zaïre, killed by competing ideological interests. Lumumba had been in one sense a victim of Tshombe's Katangese secession of 1960, in another the victim of foreign interests masquerading under the disguise of a political programme. Okigbo prefers to see him as the victim of narrow thinking, of ideological systems promulgated by those who say 'yes' too shrilly and wrongheadedly. Thus not only does he feature, like Tammuz, as a tragic protagonist, but also, like the Christ whose fate his recalls, as the prey of unscrupulous and shallow interests:

> They struck him in the ear they struck him in the eye;
> They picked his bones for scavenging:   (*Labyrinths*, p. 40)

The allusions to Christ the pascal lamb may seem odd in the context

---

[20] Merrell R. Davies and William H. Gilman (eds.), *The Letters of Herman Melville* (New Haven: Yale University Press, 1960), Letter 83, 16 April 1851, p. 125.

of a poem partially concerned with bewailing the trampling by his followers over African religious susceptibilities. The texture of *Silences*, however, reveals other Christian elements. In their capacity as drowning Franciscan nuns the Silent Sisters begin by invoking the crucifix:

> The cross to us we still call to us,
> In this jubilee dance above the carrion     (*Labyrinths*, p. 39)

The redemptive processes of Christianity are therefore revealed as one strand in the tragic exultation through which the Sisters affirm the victory of life over death, joy over suffering. In the choral antiphon which constitutes the last section of 'Lament of the Silent Sisters', the chorus invokes the contours of Gothic ecclesiastical architecture:

> Pointed arches:
> Pieces in the form of a pear     (*Labyrinths*, p. 43)

*Pointed Arches* was the title of Okigbo's projected work on the aesthetics of poetry on which he was engaged when felled in action. All of these allusions suggest that while, on the simplest polemical level, Christianity is condemned as the violator of traditional African Sanctity, at another, higher level it is seen as one element in an inclusive higher religious consciousness, bordering on the tragic sense, which is continually held at bay by the forces of intellectual and political bigotry. It is in this light that the extracts from Ishtar's lament for Tammuz quoted in Section v of 'Lament of the Drums' can be viewed, not so much as a dirge for the passing of traditional Igbo religious certainties as a lament for the dwindling of the totality of man's spirituality in the face of ruthless and prejudiced forces.

Armed with these observations on the overall scheme of *Silences*, we can now turn to examine the individual sections. The fragmented and storm-tossed syntax of the opening strains of 'Lament of the Silent Sisters' evokes a state of chaos and panic in which the mind gropes after consoling certainties, such as those offered by the Christian crucifix. These offer a 'difference' rather than an escape ladder because, though supplying an explanation for the necessity of suffering, they supply no means of avoidance. Suffering has to be lived through, whether in the berth of a sinking ship or in the perturbations of the religious vocation. The intervention of the chorus in paragraph five reminds us for the first time of the threatening forces of ideological restraint, associated at this stage with the predators of 'Fragments out of the Deluge'. Yet the chorus leader is not distracted in his task of leading the intoxicated dance and ode in which the worshippers in a manner reminiscent of the choruses of Attic tragedy, celebrate the triumph of the tragic spirit over the reality of death; 'this jubilee dance above the carrion'.

In Section II the chorus identifies itself more clearly with a group of village women bound for the communal well, their classic lament merging with the strains of a traditional Igbo dirge. Their opening statement harks back to the previous section, in its concern with the celebratory power of music and dance over the fact of death, and its reiteration of the nightmare of violent oppression. Moloch was the Carthaginian sun god to whom devotees fed their firstborn in an attempt to placate his wrath. His presence reminds us of the persistence of a male sun cult in the midst of the traditional feminine mysteries: the Sister's cry is both to Moloch (to save them from immolation) and on behalf of Moloch (as a gesture of further religious integration). The grammar of the last sentence of Section II and the opening lines of Section III is continuous, as the plaintive sentiments of the latter represent the burden of the Sisters' complaint. Silence here is regarded as the consummation of music. The Sisters are 'dumb' because they neither speak nor sing; yet this very silence is more eloquent of memory, regret and determination than the 'shriek' torn from them by the menacing 'shadows' of circumstance. The shadows are compared to the 'long-fingered winds' which, in the following section, also continuous with the foregoing, reappear as the 'wild winds' which 'cry out against us'. The Sisters' only defence, once again, lies in their silence, which, like the rainbow and the sea's froth, offers an infinity of chromatic shading.

Much attention is paid to form in these sections. Section III is for full chorus with an occasional interpolation by the leader in the form of a refrain. Sections IV and V are antiphons proper: that is, the leader and his acolytes speak alternately, sharing the burden and privilege of statement. There is also a progression of theme: Section IV contents itself with an analysis of the subtle nuances of 'silence' as a weapon against misfortune, while Section V concerns itself more positively with the transcendental power of art, the 'Pointed arches: / pieces in the form of a pear' to which all poetry aspires. This power is of a kind to transform and subsume all tragic manifestations: even Judas Iscariot here numbers magnificently amongst the performers of the choric dance. In the true and absolute silence that lies beyond achieved artistic statement all lesser forms and means of expression, the constituent 'melodies' which make up the final tranquillity, fall into place and can be observed nostalgically in long-view:

> Silences are melodies
> Heard in retrospect:                    (*Labyrinths*, p. 43)

The effect of this turn of thought is to transform the context of the quotation from Melville's letter, so that when the question appears for the second time it seems to have accumulated its own answer: the finest way to assert the power that lies beyond negativity, to 'say NO in thunder', is to keep one's peace. Frenetic assertion of an attitude is of no use here. What is required of the artist, as of the truly tragic spirit, is to keep counsel with his own inspiration, to dig deep down into the resources of the personality so as to tap the inner serenity into which all effort and all expression ultimately reaches. In the closing lines of Section v the miracle of the tragic exultation which conquers despair is explained as an achievement of the complete human personality at ease with itself.

'Lament of the Drums' also celebrates the tragic event, but from a different angle, and largely in prospect. Lyric v finds the drummers limbering up for their performance, invoking the various materials that go towards the construction of their instruments in a manner characteristic of a number of West African drum literatures, Igbo, Yoruba and Akan. They also aim to keep at a distance the tragic facts of dissolution which underlie the impending catastrophe ('Thunder of tanks of giant iron steps of detonators') but the effort is inevitably frustrated, and Section II finds them in full spate proclaiming the sacrifice which will be necessary to lend full savour to the threatening disaster. Okigbo says somewhat tantalizingly in his Introduction of 1965 that 'Babylonian capture', 'martyrdom' and 'chaliced vintage' suggest that someone may have been betrayed by his disciples. Certainly the Christian liturgical element is there, underpinning the wealth of traditional Igbo references. Yet an earlier paragraph suggests that he had something much more specific in mind, namely the incarceration of Obafemi Awolowo, the first premier of Nigeria's Western Region, in September 1963 on charges of attempting to undermine the Federal leadership, and his desertion in his hour of distress by such as Chief Akintola, the deputy whom he had left in charge of regional politics while he fought his campaign at the national level. Thus Awolowo joins Patrice Lumumba, Tammuz and Christ to form a pantheon of tragic figures whose demise the drums, as the Sisters before them, lament. They are joined, at the beginning of Lyric III by Palinurus, Aeneas' homesick helmsman in his voyage across the Mediterranean back from Troy, who, washed ashore near Velia after three days' exposure at sea, was cruelly murdered by the local inhabitants and left unburied on the foreshore. He hence wanders for ever in a limbo of non-entity, far from the comforts of interment and the safe port of entry into Hades. The whole of Lyric III is a lament for his fate, half-elegy and half-recreation of that hideous state of non-being endured only by those disowned by all of their fellows, journeying endlessly. As such, in his unredeemed condition, Palinurus is prey to the full force of divine vengeance, operated on by the infernal agency of the harpies, weird ravenous creatures with womens' faces who hound him down under the eye of the vengeful Calaeno, daughter of Neptune and Terra. He is thus a perfect subject for the 'Lament of the Drums' in their sacrificial plea for mercy and divine forgiveness. The possibility of release from the prison of endless torment, wished upon Palinurus by his master Aeneas during a visit to him in the underworld in *Aeneid* VI, leads us on to the limpid beauty of lines 19 and 20 of this matchless lyric:

> *Tears of grace, not of sorrow, broken*
> *In two, protest your inviolable image.*     (*Labyrinths*, p. 47)

The tears are of grace because the drums, in their sacrificial, cleansing function, have worked the miracle of ultimate release from divine displeasure. Their music is thus an act of grace. The tears are hence broken in two, and each half bears etched on its trembling surface a permanent picture of Palinurus in his lasting significance as redeemed victim. These lines give an extra poignancy to the previous paragraph's 'It is over, Palinurus, at least for you': for Palinurus, life is over, but so, at last, is Purgatory.

The Palinurus motif, in its insistence on the final power of grace, leads us quite naturally on to the next section in which the drums thunder out once more in an ecstasy of complaint, only to be rebuked by a conciliatory note which informs us that the shrill hysteria of full-throated protest ('our rococo / choir of insects') is powerless beside the still, sad music of antiphonal understatement. This takes us once more back to the calm of the conclusion of the 'Lament of the Silent Sisters' to which this verse is evidently an allusion. As *Silences* rises to its culmination, Sisters and drums join their voices in one common hymn of praise which blends with the inherited strains of Ishtar's lament for Tammuz, in which the Babylonian god, victim of his mistress's lust and destructiveness, is coaxed back to life with the seductive, gentle inflections of the flutes. The quotation from the Babylonian hymn, which has an important historical connection with the text of the *Epic of Gilgamesh* so important to *Limits*, constitutes, as Okigbo puts it, a 'variation' in rephrased language on the 'Lament of the Flutes of Tammuz', translated for the general reader in James Frazer's *The Golden Bough*. Despite its heart-breaking solemnity it is a song of hope: Tammuz will rise from the dead, the shrubs will flower, the fields, the river and the men come back to life. In this rapt moment of tragic invocation, we have a perfect distillation of that power, shared by mystic and artist alike, to triumph over sheer negativity, which Okigbo found so appealing in Melville's comments in his letter to Hawthorne. Only one discordant note intrudes, in the concluding couplet, in which the 'pot-bellied watchers', the overfed ministrants of the shrine, are admonished for their cupidity and greed which, going unchecked, will ruin the redemptive process once again. In this word of warning, seemingly out of place in the calm of the close, lies one of the few sinister political overtones of *Silences*, a reference back to the wholesale destruction of 'Fragments out of the Deluge' and a foreboding of the holocaust to come in the yet unwritten 'Path of Thunder'.

Okigbo left us two distinct clues to the interpretation of *Distances*. The first is its integral relationship with the sequence which precedes *Silences*, namely *Limits*, to which it affords an inner, psychological equivalent; the second being its origin in the experience of undergoing surgery. It is quite plain that, on a simple narrative level, the whole piece may be read as a literal description of the mind's turmoil during a course of anaesthesia. Section I finds the poet prostrate on the surgery table, looking up at the immense lamps hanging above him ('serene lights on the other balcony'). As the anaesthetic takes hold he drifts off into a world of phantasy in which he joins a procession of pilgrims from an island where 'death lay in ambush', through a lintel over which hangs a magic inscription, and into an inner sanctum where he experiences a complete, and possibly erotic, possession of the goddess whom he had sought throughout *Limits*. It would be wrong, however, to see this as nothing but phantasy: the journey has its symbolic connotations, and, though *Distances* is mythologically less dense than the earlier sequence, opens out on to a world of cosmological cultural reference.

Section 1, I would suggest, finds the poet in the same abject position as that described in *Limits* v, though there he was stretched out in the tomb, here on a 'horizontal slab' which, while recalling the 'empty sarcophagus' of the earlier piece, seems also to hold out the possibility of resurrection. It is interesting that Okigbo interdisperses the lyrics of this sequence with the line 'I was the sole witness to my homecoming', thus seeing the whole process in optimistic long-shot. Unlike *Limits*, *Distances* is to be read as a song of hope and rejoicing. As such it takes its lead from the relative positiveness of the closing lines of *Silences*, in which Tammuz's revival seems imminent; it can even, like *Heavensgate* before it, be regarded as an Easter sequence. On the symbolic level the 'lights on the other balcony' are clearly those of Heaven, but before he reaches them the poet must experience entry into the underworld of fear and death, the 'dark labyrinth' that leads eventually out into the clear light of day. In this journey the poet is both pilgrim and onlooker, simultaneously involved, and, in a manner very typical of dream experience, completely detached from the process. It is in the latter capacity that, in the closing lines of Section 1, he addresses his own voice as it sings the liturgy of self-immolation and renewal:

> Miner into my solitude,
> incarnate voice of the dream,
> you will go,
> with me as your chief acolyte,
> again into the anti-hill . . .

Section 11 finds us straight away plunged into the nightmare world of a *danse macabre* presided over by 'Death herself, the chief celebrant', seen as a murderous woman whose blood-lust reeks of the goddess's less savoury characteristics. It is a black mass, attended by incense, flesh and blood, in which the poet features as the member of a band of travellers, trapped on the island, hounded by fear of 'such great events' and talking incessantly to keep their spirits up. He is also one of the allotted sacrificial victims tied to a slab. (The link between this and fears induced by a surgical operation is straightforward.) The splitting of personal identity here is another feature of the dream, but also reflects the symbolic ambivalence of the poet's meaning, since he is concerned to see himself both as forfeit to death and destruction and as capable of rising above these limitations. He will only achieve this, however, if he subjects himself to a long process of initiation, and

Section III finds him again as one of the select band of pilgrims bound 'from Dan to Beersheba', the formula used, in the Books of Judges and Samuel, to describe the outer limits of the Kingdom of Israel.[21] The reference to Shibboleth in the first stanza is also to the Book of Judges, this time to the incident described in the twelfth chapter, in which Jephthah, in an attempt to distinguish his own people, the Gilleadites, from the fleeing Ephraimites, used the pass-word 'Shibboleth' whose soft opening syllable the enemy could not pronounce. Both allusions fix the idea of an utter exclusiveness reinforced by the use of special emblems: the crucifix, the censer, the medicaments of camphor and iodine. The poet then is numbered amongst a unique band of postulants whose way lies up stone steps, across a balcony inhabited by the manic and the inspired, to a clearing where, blocking their path, they encounter 'dilletanti; / vendors princes negritude', the reincarnations, it would seem of the 'brothers and deacons, liberal politicians, selfish self-seekers' who tortured the poet's progress in *Heavensgate*.

At last they reach the inner sanctum, the threshold of which is marked by a sign comprising the three principal geometrical figures: square, circle and triangle. Beyond hang the orbs whose tantalizing presence the poet had observed at the beginning of his quest 'on the other balcony'. The cryptic phrases of the italicized refrain

> *after we had formed*
> *then only the forms were formed*
> *and all forms*
> *were formed after our forming*

almost seem to justify Sunday Anozie's account of the sequence as concerned with the number 3, reflected in crucifix, lintel and other recurrent patterns. Anozie, however, builds too elaborate a superstructure on this.[22] The trinitarian concept is fundamental to the Christian as to other religions: I can see no more significance in it here than attaches to the Biblical allusions in the previous section, as mystical emblems which enforce the idea of a cult. The poet, it will be remembered, is under an anaesthetic: thus his intimations which in earlier sequences were conveyed by a multiplicity of literary references, here assume a vivid visual shape suggestive of the forms of dream. There is a sense of mystery, and of closed, hermetic codes, culminating in Sec-

---

[21] Cf. Judges 20, 1; 1 Samuel 3, 20; 2 Samuel 3, 10.
[22] Anozie, *Christopher Okigbo*, pp. 158–68.

tion v in the posing of 'the unanswerable question in the tabernacle's silence'. The censers which swing in the sanctuary come 'from the cradle / of a nameless religion'. The poet is fumbling his way towards a truth which he cannot articulate, and which certainly does not attach itself immediately to any of the great recognizable religious systems. This accounts, I believe, for the surrealistic method of Lyric v with its intriguing references to 'sweat over hoof in ascending gestures' and 'the question in the inkwell'. The general shape of events is clear enough: the poet, possibly mounted, like Christ, on a donkey, is ascending the steps of a shrine, which, when he enters, shimmers with light and water. The refrain 'each sign is the stillness of the kiss' takes us back to the language of 'Lament of the Silent Sisters'. Clearly, just as in that sequence, silence was the consummation of music, so here the intimacies of a kiss, imprinted perhaps on the goddess's at last receptive body, is the culmination of the religious rite. There are other side glances at the possible sexual nature of this final reunion, as in the words 'mated and sealed / in a proud oblation', as if, in making love to the goddess, the poet has redeemed himself from the taint of sin and death which earlier encumbered him. Yet the distance set between this and any recognizable theology is emphasized by such lines as 'the burden of the pawn' and 'the scar of the kiss and of the two swords', where Okigbo seems to be constructing his own myth, not surprisingly in this freely floating world of dream, the irrationality of which reaches its climax at the end of this section.

Section vi, by contrast, discovers the poet coming back to consciousness and reassembling his bearings. 'Homecoming' here carries, among other connotations, the simple sense of growing lucidity to one's surroundings. As his external circumstances sort themselves out, so the poet begins to make sense of the wild *pot-pourri* of myth, emblem and phantasy which has accompanied him on his inner voyage. Where the previous section emphasized discrepancy, diversity and imagistic innovation, the stress here is on the reconciling homogeneity of all myth:

> For it is the same blood,
> through the same orifices,
> the same branches
> and the same faces
> trembling, intertwined
> in the interspaces.     (*Labyrinths*, p. 59)

Thus the 'proud oblation' of the previous section blends itself with the redemptive processes of other great religions, including the Hebraic and Christian. The call of the goddess becomes recognizably that of the inscrutable lady in Eliot's early poem 'La Figlia Che Piange':

> Stand on the highest pavement of the stair –
> Lean on a garden urn –
> Weave, weave the sunlight in your hair –[23]

Gradually the elements of the dream sort themselves out: the season (which is also the season of Tammuz's uprising), the tall wood in which the politicians lower, the stone steps to the altar, the dark labyrinths of the poet's passage, the oblong inscribed above the lintel to the shrine. It is a kind of resumé, but also an act of recognition. And the culmination of this progressive enlightenment is the poet's delighted identification of his mistress, embraced in the enchanted recesses of the shrine, with the white queen, for whom he had previously felt a chaste dedication. Only when he has recognized both her and rites attending her is he free at last to recognize himself in his new state of spiritual apotheosis:

> I am the sole witness to my homecoming
> (*Labyrinths*, p. 60)

With this line we reach the conclusion of *Labyrinths* as originally evisaged in the revisions of 1965. The Heinemann volume, however, goes on to include a further sequence, written in the aftermath of the first 1966 *coup*, and published posthumously, called *Path of Thunder*. Sunday Anozie, in the monograph published five years after Okigbo's death, devotes much space to a discussion as to whether the eventual decision to publish these two rather different works in one volume was justified. His reasons for deciding against – that Okigbo had clearly come to the end of one phase of his development and was about to start another; that the poetic language of *Path of Thunder* is in a different register and addresses itself to different ends – seem cogent enough. *Path of Thunder* can clearly be viewed in two ways: as an immediate response to the political crisis of 1966 and as a further, and as it happened final, stage in the evolution of Okigbo's *oeuvre*. I have chosen here to postpone a discussion of the poem's political ramifications until chapter 10, preferring to concentrate in the present chap-

---

[23] T. S. Eliot, *Collected Poetry and Plays* (London: Faber, 1969), p. 34.

ter on the extent to which this last sequence may be interpreted as an outcrop and extension of the earlier work.

First, I think that we have to consider the meaning of Okigbo's concluding statement at the end of *Distances*: to what does this state of homecoming correspond? A nebulous answer could be returned: a state of spiritual perfectedness perhaps, or a state of grace. However, if we consider the statement, not merely in the context of *Distances* alone, but of *Labyrinths* as a whole, I think we may elicit the more positive answer that he has returned precisely to the geographical and vocational circumstances evoked at the very beginning of *Heavensgate*:

> BEFORE YOU, mother Idoto,
> naked I stand;
> before your watery presence.

Idoto, as we have already seen, was the riverside goddess whom Okigbo's grandfather served as priest and whose ministry he himself was expected to inherit. In other words, Okigbo has returned to his ancestral state of priesthood. And this leaves him with the pressing problem of his function. What is the best and most effective way, in the context of modern Nigeria, to serve the ancient gods and hence render an honest account of one's ministry? If we turn to *Path of Thunder* written immediately after the eruption of the ominous events of January 1966, we can find one possible answer: to warn, to preach, to exhort. This is the unpopular rôle for which Okigbo has elected, a rôle rife with misunderstandings, but the only one in which he can adequately fulfil his triple initiation, by Kepkanly, by Upandru, by Jadum:

> If I don't learn to shut my mouth I'll soon go to hell,
> I, Okigbo, town-crier, together with my iron bell.

*Path of Thunder* is strident, explicit, outright art: its reiterated images and ritualistic repetitions speak of a state of rapt possession in which a priest, one gifted with divine knowledge, utters his declamations and judgements. It is poetry of foresight and warning: in the full Old Testament sense, poetry of prophecy. Just as the Hebrew prophet Amos warned the people of God that, unless they changed their ways, their city would be made a desolation, so Okigbo is telling his fellow countrymen that, unless they put their house in order, the newly won state of independent Nigeria will fall about their ears. Okigbo is sometimes accused towards the end of his life of having foresaken the primrose path of the pure art and plunged himself into full-blooded political statement and action, degrading his calling in the process. Indeed one extremely fine philosophical novel, Ali Mazrui's *The Trial of Christopher Okigbo* is constructed around a dialectic generated by this view.[24] The most effective riposte to this criticism is that increasingly, as his art matured and the political environment in which he was working swam into finer focus, Okigbo came to see poetry and priesthood as synonymous, and priesthood as constituting a state of possession which, in modern Africa as in traditional Igboland, carried a strong political prerogative.

We have already noted that the constituent poems of *Labyrinths* carry implications of tempo and mood which suggest a musical framework. *Path of Thunder* takes this principle further by envisaging a score for percussion instruments against which it may be performed. Sometimes, as in the very opening lines, the instructions are included in the text:

> Fanfare of drums, wooden bells, iron chapter.

Otherwise, especially in the last two sections, they appear in the titles as suggestions for scoring. Throughout, however, there is a strong implied background supplied by a flexible musical pulse, lending the rolling lines and repeated cadences dignity and weight.

The opening salvo, for instance, *fortissimo*, envisages a holocaust of cataclysmic proportions, conveyed by clashing metal and deep drums. Then at line seven the volume suddenly drops, and we are left surveying a desolate ruined landscape:

> Barbicans alone tell one tale the winds scatter.
> (*Labyrinths*, p. 63)

Gradually the audience fall into place as 'hostages' to an occupying army, which is as yet unidentified. Yet of one fact we are assured, that the monumental events described are part of a pattern older than the present crisis, older than the society involved, older even than the written verse or the individual speaking voice. They belong rather to that larger backdrop of legend and myth upon which Okigbo's earlier sequences, and *Limits* in particular, drew so freely:

> Bring them out we say, bring them out
> Faces and hands and feet,
> The stories behind the myth, the plot
> Which the ritual enacts.   (*Labyrinths*, p. 63)

---

[24] Ali Mazrui, *The Trial of Christopher Okigbo* (London: Heinemann, 1971).

Seen thus, the precise political context of the present troubles, soon to identify itself as that attending the first Nigerian *coup d'état* of 1966, falls into place as an instance of that ageless history of oppression and betrayal which concerned Okigbo in 'Fragments out of the Deluge'. Viewed thus, the connections between *Path of Thunder* and the poetry of *Labyrinths* become increasingly clear.

Meanwhile Okigbo interpolates an interlude, 'Elegy of the Wind', which has less to do with the political events under consideration, or with their mythological backdrop, than with the poet's perspective on history. The kernel of the piece is a reworking of Wordsworth's famous lines in 'My Heart Leaps Up':

> So was it when my life began
> So is it now that I am a man;
> So be it when I shall grow old
>     Or let me die!
> The Child is father to the Man;
> And I could wish my days to be
> Bound each to each by natural piety.[25]

In Okigbo's variation this becomes:

> The man embodies the child
> The child embodies the man; the man remembers
> The song of the innocent,
> Of the uncircumcised at the sight of the flaming razor –
> The chief priest of the sanctuary has uttered
>     the enchanted words;
> The bleeding phallus,
> Dripping fresh from the carnage cries out
>     for the medicinal leaf . . .

> (*Labyrinths*, p. 64-5)

Seen against the Wordsworth original, 'Elegy of the Wind' becomes a meditation on innocence and experience. It is organized around two image clusters: one concerning the hard surfaces and sounds of metal; the other, concerning the gentle unforced processes of organic growth. The latter are throughout connected with intimations of childhood which blend fetchingly with the poet's own adult voice. Thus the poet begins with a determination to break the 'iron gate' of experience and suffering against the 'twin tremulous cotyledons' of his own tender exploratory yearnings. He is a 'man of iron throat', who has had, after all, to come to terms with the abrasive facts of experience;

[25] *The Poetical Works of William Wordsworth*, Vol. 1, ed. Ernest de Selincourt (Oxford University Press, 1940), p. 226.

yet it has been his constant endeavour to win through the dull blanket of adult conformity to 'chlorophyll', to the healing processes which have been his imaginative mainstay since early childhood. In his capacity as perennial child he can afford to relive his early adolescent fear of the 'flaming razor', the heated knife which circumcised him, and, in so doing, in crying out for the 'medicinal leaf' which serves as a balm for necessary suffering, to find a way through violence, upheaval and pain to the peace that lies beyond. Inevitably he shrinks from the ordeal, from 'the narrow neck of the calabash', but a fully mature attitude for him seems to lie in an acceptance of these facts and a transcendence of them. (Once again, links with the wisdom of 'Lament of the Silent Sisters' are manifest.) It will be seen here that Okigbo is concerned with *necessary* suffering, just as circumcision is necessary to adult manhood. The implication of this for what is to follow is important. The sufferings of Nigeria during the *coup* are to be viewed, not as an unwarranted interruption of an orderly progress, but as part of an inevitable process of cleansing and renewal without which Nigeria will never be whole.

Consequently the next section 'Come Thunder' begins on a welcoming note:

> NOW THAT the triumphal arch has entered the last street corners,
> Remember, O dancers, the thunder among the clouds.
> (*Labyrinths*, p. 66)

The reference to thunder takes us back to 'Lament of the Silent Sisters', where 'to say NO in thunder' was a sign of the acceptance of the negation underlying all experience. Here Okigbo is torn between his advocacy of cleansing violence, 'the Lightning beyond the earth', and an irresistable sense of foreboding. Clearly the *coup* is a welcome act of deliverance, yet, once accepted, the way lies through the escalating violence of unprecedented proportions:

> And a great fearful thing already tugs at the cables of the open air,
> A nebula immense and immeasurable, a night of deep waters –
> An iron dream unnamed and unprintable, a path of stone.

Once again the hard, unyielding surfaces of stone, the 'iron mask' worn by history, threatens to throttle the unhurried processes of growth which lead to natural, unforced maturity.

In the lyric which follows, 'Hurrah for Thunder', the political context of the current crisis comes more clearly into view. The elephant, 'tetrarch of the jungle', felled by the caustic intervention of thunder, can be no other than the Federal prime minister, Sir Abubakar Tafawa Balewa, killed on the night of 15 January 1966 by a group of young army officers, inspired by increasing resentment at his régime, at the Eastern / Northern domination of the Federation, and at irregularities in the Western Regional election of 1965. His death is welcomed as a release from his 'obduracy', yet, prophet and priest as Okigbo was, he cannot help but warn that this recourse to blood, once accepted and vindicated, may lead to untold consequences which will fall on the heads of the perpetrators.

> But already the hunters are talking about pumpkins:
> If they share the meat let them remember thunder.
> (*Labyrinths*, p. 67)

The following lyric, 'Elegy for Slit-drum' is dominated by a tone of ironic celebration. As the civil constitution is rescinded, and soldiers assume the day, the poet indulges in a moment of mock rejoicing:

> parliament has gone on leave
> the members are now on bail
> parliament is now on sale
> the voters are lying in wait – (*Labyrinths*, p. 68)

The action of General Aguiyi-Ironsi of taking over the leadership of the *coup* after its successful enactment by junior officers is likewise fêted in lines which, nevertheless, draw attention to the 'iron mask' he wears, the same mask as indicated the cruel face of human history in its path of retribution and mutual destruction (prophetically, as it happens, since Ironsi was himself assassinated in a subsequent *coup* that very July):

> The General is near the throne
> an iron mask covers his face
> the General has carried the day
> the mortars are far away – (*Labyrinths*, p. 69)

In the collage of references which follow Okigbo pauses for a perfect parody of a tabloid headline announcing the collapse at the hands of the military of Britain's carefully promoted legacy of parliamentary democracy:

> Jungle tanks blast Britain's last stand –

As the pitch rises, Okigbo warns of an accelerating pace of destruction in which animal feeds on animal, violence begets violence, and the cleansing path of thunder widens into a wilderness of destruction.

Then, with the last lyric, envisaged as a slow plaintive lament for alto saxophone accompanied by the solemn beat of drums, Okigbo comes to the heart of his message. The growing holocaust which is about to envelope Nigeria is here seen, less as a new and unforeseen danger, than as the re-establishing of an ancient pattern, the return of those 'eagles' and 'robbers' who carved so unmistakable a wake of despoliation in the annals of 'Fragments out of the Deluge':

> THE EAGLES have come again,
> The eagles rain down on us –          (*Labyrinths*, p. 71)

This is one of the earliest entrances into West African poetry of that theme of neo-colonialism which later was to become such a mainstay of political lament. Yet even here Okigbo is concerned less with topicality than with an effort to view the whole process historically as part of that endless cycle of destruction, renewal and perpetuated strife which has interested him ever since the outset of *Labyrinths*. As the sequence draws to a close he brings together threads and images from previous stages of his development in a culminating vision of the 'dream' of wholeness and human integrity beset with forces which would set upon and devour it. And, as, gazing up at the night sky, he seizes on the image of a pulsing star as a symbol of man's intermittent, frustrated fumbling for peace, order and fulfilment, it is hard to resist the conclusion that here he had achieved a definitive vision, not merely of the historical period on which he was commenting, but also of the themes which inspired his life's work.

Seen thus, Okigbo's *oeuvre* reveals itself as a prolonged meditation on the processes of decay and renewal, processes with both personal and societal dimensions which come to the fore at different times. *Heavensgate* concerns the initiation of a would-be priest into the mysteries of his vocation. In *Limits*, this development is carried through to a stage at which contradictions begin to emerge. The poet's dedication to his muse leads him into alienation from himself and rivalry with other dedicatees. In historical terms, explored in 'Fragments out of the Deluge', this may involve the appearance of a rival religion whose influence results in the destruction of the very shrines at which the priest ministers. The havoc thus wrought may not be avoided or explained away by complacent and trite systems of thought, whether political or philosophical. The only true poetic response to misfortune is to 'say NO in thunder', that is to accept the negation and to thrive upon it. It is to this task that the dual choric ode known as *Silences* addresses itself.

Once reconciled with the facts of suffering, the priest is free to retrace his steps, and, triumphing over death, to meet his divine mistress in an erotic embrace. As *Distances* draws to its conclusion the poet signals his awareness of his homecoming, thus begging the question of the rôle that he is now fit to play. With the final assumption of his priestly mantle, the poet–priest now realizes that it is incumbent on him to warn and to teach. Yet what message can he convey save the experience which he has lived through in his own person? Thus he meditates on the fluctuation between joy and despair, fulfilment and devastation which operates as an invariable law both within the individual and the society which he creates. In *Path of Thunder* the tribulations of contemporary Nigeria come to be viewed as one phase in the pulsing pattern of human history, a sudden but necessary eclipse in the 'going and coming that goes on for ever'.

To speak thus is to simplify, but it is worth while reminding oneself that Okigbo's preoccupations constitute grand themes which have obsessed poets through the ages. Of all the poets dealt with in this volume Okigbo has the strongest claim to be considered a writer of permanent standing, since, though firmly grounded in the traditions and realities of the region in which he grew up, his talent was of the sort which reaches out and embraces every time and place. He also possessed to a marked degree that authentic poetic *mania*, the spirit which drives an individual to express himself even at the cost of his sanity, life and self-respect. Okigbo is said to have given his life for a political cause. It might be truer to say that he gave his death to Biafra, his life to the creation of some of the most delicate lyrics written in the English language in Africa.

# CHAPTER 6

# Continuity and Adaptation in Ghanaian Verse, 1952–71

When we turn from Nigeria to look at the poetry which had emerged in Ghana since the 1950s we enter an atmosphere at once akin and sharply different. No traveller from one country to the other can fail to notice a communality of cultural response, custom, gesture, expression, aspiration and attitude. At the same time no one who has lived or worked in both countries can also fail to be aware after a time of a fundamental difference of tempo, a different level of tension that marks one nation from the other, however arbitrary the boundaries of each may be. Ghana and Nigeria were both British colonies. Both were exposed from a period not long after the closing of the European middle ages to tentative but occasionally brutal incursions along the coast. Both were subject to the debilitating slave trade, the tentacles of which reached from trading posts and forts in the south into the remotest hinterland. Both were formerly occupied from the end of the nineteenth century, and were fed with a palliative promise of self-government throughout the 1930s and 1940s. Both attained independence at approximately the same period (Ghana, 1957; Nigeria, 1960), and have subsequently largely abandoned the Westminster model of legislative democracy for alternating phases of experimental democracy and military control.

To remind oneself of these similarities is, however, at once to summon up areas of vivid divergence. Ghana is a far smaller country than Nigeria, less ethnically diverse and rent by fewer divisions of local loyalty. Whereas, thanks to oil revenues, the prosperity of Nigeria steadily increased until 1982, in Ghana the opposite has occurred. Riding high on a surfeit of cocoa wealth throughout the thirties and forties, she inherited a massive financial surplus at Independence much of which went to furnish the splendid university campus at Legon a few miles north of Accra. The late forties saw the arrival from America via London of Kwame Nkrumah, a Nzima and a politician of genius. Under his inspired leadership Ghana entered the condition of Independence full of promise, a model Africa regarded with envy and respect by the rest of the continent. After the *coup d'état* in 1966, however, she gradually drifted further into debt, and with the consequent sapping of confidence, institutions and morale began to crumble. After two further attempts at civilian rule stability now seems as far away as ever, with the result that Ghana, in 1957 the richest and most buoyant country in the region, is now one of the poorest. By 1972, when this chapter closes, the process was already well advanced, and the mood of the national literature had been effected decisively.

*[handwritten margin note: strange version of political events.]*

Both the relative smallness of the country and the course of its recent history have been conditioning factors in the sensibility of its writers. The steep decline in the national fortunes has sent a series of shock waves through the collective consciousness which have been experienced as an astringent wounding of the communal mind. Thus, if in Nigeria the observer has been struck by the diversity of forms and talents, in Ghana there has often seemed to be a cohesiveness of the national mood which has led to a recognizable national literary personality. The period of flagwaving described in chapter 2 was soon followed by a quickening of hope which was in turn followed by a slide into disillusionment. By the mid-sixties the dominant characteristic of Ghanaian literature, whether prose or verse, was a deeply moving sense of loss. Though touched up in different colours, the sensation is pervasive to a variety of authors and expressed in a surprisingly consistent imaginative language. The reason for this is not difficult to fathom. Less distracted by passing fashion than some of their neighbours, less prone to gather into opposing cabals or groups, and, with notable exceptions, less prone to the airing of quarrels, Ghanaian writers have from the early fifties felt able to turn to an abiding heritage of poetry and song which has fed their work with unifying strengths. The indebtedness is easy to demonstrate:

> (1) Lonely bird flitting away to the forest so fast,
> Gold-speckled finch, your feathers wet all fading,
> Tell me, shivering bird, have you seen her –
> Have you seen my crying baby's mother?
>
> She went to the river at early dew,
> A pot on her head;
> But down the water floats her pot,
> And the path from the river is empty.[1]

[1] Joe de Graft, *Beneath the Jazz and Brass* (London: Heinemann, 1975), p. 4.

> (2)  Thou vast forest,
>       Helper, please help us.
>       I told mother to come with me
>       To the head of the river; but
>       South of the river was better, she said.
>       Darkness falls and mother cannot be found.[2]

The first of these extracts is from an early lyric of the late Joe de Graft, grand old man of Ghanaian letters and a founder of the modern Ghanaian theatre. The second is a translation of part of a traditional lament sung round the corpse of the deceased at an Akan funeral to the wailing tones of the *oduragya* pipe. De Graft came from a long-established and high-born Fante family and would have heard many such laments in the streets of Cape Coast during his childhood. As a baby he was also soothed to sleep by the strains of a Fante lullaby. In this poem, written not long after assuming the Directorship of the Ghana Drama Studio in Accra, he has had the idea of combining the two forms. Such reliance on inherited modes of expression is all the more significant in a writer noted among his compatriots for resisting the narrower claims of national loyalty. De Graft proclaimed himself an internationalist, yet he often wrote most effectively when drawing from a proverbial well in his mother's courtyard.

A tradition of dirge-singing is prominent not only throughout the areas occupied by the various sub-groups of the Akan, but also among the Ewe and other ethnic groups. Though unusual for its frequency the lament is furthermore only one of the genres which proliferate in Ghanaian tradition. The very phrase 'Ghanaian tradition' is itself sufficient to suggest the relative cohesiveness of this remarkable legacy. To talk of a 'Nigerian poetic tradition' in either the context of oral literature or of English language verse would make little sense. Yoruba writers have learnt from the hunter's *ijala* chant and from the *odu* of the *babalawo* or diviner, Igbo writers from the riddle poem and antiphonal chant; yet, though parallels occur, the streams are distinct. The affinity of the Akan dirge to the Ewe lament has contributed to a shared language of disappointment which has in turn fed a widespread elegiac strain. The roots run deep, and few writers, however experimental and far-ranging in their extraneous influences, have failed to be affected.

---

[2] J. H. Kwabena Nketia, *Funeral Dirges of the Akan People* (Achimota, 1955), p. 126.

It was this active willingness to sit at the feet of the elders that distinguished the generation of Ghanaian writers who came to the fore in the sixties from earlier versifiers such as Raphael Armattoe and Michael Dei-Anang, for whom the ancestors were an abstraction to be invoked when local colour was required. The initiative in this direction came less from ethnographic contributions to periodicals – Ghana had no equivalent to *Black Orpheus* – than from the painstaking work of scholars and academics.[3] Soon after its establishment as a semi-autonomous institution of higher learning the University College of the Gold Coast was graced by the presence of members of staff, principally attached to the Institute of African Studies, concerned with recording, translating and publishing findings in this field. The distinguished musicologist Kwabena Nketia, himself a published poet in the Fante tongue, brought out his *Funeral Dirges of the Akan People* in 1954, thus continuing a distinguished ethnographic tradition going back to the pioneering efforts of expatriate scholars such as Robert Rattray. In the years that followed Nketia was to be joined at the Institute by others with interests in the practical and dramatic arts: Efua Sutherland, De Graft, and, before her move to Cape Coast, Ama Atta Aidoo, writers who were to infuse into Ghanaian poetry and drama in English an energy which came from their own grounding in traditional forms.

Of these Joe de Graft and Efua Sutherland may be said to span the generations. Already in their thirties by 1957, both retained a foothold in the genteel colonial world of the Gold Coast, a steadying poise which their successors would not enjoy. Both were brought up and initially educated in Cape Coast, the respectable but rather dilapidated former capital – Sutherland at St Monica's School and De Graft at Mfantsipim, a Methodist foundation with connections as old as the missionary movement itself. Both were brought up on a solid diet of the English Classics before the Modernist craze hit African academe in the late fifties. If this released them from the affectations of the new intelligentsia, it also left them with mannerisms of their own, on the one hand a sort of tea-sipping delicacy, on the other a rumbustious, back-slapping heartiness.

[3] An important exception to this rule was *Okyeame*, edited by Efua Sutherland and Kofi Awoonor in Accra from 1964.

Efua Sutherland's work for the Ghanaian stage has authenticity and distinction, but her published verses possess more than a whiff of the drawing room and the Edwardian salon. Her poetry has been mercilessly parodied by the novelist Ayi Kwei Armah in his second book *Fragments*[4] and the eight poems published in 1971 in the anthology *Messages* tend rather to endorse the charge. Her vice is a kind of neo-Protestant sentimentality tricked out by local symbolism and shot through with a weepy moral significance. 'The Redeemed' is overtly a folk tale about a village woman's escape from a hidden snake with intentions on 'those orbs dancing / In the fold across your breast', but covertly a parable in which Eve for once gets the better of the serpent.[5] 'The Dedication' concerns the hypocrisy behind the church's call to patriotic violence, but, though the poet starts by asking awkward questions from the back row of the Sunday School, she ends by playing the harmonium with the *tremolo* stop full out.[6] In 'Observations on on a Cockerel About to Crow, for a Young Man' she has learned from her own dramatic work for children and produces a nursery rhyme with a hint of Fante childrens' verse. But she is only really successful when in 'Song of the Fishing Ghosts' she steps down from the organ loft, walks out of the church, crosses the road to the lagoon and *listens*:

> Skulls are nets for phantom fishes,
>   Flows the river,
> Phantom red on a phantom river
> Dark flows the river.[7]

Joe de Graft is another writer whose august contribution to the Ghanaian stage has overshadowed his poetic output. In Sutherland's case the imbalance was perhaps inevitable; her published verse shows her to have little talent in this direction. Surveying de Graft's poetry, however, one comes away with a strong sense of gifts squandered. Some of his earliest pieces demonstrate a control of form and language quite lacking in the later work:

CLAY

> Early I fell among the potters,
> And so like feathers were their fingers.
> I was the clay, they the makers,

[4] Ayi Kwei Armah, *Fragments* (London: Heinemann, 1974), pp. 160–2.
[5] *Messages: Poems from Ghana*, eds. Kofi Awoonor and G. Adali-Mortty (London: Heinemann, 1971), pp. 158–9.    [6] *Ibid*, pp. 163–4.    [7] *Ibid.*, p. 165.

And as the wheel turned so I turned.
Oh, I loved their soft caresses,
Their sleekness, form- and beauty-giving fingers.[8]

This piece, dated November 1952, has a purity and grace of diction which spring from an experience perfectly realized, drawing on depths of suggestion made still deeper by the very ease of the technique and the supple use of half-rhymes. The first person singular of the poem may freely be associated with the human embryo, the crude matter of the universe, the poet's mind, or indeed the poem itself. On another level it is simply clay given voice. Any one of these alternatives would limit our response, but in conjunction the various possibilities add up to a strongly evocative sense of creation as a conscious, ethically directed process. There is a distance and an impersonal elegance about this piece, as there is about a perfectly realized theatrical plot, which raises it above the pettiness of the poet's self-concern while permitting the reader a range of interpretative possibility which in no way detracts from the poem's definiteness. It was a kind of achievement which de Graft learned early, and promptly abandoned for another tone of voice entirely:

Sometimes I have felt myself growing old
Lying there in my faded pyjamas
Listening to the cricket in the grass.
The cricket is always there
Jingling through the night.
And the mosquito comes singing very close
And vexes me rubbing his feet on the tip of my nose;
And the late cars keep droning home
One at a time, always one at a time,
While the Smith clock ticks.[9]

There is a candour of the reflective mind and a naturalness in this poem 'Night Thoughts' which undeniably impresses. It is a poem which takes the reader fully into its confidence. There are also touches of great vividness such as the weary, sleep-inducing insistence of passing traffic in the last three quoted lines. Despite this, its technique of recollection in tranquillity is a lesser achievement because it fails to transcend the particularity of the prematurely aging individual who writes it. The reader is unable to extrapolate from this instance of the poet's own resigned insomnia – Joe de Graft lying passively, bored but

[8] de Graft, *Beneath the Jazz and Brass*, p. 87.   [9] *Ibid.*, p. 83.

serene, on his bed in one of the mining towns of south west Ghana in November 1952 – nothing else asserts its presence.

This was henceforth to be de Graft's limitation. He possessed a personality ideally suited to his chosen rôle of theatrical impresario. A poet, however, needs a mask; without an element of disguise he becomes one with a man we meet during the daily round, tolerable only for limited periods. De Graft was born into a lucky generation, heir to the confidence and affluent self-assurance of the immediate post-Independence era. It was a confidence which he was able to transmit to his juniors but which, as a poet, confined him. There is a bonhomie, a hail-fellow-well-met cock-suredness about much of his later writing that lifts it scarcely higher than cultivated banter over the bar of a Senior Common Room. Only occasionally does the assurance slip to suggest the shyness lurking beneath. Consequently his verse is at its finest when at its most reticent. Indeed he writes most effectively of all on those rare occasions when we are hardly aware of his presence at all. During the 1960s and 1970s his themes were the self-deception of the new power-seeking élite, and the silliness of the more demonstrative kinds of ethnic loyalty. Yet, though he liked to proclaim himself a citizen of the world, he wrote his best poetry when anchored in traditional forms which allowed him little room for his habitual flights of rollicking self-indulgence.

There is one other reason for de Graft's relative failure as a poet which his selected poems make abundantly clear. It was his practice to date every poem in his notebook, detailing also the date of subsequent revisions. Of the sixty-eight poems eventually collected in *Behind the Jazz and Brass* in 1975 only six show any such evidence of revision, the rest having apparently been dashed off in one session. While there have been poets whose instinctive fluency has enabled them to perform with equivalent heedless speed – the Ulster poet Louis MacNeice in his younger years being a good example – it is very seldom that their best work was produced under such conditions. In such poets excellence more often occurs when something unaccountably happens to block the flow, causing the poet to revise his first thoughts in the interests of a finer texture. Significantly the most accomplished poem in de Graft's book is entitled simply 'The Poem I Cannot Write':

> I would mould a poem
>    about you;
> Only
>    Words snap in the shaping

> Too brittle-coarse to take your form.
> The mystic serenity of you
> So I am left with the memory of
> A lady giving alms –
>     Vision of grace
>     among beggars –
> Inimitably you
>     Giving alms.[10]

The poem refers to a woman of whom de Graft was clearly very fond, her 'alms' being those of love as well as 'alms' of charity. One senses that the poet wishes to say more, but the very depth of his feeling arrests him. The result is a lucid Poundean vignette, as clear-cut and satisfying as a Japanese print. The two lines 'Vision of grace / among beggars' are probably worth the rest of de Graft's *oeuvre*. Blocked for once in his complacent self-expression. he has had no alternative but to let the poem speak for itself.

If the career of Joe de Graft illustrates the dangers of fluency, the work of Geormbeeyi Adali-Mortty is beset by dangers of quite another kind. In de Graft the poet is drowned by the convivial man of letters; in Adali-Mortty he is smothered in the sentimental man of affairs. Adali-Mortty has spent his professional life in the worlds of business and administration, but his loyalties belong to the Ewe countryside where he was born. His poetry invokes the rural environment of his childhood in terms which imply genuine regret for leaving while betraying something quite different – the compensatory nostalgia of one who could not wait to get away:

> Fearsome and dark are village nights!
> How odd of me
> To near-forget those village nights.
> Here, seen through baccy smoke
> The spectred looming gloom
> Here, in Aloka, harrowed by the hush,
> Reminds me.[11]

Adali-Mortty has 'half-' forgotten, but remembers just enough to keep him comfortably in Accra. 'Where are they, the spirits of the night / Where?' he cries, echoing François Villon's 'Ou sont les neiges d'antan?' Adali-Mortty is wise enough not to attempt the move back to the country, just as Villon knew that in reality 'les neiges d'antan'

---

[10] *Ibid.*, p. 14.    [11] *Messages*, p. 50.

No + ?

had long since turned into unsightly slush. There is in much of Adali-Mortty's poetry a narrow balance between the sentimental vein and the realism of one who knows just where his advantage, and his heart, really lies. It is this merciless realism that enabled him to write one of the most penetrating lyrics ever written on the relationship between the African poet of English expression and the language he employs:

> You may excel
> in knowledge of their tongue,
> and universal ties may bind you close to them;
> but what they say, and how they feel –
> the subtler details of meaning,
> thinking, feeling, reaching –
> these are closed to you and me forever more;
> As are, indeed, the interleaves of speech
> – our speech – which falls on them
> no more than were they dead leaves
> in dust-dry harmattan[12]

These are lines which challenge the critic just as sharply as they do the poet. In fact the poem raises questions very close to the heart of this book, questions about the extent to which any given tongue, inescapably embedded as it necessarily is in the mentality of the people among whom it evolved, can viably serve the interests of another people accustomed to very different cultural conditions.

꩜          ꩜          ꩜

It was the critic A. A. Alvarez who in the fighting introduction to his anthology *New Poetry* of 1961 attacked what he termed the 'gentility principle' in contemporary British verse.[13] Reading the work of Sutherland, de Graft and Adali-Mortty one is driven to the conclusion that if the term 'gentility' pertains to any literature it is to Ghanaian poetry between the fifties and the early sixties. There is a pervasive niceness (as opposed to nicety) about the work of many of these writers which often makes it appear as if it were holding life at arm's length in well-bred distaste. It is not a reaction which makes for gut-felt writing, nor a reaction which often gives rise to substantial work in any imaginative medium. Ghanaian verse in English only picked up

[12] 'Belonging' in *Messages*, p. 42.
[13] 'Beyond the Gentility Principle' in *The New Poetry*, ed. A. A. Alvarez (Harmondsworth: Penguin, 1962).

146

its strength with the arrival of a new generation of writers who, reject-ing the refinements of an imperial past, plunged into the difficult busi-ness of interpreting the perplexities of the present in language which drew on older sources of self-awareness.

The work of Frank Kobina Parkes marks an improvement in this direction. Unfortunately, if the work of de Graft and Sutherland was undermined by gentility, the work of Parkes occasionally sags under the weight of another tendency: an over-willingness to espouse the myth of progress. *Songs of the Wilderness* (1965) commences with a note to 'The Critics' requesting them to relinquish their demand for local authenticity so as to allow the poet to soar 'heaven-bound'.[14] The sort of destination Parkes has in mind is implied by the poem 'African Heaven' in which the celestial mansions of the Akan deity Odoman-koma resound to a distinctly Negritudinous drum.[15] Yet the slackness of the phraseology in that piece suggests that the poet's heart is else-where, in the sub-Wellsian vision of scientific self-improvement expressed in 'Twentieth Century Epiphany':

> Angels depart
> Your rule of peace lies cold
> Your message now is stale
> No longer raise your voice
> For from the new voice of the white man's mind
> Shall new angels sing us the beauteous birth
> Here is the news, the new saint john shall cry
> And then, the atoms split and split again
> Shall sit upon Christ's throne.[16]

Round about the throne African acolytes stand in rapt agreement, but the focus of the poem is on a future benevolently controlled by a sort of celestial UNESCO carrying out its orderly, beneficent plans while 'the rude, the black' literally dance attendance.

Frank Parkes was born in Sierra Leone of mixed parentage but returned to the Gold Coast in his early teens to attend Adisadel, the Anglican secondary school in Cape Coast. He subsequently worked for the Ghana Broadcasting Corporation as a radio editor for Radio Ghana before coming to London in the mid-sixties to act as an agent for the ruling Convention People's Party. Parkes's tragedy is that the nature of his training and the political atmosphere of the period in

---

[14] Frank Kobina Parkes, *Songs from the Wilderness* (London: University of London Press, 1965), p. 7.
[15] *Ibid.*, pp. 26–8.     [16] *Ibid.*, pp. 24–5.

which he reached adulthood caused him totally to mistake the direction of his talent. He takes himself for a poet of ideas, but is something much rarer: a poet of the imagination. His long dissertations on ideological issues 'The Spectre and the Talking Drum', 'Twentieth Century Epiphany', 'Two Deaths, One Grave' and 'Monsters' all drag their feet, a tendency not improved by their physical arrangement on the page. Indentation can be a useful device, but Parkes's flagrant overuse of it is a mannerism completely unjustified by any corresponding bifurcation either of sound or meaning.

When he abandons the realm of the rational ordering intelligence, and takes to the occult, his instinctual habitat, Parkes suddenly and unexpectedly comes into his own. In his best work we find a late flowering of the Gothic imagination unusual in an African poet. The genre has, of course, distinct literary antecedents: the creaking machinery of ghosts, goblins and wailing spectres bequeathed by the late eighteenth century. In most twentieth-century poets a reliance on this legacy would produce disastrous results. There is in some writers, however, a cast of mind that enables them to make personal use of properties abandoned by others to great effect: it is one reason why Baudelaire's diabolism, for instance, is so much more meaningful than that of his contemporaries. Such is the hold of the Gothic shadows on Parkes's imagination that in his strongest pieces they cease for a moment to howl in borrowed accents and take on flesh and blood. It is noticeable that when the poets Kofi Awoonor and Adali-Mortty came to edit the Ghanaian anthology *Messages* in 1971 they omitted all of Parkes's progressivist vistas and clung to the real evidence of his talent: 'The Unlaid Ghost', 'Redemption' and 'Strange Harvest'. Each of these poems is spoken in the first person singular by a spirit haunting the desolate realms of its past existence. In 'Redemption' it becomes the victim of 'past oppression' evoking in Biblical tones the decay of a forsaken city:

> My world pines in your marble breasts, daughter of woe
> Green buds crack in the dry harmattan wind
> Sun beats down on the city of a million dead
> Men wove hats with their hands for shelter
> And monkeys, from tree-tops bare, mock
> With crown-capped glee
> Bare headed among the despoiled flowers I stand
> Empty-handed, in built-up deserts

> I groan mankind's loss
> And search wide heavens for a sign not written there.[17]

With this we discern the entry into Ghanaian verse of an entirely new tone. Gone is the false exhilaration of hopes not to be realized, gone the eyes lifted up towards heaven. God is dead, and the shrines empty, and around the poet lies a scorched terrain bereft of familiar comfort. It is a vision at once strange and very old, leaning on the inflections of an elegiac tradition with roots deep in the collective mind. 'Shall these bones live? / Shall these bones live?' cries Parkes's prophet, echoing Eliot's *Ash Wednesday*, itself echoing Ecclesiastes, but the answer echoes in the blank space between the verse paragraphs, an emptiness which suggests the desolation of the Nkrumahist panacea. In 'Strange Harvest' the ghost is that of the poet himself haunting the foreign metropolis, impotently bewailing the fate of his distant people. Once again the Bible is in evidence, this time the opening of Psalm 137:

> By the waters of London, there I sat, and sang
> Adding salt waters to fresh waters
> Multiplying woe by woe
> For those silent, unborn lips
>
> And you, full of anger, ask:
> How dare you sing the Lord's song in this strange city?
> Where cold corpses feed on humans
> And the womb's visitation, thorns?[18]

Though London is here glimpsed with something of the disaffection of Eliot's *Waste Land*, the writing is none the worse for that. Borrowing may encumber a poet, or it may, as with Parkes's biblical and Eliotic allusions, release him. These lines have a simplicity of lyrical directness and a consequent melancholy rare in Parkes's work. The image of 'cold corpses' feeding on humans is genuinely chilling, while 'the womb's visitation, thorns' has a compressed sadness which redeems Parkes's habitual fustian. The reason is that here at last he is responding to promptings deep within himself: he is moved by a memory, dimly stirring within the imagination, of a desolation much more ancient than that caused by the mere collapse of a questionable political programme. Much Ghanaian oral verse dwells on the spectacle of a deserted compound, crumbling and eaten by termites, its inhabitants either fled or sold into slavery. It is a flickering shadow thrown up by

---

[17] *Ibid.*, p. 52.     [18] *Ibid.*, p. 55.

the ancestral imagination, a fugitive image from an earlier age of mass migrations, wars, disruption and bondage. If Parkes's echoes of the exilic Psalms are effective it is because they allow him to participate in a Hebraic lament for Babylonian exile which has much in common with the indigenous laments of his own people.

Despite the failure of Nkrumah's government, throughout the late sixties and early seventies the progressivist myth retained its seductive hold on the Ghanaian mind. In the case of Albert Kayper-Mensah its grip was strengthened by a scientific education. Born in Sekondi Mensah read Natural Sciences at Cambridge before embarking on a teaching and later administrative career which eventually took him abroad in the ranks of the diplomatic corps. Poetry for Mensah has always been a passionate pastime into which he has poured all the pent-up energy of a curious, quizzical but often sentimental mind. His distinct strengths are less easily observable in his second volume *The Drummer in Our Time*,[19] than in his first *The Dark Wanderer* (1970) published when the author was stationed in Germany. Rereading the earlier volume the reason for its superiority is not difficult to detect. The poetry in *The Dark Wanderer* was written during the first years of an initially happy marriage to a German wife. The contentedness pays dividends in an easy naturalness of style, an absence of affectation and directness of feeling which are at times very attractive. In this respect Kayper-Mensah is highly unusual: the majority of poets write most effectively out of a sense of unease with the world or themselves. Of all the subjects to which poets are habitually drawn, fulfilled monogamous love is perhaps the most difficult to evoke without self-consciousness. Despite this, the section entitled 'Germany' in Mensah's first book, which is virtually a portrait of his marriage, works at times wonderfully well. Mensah's love for his wife mirrored his passion for German culture, and more especially the music of Bach and Beethoven. It is to the German seventeenth and nineteenth centuries to which he seems especially attracted. It is not the rococo which draws Mensah but *Sturm und Drang* and the German sublime, an affinity of feeling which he expresses with great sensitivity. By the time he came to write the pieces included in *A Drummer in Our Time* Mensah had lost sight of his happiness, and his marriage, as one or two bitter

[19] A. W. Kayper-Mensah, *The Drummer in our Time* (London: Heinemann, 1975).

*No self consciousness on Fraser's part about imagery of temperate zone seasons.*

poems make clear, was on the rocks. The resulting *angst* distorts his view of everything: politics, women, art. Suddenly everyone, and everything becomes a deceiver. Mensah has no gift for the tragic vein, and the poetry inevitably suffers. If we wish for an account of Mensah's strength, then, it is to *The Dark Wanderer* that we must turn.

The German section of Mensah's first book begins with a set of poems on the seasons done with an unhurried grace:

> Spring came in newest greens
> In rainbow coloured crocuses
> In flaming tulips, gold of dancing
> Daffodils, and warm wine-red Easter roses.[20]

Though the 'dancing daffodils' are, of course, Wordsworthian they are not intrusive. The pace of recollection is natural and unforced, untroubled by any desire to pull adjectival plums or to impress by descriptive display. Rhymes where they occur come without fuss, almost as if by oversight:

> Summer dressed in warmer colours
> Darker greens and deeper reds
> White, gold on mixed beds
> In colours vanishing in Summer fruits.

The landscape and artistic life of Germany are conveyed with a warmth which carries the writing beyond travelogue towards tender celebration. One feels that the author's stay in his wife's country has been a voyage of exploration, and that we are invited to join him for the ride. 'Departures and Arrivals',[21] for instance, lets us in on the impact of a foreign rhythm of life on one not bred to seasonal extremes; in short, rapidly moving lines 'Fasching'[22] allows us to participate in the joy and release of the annual Lenten festival. In 'Light in the Nude'[23] spring and a beloved spouse come to life as both divest themselves. It is in their descriptions of cultural life that these poems most excel. No African poet to date has so successfully registered the delights of discovering classical music. 'Into Easter with Bach'[24] is a thoughtful meditation on the Easter Oratorio, while 'Beethoven and Us' attempts, perhaps rather arbitrarily, to interpret Beethoven's life through his music. It is not Beethoven's mood which the poet

[20] A. W. Kayper-Mensah, *The Dark Wanderer* (Tübingen: Horst Erdmann Verlag), p. 9.
[21] *Ibid.*, pp. 10–11.     [22] *Ibid.*, p. 28.     [23] *Ibid.*, pp. 22–3.     [24] *Ibid.*, pp. 60–3.

discerns, however, but his own, since Mensah attributes to the German composer a fulfilment and a completeness in love he never knew. The most sustained of these pieces is 'Germany in Music' in which an account of a concert given in a private house provides an occasion both for a compliment to the host and a portrait of a land and its people. Though the tone sometimes waxes over-philosophical, the reader is constantly buoyed up by Mensah's description of aural delights as one by one they assault the imagination:

> Time for new music and new shapes
> New colours of sound from voice to noise:
> The one pure note's pirouette,
> Its beauty showing through, in light;
> The mixed notes, which overlapping,
> Yield, for joy and sad reflection,
> Wider, steep perspectives of the spirit.[25]

The balance maintained in this description of baroque counterpoint between physical almost dizzying sensation and intellectual interpretation of musical structure is a delicate one, depending on a willingness to let feeling follow its course before the mind intervenes.

Though of much the same generation, by poetic temperament Frank Kobina Parkes and Kayper-Mensah are almost precise opposites. Where Mensah writes most convincingly when buoyed up by serene circumstances, Parkes's strengths only become apparent when passing through the valley of the shadow of death. In manifesting his gift in this way, Parkes comes very much the nearest of the two to one essential reflex of Ghanaian poetry, and in so doing helps to highlight an important generalization. With very few exceptions the verse which emerged from Ghana's short period of prosperity and progress was enfeebled, apathetic and derivative. The verse of the seventies, when Ghana went into decline, was by contrast eloquent to an extraordinary degree. Despite the prognostications of the administrators, material progress and cultural vigour flourished in inverse ratio. Ghana's economical ruin was her artistic salvation.

Beginning in the mid-sixties, when the Convention People's Party government first showed signs of faltering, one began to notice a

[25] *Ibid.*, pp. 43–4.

sombre undertow beneath the best of Ghanaian poetry. The strain was not exclusive to verse; some of the most notable expressions of it were later to be found in the novels of Ayi Kwei Armah and the short stories of Ama Atta Aidoo. The resulting literature was very far from the self-lacerating world-weariness of the European intelligentsia, arrested in an emotional and cultural impasse. The prose and verse of Ghana's declining years was the cry of a people who, arriving in the land of exile, look around them and realize with a horrified shudder that they have been here before. It is the complaint of a migrant people forced once more to pack their belongings and set off into an uncertain future, leaving in their wake shattered homesteads washed by the sound of the sea. At first, the sea's advance is only a tremor heard in the far distance, but as time goes on and the national fortunes further fade, it becomes more and more insistent, until in the poetry discussed in chapter 11 of this history, it threatens to drown everything else. The first signs were, however, not easy to detect. They were evident in one of the most accomplished collections of verse to have been written in Africa during the whole period: Kwesi Brew's *The Shadows of Laughter* (1968).

Though emerging from a very similar professional and ethnic background as Kayper-Mensah, Brew displays very different imaginative tendencies, and in so doing reaffirms the continuity of the mainstream of Ghanaian verse. Like Kayper-Mensah, Brew can claim descent from an old Gold Coast family. There have been Brews in Fanteland since 1745 when Richard Brew, a vintner's son, journeyed from County Clare to Anomabu where to this day his 'castle' lies in the shade of the trading fort of which he was one time governor. Like Mensah too, Brew has spent the major part of his professional life as a diplomat attached to missions in Britain, France, India, Germany and Russia. Yet one looks in vain for any reflection of all this cosmopolitan experience in his verse. Indeed one of the first pieces in his book is a disavowal of the advantages of travel, phrased in language which suggests a traditional Fante lyric such as that quoted at the beginning of this chapter:

> The mud of my feet, mother,
> Is from the long journey
> I made, deluded that at the end
> I should find wisdom and peace.
> I trudged the hot red roads
> And the hills that strive to touch the stars,

And came upon a clear river
In the folds of a valley.[26]

This is a poem which impresses by the sheer strength of its simplicity. The language is straightforward and unforced, the images commonplace, but Brew's scrupulous ordering of basic elements is utterly convincing in its outlining both of situation and of emotional logic. Standing at his mother's threshold, the son announces his arrival without ceremony or undue fuss. The 'hot red roads' bring to mind the dusty laterite paths of West Africa while implying an infinite extension beyond. There is nothing very original about the 'stars' as an emblem of youthful ambition, but placed as they are at the summit of the upward climb before a relaxed descent into the valley, their inclusion is perfectly judged. Lastly, the 'folds' in the landscape evoke the maternal breasts and thus lead with complete naturalness to the domestic reconciliation of the last stanza.

Brew is not confined to homespun themes. To suggest this would do a great disservice not only to Brew but to traditional Akan literature from which he has learned so much. Brew's indebtedness to oral poetry is not just a matter of surface similarity: underneath lie depths of feeling of a difficult and often contradictory kind. The skill of such writing, as the skill of a Fante lyric, consists in the deployment of minimal contours in such a way as to summon up a whole penumbra of liquid and often threatening association. To read Brew is to be delighted and disturbed in equal measure. On first reading the anthology piece 'A Plea for Mercy', for instance, the reader may very well come away with an impression of a neatly etched homeward bound piece. A closer look, however, and he notices the way in which the confidence of the supplicants is sapped by their sense both of their own insufficiency and of the inadequacy of the faith in which they have plighted their trust:

Why should we the sons of the land
Plead unheeded before your shrine,
When our hearts are full of song
And our lips tremble with sadness[27]

There is a suppressed urgency of complaint here which passes beyond mundane resentment to express hurt incredulity. Though the text ends with a gesture of deference to the 'master', the 'tattered penury'

[26] Kwesi Brew, *The Shadows of Laughter* (London: Longman, 1968), p. 6.
[27] *Ibid.*, p. 55.

of the pilgrims betrays a state of dilapidation which calls the object of their homage into question.

Throughout the poetry collected in *The Shadows of Laughter* Brew's view of the abiding Akan scene is similarly poised between reverence and scepticism. In the finest pieces there is a superimposition of a picturesque and settled foreground – like an attractive watercolour of the rainforest – over an intermittently perceived background dark with forces which threaten to undermine it. The pictorial analogy seems peculiarly fitting since some of Brew's most sinister effects come from a juxtaposition of visual elements. Take the arresting opening image in the first stanza of 'The Executioner's Dream' in which the disembodied eye of a sacrificial victim appears stark but beautiful in its frame of lashes:

> I dreamt I saw an eye, a pretty eye,
> In your hands,
> Glittering, wet and sickening
> Like a dull onyx set in a crown of thorns.[28]

Though the poem is called 'The Executioner's Dream' it is the narrator who is at first dreaming, and the executioner his subject. We soon, however, pass on from the surreal first image to an evocation of the executioner's own guilty nocturnal agony in which the eye reappears as that of a living victim 'hot, imploring'. With the insane logic of nightmare we then switch to a beach scene in which a surfboat is seen ploughing landwards with the executioner himself standing grimly at the helm. Mysteriously he is then transferred to *terra firma* where he plays in the sand with a little child who is gradually transformed into the speaker's infant self, lost in innocent wonder at the flamboyant beauty of bougainvillaeas which, 'blood-bright' prefigure his choice of adult occupation. And so back we come to the gift of an eye set in a foil which intensifies its horror even as it decorates it. Lastly, who is the donor and who the recipient? Is the victim placating the executioner or the other way round? Whose eye is it, and what is its relationship to the eye which perceives the reality of the poem? There is a careful balance between attraction and repulsion here, and an entire fidelity to bizarre subjective forces which mark this out as one of Brew's most effective poems.

Though elsewhere Brew is more sparing in his treatment of menace and less audacious in his choice of image, the underlying disturbance

[28] *Ibid.*, p. 11

of an apparently calm surface is never absent. Everywhere is the elegance of descriptive line; everywhere too the odd displacement of detail which serves to delineate a residual unease. In 'Dry Season',[29] for instance, the autumnal serenity of the harmattan is depicted with a confidence worthy of Constable. The reader is entirely seduced by the seasonal dignity of the scene the poet describes, until that is he happens to notice the hare scurrying off the bottom right hand corner of the canvas about to be torn in pieces by the dogs. In 'The Vulture'[30] the inhabitants of the homestead seem frozen in an attitude of decorous anticipation until the last line suggests that they are themselves the bird's intended victims. In 'Locusts'[31] the sudden flushing of the sky-line seems to predict an early sunset full of abundance and repose, while the image 'like salmon' is rich with the promise of food and plenty. But as the fishermen set out towards the horizon in the hope of a miraculous catch, the billowing cloud before them reveals itself for what it is: a flight of scavengers intent on depriving the villagers of their last morsel. Once again there is pictorial beauty behind which lingers disappointment and ugliness. The sky's colour is gorgeous while in the imagined sea the herrings 'dye themselves' into a still deeper shade of indigo to feast the eye. But if the eye is flattered, the stomach contracts in anticipated hunger, and behind the voluptuous prettiness death hangs in the air.

Throughout Brew's poetry this sort of layering effect is meticulously deployed so as to keep the reader alert until he has taken the full measure of the author's disquiet. The deeper levels only reveal themselves at moments and under certain lights: often it is no more than one or two words that do the trick. 'Hot Day'[32] seems at first nothing but a drowsy picture of torrid noon, but then the reader looks at the choice of words in the last two lines and asks himself why the starling's shoulders should 'roll', and why the midday hush is described as 'mumbling'. There is a kind of lolling obsessiveness about these two verbs which finally conveys the fact that the afternoon stands poised on the edge of an extremity in which the searing heat will claim not merely man-hours but soon also the demented death of the very men and women who now indolently haunt the shade.

It is only in the longish piece 'Questions of Our Time' which lends its name to the last section of *The Shadows of Laughter* that the nagging undercurrent beneath the even flow of Brew's verse makes itself felt

---

[29] *Ibid.*, p. 38    [30] *Ibid.*, p. 39    [31] *Ibid.*, p. 40.    [32] *Ibid.*, p. 35

with any explicitness. The poem begins by setting the efforts of the present time in the context of natural rhythms which endow it with significance and an appearance of auspiciousness. As the sun rises and falls, orchestrating a sequence of work and rest in which all men take reassurance and consolation, a traditional wisdom insinuates itself in the reader's mind, a wisdom attuned to the absolute certainties of rural life: a philosophy which trembles on the brink of moral complacency. Instead of apathetic calm, however, the concluding lines of the first verse paragraph offer a question which threatens the very security in which the opening lines delighted:

> Do we know indeed what has gone before
> And what is to come after?[33]

The 'fighting warriors' who come back laden with spoils are in reality no more certain of lasting prosperity than the poverty-stricken 'sons of the land' in 'A Plea for Mercy'. Like them they stand at the beck and call of natural accident and of 'the colour of the sky' which, as we have already seen in 'Locusts', often lours with an ominous red. Thus it is to a tiny child wandering in the market place rather than to the elders that the questioner turns for enlightenment, only to be greeted with the unsettling answer 'perhaps, only perhaps': again the re-iterated uncertainty. It is an answer too easily discounted: after all, the speaker reassures himself 'he has seen nothing of life' and has no access to adult serenity. But as the boy scours the horizon of the future, like the fishermen searching the skyline in 'Locusts' or the infant executioner peering into his sinister destiny in the shape of a flower, what does he see but 'the fighting tribes' permanently caught between enthusiasm for the task at hand and a cynical world-weariness which undermines it? Really, there is nothing to look forward to but perpetuated doubt endlessly reinterpreted, purposes endlessly thwarted.

For a poet so close to the rhythms of rural life Brew has strangely little faith in the solidity of inherited wisdom. All that he seems to be able to discern beyond the elegant complacency of custom, is flux and directionless change. One of his poems is entitled 'The Woods Decay' after the pervading mutability which Tennyson's Tithonus found in the world around him. Tithonus had found himself exempt from

---

[33] *Ibid.*, p. 64.

death, protected unwillingly from mortality by a besotted goddess. But in Brew's universe not even the gods are exempt, and any appeal for stability can be addressed only to a callous destiny which in extreme moments seems itself to have been swept away.

For several Ghanaian poets looking for a symbol of this kind of remorseless change there has seemed to be a symbol ready at hand in the shape of the Ewe town of Keta, poised precariously on an isthmus between lagoon and sea eleven miles south of Wheta, and for generations imperilled by ceaseless erosion from the sea. Many poems have been written about Keta, but few more effective than Brew's own 'The Sea Eats Our Lands'.[34] Brew is not an Ewe, yet few have captured with such veracity the experience of growing up in a place where the very soil under one's feet is threatened with dissolution. In a remarkable expression of the theme of the decaying compound already noted as a recurrent motif in Ghanaian verse, Brew imagines the sight of a family homestead now reduced to rubble, the futile acts of propitiation to gods apparently indifferent to the community's fate. As the material of the house dissolves into the advancing tide, the moral fabric of the society wilts with it, dispatching young girls to Accra and nearby Lomé in search of easy money. Once again the thrust of Brew's disquiet is conveyed by a handful of words. The daughters in the concluding quatrain are 'golden' because both beautiful and prey to commercial exploitation. Like the town itself they 'erode', melting into 'arms' which belong both to the sugar-daddies of the new élite and, more notionally, to the cash economy which their buying power represents.

Brew's requiem for Keta is an act of empathy rather than an autobiographical record. Fante-born, he uses the dilemma of one imperilled, distant community as a symbol for his personal sense of time's threat. For Kofi Awoonor, by contrast, a relationship with the area of the Keta lagoon has been essential and profound. Born in Wheta, in 1935 of mixed Togolese and Sierra Leonian parentage, he attended as a child local funeral celebrations presided over by the great dirge-singer Vinoko Akpalu, imbibing in the process the elegiac tradition of the Anlos, the Ewe sub-group predominant in the region. When his

[34] *Ibid.*, p. 41.

apprentice volume *Rediscovery and Other Poems* appeared under the Mbari imprint in 1964, many of the pieces were recognized by Ewe speakers as reworkings of Akpalu lyrics. In some quarters he was even accused unofficially of a mild form of plagiarism.[35] The charge is unjust, since the book's title is clear acknowledgement of a debt owed to a long and distinguished tradition within which textual ownership has little meaning. When seven years later a selection from the pieces in *Rediscovery* was interspersed amongst other poems composed in the interval to form the volume *Night of My Blood* (1971) Awoonor's intention became clearer. As a young poet he had sat at the feet of the Anlo masters, attempting to render the sentiments of their tonal verse in the strains of an imported, accentual tongue. Later he felt able to proceed beyond 'rediscovery' and extend the dirge tradition into a medium for comment both political and private.

Though the Akpalu versions in *Rediscovery* were in some cases very close to the originals, their indebtedness to Ewe tradition was the result of influences imbibed during childhood rather than of deliberate research. It was not until after their publication and the inception of many of the poems included in *Night of My Blood*, that, in the rainy season of 1970, Awoonor was able to make a visit to Wheta systematically to investigate the sources of his own inspiration. The study which resulted, *Guardians of the Sacred Word* (1974),[36] is both a remarkable source-book and a prolonged meditation on the social position and skills of the vernacular Ewe poet or *heno*, translations from the work of three of whom he was able to include. Though a general reliance on an indigenous form has long been recognized as a feature of Awoonor's achievement it was not until the comparison of related texts thus made possible that the exact extent of his indebtedness became clear.

In the first chapter I quoted an extract from an Akpalu dirge with a short extract from one of the 'Songs of Sorrow' from *Rediscovery*.[37] Here to extend the point is a section of a different dirge taken from the introduction to *Guardians of the Sacred Word* followed by the first four lines of the second verse paragraph of the first 'Song of Sorrow' which duplicates in almost every particular the literal English translation given by Awoonor himself in 1974:

[35] Cf. letter in *West Africa*, 26 March 1985.
[36] Kofi Awoonor, *Guardians of the Sacred Word: Ewe Poetry* (New York: Nok Publications, (1974).     [37] See pp. 9-11 and 16-18.

### EWE ORIGINAL

Xexeame fe dzogoedzi nyea mele
Nye mele amewoamewo kasa o
Amesiwo nye aklamatowo wokpo dome no
Heno anyi de me nu
Wogblobe nudzi gee nyea meyi
Vinoko, mayi tsyie made nu di[38]

[I am on the world's extreme corner / I am not sitting in the row with the eminent / Those who are lucky sit in the middle / Sitting and leaning against a wall / They say I came to search, / I, Vinoko, can only go beyond and forget.]

### SONG OF SORROW

I am on the world's extreme corner,
I am not sitting in the row with the eminent
Those who are lucky
Sit in the middle and forget

Read in the context of *Rediscovery* the words of Awoonor's poem, moving as they are, appear as a conventional expression of isolation by a scorned artist, and, as such, are applicable to the condition of the poet in almost every time and place. The gain in universality thus achieved, however, involves a corresponding loss of *locale*, for in the Ewe original Akpalu is concerned less with the recurrent fact of artistic alienation than, first and foremost, a sense of himself as one who, childless and an orphan, must live, like the deceased soul whom he mourns, on the very edge of his community. Awoonor's comments in *Guardians of the Sacred Word* allow us access to an additional dimension, for Akpalu's self-portrait makes further sense when related to the social and economic position of the *heno* in Anlo society: 'Most poet–cantors are ... plagued by ennui and a deep feeling that they are not in the mainstream of the human family. They make neither great farmers nor great fishermen; and in a society where leaders are men of action and of measurable success, poet–cantors, even though they may be respected, are never among the aristocracy of leaders.'[39]

A consideration of the Akpalu poem or song against its social and biographical background raises questions relevant, not only to the relationship of the oral artist to his society, but to the activity and sense of purpose of those writers who, like Awoonor, have attempted to reproduce part of the effect. In Akpalu, the equation between a par-

[38] Awoonor, *Guardians*, p. 19. (I have used Awoonor's own transcription conventions.)
[39] *Ibid.*

ticularized foreground and the eternal verities perceived in the far distance, is moderately clear. In the case of Awoonor, leaning on a local tradition which he half-acknowledges, and yet attempting to articulate realities relevant to the urban world in which he lives, the equation is at first less clear. Does Awoonor see himself as a *heno*? When he gives expression, as in 'Songs of Sorrow', to a personal sense of alienation, is he speaking of his seclusion from the Anlo community from which he emerged, of his hostility to contemporary cosmopolitan *moeurs*, of his disgruntlement at private misfortune, or of his feeling of political chagrin? Where does he stand in relation to a tradition for which he has undertaken to act as both chronicler and interpretative mouthpiece?

Awoonor's views as to the relationship between a modern artist and his community are explained with some care both in his historical survey *The Breast of the Earth*[40] and in interviews which he has given from time to time. His statements here show him to be as wary of sentimental over-simplification as he is of a cynical denigration of tradition. Africa is involved in a continuous process of cultural transformation – she continues to 'expand, change, adapt' – and yet the way in which she responds to these challenges reflects deeply her own complex personality. In the slow, unravelling process of 'growth and elimination' undergone by every modern African community, the poet has a vital rôle to play, for it is only through the disruptive consciousness of the poet, revealed in blinding flashes, that the zigzagging direction of the future may be seen. Thus, though relating to a community in some respects more complicated than that of the village, the contemporary literary artist may revive within himself the function of the *heno*: he too may be scorned and ignored, but only through him, as through the indigenous cantor, may the community dimly define itself.

Thus, in all of Kofi Awoonor's work, personal self-expression and social criticism proceed hand-in-hand. There are two principal reasons for this. The first is that the Anlo tradition itself embraces both norms: the 'I' of an Akpalu dirge is both the suffering individual artist, despised and often a little ridiculous, and the whole society which has

[40] Kofi Awoonor, *The Breast of the Earth: A Survey of the History, Culture and Literatures of Africa South of the Sahara* (New York: Anchor Doubleday, 1975) p. 355.

suddenly and inexplicably been plunged into mourning. The English-language poet who draws on this convention soon learns to operate in both capacities. The second is Awoonor's deep sense of responsibility toward the nation as a whole, a responsibility which extends way beyond the boundaries of Eweland to embrace the whole of suffering Ghana.

The public axis was evident in Awoonor's earliest work:

> The weaver bird built in our house
> And laid its eggs on our only tree.
> We did not want to send it away
> We watched the building of the nest
> And supervised the egg-laying.[41]

'The Weaver Bird' is a parable about missionary intrusion and colonial under-development. More specifically it is a poem about the relationship between the two: the way in which the venally-minded constantly dress up their foulest intentions in neat-fitting robes of benevolence. The poet envisages a contest between two religious systems, one securely earthed in the 'old shrines', and another which, though proclaiming its presence in the language of God and enlightened self-knowledge, manages to bring in its train the yoke of tyranny. Both appear on the surface to enjoy a basic sincerity of intention; both are described in terms of 'prayers', 'communicants' and 'altars'. It is only in the effect of their ministrations that the sharply differing aims of the two creeds may finally be seen.

Though 'The Weaver Bird' concerns a particular phase in the history of the Gold Coast, its thought processes are fundamental to the way in which Awoonor regards all periods and kinds of historical stress. There is, running through a great deal of his work, a strong concern with the language of idealism, and the way that this may be undermined by systematic misuse. The poem 'We Have Found a New Land', for instance, takes the form of a dialogue between two contrasted groups: the new élite of pampered professionals on the one hand, and, on the other, those who have remained faithful to 'the wisdom of our fathers'. Though travelling in opposite directions, both groups phrase their aspirations in the litany of meaningful pilgrimage. Say the 'smart professionals':

---

[41] Kofi Awoonor, *Night of My Blood* (New York: Anchor Doubleday, 1971), p. 37.

> We have found a new land
> This side of eternity
> Where our blackness does not matter[42]

Reply the advocates of tradition:

> Our songs are dead and we sell them dead to
>   the other side
> Reaching for the Stars we stop at the house
>   of the Moon
> And pause to relearn the wisdom of our fathers.

Even if Awoonor has weighted his account substantially in favour of the *indigènes*, the argument is potentially unending, for, however strong the claims of their opponents, the exiles are never likely to abandon either their case or their attempts to pass muster as genuine pilgrims. This, in Awoonor's eyes, is the crux of the problem. In post-colonial Africa every party or pressure group desirous of respect automatically expressed its convictions in identical language lifted from a combination of religion and left-wing polemics. To fail to dress one's claims in these borrowed robes is to admit defeat in advance. Thus the cry for justice is taken up in the slogans of the political rally which in turn disguise the haggling of the market place. There is a vivid instance of such debasement in Awoonor's poem 'March, Kind Comrade, Abreast Him'[43] where, in the streets of the new Utopia, a beggar boy slumps away from the narrator and his companions, betrayed both by their lack of charity and by 'this talk of our people and salvation'. In the closing lines, Awoonor, poet and propagandist, invites the readers to club together for a consoling donation intended to convince the vagrant of their good earnest towards 'a better world, a social world'. With everything that has gone before, however, the sentiments sound insincere even in the poet's mouth.

What hope then has the poet if even his best intentions can be undermined by precisely that process of linguistic debasement it has been his purpose to decry? For Awoonor the answer is plain. Unless he wishes to be caught up on the treadmill of recurrent apologetics, he must reach for an imagistic language which carries him well beyond the run-of-the-mill political debate. For a writer with no stock of indigenous images on which to draw, the problem would be insuperable, but for one as securely rooted as Awoonor in a precise local convention, there is material at hand. It is thus that the Anlo dirge

---

[42] *Ibid.*, p. 28.    [43] *Ibid.*, p. 30.

Anlo dirge tradition

tradition, with its established discourse of earthly disappointment, has come to play so crucial a part in Awoonor's work, supplying as it does a funereal imagery ready for transposition to the dwindling of transitory hopes, the temporal invasion of negation and despair.

The Anlos are a sub-group of the Ewe who, though now settled in the area between the rivers Volta and Mono, are believed to be a migrant people originally from Oyo in present-day Nigeria. Though there are many strands in their folklore, none has exercised a greater influence than the mythology of the journey, drawing as it does on a deeply embedded memory of a gruelling march in search of a place of lasting settlement. In much of Awoonor's work the odyssey appears in one form or another. Perhaps the most moving instance occurs in the penultimate chapter of his novel *This Earth My Brother* published in the same year as *Night of My Blood*. In the following passage Amamu, the young but much-travelled protagonist, breaks down after a stressful evening in Accra, and, tired of the buffetings of urban competition, retraces his forefathers' steps back to the village lagoon, the familiar billows bursting on the foreshore:

He had arrived home at last. The Atlantic breakers boomed across the memory of years; sea gulls careered upwards and downwards above the surf, and rose and crashed into the sand like a madman at the rise of a new moon. The tumult was the signal for the calm that was promised, it was the legend of a final peace.[44]

Needless to say, the madman to whom the gulls are compared is Amamu himself. Amamu's solace turns out to be pure illusion. He enjoys a momentary vision of his female cousin rising from the sea like Aphrodite – that creature of another myth – her young breasts swaying invitingly above the foam, but when found by children playing under the old almond tree, his body is stiff, his eyes glazed over by premature death.

Throughout much Ewe dirge poetry we find this surviving sense of an ancestral pilgrimage back to a land which on arrival is found to be desolate, its fences eaten by termites. It is a theme which the great Vinoko Akpalu turned to his private sense of futility and abandonment, and which Awoonor, late offspring of an identical tradition, has resurrected and applied both to his personal feeling of alienation and to the current plight of the people of Ghana, severed from their ancestral ties and drifting towards the rocks of ineptitude.

In Awoonor's poetry the myth of the thwarted return occurs with

[44] Kofi Awoonor, *This Earth My Brother* (London: Heinemann 1971), p. 179.

peculiar poignancy in 'Exiles',[45] one of the pieces taken into *Night of My Blood* from the earlier volume *Rediscovery*. Here, in an African reversal of a common Greek legend, Awoonor envisages the spirits of the new Africans crowding the foreshore and performing a travesty of the old dances in a pained effort to persuade the forces of life and death to allow them waftage back to the land of their birth. But the effort is futile, their cause lost in advance. Not only are the migrants already aware that the town to which they wish to return is devastated and ant-ridden, but the very language in which they are forced to express their plea is sullied by commerce with the urban society from which they are trying to escape: 'At the star's entrance the night revellers gather / To sell their chatter and inhuman sweat to the gateman.' Unable to discourse freely in their own language, their very conversation has become a means of barter. There is nothing left but to 'shuffle their feet in agonies of birth', to perform a recurrent and pointless parody of their mother's birthpangs like a neurotically obsessive rite repeated in the vain hope of readmission to their own childhood.

The 'Songs of Sorrow' originally included in *Rediscovery* were reworkings of Akpalu dirges which drew on similar feelings of exclusion and loss. In *Night of My Blood* these pieces were excluded possibly as much because of their status as near-translations as the obscurity of some of their references. Instead individual sections were inserted in the flow of a much longer poem 'Hymn to My Dumb Earth'.[46] This is an effective piece which exploits a number of different sources: childhood memories, quotations from Protestant hymns and from the Coverdale translation of the Psalms as well as from the Ewe church 'cantatas', morality plays performed locally to this day. There are also references to the modern worlds of jazz and national politics. The whole poem is a sort of poetic patchwork into which are sewn pieces of diverse origin around a recurring verbal motif: the half-trusting, half-cynical 'Everything Comes from God'. The poem is thus a simultaneous appeal to the Ewe ancestors and to the Jehovah of the missions, both of whom have decamped and fled. It is a hymn to an empty shrine couched in the language of the Anlo laments, itself the product of a faith which now appears groundless. Although based partly on the author's life, the sequence of events has a randomness of direction which comes from a drifting sense of loss barely controlled. We begin with a ragged church choir performing an anthem under the

---

[45] Awoonor, *Night of My Blood*, p. 23.    [46] *Ibid.*, pp. 82–96.

direction of Awoonor's own uncle, proceed through the time-serving careers of various acquaintances and the downward swoop of political hope in the black movement on both sides of the Atlantic during the ill-fated sixties – Nkrumah, Malcolm X, the 'African Personality', international socialist solidarity, military takeover, bankruptcy – to a funeral ceremony in which the aspirations of the people are buried once and for all. Here, across the deserts of disappointment, migration is felt as a futile gesture, and the argument of the poem is thus like the progress of a caravan in which sore-footed travellers stagger from oasis to oasis, each of which dries up as they reach it.

'Hymn to My Dumb Earth' is one of two long episodic poems which feature in *Night of My Blood*. The other is 'I Heard a Bird Cry', which tells us of a mass exodus from a country of spiritual exile back to the Promised Land. The form – narrative interspersed with meditation – is similar to that of the Hebraic Psalms 78 and 105 in which David sings of the Israelites' sojourn in the wilderness. In it Awoonor plies his customary symbols to great effect: the tree blasted by birds of prey, the sacrifice, the river crossing. The parallels with the Psalms and Anlo dirge are well conceived, since both bequeath upon the cantor a rôle as seer and judge:

> That day when they opened the sacred hut
> And made pledges to the gone-befores
> I was there.
> They wound a cloth around my loins,
> A fly-whisk in my right
> And a calabash in my left hand,
> I was there
> When we pledged to the ancestors . . . [47]

The fly-whisk is the *heno*'s staff of office: *Guardians of the Sacred Word* has a photograph of Amega Dunyo (b. 1888), another exponent of the profession, brandishing one in mock-threatening fashion at the camera. In this passage the *heno* and by implication Awoonor his successor is seen to claim authority as custodian of the covenant which the Ewes plighted with the ancestors when re-establishing the shrines at the culmination of their historic odyssey from the east. The *heno* acts as the people's memory and conscience, for in him is vested the responsibility of securing that, however far the sons and daughters of the clan roam in search of wealth and opportunity, the homeland will not be destroyed. Through him poetry becomes a means of continuity

[47] *Ibid.*, pp. 44–5.

and hence a channel of grace. It is a poetic prerogative unknown for centuries in Europe, but still in Africa conferring upon the artist a power enabling him to subsume transient considerations of style, school, theme or affiliation.

In reasserting this prerogative and this tradition, rooted in the historical imagination and deeply committed to the affirmation of life-giving values, the poetry of Kofi Awoonor illustrates Ghanaian literature at its oldest, most original and best.

# CHAPTER 7

# Two Ijǫ poets

It is possible to argue that the English-language poet in West Africa is subject to two very different kinds of pressure. The first, arising from his geographical and cultural situation, is a sense of responsibility towards the nation, the ethnic group, the intimate realities of a shared ancestral culture. The second, arising partly from the use of an international language, and partly from a heightened awareness of the cosmopolitical world of letters to which that language amongst other factors gives access, is an ambition to address a world audience in terms amenable to it. Though dying ultimately for a sectarian and local cause, Christopher Okigbo in his literary activity may be seen as an artist who succumbed to the latter temptation, and who in his determination to draw deeply on ancient springs of poetic thought and inspiration neglected an opportunity to speak more directly and unambiguously to a local audience through a language accessible to it. There are, of course, reservations that one must put: Okigbo is profoundly Igbo even at those moments, which are not rare, when he seems to have wandered far and wide in search of a Holy Grail of quintessential human wisdom. Yet for Okigbo his indebtedness to local knowledge and tradition always seems to have been something which, perhaps because of his confident possession of it, he could afford to take for granted rather than stressing as part of a deliberate programme. There are other artists, who came to the fore at the same time and via the same organs of dissemination such as the magazine *Black Orpheus*, who experienced their relationship with their own ethnic base and language in a very different way. Prominent amongst these were two men, very different in temperament and training, who came from the Ijǫ people inhabiting the mass of creeks around the mouth of the Niger delta. These were John Pepper Clark, born in 1935, university graduate, journalist, university professor, dramatist and critic; and Gabriel Okara, born in 1921, book-binder, autodidact, administrator, Biafran nationalist.

An analysis of the work of these two poets of the creeks can only be a study in contrast. It represents, however, one meaningful way of exploring the multitude of options open to those poets from West Africa who, emerging into the light of independence in the 1960s, chose to devote a large part of their energies to writing in the English tongue. To use this official, though originally borrowed language was to beset oneself with contradictions, to pose inconvenient questions both for oneself and for one's readership, to adopt an awkward and potentially contentious stance. Above all it was to involve oneself in a troubled relationship with the culture of one's first language and constantly to confront oneself with the question of how best to render an account of one's birthright through accents and inflections which derived from elsewhere. To this question the two poets here treated returned two very dissimilar answers, and a study of their work therefore pays dividends not only for our knowledge of the literary history of the period, but also for the continuing debate about the rôle of the metropolitan languages in the states of independent Africa.

The contrasting styles of these two artists is evidenced by the shape which their careers have taken. Alert to the need to establish a reputation, Clark got off to an early start: he co-founded *The Horn* while still an undergraduate, and, while still in his twenties, became co-editor of *Black Orpheus* while publishing an early volume (*Poems*) with Mbari.[1] By his early thirties he had also brought out a highly influential trilogy of plays, an account of a year's sojourn in America, and a full-length book of poetry, *A Reed in the Tide* (1965). Okara, on the other hand, careless of public esteem, also began writing early, but published nothing until the sixties when he was already well into middle age. He was forty-four when his first book, the innovative novel *The Voice*, saw the light of day,[2] and had to wait until 1978 before Heinemann brought together those pieces extant after a career of mishaps and delays into the volume *The Fisherman's Invocation* which immediately became joint winner of the Commonwealth Poetry Prize.

There is one other factor besides historical coincidence which makes a comparative study between these writers an instructive exercise: a similar ethnic background. To a very real extent, though in two different senses, both Clark and Okara are poets of landscape. Continually alert to those factors in the environment which have shaped the lives of the people about whom they write, both of them have been markedly affected by the sights, smells and sounds of the creeks

[1] John Pepper Clark, *Poems* (Ibadan: Mbari, 1962).
[2] Gabriel Okara, *The Voice* (London: André Deutsch, 1964).

amongst which they grew up, and which have supplied them with continuing metaphors of the human condition. Beyond that one cannot go. There are essential ways in which the phrase 'poet of land-scape' has to be defined so as to highlight the difference in the way that these two writers have responded to similar physical stimuli. The effort to refine this distinction is a task which will absorb us for the rest of this chapter. It would be no exaggeration to state that to grasp the diverging ways in which these two writers respond to a shared geography is to focus on the quintessential difference between them.

Undoubtedly Clark is the more literary artist of the two: the better read, the more conscious of antecedents, the more critically perspicacious. Clark has spent much of his professional life as a university teacher of English, and a familiarity with the landmarks of the British literary tradition is evident for all to see in his published work. In the Preface to *A Reed in the Tide* he goes so far as to acknowledge himself as 'that fashionable cultural phenomenon they call "mulatto" – not in flesh but in mind.' He then expands this by adding:

Coming of an ancient multiple stock in the Niger Delta area of Nigeria from which I have never quite felt myself severed, and going through the usual educational mill with the regular grind of an English school at its end, I sometimes wonder what in my make-up is 'traditional' and 'native', and what 'derived' and 'modern'.[3]

The 'usual educational grind' which Clark would have experienced in the forties and fifties in colonial Nigeria, would have consisted of the stock subjects examined by the British syllabuses then set with little or no concession to local needs; the 'grind' of the Ibadan English school consisted, as we have seen, of a chronological trek through the great English authors culminating in a study of the classics of modern English poetry: Eliot, Yeats and Hopkins. In a letter to Sunday Anozie, quoted in that critic's study of the poet Christopher Okigbo,[4] Clark mentions the fact that, in the Ibadan of the late fifties, he was often to be found urging upon the impressionable young Okigbo the necessity of writing in the style of the New Greats, by which he meant the style of twentieth-century English poetry associated with Eliot, Pound, Yeats, and especially Gerard Manley Hopkins, who, though he died in 1889, was not published in full until 1918 and whose influence therefore mainly falls within this century. It is interesting

---

[3] John Pepper Clark, *A Reed in the Tide* (London: Longman, 1965), p. vii.
[4] Sunday O. Anozie, *Christopher Okigbo: Creative Rhetoric* (London: Evans, 1972), p. 12.

that, in the above quotation, Clark associates what is 'derived' with what is 'modern', thus excluding any consideration of 'traditional' European influence. It is therefore with all the more fascination that one finds oneself scouring the texts of Clark's early poetry for evidence of the impact on his writing of the manner of the European Modernist school.

With poets of Clark's academic background and eclecticism of taste the question of the assimilation of influence often raises its head. It is a question anticipated by T. S. Eliot, a leading figure in the Modern school who had himself felt the need in his own work to come to terms with influences from earlier periods of European literature. Since Eliot is a writer whom Clark takes seriously, his words on the subject are worth quoting. In a set of lectures published in 1933 under the title *The Use of Poetry and the Use of Criticism* he has this to say about poets who feel a need to draw significantly on the achievement of earlier periods:

Just as Pope, who used what is nominally the same form as Dryden's couplet, bears little resemblance to Dryden, and as the writer today who was influenced by Pope would hardly want to use that couplet at all, so the writers who were significantly influenced by Spenser are not those who have attempted to use his stanza, which is inimitable.[5]

*! silly*

It will be seen that, in this passage, although Eliot is talking about the spreading of influence from one period of English literature to another, his point is of wider application. It has to do with the ways in which the influence of any writer permeates the skin of another. 'Influence' here is seen, not as the abrogation of the creative will and personality, the submission of one's private voice to the mannerisms of another, but as the deep-seated absorption of various technical strengths, which, when translated into the sometimes very distinct personal idiom of another writer may produce unpredictable but worthwhile results. In other words an author who exposes himself to the influence of one whom he admires may, and, if gifted with genuine originality most probably will, finish by sounding quite unlike him. And the distance he sets between his own tone and cultural bearing and those of his mentor will be the measure of the extent to which he has assimilated the influence.

Many echoes of the English poets are present in the poems included in *A Reed in the Tide*: Keats, Yeats, Eliot, but above all Gerard Manley Hopkins, whom Clark not only obviously much admires, but whom in

---

[5] T. S. Eliot, *The Use of Poetry and the Use of Criticism* (London: Faber, 1933), p. 45.

one case he explicitly imitates. 'Ibadan Dawn (after *Pied Beauty*)' is almost an academic exercise in the reproduction of an influence.

> Mist-hung curtains, adrizzle-damp, draw, fall
> Apart, spring a forward catch in the sky
> That swift over us spreads, all
> Of a lift, this fresh burst of blue, freckled dye
> In running decks
> Of quicksilver flakes and flecks.
> It is pageant fit for a bride
> Who, ah, look at! walks over there wide
> Velvet greens dipping out of sight:
> Rush outdoor concession-strong,
> Greet her with cockerel song,
> For blushing calm from flush of cam,
> Morning comes breathing flowers, warm and light
> Of limb, to charm earth from vice of night –
>     Tumble in her flaming tan!

It may be helpful then to examine the text of Clark's much anthologized poem against Hopkins's original:

> Glory be to God for dappled things –
>   For skies of couple-colour like a brinded cow;
>   For rose-moles all in stipple upon trout that swim;
> Fresh firecoal chestnut-falls; finches' wings;
>   Landscape plotted and pieced – fold, fallow, and plough;
>   And áll trádes, their gear and tackle and trim.
>
> All things counter, original, spare, strange;
>   Whatever is fickle, freckled (who knows how?)
>   With swift, slow; sweet, sour; adazzle, dim;
> He fathers-forth whose beauty is past change:
>     Praise him.[6]

It will immediately be seen that, while both poets are praising natural beauty, Hopkins is praising its general diversity grounded in God's unchanging wisdom, while Clark is praising one particular instance of it: dawn over the great southern Nigerian city which he compares to an Ijọ bride coming out in all her camwood-dyed splendour. This contrast in itself is sufficient clue to the different mental cast of the two poets, one the theologian of nature, drenched in Duns Scotus and the scholastic Fathers, the other a lover of his native landscape which he rightly interprets by comparison with

---

[6] Clark, *A Reed in the Tide*, p. 13. *A Decade of Tongues, Selected Poems 1958–1968* (London: Longman, 1981), p. 61, *The Poems of Gerard Manley Hopkins*, eds. W. H. Gardner and N. H. Mackenzie (Oxford University Press, 1967), pp. 69–70.

sights and customs with which he is intimately familiar. What they share is an instinct for *particularity*, which Hopkins with his theories of 'inscape' and 'instress' sees as the token of God's concern for particular creatures, and Clark as the hallmark of a special kind of local authenticity. There are then grounds of genuine, though partial, affinity. But Clark has gone one step further – as he is entitled to do in what is, after all, an academic exercise – and borrowed from Hopkins certain verbal and stylistic tricks. These are a marked syntactical concentration, particularly in the opening lines, a profusion of short words of Anglo-Saxon origin, an ample use of alliteration ('flakes and flecks'), and the imperative clause tacked on to the end. With the possible exception of the last line, no parts of the poem are, however, recognizably modelled on 'Pied Beauty' itself. The detectable echoes from Hopkins are from other poems, from 'The Windhover' and 'Hurrahing in Harvest'. Above all, however, there is little organizational affinity, no clear sense in which the Clark poem works like the Hopkins, or even addresses itself to the same end. Thus, both as a deliberate attempt at imitation, and an example of the deeper assimilation of an influence 'Ibadan Dawn' fails. There is not even any clear indication that Clark has seized on the essence of 'Pied Beauty' and tried to do something of interest with it. What we have is a slight similarity of theme, decked out in borrowed colours which do scant justice to the real originality of the Hopkins poem, the ways in which it genuinely experiments with language, metre and other poetic resources.

By contrast, examine the complementary poem 'Ibadan' printed on the opposite page of the original Longman edition. Here is no encrusted syntax, no verbal affectation, no flourish in the direction of a half-digested influence. 'Ibadan' too is a deliberate exercise after another model: the Imagist school which inspired so many of the French poets towards the end of the nineteenth century. The Imagists believed that, in the text of a poem, the image should stand stark and efficient, unsupported by explanation, extrapolation, or any other means of teasing out its hidden meaning. This 'Ibadan' manages to achieve perfectly, though the impression, it is true, is purely visual, and Clark has elected for the more explicit medium of the simile rather than the sharper device of direct metaphor. Nevertheless it is a poem which exploits perfectly what, at this stage in his career, must be seen as Clark's supreme gift: his ability to convey sensual impressions through the use of carefully selected images.

*facile judgement*

That Clark is quite conscious of this as his main strength is obvious from the line of argument in his essay 'The Legacy of Caliban', originally printed in *Black Orpheus*, and later collected in his important volume of essays *The Example of Shakespeare*.[7] Here he argues that, for an African poet writing in English, there are two ways of conveying local flavour: the disruption of the natural flow of the English language so as to suggest indigenous idiomatic patterns, and the injection into the bloodstream of English of images which derive from the poet's own environment. The former technique he believes to be fraught with dangers and absurdities, many of which he illustrates from the work of Gabriel Okara. On the contrary, he comes down very firmly in favour of the imagistic method as a means of guaranteeing local self-respect and relevance. When writing this essay Clark was clearly more concerned about the problems of a working dramatist than the dilemma of the lyric poet, and much of his argument centres on the need to delineate character and the social shading between different classes and national and professional groups. Nevertheless, the relevance of his remarks to the task of the poet is obvious, and helps alert us to the mainstay of his own poetic strength.

Of the pertinacity of these observations, the justly much anthologized 'Night Rain' stands as supreme exemplar. Clark's object here is to achieve the immediacy of impressions felt by a pre-pubescent child safe within his mother's hut against the challenges and mystery of the world outside. The present tense plays a vital rôle here, as does the use of the first person singular for a vividly remembered earlier self. The first sentence demonstrates just how, at his very best, Clark manages to assimilate a specific influence into the lyric flow of naturally expressed feeling. 'And no cocks crow' is clearly indebted to the line 'and no birds sing' from Keats's 'La Belle Dame Sans Merci', yet the sense of desolation is so similar, and the progress of the syntax so inevitable, that we are able to recall the influence without being in any sense startled by it. The image of the fish, anaesthetized for easy catching, falls both within the experience of the Delta community described, and of a child who, growing up beside the creeks, must have observed this fishing method daily and is hence able, in the dim twilight world between dream and waking, to apply it to himself without any sense of strain. The rhythm too is of much assistance here, conveying, without artifice or a deliberate break of stride, the contrast between the regular droning insistence of the

[7] John Pepper Clark, *The Example of Shakespeare* (London: Longman, 1970).

downpour on the roof, and the dribbling motion of the water as it finds its way around the eaves. Thus lines like

> And nó cócks crów

and

> Our roóf thatćh and shéd[8]

provide a background pulse against which the insinuated graphic diffuseness of

> Fruits showered forth in the wind
> Or perhaps I should say so
> Much like beads I could in prayer tell
> Them on a string[9]

can make itself felt. There is a great sense of awe here, but no sense of alarm, since the spiritual sensations of the child are firmly anchored in the reassuring presence of the mother, who herself appears disarmingly mid-sentence at line 22. Whether a word like 'deploying' is fit parlance for a ten-year-old child hardly matters, since Clark is not indulging in direct speech, however expertly deflected: he is concerned with conveying an equivalent, expressed in skilful adult language (and, coincidentally in English) for the perplexed, half-formulated thought-processes of a young boy. The boy's senses are alive to all around him, yet it is less his sensual perceptions than his state of mind which Clark is ultimately aiming to reproduce. Those who follow the logic of the poem through from the line 'I know her practised step' will notice that the 'spell deeper than the owl's or bat's' of which the child speaks in the concluding peroration is less the haunting experience of the rainstorm itself – though that is important – than the experience of security and wholesomeness provided by the mother, who in her reliability and resourcefulness is able to give her children a sensation of unity and belonging of which the insects on the *iroko* outside know nothing. The finest moment in the piece occurs at the end, where the telepathic movements of the brothers as they turn over together on the mat combines perfectly and naturally with the heaving of the familiar waves and the rush and lull of the rain outside. This sense of pervading motion, of elemental natural forces combining with the intimate movements of the household, gives these lines a compulsive strength rare in Clark's output.

[8] Clark, *A Reed in the Tide*, p. 2. (*A Decade of Tongues*, p. 6.)
[9] *Ibid.*, p. 2 (*A Decade of Tongues*, p. 6.)

It is an irresistible thought that this poem, which has as its theme the security and peace achieved by the shared values and a settled environment, is most successful because it rests on poetic resources in which Clark the poet is himself most secure: direct, unadulterated local imagery and unambiguous syntax. It is a technique employed with almost equal success when reaching out from a basis of confident, shared experience, he manages to confront the mystery of personalities which, while inhabiting the poet's geographical space, partake of elements of suffering or tragedy to which he has no private access. The most successful of these are 'Fulani Cattle' and 'Abiku', printed opposite one another in the original edition. 'Fulani Cattle' is a piece in which the straggling, undulating motion of a cattle train as it meanders from the far north to the markets of the south is imitated by a subtle system of staggered rhymes and half-rhymes. The rhyme scheme itself is irregular and complicated (a/a/b/c/c/d/b/d/b/e/f/e/e etc.), yet the effect is due less to its eccentricity than the way in which the repeated elements (notably b, d and e) are driven through the text, much like a drover urging on the reluctant members of a herd. The theme of the poem comes from the fusion of the cattles' pain, intimated at second hand, with the guilt which the poet feels as one who, as a participant in the market economy, has collaborated in bringing the animals to this pass. A niggling doubt here is as to whether this sentiment, with its elevation of transient 'contrition' to the status of a tragic emotion, is sufficient to support the weight of the poem. The enterprise is only feasible if its message is taken to include, not merely casually inflicted guilt, but the eventual confrontation with death which the poet must also endure. There is a strenuousness of feeling, a bracing of the spiritual sinews, which lends support to this interpretation, as well as enabling us to appreciate the force of some of the poem's rhythms:

> Sŏ mūte ănd fiērce ănd wān . . .
> Ăs trūe thĕ long kñife mūst prĕvāil[10]

These are lines which speak of a certain heroic torsion in the face of inexplicable suffering which lends the piece more dignity than it seems at first to possess. The last but one line in particular, with its sense of indefinitely suspended nemesis lends the seeming pathetic fallacy of the end the sort of gravity which redeems it from triviality or wistfulness.

[10] *Ibid.*, p. 2. (*A Decade of Tongues*, p. 4.)

'Abiku', addressed to the shade of a repeatedly stillborn child, takes us back to the voice and manner of 'Night Rain'; yet it too is directed at a source of mystery outside the community's immediate comprehension. The dead child with its unearthly appearances and disappearances, is of the family and yet not of it, and it is the attempt to resolve this paradox and to bring the threatening phenomenon safely within the confines of the accountable, that occupies the poet. The logic of the first sentence is cogent and irrefutable: either the child accepts the invitation to stay, or else proves itself 'kindred' not to the family but to a society of malign spirits. Beyond this the poem does not go, since, though rooted in traditional Nigerian belief, it makes explicit no theology, relying for its enticements simply on the child's natural preference for warmth and protection. It is thus that the familiar scents and sounds which Clark is so good at conveying prove integral to the thought of the poem: if the *abiku* rejects these comforts it proves itself no worthy guest. The symmetry of the poem, its balance of inclusiveness and exclusiveness, is once again helpfully underscored by the line movement. The welcoming gesture of the closing invitation, for instance, is counterposed by a warning which lends the break in the middle of line 17 the significance of a fulcrum between reassurance and threat:

> But step in and stay
> For good. We know the knife scars[11]

The urgency of the argument issues in the repetition of the last four lines with their imitation of a fretful voice torn between exhortation and conciliation.

The further he moves away from the intimacies of inherited geography and thought, the less successful Clark is. 'The Imprisonment of Obatala', for example, is an attempt to render a Yoruba myth within densely packed regular stanzas. Yet the theology of the *orisas*, amongst whom Obatala, god of creation, numbers, belongs to the forest world of south western Nigeria rather than the creeks, and Clark is less purveying a legend integral to his people than describing a picture.

Susanne Wenger, wife of the critic and literary entrepreneur Ulli Beier, had in the early sixties set up a studio at Oshogbo close to Ibadan where Clark had studied. Her style of batik painting and copper relief were to influence a whole generation of Nigerian artists

---

[11] *Ibid.*, p. 5. (*A Decade of Tongues*, p. 3.)

to whom she contributed a visual language to flesh out images already welling within the mythical imagination. Yet it is not on the mythical imagination that this poem with its convoluted syntax, its apostrophes and ellipses, relies. The convolutedness of the first stanza is justifiable as a reaction to the complex visual impact of the figures themselves, all waving arms and legs. Yet there is something perverse about the phrase 'in His front' meaning 'in front of him' and the way in which such an ill-assorted sentence prepares the way for so fine a line, its relative length imitative of complete prostration, as 'Invincible limbs cramped by love of their strength'. The second stanza, which describes the spilling of Eṣu's pot of misfortunes, moves with more assurance, yet overdoes its alliteration, 'spilt' suggesting the rhyme 'stilt' which necessitates 'stagnant' which brings in its train a whole bunch of subsidiary alliterations throughout the last three lines. Here once again, one cannot help but feel, is the baneful influence of Hopkins, whose dead hand lies too on the very last line of the poem with its dense conjunction of 'droop, mud-crack and clot'. Other doubts persist: how conscious, for example, is the pun on 'trebly' as applied to a child's cry? How can a 'tattoo', which means either a carefully marshalled military entertainment, or a dexterous pattern of pigment applied under the skin, be kicked 'impatiently'? Once again, the simplest line 'generations unborn spared the wrong', applied to exemption from Obatala's occasional bungling creation of cripples and lunatics, is the most effective. Once again also, however, the poem leaves behind in the mouth the dry taste of an academic exercise, with its painful negotiation of stanzaic structure, its inversions, its remoteness, its aping of a borrowed manner.

Two poems in honour of women, 'Agbor Dancer' and 'Girl Bathing' find Clark struggling, not this time with Hopkins, but with the ghost of the English Romantic Revival. Both are village women, yet seen with the alienated eye of educated adulthood rather than the quick insight of the child which informs the passages of the mother in 'Night Rain'. Caught by the contradiction between his evident homage and his sense of having moved beyond a community where simple admiration is possible, Clark is forced back on the posture of Wordsworth's 'Highland Lass' with its wistful seeking after a lost innocence. 'In 'Agbor Dancer' Clark protests that he wishes to 'lose' himself in the embrace both of the girl and of enveloping nature, both of which seem to correspond to the 'ancestral core' of which he abstractly speaks in the first stanza. Yet the core of the earth and of tradition, the abundance of nature and a woman's flesh have links only valid in the over-heated romantic imagination. The poem thus possesses a wobbly moral focus which explains its flushed phraseology, its 'hide-brimmed stem', its 'tremulous beats', its 'virginal habits' (clothes, customs?). There is throughout a debilitating sense that Clark is seeking to persuade us of something of which he is himself inadequately convinced, namely that the girl in her naïve unsophistication possesses a freedom which he, with his advantages of education and status, does not have. There is also something dishonest about the way in which the fall of the apostrophes of 'sequester'd' and 'lead-tether'd' contrive to persuade us of the constraints of a 'lead-tethered' style, when Clark is so obviously able to write directly and out of his own immediate experience when he wishes to. When dealing with such subjects, with their inbuilt overload of romantic association, Clark too easily reclines on bad habits he is elsewhere free of, the self-conscious rhyming couplets of 'Girl Bathing' being a case in point. 'Rearing breast' suggests 'blest', an adjective quite alien to the subject of the poem, except in its bathetic sense of 'those who are fortunate enough to get close to her'. This falsity of association, however, is not unique to the end rhymes. 'Splash, splash', itself anticlimactic, brings in its train the clichéd description of her teeth as 'flashing pearls'. It is a relief to turn to the direct childrens' play song 'Hands over Head' with its warning against the dangers of smallpox. Here the actions suggested by written-in stage directions justify the jaunty regularity of the stanza form, making exclamations and abbreviations seem natural and part of a shared vital lore. Clark has ceased to gloat and admire from a distance, throwing himself once again into the hurly-burly of what he knows and loves.

Clark's talent then, at least in this volume, seems to consist in an ability to summon up the sights and sounds which derive from a specific geography. At his best he relies on the techniques over which he has complete control: a colourful use of adjective, of image, of cultural reference, and a coherent, locally derived symbolism. Two further poems, 'The Year's First Rain' and 'Flight Across Africa', illustrate the rewards and risks of the symbolic method. 'The Year's First Rain' compares the eruption of the rainy season to an act of sexual intercourse, possibly between two human beings, but more probably between a woman (the earth) and a god. There is something about the energy and momentousness of the description which recalls Yeats's famous sonnet 'Leda and the Swan' in which the sensation of absolute possession is much the same. The energy of the first few lines derives from a sense of taut expectation, achieved by careful repetition and the emphasized use of adjective and adjectival phrase. At this point Clark wants to weigh us down with a sense of burdensome deprivation: he does this by coupling adjectives together in multiple phrases which intensify their effect. This is useful when the inspiration originates in his own mind: 'hot-breathing' is fine, but 'kestrel-together-leaf flaps' goes too far and is again too reminiscent of Hopkins. He then releases the tension by suggesting the amorous foreplay of the lovers in a series of shorter lines, unfortunately ruining the effect by the application of one contrived rhyme; 'tingles to the trump' is pompous and comes from a different mythical universe from that which Clark is invoking. The poem is saved in the last few lines where the delighted, lithe movements of the triumphant male are perfectly caught in the rolling movement of the lines

> Thrusts, he strokes her, swamps her,
> Enters all of him beyond her fell.[12]

The sense of post-coital ease too is wonderfully distilled as the last two lines open up to a mood of relaxed fulfilment.

'Flight Across Africa' compares the landscape seen from an aeroplane window to the carcass of an animal sacrificed to ensure a safe journey. The idea is a difficult one, and the treatment less than convincing. A 'calf' is either a young animal or the lower section of its leg. If the former, it is too frail and too vulnerable for this setting; if the latter, it is hard to see to which element in the landscape it is supposed to correspond. Moreover, the second half of the poem seems to contradict the beginning, for the earth is a sacrifice which obeys few of the specified conditions. There are admittedly some vivid words which tell us much about the impression of virgin bush seen from the air: 'pummel', 'ulcerated', 'carved'. The imbalance lies in the weakness of the organizing idea. Who, carrying the symbolism through, are the 'butchers' that kill the beast for this 'strange sacrifice'? 'Butchers' too is an inappropriate word for the attendants at a solemn ritual such as that envisaged. Clark is in the grip of an idea which he evidently finds it hard to sustain. We are thus left with the impression of a vivid but spoiled poem.

Apart from 'Flight Over Africa' all of the above poems originally appeared in Clark's apprentice volume *Poems* (Mbari, 1962) and were

---

[12] *Ibid.*, p. 14. (*A Decade of Tongues*, p. 17.)

later reprinted in *A Reed in the Tide* (1965). Virtually all of the better pieces from the earlier book were taken over into the later volume, where most were reproduced without alteration. However, there is one notable exception. One of the triumphs of the earlier book was the long sequence in six movements entitled 'Ivbie: A Song of Wrong'. When Clark came to issue *A Reed in the Tide* he unaccountably decided to confine his selection from 'Ivbie' to movements 4 and 6, and to omit its helpful sub-title. As a result, even the extensive notes which he provided could not redeem this impressive poem from the general incomprehensibility caused solely by its severe truncation. The omission was not redressed until the appearance in 1981 of Clark's retrospective volume *A Decade of Tongues*[13] where 'Ivbie: A Song of Wrong' elucidates itself as a prolonged meditation on the theme of colonial intervention seen from the vantage point of the inhabitants of an Ijọ village. Clark obviously felt that it was the apprehension of communal threat, expressed by the villagers in movements 4 and 6, which represented the strength of the poem. He thus confined himself in 1965 to these movements without realizing that without the inclusion of the remainder the nature of the threat itself was entirely unclear.

The structure of 'Ivbie', with its six 'movements' and its theme of the passing away of the ancient certainties of a civilization, recalls T. S. Eliot's *The Waste Land* (1922). Similar too is its poetic method, the assembling of a collage of many voices: a traditional woman's lament, a lullaby, the recreated proclamations of Oyin, the creator goddess. There are also recognizable echoes, the 'Sweet Mrs Gamp, not a coward', of movement 2 recalling 'Mrs Porter and her daughter' from 'The Fire Sermon', and the prophetic strains of Oyin at the very end coming very close both in their sense of patient foreboding and even a certain turn of phrase to the passage, also from 'The Fire Sermon', in which Tiresias, the blind seer, foresuffers the fate of modern industrial civilization. Clark is, however, a great deal more in control of his borrowings here than in his Hopkinsesque pieces, managing to recruit the gravity of Eliot without subordinating himself to it. He has taken on a large theme, and by so doing courts the dangers of pretentiousness to which he is elsewhere prone. If there are moments when the poem sinks under the weight of its philosophical speculation, Clark's talent is seen at its most impressive when it alights on detail and thereby enhances the immediacy of his meaning. Take, from the

---

[13] 'Two decades' might have been a more apt title for this volume, which conveniently collects most of Clark's poetry since 1958.

first movement, the marvellous lines:

> How can they catch
> the thousand
>      intricacies
> Tucked away in crannies
> And corners known perhaps only
>      to rats?
> How can they tell the loin-cloth
> Cast away in the heat of desire
> The shifts hanging in the wind
> Now groins want oiling?[14]

These attack the eye and gut, where the opening lines of the second movement with their cumbersome moralizing merely dizzy the head:

> In the irresolution
> Of one unguarded moment
> Thereby hangs a tale
> A tale so tall in implications
> Universal void cannot contain
> The terrible immensity
> Nor its permanence dissolve
> In the flux wash of eternity.[15]

The former makes of the cultural myopia of the invaders something vivid and real; in its cerebral effort to convince us of the complacency of the villagers in their own defence, the latter merely loses us in a welter of abstraction.

With this contrast in mind we can see why, in selecting extracts for the 1965 volume, Clark's preference fell on movement 4, where generalization is kept to a minimum. This movement portrays the violation of communal proprieties in the guise of a visitation by an evil spirit, an experience Clark conveys from three related points of view: the village folk in general, the mothers of the town, and lastly but most ominously, Oyin herself. The opening, with its solemn tone of rapt supplication, is marred only by an untimely quotation from Robert Burns. Otherwise it captures perfectly that sense of ambiguous reverence – half-respectful, half-resentful – with which the faithful regard those forces which have complete control over their destiny. A change of tone in the second verse paragraph immerses us once again in the intimacies of communal life. At line 16 we revert to the por-

---

[14] Clark, *A Decade of Tongues*, p. 24. The poem first appeared in *The Horn*, Vol. 2, No. 2, 1958, pp. 2–15.      [15] *Ibid.*, p. 25.

tentous inflections of a goddess addressing her devotees. Remarkable is the way in which in lines 20 to 26 the voice of Oyin blends with those of the town's women-folk to create an overwhelming sense of shared loss and taboo. Here the movement of the verse picks up the light, stealthy tread of the ghost as it edges its way past traditional defences:

> Fear him his footfall soft light
> As a cat's, his shadow far darker
> Than forest gloom or night.[16]

Movements 5 and 6 once again change perspective; this time to the educated élite of contemporary Nigeria with their new-found affluence and lack of ease with traditional manners. It is an attitude with which Clark both associates and disassociates himself, the 'you and I' of the beginning of the fifth movement, addressed to a fellow bourgeois, counter-balancing the tone of lofty distance in the closing lines of the poem:

> Pass on in mad headlong flight
> O pass on, your ears right
> Full of throttle sound[17]

In this closing section Clark once again falls foul of his wilful romanticism, portraying himself as 'an innocent in sleep of ages', one who has been 'reared here on cow-dung floor'. No two phrases could highlight to greater effect the difference between Clark the authentic chronicler of local life witnessed in 'Night Rain' and the stronger passages from 'Ivbie', and Clark the bogus expostulator of the virtues of naïveté as seen in 'Girl Bathing' and in this the last section of 'Ivbie', in other ways his most sustained and substantial achievement.

'Ivbie' is the longest of the poems taken over from *Poems* (1962) and part transplanted into *A Reed in the Tide*. The rest of the later volume is largely devoted to pieces written during Clark's tenure of the Parvin Fellowship at the University of Princeton, USA during the academic year 1963–4. This group of poems is extracted from the text of Clark's prose account of his transatlantic voyage *America, Their America* (1964) in which they act as a trenchant poetic commentary.[18]

*America, Their America* is a highly personal record of eight turbulent months. In the States Clark was an honest and energetic observer who though, as he himself admits, weighed down with prejudices which

---

[16] *Ibid.*, p. 28.     [17] *Ibid.*, p. 32.
[18] John Pepper Clark, *America, Their America* (London: André Deutsch, 1964).

stemmed from his own environment, was initially prepared to put these feelings aside and to judge of things as he found them. He was expected to follow a concentrated programme of lectures and classes designed to impress upon him the superiority of the American way of life. Instead he preferred to take his time, establish his own elbow room, gather impressions – and write. The result was official displeasure and the abrupt termination of his fellowship. The tone of the book is somewhat affected by this disastrous débâcle, and there are those who find *America, Their America* a rambling, tetchy, ill-mannered diatribe. On re-reading it, however, one is struck by the candour of Clark's manner, his willingness to give honour where it is due, and by the fact that the worst strictures which he metes out to the host country amount to no more than a demand that it should live up to its professed democratic principles. Throughout he pays tribute to the courage and friendliness of Afro-American friends in whom he found all the warmth and good humour lacking elsewhere. Moreover, his months in America were far from wasted, since as he informs his Director of Programme in the closing pages of his account he had 'done a couple of plays and written a number of poems'. The plays – *The Masquerade* and *The Raft* – are now a permanent part of the African repertoire.[19] The poems found their way into *A Reed in the Tide*.

The American poems follow faithfully the course of Clark's progressive alienation and disillusionment. 'Boeing Crossing', which does not appear in his prose account, records the mood of bustling expectation with which Clark, then a novice journalist, approached the shores of the New World. There is excitement at the variety of human activity on board the aeroplane, each passenger bound on private adventures of his own, each man and woman in the American sense their own pioneer. It is an occasional journalistic piece which nevertheless succeeds in establishing two important facts. The first is Clark's initial fascination with the diversity of types which make up American society from self-made tycoon to self-styled adventurer. The second is his grim compensatory determination not to be taken in by what he finds on his arrival. The very last line, with its rejuvenation of a piece of stock proverbial wisdom, acts as a note of foreboding for what is to follow.

'Three Moods of Princeton', written shortly after Clark had installed

---

[19] John Pepper Clark, *Three Plays: Song of a Goat, The Masquerade, The Raft* (London and Ibadan: Oxford University Press, 1964).

himself on the campus, and published in an earlier version at the end of the first chapter of *America, Their America*, represents a goodnatured attempt to pay the expected compliment. The pieces were nevertheless, as Clark records, 'considered brickbats by those who regard the place as a shrine'. It is hard to see why. The theme of these pieces, intimately related to the concerns of Clark's Nigerian poems, is the fact and the metaphor of rootedness. Clark notes the stark beauty of the Autumn landscape with its great drifts of burnished leaves and the austere eloquence of denuded tree trunks piercing the desolate skyline. Yet the image of antlers and the verb 'prick' contrive to suggest a hidden violence, a harsh abrasiveness from which the poet wishes to dissociate himself, and which he fancifully connects with the withering of the leaves themselves. Both seem manifestations of a latent threat which the poet, himself rooted in a kinder soil, must hold at a distance if he wishes to retain his integrity. The image of the hands, which recurs in the second piece, conjures up a procession of memories: of the soft hands which hypocritically welcomed him on his arrival, soon to withdraw into stiffness (an almost invariable pattern in his American relationships as Clark himself sourly notes), the hands of the woman who seduced him on his arrival in his New York hotel room with a routine of instant, processed sex; and, lastly, as the strategic verb 'lash' makes clear, the hands which have enslaved his brothers over the centuries. The closing lines express the poet's determination to remain true to his natural spontaneity and to resist the habits of rejection which seem natural in the host country.

The second poem compares the snow-coated elm trees seen outside his room window to the *alufa*, Fulani traders of northern Nigeria, but then goes on in the original version, which links sections 2 and 3 with the words 'and ask of', to connect the fall of snow with the leaf fall described earlier, both of which are seen as being engineered by alluring hands which spread over the sufferer 'this bed / of bile'. As the snow metamorphoses first into a sheet and then into a shroud, he is prompted to ask whether this foreshadows his own death since 'all the world is a mushroom pie', vulnerable to instant extinction by nuclear holocaust. It is at this stage that a muted political note makes itself felt, anticipating the concerns of the rest of the volume.

The poem 'Cuba Confrontation' was, as Clark's documentary account makes clear, written shortly after a visit to the offices of *The Washington Post*, arranged for him as a foreign journalist by the organizers of his programme, at which the merits and demerits of President Kennedy's Cuba blockade were discussed.[20] Clark was asked for his opinion of the official American reaction to the discovery of Soviet bases in the Caribbean, and replied that, though an understandable rejoinder to detected danger, the decision to confront the Russian government openly could only endanger the cause of world peace for which the Administration ostensibly stood. The poem itself puts the matter more forcefully. Kennedy, and behind him the might of America, is compared to a lizard – not, of course, the small skittish variety common in Europe, but the large ornate monster with the gorgeous orange head familiar throughout West Africa. The lizard threatens, yet when the blow falls, its head, with its vivid encrustations, transforms itself into a prostitute's tiara, laid down for mere gain. The theme is taken up again in the next but one poem 'Home from Hiroshima', written during a sponsored visit to Washington. Clark had heard much, during his stay in the States, of Kennedy's famous New Frontier programme and the vaunted attempts by officials of the State Department to foster in international affairs a fresh policy of meaningful co-existence. Yet his months in the States coincided with a series of events which combined to give this rationale the lie: first the Cuba incident, then increasing friction with blacks in the south and in the northern cities. His poem neatly points to the discrepancy, summoning up the presidential (and, by association, imperial) image of the eagle, then shedding its feathers to remind us of the death of thousands of native Americans and those slaughtered in the search for an earlier frontier. Thus the violence of the pioneers of the old West merges with the implied violence of the new breed of liberal politicians as they remorselessly assert national claims in the name of peace and progress.[21]

As the sequence progresses, Clark's view of the state of modern America comes to be dominated increasingly by the perspective of the victim, whether imprisoned black, disinherited Indian, alienated city-dweller or simply lonely, frustrated outsider. In his first few months Clark had been much affected by the case of James Meredith, the black southern student who, taking the new government's open-door educational policy at face value, had the temerity to register at the all-white University of Mississippi, only to be greeted by a hail of abuse and missiles. After a day visiting black friends, during which he saw television news footage of Meredith's protective body-guard, Clark

[20] Clark, *America*, p. 32.     [21] *Ibid.*, p. 47–9.

woke from a period of fitful sleep to write 'I wake to the touch'. The poem is a re-creation of his dream which 'turned out to be one nightmare featuring my brother and James Meredith all mixed up in one terrible rôle and struggle for identity and survival'.[22] At the time Clark's brother was serving in the Nigerian diplomatic mission in Delhi; it is he who in the poem is seen as brandishing a stick, a weapon in his fight for Third World solidarity, only to be victimized by the very language he is obliged to employ. Stick into snake: it is a metamorphosis familiar from the Book of Exodus. Yet here the deadliness of the snake the brother finds himself holding is suffused with the hideous novelty of threatening nuclear extinction. The irrationality of the symbolism disguises the rigour of the underlying thought. In a world in which the slogans of liberation are used by self-seeking politicians to justify crude acts of aggression, any statement of revolutionary intent, however earnest, may turn out to be a two-edged weapon in the service of imperial interests. As his head clears and the nightmare recedes, the poet is able to make sense of his surroundings, hemmed in by presences deceptively fair, yet for all that a potential victim in this land, ruled as it still apparently is by the code of the Wild West.

The conflation of the legend of Moses with the theme of nuclear threat reappears in the poem 'Service' in which, under cover of a light *jeu d'esprit* at the expense of America's instant pre-packed culture, Clark comments on the technological menace underlying a society which requires immediate remote-controlled gratification of its every fad and whim. The preference which leads to the monopolization by advertising of television space that could be more humanely allotted to sympathetic coverage of massacres in the Congo (or retrospectively to a programme about the Spanish Civil War) can only lead to a casual dismissal of the realities of violence. This thought is itself part of a critique, persistent in these closing pages, of a kind of cowardice embedded in American culture, an inability to face life straight and consequent reliance on easy substitutes. This strain in the national psyche affects not only politics but personal relationships as well, as the poems about Marilyn Monroe and Times Square make clear. Clark, together with many West Africans of his generation, had been reared on the celluloid myth of the infinite desirability of American women, epitomized by Monroe. Yet, arriving in this reputed sexual paradise, he found himself deeply disappointed by the girls he met whom he found tasteless, spineless and ultimately without appeal.

[22] *Ibid.*, p. 62.

The first of the views of Monroe is a lament, a poem of loss, in which he records the death of his teenage dream of ultimate satisfaction. The sirens still call down the crowded avenues, yet Clark is left mourning the demise of that unique symbol who might help revive his adolescent fantasies. Consummation when it comes arrives in the form of a pneumatic pillow offering superficial sensual solace without feeling or tenderness. As Clark records the destruction of his dream, the image of the hands, familiar from 'Three Moods of Princeton', returns, this time nicotine-stained and flagrant in their hypocrisy.

Clark spent much of the time in the period between the cessation of his fellowship and his departure for Africa nosing around New York The result was two pieces, 'Times Square' and 'Cave Call', which have to do with the feeling of neutrality experienced in a large city. Of the two 'Times Square' is the more effective. By portraying dawn as a corpse, victim perhaps in some 'B' movie, and then conveying the emptiness of the early morning scene through a parody of meaningless, bleary-eyed sex, he selects the perfect images for the essential sterility that lies behind the paste-board façade of midtown Manhattan. Then by comparing his sight-seeing self to a scarecrow abandoned in a lonely Nigerian homestead, he brings into play a network of associations from earlier in the volume to persuade us of the essential superiority of the rural way of life. By contrast 'Cave Call' is an essay in farce, a tragi-comic account of an attempt to disembark from a crowded subway train, beginning with a pointless importation from Matthew Arnold's 'Dover Beach', and ending with a sense of relief clumsily etched out with forced grammatical inversions. There could be fewer more conclusive demonstrations than this of the narrow boundary between Clark's strengths and his weaknesses, his ability, grounded in 'the example of Shakespeare', to bring detail to life through a sharp choice of images, contrasted with his calamitous tendency, when wishing to impress us with his versatility, of overloading his canvas with colour and incident to the point at which perspective fails and a general dinginess prevails.

        ☽                ☽                ☽

Clark is himself aware of the sources of his main strength, as we can see from this summary of the options open to the African poet of English expression:

His best way to a new and genuine mode of expression seems to lie in a reliance upon the inner resources of language. These are images, figures of meaning and speech, which with expert handling can achieve a kind of blood transfusion, reviving the English language by the living adaptable properties of another language.[23]

This, however, is less by way of confirming his own success in this direction than of laying down the law to his fellow Ijǫ writer Gabriel Okara, whom he is accusing of a special sort of linguistic pretentiousness. For Clark, Okara's cardinal sins, as exemplified in his novel *The Voice* (1964), are occasion for strictures of potentially universal application:

For the African writer in a European language, the use of external and formalistic devices like special syntax and sentence structures from the vernacular, although tempting, carries with it risks that can lead even the genius to disaster.[24]

Okara, it is perhaps needless to add, is not regarded by Clark as a genius, or his novel as being anything but patchily successful. *The Voice*, however, does provide him with an interesting test case of an intriguing but he believes doomed experiment: the surgical transplantation of idioms, phrases and actual syntax from one language, to another. Clark urges transfusion as opposed to transplantation, a more subtle and altogether less dramatic process.

These remarks are significant here insofar as they impinge on Okara's activity as a poet. *The Voice*, though its publication preceded that of *The Fisherman's Invocation* by fourteen years, is contemporary with the best pieces in that book. It is also, as Arthur Ravenscroft maintains, very much a poet's novel. The density of the poetic charge, and the insistent reliance on such devices as ellipsis can be observed in a passage such as this:

'Do not ask the bottom of things,' Chief Izongo said after laughing a surface water laugh. 'Do not ask the bottom of things, my friend. I want you and that is the end.' 'You have to tell me the bottom of *it*,' Okolo insisted. 'Do not ask the bottom of things. I have told you so many times. Now let me give you some teaching words,' Chief Izongo said, lowering his voice. 'Listen. Asking the bottom of things in this town will get you no place. Hook this with your little finger. Put it in your inside's box and lock it up.' 'Your teaching words do not enter my inside. If it is a thing with a good bottom. Why not send a messenger?' Okolo asked.

[23] Clark, *The Example of Shakespeare*, p. 37.      [24] *Ibid.*, p. 37.

'You mean my wanting you has a bad bottom', Chief Izongo said, laughing a laugh that was no laughter. 'Was it not you who one day gave us such teaching words from your books which say what I may eat may be a man-killing medicine to another person? My wanting you may be man-killing medicine to you, but it is the best food for my body.'

He then looked at Okolo and laughed. 'I have held him with his own teaching words,' he said turning to the crowd and raising his hands in triumph.[25]

John Pepper Clark's objections to such a passage are first that expressions like 'my wanting you has a bad bottom' represents an entirely unreliable translation out of the Ijọ, and secondly that, in the context of a passage in which Okara is clearly trying to achieve weird and wonderful things with the English language, straightforward formulations like 'turning to the crowd raising his hands in triumph' sit awkwardly, as do half-baked Americanisms like 'asking the bottom of things in this town will get you no place'. Both criticisms are probably just but Clark's comments do scant justice to another essential aspect of Okara's art: his attempt to reproduce an entire world-view through a manipulation of key expressions, rooted elsewhere than in standard usage, gradually refining their meaning through a process of structured repetition. *The Voice* is a book about a clash of value systems, and this conflict is registered most keenly in the arresting use of such expressions as 'inside' (Ijọ: *biri*), it (Ijọ: *iye*), 'bottom' and 'chests'. The 'inside' is the inner hall of a man's integrity wherein he judges and is judged; 'it' is the unknown ingredient of ultimate moral knowledge, and 'bottom' the root cause of personal behaviour. 'Chests' would seem to correspond to the outward visible sign of a man's inner spiritual stature. These are less symbols proper than moral counters deployed with great skill throughout the text to convey the root significance of the ethical impasse between the defiant young Okolo in his determined search for *iye* and the elders with their pompous protestations founded on nothing but vested interest. It is a technique practically unique to Okara and one which proves illuminating when we turn to the poetry collected in *The Fisherman's Invocation*.[26]

The title poem of this volume is a dialogue between two voices, one the voice of instruction and patient homily, the other the voice of experiment and inductive experience. The first supplies clues for action. The second acts on these and reports its findings. Throughout the argument the significance of what is occurring is debated by the use of

[25] Gabriel Okara, *The Voice* (London: André Deutsch, 1964), pp. 36–7.
[26] Gabriel Okara, *The Fisherman's Invocation* (London: Heinemann, 1978).

terms understood by both speakers: 'the Back', 'the Child-Front', 'the stump' and so forth. The connotation of these phrases may elude immediate understanding, but a rereading soon establishes their meaning. 'The Back' represents the force of received tradition, the past with its insistent claims; 'the Front', the future towards which all purposeful effort must be directed. The relationship between these two quantities is suggested by the lines:

> The Front grows from the Back
> like buds from a tree stump[27]

Hence the 'stump' is the point at which the past attempts to release itself from its constraints and grow into a more positive relationship with the present. Throughout the opening section, the search for a meaningful equilibrium between these phases of a society's history is realized through the local metaphor of fishing in the Niger delta creeks. As the net is hauled through the water it experiences both the resistance of the Back (the back-current of the water as it flows past the canoe), and the mysterious eddying attraction of the Front. The net is powerless to evade this tug of forces: if it frees itself from the cross-currents of the stream there will be no chance of a catch. As the first voice advises, paying a passing tribute to the terminology of *The Voice*:

> Dig deep at the back
> of the womb. There's water
> there's water from a river
> flowing from the bottom of the Back
> of the womb. So draw up the Back caught
> in the net. Draw it up and let's look it over
> in our insides, in our heads.[28]

This also issues in a fresh image, the 'womb', which will enlarge into one of the key organizing ideas of the sequence. Increasingly as the poem progresses the emphasis is on the need to placate the past and bring a new, unencumbered future into being. This, however, cannot be done through evasion or disrespect. As the teaching voice reminds its companion, the past has to be dealt with skilfully and with reverence, lest a general blight result:

> You'll no more be man among
> men, for you have defiled the Back

[27] *Ibid.*, p. 4.    [28] *Ibid.*, p. 5.

and the things of the ground
and have killed the gods of the Back[29]

Provided the past has its due, however, the way lies forward to an uninhibited and responsible future. In section 2 the image of child-birth comes to full fruition, as voice 1 assumes the rôle of midwife at the delivery of the Future, now identified as the child of the second voice. The change of rhythmic momentum here is perfect with the simplified repetitions of voice 1 and the reiterated dependent rejoin-der from voice 2, 'I see', suggesting hypnosis or a technique of care-fully induced birth. As the moment of delivery approaches the suppressed hysteria of voice 2, in the grip of painful contractions, counterpoints with the reassuring tones of the midwife as she guides the Future into being while staying the mother's impatience. Section 3 begins with a moment of pure horror. What is this monster which has emerged from the womb, and why does it bear so little resemblance to past children? Again the tetchy reactions of voice 2, increasingly stri-dent in their maternal disappointment, contrast with the serene confi-dence of voice 1 with its calm certainty that the unfamiliar appearance of this new creature, so alien to established taste, must and will trans-form itself into something whole and loveable. With that the images of fishing and childbirth are discarded and the poem proceeds to a fresh stage.

As so often when Okara wishes us to take fresh stock of his theme, the effect is achieved through a break in rhythm. The constant two-stress metre of the next section – sub-titled 'Birth Dance of the Child-Front' – expresses, through its guileless stamping gait, the sheer exultation which greets the community's certainty that a healthy access to a buoyant future is assured. There are very few poets who can afford to inform us so explicitly of the technique they are using without involving any interruption in the spontaneity of the effect:

> And so the rhythm has changed
> but not the theme –
> Dance in circles
> stamp your feet
> to the circular drums.[30]

At section 5 the dichotomy between the two voices caused by a dis-parity of wisdom and experience disappears. There is a sense of shared security and fulfilment evoked by the lessening momentum of

[29] *Ibid.*, p. 6.    [30] *Ibid.*, p. 13.

relatively long lines as the crowds disperse from the dancing arena, leaving the new child free from the persistent demands of a remorseless past and free to develop through untrammelled years of growth. The plural of the closing lines ('We learn to dance') betokens a determination by teacher and ward alike to adjust to the new realities of a present responsive to tradition, yet sensitive to the need for change.

How to achieve a meaningful relationship with the past? It is a question central to Okara's thinking, and has inspired some of his best poems, as well as a few where his grasp is less certain. It would be no exaggeration to say that the successful poems are those in which such a relationship is perfected during the course of the writing, the less successful those in which he fails to come to terms with the pressures of history, taking recourse in either sentimentality or preaching. The lapses, however, are rare, and even then are interesting. It is a theme too which he tackles from a number of different angles, either speaking in his own tender lyrical voice, as in the strongly romantic 'Call of the River Nun', or, as in 'You Laughed and Laughed and Laughed', parodying an attitude. Even when he distances himself from the speaker, however, one senses that a great deal of himself is still present. In 'You Laughed and Laughed and Laughed', for example, the speaker is a rural naïf, a bumpkin with insufficient social graces to impress a patronizing townee.[31] Yet, though the poem might be considered a comparative study in personality, the countryman's sentiments possess enough conviction eventually to carry the day and to convince us that their routing of the city-dweller's amused condescension is vindicated by Okara, himself, one senses, a man strongly sensitive to ridicule. There is one marvellous moment at which the poem really takes off, when the countryman, tired at last of his friend's disdain, decides to turn the tables and laugh in his turn. At this point the dimensions of the poem open out, as so often in Okara, to let in a mystical and cosmic strain which carries everything in its path. With that the townsman's attitude shrivels to 'meek wonder', allowing the erstwhile bumpkin, confident now of the validity of his views, to deliver a clinching final riposte.

There is one image which dominates all of Okara's writing on the relationship of past to present, and that, not surprisingly for one from the Niger delta, is a riverbank. For Okara, the river is the curve inscribed by history as it meanders between the heritage of the past and the challenge of the future. The river too possesses a personal

[31] *Ibid.*, p. 24.

dimension: it is the point of decision, the Rubicon that must be crossed before an individual destiny may find fulfilment. 'The Call of the River Nun' explores this theme less adequately I fear than most of his poems.[32] The poem won Okara a prize early in his career, and has been much anthologized, but for this reader there is a fatal flaw caused by a mismatch in the symbolism. The river features in the first three verse paragraphs as the domain of childhood – in A. E. Housman's phrase 'the land of lost content' – towards which the land-locked adult nostalgically aspires. By paragraph 4 it has changed its significance to that of the shape of a person's entire destiny, with the source inland as birth, and the delta, open to the ocean, as death. The direction taken by the current is said to be 'inevitable' with a determinism stemming from uncontrollable physical forces. However, the closing lines find the poet wondering whether he is controlled, not by the environment he inhabits, but by some private force of temperament ('my inner stars'). The intrusion of the Christian God in the last verse, moreover, seems forced and sentimental.

Better is 'Piano and Drums' which finds the poet 'at the break of day at a riverside', buffeted by the cross-rhythms of traditional drums and the convoluted strains of a piano concerto, which Okara once kindly identified for me as the Rachmaninov First.[33] Rachmaninov, somehow, seems an ideal choice: tortured, indulgent, ravenously passionate. 'Tear-furrowed' too is the perfect compound adjective to describe this sort of ruthlessly self-pitying romanticism. Indeed the poem finally resolves itself into a debate not so much between competing kinds of music as between competing kinds of violence. The disadvantage, as even the most sympathetic reader is likely to appreciate, is that the 'jungle drums' of the first paragraph come less from an exactly recalled childhood, such as Clark might have evoked, as from a mental re-run of films such as *Sanders of the River*, which themselves represent another sour by-product of the long stale dream of European romanticism. Okara, in many respects still a product of his colonial generation, writes better when, instead of reproducing stock romantic attitudes, he seeks to describe the romantic artifact itself: his rhythmic modulations in the lines 'coaxing diminuendo, counterpoint/ crescendo' are masterly. When he attempts to portray the essence of African authenticity, which he manages so well elsewhere, his ingrained romantic habits of thought, far from sustaining

[32] *Ibid.*, p. 16.   [33] *Ibid.*, p. 20.

him, trip him up so that he is left clutching a pathetic rubber spear, like a film extra who has arrived too late to take part in the shooting. It is said that Jomo Kenyatta once had a part-time job on the film-set of the 'Sanders' film; let us hope that he was more quizzical about the antics of Paul Robeson than Okara seems to be about his 'panther ready to pounce' and his 'leopard snarling about to leap'. Despite all this, how-ever, Okara's point is an important one: to decide between the Rach-maninov and the drum is to arbitrate between alternative methods of carnage. It is to the poem's credit that, in the moving closing lines, he signals his inability to choose.

Okara is a gentle man, and gentle men (even gentlemen) often seem irresistibly drawn to themes of violence as if by horrified fascination or perhaps puritanical disapproval. 'Were I to choose', sensibly printed opposite the foregoing, has a right to be considered Okara's most fin-ished poem.[34] It is a poem of movement: from immobility to immobil-ity, stone to stone, and the rhythm of the movement is the rhythm of history. Adam breaks the stone and with it the silence of eternity. By the same gesture he releases the torrents of violence in which the poet, trapped like Cain inside history, is involved. 'Mewed' here is a lovely word, coming originally from a mediaeval term for the wicker cage inside which hawks were kept while moulting. Hawks are birds of prey, and I don't think that I'm being entirely fanciful in supposing that Okara means to indicate a recognition of a sort of violence even in the frightened self. Be that as it may, violence leads to dissension which leads to non-communication, which in turn leads to the night-mare of nationalism and colour consciousness (of which Okara, again a representative of his generation, is both aware and ashamed: see the conclusion to his next poem, 'Spirit of the Wind'). Slowly the darkness of the self-involved black soul becomes the darkness of death, leaving the poet in his headlong flight to dissolution longing for the original immobility, the stable anonymity which Adam, the first self-conscious man, has broken for ever. The poet would opt for a soothing imper-sonal peace if he could ('were I to choose'), but the point is that he cannot. Like everybody else he is stuck with the mess and contradic-tions of human history. The poem comes close to being a masterpiece; it is also (quite unconnectedly) the closest any West African poet comes to Blake, not a common model.

Okara writes well on a number of themes, but on few better than unrequited love, a malaise from which he seems especially to suffer.

[34] *Ibid.*, p. 21.

There is almost a history of his unlucky love-life in this volume, start-ing with 'The Mystic Drum' which, contrary to public opinion, is a poem about how poets often alienate lovers by the very vigour of their protestations. If it contented itself with this observation, 'The Mystic Drum' would, however, constitute no more than a poignant piece of autobiography.[35] The miracle of the poem, however, occurs when the poet *stops* speaking, and suddenly the girl, until then limp and pout-ing, comes to life, assuming a grandeur commensurate with the language that previously has been wasted on her. At this the poet gives up, for this is an exchange in which he can only lose, lending the girl a magnificence she does not deserve, while exhausting himself in unsatisfaction. He decides never again to waste words on an unworthy subject, but 'To Paveba' finds him at his tricks again.[36] By this time he is middle-aged, less easy to rouse, but verse 3 again finds him serenading in fine style. By now, however, the poet has learned something: his words, even if erotically ineffective, are not wasted, because they are of value in themselves. Even if he loses the girl, he keeps the poems (even Okara, who, as Theo Vincent informs us in his Introduction, has a sad tendency to mislay them). He also realizes that 'they die in the telling', that by expending verbal energy in the common coin of amorous discourse, the poet is devaluing his gift. He had better keep it 'smouldering' beneath the ashes. The poet, then, need only speak when his partner is silent, supplying a meaning he dimly intuits behind her reticence, as in the poem 'Silent Girl', written in 1969 in Ogwa, where Okara seems at last to have struck lucky.[37] This, however, is a weak poem, as are so many poems about satisfied love. Okara is not a poet of fulfilment, but of contradiction and of raging in the dark. He is best when puzzled, alarmed, wide awake to the paradoxes of an existence which is forever moving against the grain.

These remarks prove helpful when we come to consider two poems with religious themes, 'The Snowflakes Sail Gently Down', written during a visit to America, and 'One Night At Victoria Beach', which describes the activities of a revivalist religious sect on Lagos beach. 'The Snowflakes Sail Gently Down' makes an instructive contrast with Clark's 'Three Moods of Princeton', since both have the same starting point, a feeling of alienation while away from the Nigerian scene in

---

[35] *Ibid.*, p. 26.  [36] *Ibid.*, p. 33.  [37] *Ibid.*, p. 44.

winter-torn America, and both use the starkness of the landscape as an emblem of some subterranean violence.[38] Clark, as is his wont, lets his images do the work: 'hands' proceeding from gentleness to abuse, 'antlers' beginning as a picturesque decoration and then butting at the poet's entrails. Okara, again typically, is more systematically philosophical, letting his images assume the weight of symbols and then using them as counters to advance his argument. He is good at using simple words to arrest our attention: the 'weight' of the 'weightless snow' providing the basis for a paradox which carries over into the notion of a funeral for the earth which is, at least in terms of human expectation, 'deathless'. So the whole of the first verse paragraph turns into an indictment of a society which too easily consigns life to the rubbish tip, and blasts everything which it touches with chilling finality (compare the polemicism of Clark's 'mushroom pie'). This issues in an allegory of colonial exploitation, of the wearying of the despoilers, emerging from the tiredness of their ancestral landscape, and contrasted with the invigorating intervention of birds black with the poet's own buoyant racial consciousness, of which he is for once not ashamed. The despoilers refuse the gift of the sun, since it cannot readily be exchanged for hard cash. With that the poem springs to life. Once again, had Okara left his poem at this point we would have had a vivid parable of colonialism and no more. But Okara's habitual excellence lies in the fact that, at precisely the moment when we believe him to have concluded his argument, he then pulls the rug from under our feet and exposes us to unsuspected depths of meaning. Thus, at the very instant at which we expect the sleeper's sense of isolation and disappointment to find waking confirmation, daylight finds the landscape outside his window transformed into a holy of holies, and the trees bending their heads in genuine obeisance. It is the equivalent of that marvellous moment at the end of 'The Mystic Drum' when the girl magically assumes new life and dignity and the poet recognizes his gift to transform unresponsive normality into something more interesting. So here, the poet's transforming gift is seen in his ability to turn a prosaic, depressing scene into a place of awe and wonder.

Running through all these poems there is this fundamental theme of the dynamism active between the poet and his material. Thus 'One Night at Victoria Beach' reads at first as just a rather absorbing description of a minority sect enacting its strange baptismal rites in a corner of

[38] *Ibid.*, p. 30.

a popular stretch of sand.[39] But then we notice the poet standing on his own patch of sand, and catch ourselves wondering how much of the energy ascribed to the Aladuras is their own and how much due to the invigorating consciousness of the narrator. The poet is alone and unheeded, like the lover in 'The Mystic Drum', yet it is his words which kindle our imagination in reading, even if they are symbolically nipped in the bud. And what, one asks, is this chilling draft which has 'killed the budding words' if not the unresponsiveness of the onlookers to his presence, and his own belated recognition that the spiritual consciousness of the worshippers is in no way as profound and as subtle as he has made it out to be? Then one notices the insistence in the first three verses of the phrase 'the Aladuras pray', which comes to seem less a manifestation of devotion than a blinkered refusal to accept the bustling secular activity which surrounds them. The worshippers are 'trying to see tomorrow', yet despite their painful efforts to recruit the *babalawo*, Father of Secrets, Priest of the Yoruba god Ifa, to their ends, finally it is the fish who sit in judgement and make a mockery of them. Thus what seems at first sight an act of celebration comes closer to parody, and the poet is left pathetically (again) in his trouser turn-ups contemplating the discrepancy. Okara is ever prepared to play the fool for the sake of his art, but he has seldom risked bathos to such rich effect.

Okara completed *The Fisherman's Invocation* by endowing the theme of the power of words to make and unmake with cosmological significance. 'The Revolt of the Gods' is doubtless a fragment, a verse drama in three brief scenes, the model for which may well have been supplied by Shelley (the title recalls *The Revolt of Islam*, but the probable prototypes are Shelley's verse dramas such as *Prometheus Unbound* and the unfinished *Hellas*). Scene 1 finds the gods, taken from a wide range of different pantheons, discussing their dispensability at the hands of men, who create and then dispose of them at will. The gods have, they feel, no independent will of their own: when man's mind gropes in despair and baseness, they must grovel too. Yet there is no need: a young god illustrates his thesis by unveiling a tableau of an abjectly humble mortal begging for the life of his child.[40] Despite man's power over the mythologies created by his fickle devotion, when the chips are down he will kneel and acknowledge the heavenly powers as greater than himself. This leads into a scene where four mortals, one a

---

[39] *Ibid.*, p. 28.    [40] *Ibid.*, pp. 58–62.

prophet, one a hedonist, another a sceptic, a fourth uncommitted, debate amongst themselves the realities of the universe, each one recreating it in his own puny image. The fragment ends with an older god reaffirming the powerlessness of the immortals in the face of such insolence: the revolt of the gods has apparently been a failure. The conclusion of this sequence is quite consistent with the rest of Okara's work. The face of reality, whether physical or spiritual, is evanescent. It is only man by his gift of words who is able to interpret it so that it can be seen and judged. The human imagination possesses ultimate power over both past and future, and the awesome responsibility which goes along with it. It is a sobering lesson, but one which entirely suits the tentative, pensive nature of Okara both as man and as poet.

# 'Psalmody of sunsets':
# the career of Lenrie Peters

It can be highly misleading to see any literary tradition as an affair of groups and cabals, sects and sub-sects, pressure groups and 'schools'. The career of Lenrie Peters, with its twenty years of solid achievement, bears witness to the fact that the best work was often done alone, in a small room at dead of night with little or no active contact with other practitioners in the same art, save the perusal of printed volumes of the poets of other ages and places with whom the reader may or may not have much in common. If Peters were considered at the point of his emergence in the mid-sixties with a small pamphlet from the prestigious Mbari publishing house,[1] he might appear as a member of the same age-set as Pepper Clark, Soyinka and others of the Ibadan school. In reality, when his first poems began to appear he was far distant from the African scene working as medical student, houseman and later surgeon in the hospitals of metropolitan Britain. At Cambridge he read natural sciences with their own demands for precision and technical virtuosity, was briefly involved in student politics, but experienced limited exposure to that troubled, heart-searching debate on ways and means, fashion and precedent, which sustains literary aspirants in an English department. He learned to write in his own way, coasting around the more obvious fields of posture and protest, reading widely, coming to his own distinctive conclusions. The result, when Heinemann came to issue his first major book *Satellites* in 1967, was a volume which nobody could classify, which took on a whole range of different themes and attitudes with a secure, unflustered mastery, and which established him permanently as a voice which all respected but which few could emulate.[2]

Too much has probably been made of the fact that Peters is a doctor. To the extent that this has helped him it is due to the redeeming distance which it has set between him and those of his fellow poets who, apart from their writing, have spent most of their professional

[1] Lenrie Peters, *Poems* (Ibadan: Mbari Publications, 1964).
[2] Lenrie Peters, *Satellites* (London: Heinemann, 1967).

lives working in literature departments in universities where they are constantly exposed to critical dialogue, comparison, and the constant obligation to justify what they have done. Through his work as a surgeon, Peters has been confronted with many vital kinds of experience, but it has also given him a retreat in which to hide from the prying eyes of other literati, away from critical chatter and the obsequiousness of younger writers. The result has been a critical awareness of a much rarer kind: the ability to see through the poses of the literary elect, to wrestle with the unglamorous problems of technique, to see things with a clear, unspoiled vision. Peters has spent too much time in the mundane presence of life and death to wish to take refuge in large abstractions. His philosophical bent, which is essential to him, has had to match itself against the harsh facts of decay and decrepitude in spartan wards in the provinces. He is aware of politics, of idealism, of the pressure of history – one of his strongest themes – but he is also painfully aware of the cost of action, the debris of violence. His use of language has been somewhat glibly compared to the activity of his surgeon's scalpel, but in his most characteristic moods he seems far closer to his own patients in the dogged courage with which they maintain squalid, unfulfilled lives full of the detritus of wrecked expectations. It is somewhat remarkable that *Satellites* which was published when Peters had just turned thirty-five, and which most people would term a young man's volume, has three poems on Autumn, and one about growing older. The reason I suggest is partly the precocious maturity of a man who has had to reconcile the ardour of the artist with the resistant texture of experience, and partly the professional empathy which has enabled him, when still quite young, to discern the mental cast of his much older patients.

The title *Satellites* is amply suggestive. Sierra Leone was until recently a colony and hence a satellite of the West; its inhabitants are satellites of the world economy. The poet himself exists far from the hub of literary activity and is hence also a kind of satellite; he is constantly assailed by feelings of futility and irrelevance. More than this, in his best work he often strikes us as a satellite of his own subject matter, drawn to the large areas of political and philosophical concern, but unwilling to plunge in with happy abandon. It would be erroneous to say that, because Peters does not belong to any clearly definable school, his thematic interests are radically different from those of other African poets. National aspiration, the desire for cultural identity, a determination to undermine neo-colonialism: all of these are very close to his heart. He is, however, very wary of writing a poem which attacks these themes direct, preferring to approach them under cover of metaphor or analogy. There were, it is true, in the volume as originally published three pieces of explicit social meaning: the digest of post-colonial history printed as No. 45; the poem (No. 48) on the exploding of the Chinese atom bomb; and a tribute to Churchill written on the occasion of his funeral in 1965 (No. 31). All of these, however, were excluded from his selection from *Satellites* included in the *Selected Poetry* of 1981.[3] They are all of them too near the bone, too confident in their ability to dilate on abstract subjects, to draw on the poet's more confident manner. Peters is always best when he writes in camouflage.

A fine example of Peters's strongest work from this period is 'Sky-flood of Locusts' with which both *Satellites* and the *Selected Poetry* begin.[4] At first sight it is a descriptive piece about the devastation wreaked by a flood of rapacious insects. To the reader's surprise it waxes philosophical half way through, and ends with something close to a slogan. We are left therefore with the task of reconciling different poetic registers. Moreover, though clearly featured as predators in the opening stanzas, the locusts are finally left 'rotting / in the desert / rotting harshly / in the sun' as if felled by their own greed. The imagery drives this point home. Stanza 4 speaks of the 'castrated hope' of the afflicted farmers, but in the very next line compares the shrill screech of the insects as they set about their work to the singing of castrated male sopranos in the sixteenth-century Sistine Chapel. Though occupied in a feast of destruction, the locusts have thus forfeited their own potency through the single-mindedness of their ambition. Typical of Peters is the way in which he next converts this observation into an abstract truth – 'Ecstasy and passion / have giant wings' – and then applies it to himself. The lines

> I am reminded
> that scratching the
> sky with bare nails
> won't bring me heaven[5]

[3] Lenrie Peters, *Selected Poetry* (London: Heinemann, 1981).
[4] Peters, *Satellites*, p. 1. (*Selected Poetry*, p. 3.)     [5] *Ibid.*, p. 2. (*Selected Poetry*, p. 4.)

tell us much about the slow tempering of youthful idealism and re-
inforce the poem's salient theme: the conflict between the impulse to
act and the restraint imposed by experience. One should not ignore
the more topical comparison of the locusts to self-inflated Common-
wealth politicians clearly present in stanza 5, but it is equally import-
ant to resist the temptation to interpret the whole poem in this light as
a satire on the vanity of human wishes. There is also the poet's own in-
stinctive identification with excess and the failure to which it leads,
counterbalanced by his final recognition in the concluding lines that,
despite repeated disaster, the effort to improve human life must go
on. The writer is hence caught between his cautious mistrust of ideol-
ogy – 'Isms, deceits, vanities' – and the belief in human progress
which continues to sustain him, expressed in stanza 14 with its echoes
of the great Welsh hymn 'Guide Me O Thou Great Redeemer'. The
poet's reiterated 'I believe' in the last stanza suggests that, in the last
resort, it is the idealism which wins through. On the other hand much
in the poem, including its governing image pattern, serves to re-
inforce the pessimism which holds the warmer commitment in check.

There is a clear connection between the last piece and its companion
'Wings My Ancestors Used', published as No. 4 of *Satellites*, No. 3 in
the selected edition.[6] Again the poem has an apparent and a subter-
ranean subject. The apparent subject is apathy, and the conditions
which produce it. Though conscious of the pressure of history over his
shoulder, the poet recognizes that for him the pressure has slackened.
Technically a free man, he is nevertheless aware of the centuries of hu-
miliation and repression that lie behind his post-colonial condition.
His surface freedom, however, allows him the luxury of seeing it all as
a pre-ordained pattern over which he and his kind had and still have
little control. The image of stars 'in the immensity of chaos in space /
revolutions of desire and object faced together' takes us back to the
astronomical determinism of the book's title. There is a comforting il-
lusion that all is settled beyond power of positive action, which recom-
mends itself to the poet's own gentle disposition. Balancing this on
the other hand is a distrust of his own scepticism which leads him, in
the ante-penultimate line of the first paragraph, to brand the highly
sophisticated, urbane doubt of Socrates as 'primitive'. Such a view as-
sumes a philosophy of history according to which the civilized scepti-
cism of the Greeks was a mere blind to complicity in historical
injustice. By comparing himself to the Athenian philosopher the poet

[6] *Ibid.*, pp. 8–10. (*Selected Poetry*, pp. 6–8.)

takes on his wisdom and cultivated urbanity: he also takes on the consequent impotence, the intellectual curb to action 'wandering eternally in doubt'. The doubt is damaging because by adopting a philosophy of determinism it is able to use it as an excuse for passivity and hence avoid the moral consequences of free will. It is in this tension between competing philosophies, the one asserting the fixed destiny of all things, the other urging the autonomy of the individual conscience, that the poem's deeper meaning lies. The second paragraph holds an uneasy and finally unresolved balance between them. The determinism view, the poet suggests, belongs to a distant Utopian future in which history has relaxed its grasp. From such a perspective it might be instructive to regard the whole of history as a 'chain-reaction.' At present such a view can only be a dangerous indulgence, an invitation to indolence. There is in these lines a precarious distinction between the 'substance of things', namely the scientifically objective truth about them, and the 'guidance' of events, which, for the sake of this poem, is seen to reside in the individual human will. The poet is half persuaded of his own responsibility for the marshalling of events, but needs to convince himself further: hence the reiterated 'in me' at the end of line 56. The repetition of the line 'That is the substance of things' at the end reflects a change of heart. On its first appearance the 'substance' referred to was the model of a chain reaction; now it is the ideal of personal trusteeship. The poem has moved from complacency to determination, while retaining a vivid memory of the former state.

The poetry of *Satellites* is held in tension between the call of initiative and the need for caution, between impetuosity and restraint. Nowhere is this polarity more perfectly realized than in the two animal poems 'Consider a Snail' and 'A Sabre Shark' which may be thought of as complementary.[7] The first is a celebration of the virtues of caution spoken by one whose habitual expectations are saturated in 'the idea of energy'. Energy brings with it the notion of purpose; it is the poem's point to prove, however, that violent action can never be more than random. The burden of proof falls partly on the words chosen to evoke the state of frenetic motion ('rapaciousness', 'madness', 'luck') and partly on the central image of lightning 'ambling / through the sky' with a casualness of direction which refutes its reputation for selective malice. Here as elsewhere the poem operates by jolting inherited associations so as to pose a challenge to our thinking:

[7] *Ibid.*, pp. 29 and 91. (*Selected Poetry*, pp. 21 and 39.)

the very word 'dry' applied to a snail sets our comfortable clichés in a whirl. We are in a hushed slow-motion world where time is suspended and aspiration takes its satisfaction from the enjoyment of the moment. 'Dateless' in the last paragraph is a word which distils many of these meanings. Applied to the 'naked desert trees' it carries the idea of fruitlessness and sterility; applied to the larger time scheme it reinforces the sense of a lack of direction. The snail at least has a goal for which to strive: the very inconclusiveness of the poem's ending suggests that it may never reach it. Fulfilment in this context lies in the perpetuation of desire.

Against the advantages of stealth 'A Sabre Shark' urges the advantages of concerted speed. Appropriately in the snail poem much of the work was done by adjectives; here most of the vigour lies in the verbs: 'lifts', 'plunges', 'angles', 'ripples', 'stabs', 'tosses', 'gulps'. It is a list that suggests clear-sighted, selfish action, uncomplicated by moral compunction or doubt. As such it raises the principal moral problem of the poem, the extent to which the suppression of guilt is a price worth paying to strengthen resolve. The pivotal word of the poem is 'Truth' portrayed as a shimmering, alluring victim. The plunder of truth suggests an intellectual activity, yet the impulse behind the poem realizes itself in the realm of action. It is in the relationship between these two modes or phases of human expression that the core of the poem lies. The relationship described is complex and perplexed. The conquest of truth, for instance, serves to suggest both intellectual discovery and the suppression of inconvenient facts, the activity of the scientist and that of the propagandist. The macabre final image of the shark as hired executioner suggests perhaps that for the successful completion of either aim a certain suspension of the finer moral feelings is required, an impression strengthened by the proscription of 'acolytes and candles'. Religion and the qualms of a tender conscience are both restrictions which must be ditched if the promptings of biological survival are to be satisfied. Ultimately the ethical finesse of the poem is to be found neither in the condemnation of rash endeavour, nor in any sophistry of justified violence, but rather in the rarer sensitivity which takes cognisance of these problems without proposing easy solutions.

The extreme division of opinion between the snail and shark poems suggests that they are both elements in an incomplete dialectic which can be glimpsed elsewhere in the volume. Poem 10, for instance, is an affectionate portrait of Freetown, Peters's paternal city, which

manages to dig deeper than the travel poster image of a people colour-
ful bounteous and free to discern the tensions of a society 'poised at
the diastolic / moment of change'. The physiological metaphor is
meticulous since Peters is occupied in seeing the city from outside as a
cohesive organism pulsing under the strains of its own nature. As
such the poem is a failure: it digresses too widely and lacks the concen-
tration of image and thought which make the other poems in the
volume such a delight. In *Satellites* it seems oddly out of place like a sea
turtle left panting on dry land, but it is useful in that it points us to the
place of its first appearance as the frontispiece to Peters's novel *The
Second Round* (1965), published between the appearance of his Mbari
volume *Poems* in 1964 and *Satellites* itself. The novel's action is jerky
and unco-ordinated, its speech often artificial and its characters un-
evenly defined. Besides some strong descriptive passages, however,
it also contains a thoughtful underlying argument as to the nature of
social change as perceived by the scientifically educated mind. Dr
Kawa, a young Creole recently graduated from a London medical
school, has returned to his native Freetown after an absence of several
years. After taking up his appointment in the obstetrics department of
the local hospital he is dismayed by the rudimentary conditions he
finds there, the obsolescence of the equipment, the unwillingess of all
concerned to cope with an accelerating pace of change. Pacing round
the harbour in the cool of the evening he suddenly has a vision of
twentieth-century Freetown as a vast human cell struggling to expand
and reproduce itself:

here was a great event – the crystallization of vast energies into a mind, a per-
ception able to understand and perhaps to throw back some little influence
into the expanding whole. An organism which in a relatively short space of
time had attained a position of dominance over the psychic impulse. What
enormous opportunities opened to man and the universe for a happy remar-
riage between these opposing aspects of a fundamental reality. But rather like
the centriole in the nucleus of a living cell at the moment of its dividing, at the
very moment of its creation of new life through a process of sharing, they had
positioned themselves at opposite poles and were held together precariously
only by the flimsy threads of the artefactual spindle.[8]

The image of the twin poles resurfaces in Section III of the poem
where it is connected both with alternating wet and dry seasons and
with the 'energy which belongs to nature' in its contest with the
dominating spirit of man. It is obvious that what Peters has in mind is

[8] Lenrie Peters, *The Second Round* (London: Heinemann, 1965), p. 17.

the continuing competition between the raw evolutionary thrust embodied by the shark and the circumspection and self-awareness practised by the snail. Mankind, so he argues, has reached a staging-post in his own development where at last he is able to survey both his anatomy and his driving impulses with the objectivity of a dispassionate observer. Yet this advance in knowledge has merely confronted him with the problem of attempting to reconcile his newly found impartiality with the passion which alone can continue to fuel his progress. Though intellectually he has won an insuperable advantage, morally he has had to pay the cost of disorientation, demoralization, and all the puzzling social ills of the modern world. The novel's plot amply illustrates this thesis. On moving into his smart government bungalow, Kawa receives a visit from his neighbour Marshall, a half Lebanese of a tortured nobility of soul who has refused to leave his young wife despite her flagrant adultery with his nephew under his very own roof. Marshall's reluctance to retaliate is grounded in his fixed romantic ideal of sacrificial love and in his fond protectiveness for the ingenuous girl he once rescued from rural isolation, married, and then sent to England where she picked up a gloss of cosmopolitan sophistication. Later, when her lover dies from a malignant cancer and her husband, crazed by her infidelity, is despatched to an asylum, Clara is left facing the problem of her own guilt. Her fitful soliloquy tells us much about the way in which the novelist views her dilemma and that of her species:

All the extenuating circumstances of her life, the advent of material abundance were not enough to account for her moral diarrhoea. *It is enough to say that I could not help it. No; I knew what I was doing and had the power to change my life – to reconsider my direction but I chose not to. I enjoyed the loose griping feeling of diarrhoea. There's no one to blame; no circumstances; no Almighty; just me.*[9]

The dismissal of religion here is consonant with the feelings expressed in the shark poem; the concluding 'just me' echoes the phrase 'the guidance is in me' from 'Wings My Ancestors Used'. Fundamentally, however, the moral conflict is viewed with the diagnostic eye of the general practitioner as a malaise caused by inconsiderate living just as diarrhoea is caused by immoderate eating. Clara's impulses are hopelessly muddled up. She has wished to give free expression to her erotic energy without considering the effect this has on the feelings of others; she has tried to prove her sophistication by

[9] *The Second Round*, p. 161.

stepping above the traditional moral law. As a result her compunc-
tions come too late and too confusedly to be of any assistance. Caught
between her instincts and the directives of a hapless society, she
knows not where to turn.

As a novelist Peters seems ineluctably drawn to characters like Dr
Kawa, Marshall and Clara because their nebulous bearings reflect per-
fectly the anonymity of the world which he, as poet and man,
experiences. All of the personal pieces in *Satellites* are shot through
with a gentle despair at the possibility of saying anything which has
not to be hedged around with crippling conditions. 'Watching Some-
one Die', for instance, is a poem about the indecisiveness of what
many would regard as the most conclusive of all human events. Yet
for Peters the experience is 'fraudulent' because, promising to yield an
ultimate insight into the nature of our consciousness, death cheats us
by dwindling into an insignificant 'changing of the tide'. There are no
dramatic revelations, there is no summation. The poem is emphatic in
excluding the hope of an after-life, and in this Peters lives up to his
own passionate agnosticism. All that man has is the present, and the
faculty of free choice which enables him to muddle through. In poems
such as this Peters is very close to Existentialism with its rejection of
necessary truth and its championing of the supremacy of the moral
will. In 'The Fields are Grey with Corn' we are shown a world domi-
nated by half-shades in which all certainties end by fading into one
another. This is a mellow poem full of the sense of early middle age, of
spoiled opportunities and blasted hopes. The central image of an up-
hill path is conventional, though transformed by the associated atmos-
phere of twilit distances, delicate cadences, muted colours. The one
assertive note is the desolate, half submerged insistence on the per-
sonal choice, the determination to make the best of imperfect circum-
stances. Even this, however, is heard from the distance, like a forlorn
bugle sounding men to forgotten wars:

> There were days of glory
> before sunset; crucial with choices
> alternatives seen wistfully – married away –
> figures dancing in the rain
> against pillars of rain in moonlight
> glancing passions and turmoil of brain
> not so long ago.[10]

[10] *Satellites*, p. 15-16.

208

At such moments *Satellites* comes close to the personal statement of a man whose knowing, unimpressed stare has seen through all our pretences to heroism and glamour and accepted life at its most drab and ordinary, transfusing it with his own affectionate compassion. Nor does he exempt himself from the verdict. His is 'the silent face / in the railway compartment'; he too stands 'as all do / at the cutting chaotic edge of things', he too queues for an interview for a job and ends by returning inadequate, tongue-tied answers. It is in this light that the prevailing image of autumn, and the three poems addressed to it, must be seen; less as an expression of premature disillusionment than as the deliberate editing-out of harsher shades and sharper outlines in favour of a vision of muted possibilities, moral compromises, the slow persistence of mere effort.

The morally bleak tone is shared by Peters's next volume *Katchikali*, published shortly after Peters's return to the Gambia in 1971.[11] There is, however, a subtle change of emphasis. The shift in position can be gauged most simply by comparing two poems of sad self-scrutiny: from *Satellites*, 'Mine is the Silent Face' and, from *Katchikali* 'The Fence'. Both are attempts to align the poetic personality with the under-dog, the repressed, the mundane. In the piece from *Satellites* the effort is one of deliberate empathy with states of being initially experienced as unsavoury. The face in the railway compartment, blank with incomprehension and boredom, is something seen, rejected and then reassessed in the light of humble self-knowledge. One can feel the poet's effort to place himself on a level with those less advantaged than himself, and the sense of strain shows through. 'An empty tin rolling down / catty cobbled alleys' is an image straight out of the sleazily attractive urban underworld of Eliot's *Preludes*, and, like the Eliot poems, is tinged with a smudge of condescension. In the third stanza we find the poet trying to accept responsibility for the ills of tomorrow, yet the 'blame' he so bravely shoulders remains an abstraction, unspecified in detail, uncertain in symbolism. Even the splendidly clipped last line seems to summon up an Existentialist nightmare we have seen evoked better elsewhere in Jules Laforgue or Eliot or their imitators.

'The Fence' is a poem which invites misunderstanding.[12] The title and the wording of the opening stanzas suggest a policy of abject compromise, an impression corrected by the drift of the writing from that

[11] Lenrie Peters, *Katchikali* (London: Heinemann, 1971).     [12] *Ibid.*, No. 16.

point onwards. To lie 'where truth and untruth struggle' is not to blur ethical distinctions but to take on the battalions of distortion and to recognize that one too may fall in combat. The poet is identifying himself with the victims of history who have fallen foul of the systematic manipulation of information, the framing of laws. 'With not one moment's pause for sighing' in the next stanza is a line which banishes any suggestion of futile regret or sentimental hand-wringing over correctable injustice. The pessimistic edge of the poem derives from the writer's recognition that to partake actively in the historical process is to involve oneself in endless contradictions, to expose oneself to misconstruction, misapplication and plain abuse. In the fourth stanza the 'opposites' plaguing the embattled individual still retain their meaning, refusing to coalesce into any consoling half-truth. There is confusion, but the poet recognizes it as the product of his own strained impulses; when clarity returns, the facts are still there to be perceived. The last stanza alerts us to the most seductive misuse to which all good intentions are prone, the conversion of honest motives into an organized cause the glamour of which distracts attention from its legitimate goals. The distrust implied with the posturings of self-advertised concern sets a distance between this poem and the lip-service charity of the uninvolved observer. Where 'Mine is the Silent Face' reads as a gesture of solidarity, 'The Fence' then is finally a poem of positive commitment.

The distinction tells us much about the different atmosphere of the two volumes. For another clue we might turn to the acrostic poem 'Before / Teutonic Hatreds Marred your Grace', the initial letters of each stanza of which spell out the name of Berlin, a city whose own fence of political demarcation has turned into a wall of pure hatred.[13] The crucial term here in the third line is 'history', that word so frequently invoked by the political poets of the thirties when they wished to speak of the infringement of events on the free unfettered conscience. By contrast in the second stanza we have the word 'culture' by which Peters wishes to imply the north German civilization of Bach, Bruckner, and of Wagner before Nietzsche transformed him into a teutonic hero. 'Culture' belongs to a world of freedom in which all statements, whether literary, musical or religious, are not subverted by political pressure; 'history', in this context, is the process by which the distortion occurs. There is, however, a deeper conception of history present in the poem, signposted by the glacial image of the fourth stanza and

[13] *Ibid.*, No. 32.

the question which hangs at the end of the last line. To describe the outpourings of the nightingales in the woods above the city as 'glacier clean' is to remind the reader of the slow, inevitable movement which carries men and society towards the light. The question at the end, though an open one, points us in the direction of a future when the tensions of our own period will be resolved, when 'culture' in the sense envisaged above will once again be free to express itself unmolested by national animosities. Finally the poem addresses itself to this hope. Though necessarily the statement of an outsider, it is also the testament of a man who has set his back against petty racial loyalties including, as we shall discover, those of his own continent.

The reason for the extra explicitness of social declaration is not hard to find. Two-thirds of the poems in this volume were written prior to Peters's departure from England in the years between his qualifying as a medical practitioner, his decision to specialize in surgery and his final decision to return to work in his mother's country, the Gambia. There then follow two poems (Nos. 54 and 55) which are in effect letters posted immediately before his embarkation to friends and lovers who, in his mind, stand for the England which he is about to leave. The dividing line falls at the title poem 'Katchikali' which revives a childhood folkloric memory to tell us something of the poet's feelings on returning to the banks of the river by which he was born. The rest of the volume conveys the feelings of a man who has turned his back on the advantages and facilities of the city and gone to work, albeit temporarily, along the remoter stretches of the great river, facing the squalor and deprivation of a people with whose sufferings he is slowly learning to associate himself. They are the poems of a working doctor, a pragmatist, one who has to reconcile ideals with practice and forge a personal conception of social obligation which does justice to his humane hopes without flying in the face of his wider international ideals. It is not surprising if some of these later pieces are disfigured with anger, frustration, resentment and intolerance at the bureaucratic programmes of town-dwelling intellectuals who disguise the real problems with ample helpings of aromatic disinfectant.

The debate as to the problem of commitment is evident in many of the individual poems in the volume. Poem 17 ('The Spectator'), for instance, has to do with the position of the uncommitted in a world in which interests lie entrenched.[15] The 'silence' guarded by the uncommitted man or woman is the insignia of his reasonableness, his lack of

---

[14] *Ibid.*, No. 17

bias; yet it is bought with a heavy cost. In his rôle as spectator such a person hopes for a revelation, yet the position of his track-side seat ultimately prevents him witnessing the very things which he has come to observe. His instinctive sympathies are with the referee whose impartiality would seem to mark him as a natural ally. Yet when the enraged combatants turn on him – 'the referee is kicked' – he is powerless to intervene. To assume power or effectiveness he too must take on the responsibilities of commitment, must descend from the rarefied heights of disinterestedness to try the murkier, less-seasoned atmosphere of embattled effort (the image of the 'attic' is unfortunate here, clashing as it does with the verbal phrase 'come down'). At this stage his silence will take on another complexion, that of grim anticipation. Emerging into the open arena, his immediate response is to wish to turn aside in mimicry of his original lack of involvement, but a timely bullet draws him at once into the fray. Wounded, he is now party to the conflict whether he will or not since he is now compelled to explain his blemished condition. Now at last the 'silence' he retains becomes none other than the concentration of premeditated fury taking counsel with itself. The lesson is plain and simple: objective comment, calm meditation are the prerogatives of the privileged, the protected, the whole. If he maintains such a stance the liberal is likely to retain his personal privileges; he is also likely to deny himself the intimacy of immediate knowledge and of the power to act. To go further he must risk not only confrontation, but pain, confusion and maiming. The sole compensation is a new understanding of those who have never known the advantages to which he has previously clung. Read with an eye to Peters's own biography, the poem reads as a gesture of renunciation by one who though aware of the privileges which his élite status affords him, is deeply conscious of the limitations imposed by too easy and too complacent an acceptance of them.

The theme is extended in the poem 'How Do We Come With Rage' where, however, the dilemma is viewed from within the smoke of conflict.[15] Those who renounce the serenity of calm contemplation are vulnerable to fits of nostalgia in which the peace they have sacrificed seems like a haven of impossible fulfilment. Where the previous poem consisted of a series of statements and an analogy, this piece is in three sections, the first framed in the form of a set of questions, the second of an allegorical vision, the third, partly in French, of a warning coda.

[15] *Ibid.*, No. 19.

To read the poem with an eye only to the opening section would be to risk misinterpreting the entire drift of the argument. The first four stanzas, it is true, seem to express the desirability of reconciliation, of going beyond the hostility of the present towards a new synthesis. Yet the very way in which each question is turned is enough to suggest the impossibility of establishing agreement without by the same token reneging on the loyalties which led the conciliator into battle in the first place. 'Rage', 'Grief' are in this context warm, positive words which convey a pride in active involvement not easily assuaged by promises of peace. Adopting a soothing attitude under these circumstances would amount to a betrayal; the songs of celebration would turn into 'songs of shame'. To adopt a geophysical image, it would be to attempt to investigate a world which had not yet cooled. There then occurs what appears at first sight to be a complete break in the thought and the introduction of a fresh symbol. The female figure portrayed in stanza 5 is clearly an emblem of moral progress rather than of peace itself, since she is seen as having shed a black costume previously proper to her. But the advance towards peace and moderation is beset with complexities of an unnerving kind, suggested by the 'knotted brain' and the 'confusion of ecstasy' she displays. Though heroic in her gesture of self-sacrifice, this very restraint of hers involves a human and moral cost of which she seems dimly aware. The problem is that she has turned her back not only on the experience of war but also on its victims, whose cause she now finds difficult to champion in her new rôle as upholder of the peace. The inclusion of two lines in French seems at once to distance the sentiments of the closing epilogue and to highlight them. Literally translated 'she can only say like the wounded and blind', these lines, taken together with the rest of the sentence, convey the element of evasion in the pacifist stance, of ditching any responsibility for human suffering for which one is oneself partly accountable. Though a tempting recourse for the wounded and frightened, suing for peace may involve insensitivity to the problems of those for whom positive commitment is the only hope. Thus, far from a celebration of peace and moderation, 'How Do We Come With Rage' serves ultimately to reinforce the sense present elsewhere in the volume of the urgency of enlisted effort. Though it seems at first to come from the calmer atmosphere of *Satellites*, it ends by confirming the distance travelled from the first volume.

Indeed there are several poems in *Katchikali* which seem almost deliberately intended as a counterpoise to others in *Satellites*. 'Does

Death So Delude Us' (poem 20) is, for instance, like 'Watching Some-one Die is a Fraudulent Experience' a poem about the spectator's atti-tude to death rather than either death itself or the experience of the sufferer.[16] Whereas in the poem from *Satellites* the stress is on the nul-lity and futility of all attempts to confront the meaning of death, 'Does Death So Delude Us' chooses to concentrate on the danger of evasion present in the philosophical or stoical attitude. To take refuge in a gloomy sense of inevitability is, the poem seems to argue, to court despair, even madness. The image of the 'lunatic abyss / where the faecal air / is not sweetened by the rose' draws on Peters's own medi-cal experience. It also takes us back to the scene in *The Second Round* in which Dr Kawa, distressed at his friend Marshall's dementia, under-takes to visit him in a Freetown psychiatric hospital in the hope of obtaining for him a more lenient régime. The scene described inside the hospital is of lank figures sunk in a dejected attitude, inmates whose despondency and inertia are tokens of their inability to deal with life beyond the hospital gates. The morbidity of mental illness is aligned in the poem with the complex moral attitudes of modern Exis-tentialism, whose rigorous but ambivalent ethical concepts are com-pared with the angles, lines and systematic deformations of the modern Italian painter Modigliani. Modigliani was fond of reducing the fullness of the human face to a series of interconnecting planes and angles, a deliberate stylization of visual perception which, Peters seems to be suggesting, has its equivalent in the 'imponderable nega-tiveness' and lack of human immediacy to be found in certain contem-porary European philosophers. By contrast the poet urges a return to the instinctive responses of our natural self-assertiveness. The 'shed-ding of the heart's Autumn leaves' that the text proposes is a correc-tive to the mellowness of the autumn poems from *Satellites*, all of which had a tendency to celebrate the sober virtues of maturity. The human mind, if it is to solve the practical and social problems by which it is assailed, must pass symbolically beyond the ripeness of autumn to the violence of spring. Thus death, and the attitudes to which too close an attention to its significance often lead, comes to be dismissed in irrelevance, not regretfully as in the *Satellites* poem, but in a mood of positive defiance. 'Does Death So Delude Us' looks for-ward to an active engagement with life's ills, and, as such, underlines the volume's mood of homecoming.

There is a clear connection between the foregoing poems and the

[16] *Ibid.*, No. 20.

subsequent pieces 'Grief for Loss of Faith' (No. 23) and 'Paralyzed
Ambitions' (No. 26), each of which points in its own way to the
dangers of philosophical pessimism and cultivated docility, both atti-
tudes seen as typical of Western Europe in her state of post-industrial
ennui.[17] The image of Nietzsche's 'diamond from black coal' in the
first of these pieces focuses many of these concerns. The image of coal
seems intended to convey that passion for primitive values untamed
by Christian interference which some have seen as central to the
German philosopher's work *Beyond Good and Evil*. The loss of faith in
inherited cultural norms this involves is seen to contribute to the car-
nage unleashed by Hitler and his kind, who misread Nietzsche's
praise of sublime unrepentant energy as a pretext for senseless
slaughter. Peters is trying once again to plumb the reasons behind
Europe's prevailing demoralization to which the striptease artiste in
'Dancer', the teenage suicide victim and the lonely exile in 'He Walks
Alone' each bear witness. The last of these addresses itself to one par-
ticular historical false turning: the rejection of local and national loy-
alties in favour of a bland and tasteless internationalism. The isolated
exile in the park features as a travesty of the ideals which led him to
cross frontiers, break ties and assert a sturdy independence of every-
thing known and loved. Instead of fresh horizons and the 'new
brotherhood' of which he dreamed he has discovered loneliness,
despair and a lack of purpose and belonging. The line 'Exile go home'
at the beginning of the sixth stanza is addressed partly to the subject of
the poem and partly to the poet himself, as, drawing an inevitable con-
clusion from the exile's empty cosmopolitanism, he applies it to his
own case, yielding the corollary that his own rural roots have an unde-
niable claim on him. The alternative to this is suggested by the first
and last lines of No. 36, 'The way to nowhere lies all around'. This por-
trays a nocturnal townscape as a veritable city of death in which all
contact with the certainties of nature has been lost in a craze for utility
and quick service.[18] The moon drifts above the traffic-filled streets but
seems strangely unreal, like a picture postcard hoarded in preference
to a natural scene which it depicts. The remoteness from felt experi-
ence is stressed by the phrases 'it should be night' and 'they say the
frost was quiet', the conditional tense of the one and the reported
speech of the other passing judgement on a society deprived of all sen-
sory knowledge and dependent on the punditry of experts. Then

[17] *Ibid.*, Nos. 23 and 26. (*Selected Poetry*, pp. 55 and 57.)   [18] *Ibid.*, No. 36.

across the blank face of the city falls the filtered presence of the spring as a sign that somewhere perhaps the immediacy of unpackaged experience is still possible.

The climax of the opening phase of the volume is undoubtedly the long narrative poem 'I Heard the Firebird's Lament', in which a nightmarish scenario does much to convey the desolation of urban Europe as experienced by one whose expectations derive from elsewhere.[19] The narrator – who is related to the poet himself without necessarily duplicating his life history – is imagined looking out on a stark wintry landscape from the window of a room in which a record player is giving out the muted opening strains of Stravinsky's ballet suite *Oiseau de feu*. The second stanza with its paranoid visualization of the weapons unleashed by international conflict choking an atmosphere 'florid with missiles' is partly an indication of the narrator's state of mind and partly an interpretation of the snarling *Danse Infernale* which follows in Stravinsky's score. As the dissonance of the orchestral writing intensifies, the narrator's frightened fantasy turns against, not only the insane weaponry of industrial Europe, but also England's prevailing hedonism and self-centred morality. Suddenly the telephone rings and a stranger's voice informs him starkly of the kidnapping and death of his daughter. Whether this turn of events is seen as a realistic enactment of fact or as a further fantasy provoked by the music is hardly relevant. The important thing is the sufferer's state of mind, the increasing alienation he is coming to feel from an environment which feeds him recorded sound through a hi-fi system and deeply personal news through the impersonal medium of a telephone receiver. With this the progress of the poem assumes a disjointed feel suggestive perhaps of intermittent phobic images stimulated in the mind by deep emotional agitation. It is not clear whose loin is snapped or who has been 'larkin' about' on the sea-bed, but the factual context seems once again to be largely irrelevant. These are snatches of discordant voices clamouring, like the voices of Eliot's *The Waste Land* from the abyss of some neurotic despair. The phraseology of the penultimate stanza which speaks of 'this narrow shift / between life and death' is also distinctly Eliotian, though this time it is less the Eliot of *The Waste Land* than the poet of *The Hollow Men*. Together these elements in the poem suggest that Peters had been influenced by a reading of the poetry of Eliot's middle period, the

---

[19] *Ibid.*, No. 47.

period of agnostic despair and a search after consoling religious answers. Far from striking a discordant note, these influences are entirely fitting for a poem which marks the low point of Peters's abandonment and dejection before the reconstruction marked by the following poems of return.

'I Hear the Firebird's Lament' is the climax of the poet's argument with the Europe he is about to leave. As such it marks an ideal prelude to the poems of return proper, from 'Katchikali' on. Between these two pieces intervene two short groups of poems, one of which (Nos. 48–53) has to do with the professional activity of the doctor, and the other (Nos. 54 and 55) with the difficulty of sustaining lasting relationships in a highly urbanized society. The two groups are joined thematically by their shared concern with emotional detachment, a quality essential to the doctor in his professional rôle, but highly damaging to the warm human relationships which in his private capacity he must strive to maintain. 'You Lie There Naked' (No. 48) is addressed by a surgeon to a patient whose name he does not even know but for whom he has performed a highly personal service. There is a carefully maintained balance here between the words that highlight the doctor in his unsentimental official capacity – words like 'stranger', 'controlled', 'serene', 'dissects', 'methodically' – and words which suggest a sort of ambivalent, distanced passion – 'trembles', 'heavy', 'defiance', 'maniac', 'spatters'. There is a valid analogy to be drawn between the way in which throughout the poem and the process which it described reason keeps passion in check, and the way in which in the artistic process the critical faculty maintains an uneasy hold over the imaginative will. In form the poem resembles a piece of music: a symphony in four movements perhaps – allegro, andante, scherzo, moderato. The musical analogy is sufficiently clear for the poet to be able to detail the moment of the break between the movements. Stanzas 1 and 2 have the air of a first movement; the next two stanzas, 'controlled, serene', the *cantabile* flow of a slow movement. Then suddenly 'the metronome alters the beat' and we are into a fast, frantic scherzo before the mood subsides towards a quiet close.

Nos. 49 and 50 have a certain continuity of tone due to their shared use of the second person singular. Yet in 'You Talk To Me of Pain' there are signs of the poet's anxious awareness that the perfect detachment required of the surgeon may inflict permanent damage on his finer moral sensibilities:

I listen. My heart a graveyard
where church bells toll at midnight.[20]

The candour of these lines comes close to self-accusation, for the poet /
surgeon is uncomfortably conscious of the fact that the complacent
firmness with which he goes about his business is the ideal mask for
emotional sterility, even for a more radical emotional immaturity.
'What Do I Know of Pain' is the cry of a pre-pubescent child to whom
adult suffering is beyond comprehension. The surgeon is effective in a
limited area over which he exercises a habitual, practiced control: the
operating theatre where the 'sharp steel' of his instruments acts as a
perfect substitute for real compassion. Beyond this safe region, how-
ever, his 'steel is impotent' – above all 'across the sea', in Africa where
he has not yet had an opportunity to try his skill. This note of geo-
graphical limitation has the effect of relating the poem to the author's
concern, expressed in many of the foregoing pieces, with the ethical
demands made upon him by the prospect of returning to his rural
roots, beyond the sophisticated defences, and self-absorption of
Europe. If he fails to meet this challenge, there will be consolations
enough: the complacent success and public status described in No. 50
('Old X, you know, kills them off like flies'); the 'panelled walls, the
plush / smell of aged security' of No. 51. Yet the decision cannot be
evaded; the doctor too must descend from the calm precincts of pro-
fessional detachment into the arena where battles are lost and won.

In taking this decision he is risking, not only his prospects of pro-
fessional advancement, but also a probable violation of that essential
line which separates doctor from patient. The 'first incision' on the
supine body mentioned in the first line of No. 53 marks the acceptance
by the poet / surgeon that he too is vulnerable, and, more, that he will
never be able to cure the deeper species of pain unless he himself has
earned the capacity to suffer them.

The pair of poems numbered as 54 and 55 occupy a quite special
place in the structure of *Katchikali*. Coming as they do after a series of
pieces which fret increasingly against the constraints of Europe, these
poems mark at last a decisive break. The decision has been taken, the
knot cut, and there is now just time for the after-glow of fond memory
and calm assessment. Both celebrate fragmentary, incomplete re-
lationships which reflect perfectly the detached, take-it-or-leave-it
feeling of alliances formed in the anonymous world of the city. 'Dear

---

[20] *Ibid.*, No. 49. (*Selected Poetry*, p. 71.)

Vincent' is a poem of gratitude for a moment of transitory intimacy in which two individuals can reveal agony searing their minds to one another without taking upon themselves responsibility for the consequences. Appropriately the tone is perfectly balanced between flippant, almost cynical casualness and real concern. This balance is conveyed by a stark juxtaposition of lines of a different emotional temper:

> Here crowds gather from gloomy autumn mists
>   walk about, chatter, maul,
> Your blood dripping off the wall

The rhyme here is almost too perfect; 'maul' has just the right connotation of gluttonous self-indulgence and at the same time frenetic desperation. The result is to set Vincent's own despair in relief, and simultaneously to cast doubt on his supposition of uniqueness. When all is said and done, everybody in the city shares Vincent's problem. Moreover, is there not a touch of absurd arrogance about the impossible questions which he raises?:

> Who knows what art is all about?[21]

It is a poem of compassion and at the same time of affectionate dismissal, a fitting epilogue to life in a callous, self-tormented society.

'And So This Long Affair' illustrates perfectly the sort of provisional, conditional love which such a society typically offers as a substitute for loyalty. There is a world of affection in the poem, but at the same time no lasting regret for the dissolution of a relationship too adult to offer illusion to either party. The poem employs habitual associations and standard puns with sufficient effect to turn them into the medium for a deeply personal view not only of one woman, but of the society which frames her:

> Yet your body beside me
> smelt of the season for dying
> in summer, winter, or spring
>
> Though now and then the driving shafts impaled
> they never quite went through
> never to the bitter end[22]

'Dying' here is, of course, the female orgasm; it is also the summation of all the autumnal images in which the earlier portions of this

---

[21] *Ibid.*, No. 54.    [22] *Ibid.*, No. 55.

volume, together with the whole of *Satellites*, are so rich. 'Driving shafts' is a reference not only to the phallic thrust, but also to the hard, self-assertive mechanical processes which support a technocratic society. At the same time the cliché 'bitter end' clinches the poet's conviction that, in the context of such a relationship, commitment can only lead to disruption and disaster. Peters is wonderful at coming up with single lines which distil within themselves a whole complex of social and cultural attitudes. The line 'tortured by love like godless incense' conjures up aromatic memories of joss-sticks smouldering away in the rooms of affectedly 'radical' households in the sixties; it is also a shrewd estimate of a social milieu which rejoices in the borrowed trappings of oriental mysticism while pretending to despise an inherited Christian faith of its own. Just as memories of the myth of God hang heavy in the air of agnostic Europe, so memories of the myth of love, so central to traditional western experience, hang round the periphery of this and other such relationships, lending their cultivated detachment an atmosphere of sad, self-hurting denial. This is a poem both of parting and of transition. Like the poet it looks forward to firmer, more adequate things. The 'loneliness' with which the eighth stanza ends begs a question to which the rest of the poems in the volume represent a sort of answer. As the poem ends the poet already sees himself moving on, bowing his head in a gesture of willing self-sacrifice. It might be thought that there is an element of falsity about the way in which, in this concluding section, Peters portrays what is, after all, a quite routine decision to return to his country of origin to live and work. The word 'barbarian' in particular conveys a somewhat drastic reaction. In reality, read in the context of the volume as a whole, the melodramatic sentiments are supported and transformed by a matrix of allusions which make the tone of self-immersion perfectly proper. Peters stands on the shores of Europe looking outwards; behind him stand the centralist myth and distortions of a culture certain of its God-given right to rule the world. It is only fair that the poet should reveal for us his indebtedness to years spent studying, working and writing in England, but also the distortions inevitably wrought in his own sensitive consciousness in the process.

'Katchikali', the title poem, is based on a traditional Gambian legend which Peters, at the moment of his re-encounter with his own country, retrieves from a childhood memory.[23] In it a childless woman

---

[23] *Ibid.*, No. 6. (*Selected Poetry*, p. 74.)

comes to the shrine of the river goddess begging the gift of fertility so that she may again hold her head high in the market place. In reality, of course, the woman herself is not entirely 'traditional'; nor is her existence quite separate from that of the poet himself. The woman is asking for children; the poet is asking for the reassurance of the old loyalties, fresh as he is from another society which has destroyed its own. Yet both the woman and the poet come from a world transformed by a pace of change which has carried many of its recognized conventions away. In seeking reassurance from Katchikali they are by the same token attempting to come to terms with their own position as modern people in a society which still retains a thin, guttering memory of a quite different way of life. The poem is very much a one-way act of communication, a prayer to which 'there are no answers', the end result of which is to drive the supplicants back on their own resources. It is therefore both an act of symbolic dedication, and also a deliberate bracing of the self before facing the myriad problems the poet anticipates in his new rôle both as a doctor in a society wracked by disease and as a half-hearted apostle of progress in an environment plagued by ignorance and darkness.

The poems which follow record the encounter between this environment and the 'idea of progress' which the poet, in his professional and private rôles, carries round as part of his mental equipment. One is conscious here that not only the idea of progress but also the geography of the Gambian countryside, as described, is on one level fiction, an imaginative invention of a creative artist whose vision redraws the terrain of everything with which it is confronted. Hence the statement 'Go up the bush and learn bush medicine' is both a caricature of a stock, condescending attitude and also an angry piece of self-laceration. There is a part of the poet which accepts the need for the kind of instruction in reality which only the rural areas can provide; there is also another part, not entirely unrelated to the first, which is tempted to comply with the kind of dismissive gesture which the term 'bush' implies. The poem 'Siren-Throated Sister' both records a piquant episode and serves as a wry self-portrait of a cub doctor, newly from England, confused and not a little alarmed by the spontaneous mannerisms of a society with which he claims kinship. The line 'I withdraw to safer climes' has much to tell us about a personal habit of withdrawal from crisis and also about the personal conditioning wrought by several years exposure to British stiffness and reserve.

The ambivalence of the poet's reactions to his own homecoming are conveyed with sharp verbal density in the poem 'The Rasping Winds Lash' where a visual panorama of riverain Gambia serves as a vehicle for deeper philosophical comment. The winds of change in the first stanza are 'rasping' and redolent of the 'demented' social paranoia which Peters has already evoked in the European poems; they are also paradoxically the medium of a welcome liberation. The dance enacted by the palm trees is a thing of beauty; it is also the product of a kind of cultural rigidity from which the trees feel the need to 'unbend'. The shoots of grass which peep from the bare parched soil are tokens of a new awakening; they are also the harbingers of death. In all of this Peters recognizes 'home', the domain from which he has emerged and to which he rightfully belongs; yet his description of the 'woodman turning home with axe about his neck' reads like a reproduction of a Constable painting of the Essex countryside. The grass which the farmers burn is both 'lush' and incendiary, that is, responsible for its own incineration. The faces of Muslim worshippers are both 'sublime' and 'besmirched with dust': the erotic frenzies of which they remind the poet have their own sublime dimension, but are also the means of spiritual purgatory. The poem is remarkable for the way in which it distances and almost objectifies these reactions, at the same time telling us more about the poet's private feelings than half the pieces which employ the first person singular.

The mellow contemplativeness of the last poem is typical of many other poems in the volume, such as 'The River Flowing Soft' and 'From My Hill-Grove'; it is therefore all the more alarming to find, sandwiched between two such ambivalently affectionate landscapes, a pair of tetchy pieces in which the poet's impatience with the slowness of Africa's progress boils over in great billowing clouds of rage. But 'You Talk to Me of "Self"' and 'It is Time for Reckoning Africa' have only partly to do with the objective Africa which Peters is learning to assimilate; they have much more to do with certain political concepts of the African past, and more particularly with *négritude*.

For decades, ever since the late thirties, the intellectuals of English-speaking West Africa had held *négritude* at arm's length regarding it as a bizarre programme dreamed up by their francophone brothers to deal with their peculiar circumstances but of limited relevance to the problems of Nigeria or Sierra Leone. But now, at last, in the late 1960s and early 1970s, there was an active and continuing dialogue between English- and French-speaking writers and scholars on the relevance of Senghor's ideological scheme to post-colonial Africa. The discussion

raged in journals and conferences: these two poems are Peters's con-
tribution to the debate. 'You Talk to Me of "Self"' is the record of a
single, sullen mood: it must also be taken as an expression of one half
of Peters's mind.[24] The poem has overtones of Donne's famous
debunking song 'Go and Catch a Falling Star'. Donne wishes to illus-
trate by a process of *reductio ad absurdum* the impossibility of chastity in
women; Peters is attempting with equal self-consciousness to demon-
strate an equivalently extreme case: the primitivism of Africa unre-
deemed by scientific progress. Sharp visual images underline the
degradation of which he is attempting to convince us. The fact that
they are culled from the poet's highly personal and selective mental
world scarcely diminishes their impact. Before one categorizes this as
a piece of reactionary petulance, however, one should consider
whether the poet is talking to a radical delegate at some international
conference, or to a 'self' of which the poet repeatedly speaks. The side
of Peters's nature which found an outlet in student nationalist politics
is in no way dead, merely transmuted by age and experience. In this
poem Peters, the hard-bitten pragmatic doctor, takes Peters the stu-
dent nationalist to court and gives him a sound drubbing.

The opening of 'It is Time for Reckoning Africa' has a clear prov-
enance. Few as versed in African literature and poetry as Peters is
could fail to recognize in these first few lines the cadences of part II of
Senghor's great poem 'A New-York':

> Voici le temps des signes et des comptes
> New-York! Or voici le temps de la manne et de l'hysope.[25]

Senghor, on a fleeting visit to Manhattan, is attempting to persuade
the inhabitants of Fifth Avenue of precisely those things which he sees
missing in their civilization, despite its flaunted sophistication and
affluence. Peters, addressing his own people in a time of nationalistic
self-assertion, is pointing to failures of a different sort:

> too long we have dragged
>  our slippered feet
> through rank disorder
> incompetence, self defeat[26]

But this is just as it should be: Peters, if not exactly invalidating *négri-
tude* is at least providing a needed counterblast to its more simplistic

[24] *Ibid.*, No. 63. (*Selected Poetry*, p. 78.)
[25] Leopold Sédar Senghor, *Ethiopiques* (Paris: Editions du Seine, 1956), p. 56.
[26] Peters, *Katchikali*, No. 64. (*Selected Poetry*, p. 80.)

formulations. *Négritude* is characteristically a school of thought which concerns itself with the visionary view of the past which it then projects into the future as a basis for political action. Peters's poem is concerned with neither, but markedly with the abysmal present of neo-colonial dictatorship and monied *arrivisme*. The view is not merely in contradiction to *négritude*: Peters also sees a causal connection between the duplicities of those in power and the ideological programmes which helped bring them there:

> in the high capitals
> the angry men; angry
> with dust in their heads
> a dagger at each other's throats[27]

The 'anger' is a pose, grist to the mill of personal advancement, though it expresses itself in slogans derived from the literature of nationalist protest. At a first reading the third line of this stanza may be misconstrued as 'dust on their heads'. The confusion is useful, since it suggests that an affectation of austerity is one of the lies with which the leaders of the new Africa fill their mental vacuity. Peters is forever playing tricks like this. There is, for instance, his meticulous care with word order. In the concluding stanza:

> In this all revolutions end
> and the straight path
> from world to better world
> branded across the sky.[28]

the meaning is crucially dependent on whether the phrase 'and the straight path ... branded across the sky' is construed as apposite to 'this' or to the word 'revolutions'. If the former, the temporary disillusionment of the present is seen to give on to a dazzling vision of future revolutionary fulfilment; if the latter, the beckoning vision is also a false hope. The poem, as others in the volume, can be read in either of two ways; once again Peters the pragmatist has Peters the idealist by the throat.

The placing of these sad, angry pieces is one of the felicities of this deftly organized volume. Another complementary piece of poetic logistics is the placing of the poem 'From My Hill-Grove' immediately after them. This is a poem which can be considered at many levels. Clearly the speaker is not Peters himself. Either the poem may be

[27] *Ibid.*, No. 64. (*Selected Poetry*, p. 80.)    [28] *Ibid.*, No. 64. (*Selected Poetry*, p. 81.)

taken as a direct reply to the intemperance of the foregoing pieces, in which case the speaker is the ancestral spirit of Africa, or, more poignantly, it can be taken as a reply to the title poem, in which case the speaker is none other than Katchikali. Conceivably it is both: a reply, by the calming, abiding presence of the oldest of the continents to one who has returned full of desperation and self-rending anger. It is an attempt to see the problems posed by the rest of the volume in the longest of perspectives, one from which the torrent of 'progress' dwindles to a trickle. The vision invoked is not a reactionary one, but, in the truest sense, conservative:

> It is I who carry your past
> I forbid progress
> and I who measure
> out your future like a potion[29]

The medical image of the last line distils the poem's meaning of patient and modified comfort, accommodating at the same time the poet's thirst for his country's betterment and his sense of tradition and rootedness. What is forbidden is not enlightenment or self-improvement, but the trendy bandwagon of unthinking 'progress', an onward rush which kills as it attempts to heal. Finally, this is where the intellectual dialogue of the book comes to rest, the remaining poems being either expansions of previous material or lighthearted satires. But in allowing the goddess her own voice Peters has provided both a corrective to his own tortured discontent and a tentative answer to those problems which have beset him on his journey.

The volume *Selected Poetry* contains a representative group of new poems written since the appearance of *Katchikali* in 1971. They show Peters to have matured, mellowing into a background in which he now feels firmly at home. Fewer of them have to do with Peters's private dilemmas than in the previous volumes. Secure now in his albeit bifocal sense of identity, Peters feels free to reach out and look for analogies of the contemporary African condition which may illuminate his difficult position as one who seeks to serve the cause of a continent from which much in his education and experience has worked to alienate him. In many ways the typical poem of this phase of Peters's development is 'Some Think the Past' (No. 76), inspired by a reading of Alex Haley's *Roots* (1977), a then-fashionable epic of Afro-American

---

[29] *Ibid.*, No. 65.

history.[30] It is a poem which resists various temptations; of pitying disdain, or of too easy a compliance in Haley's well-meant but mercenary objective. Peters is able to avoid these traps because he senses in Haley's confusion a reflection of his own occasionally fraught search for meaning and place. Haley's admittedly ulterior considerations are seen as a distraction ('wall-street / hammering in your brain') rather than a cynical ploy which invalidates his deeper motives. The summation of Peters's verdict in the last stanza is carried partly by the beautifully placed proverb ('The baobab root / does not cross / the river's bend') and partly by the impeccably chosen medical word 'tendinous'. Tendons enable one, as tree roots do not, to cross continents and forge links with other climes and cultures. The image is a positive one which asserts the advantages and strengths of an interconnectedness which is the lone redeeming result of a tragic, shared history.

There is a sense in which many of the 'New Poems' have to do with ways in which the history of different peoples may be compared meaningfully. Poem 58 ('Here in the Kingdom of the Navaho') for instance is nominally set in North America, and yet there is a persistent feeling that Peters is also addressing himself to the problems of his own people:

> here, where mother is father of all,
> the concentrated gloom of all the ages,
> and all the ransomed places,
> where the dance is religious ritual
> soft stepping towards God[31]

Who else is he talking about except the dispossessed, the wretched of the earth, those enslaved by the forces of mercantile capitalism, as the Freetown creoles were before their retransportation, as the American Indians were? It is in this sense of identification with peoples and places which share this plight in its various forms that the strength of the new poems lies. There have been many poems of celebration and sympathy since the Soweto rising of 1976, but few have the power of Peters's poem which comes from his ability to see himself too as a child of South Africa, a victim of apartheid:

> But I survive
> and you are alive Soweto
> and brave and strong

---

[30] Alex Haley, *Roots* (London: Hutchinson, 1977).
[31] *Ibid.*, p. 87.

> and never alone
> never abandoned[32]

Yet if Peters simply saw himself as victim, the poem would lack the extra dimension which comes from his confession, in the last stanza but two, of implied complicity with the oppressor:

> Soweto is in my backyard
> where termites gather,
> in the offices of ten percenters
> in my envy of the next man,
> living by his sweat
> freezing his wages
> stealing his children's bread.[33]

There is a strong sense here, as elsewhere in these poems that Peters is aware of the falsity of his position as one who, while expressing solidarity with the downcast, contributes by the comparative luxury of his lifestyle towards their backwardness. This is never more honestly expressed than in poem 93, where a candid self-portrait issues in a note of self-condemnation and an admission of personal powerlessness:

> Men are roasting nuts
> on the wood fire
> their laughter like sheet-lightning
> in the night,
> girls dancing by fire light
> among green-flowing fields of rice crop.
> I, always once removed
> from their fun and laughter
> cannot reach them.[34]

There is a touch of slightly false romanticism about the social attitudes expressed here; one feels that the superior gratification attributed to the villagers is more a reflection of Peters's own nostalgic regret rather than of anything actually present in their surroundings. Nostalgia of course is one thing; guilt quite another. The poem shows abundant evidence of this. In seeking to argue in the second stanza that he is after all a product of a human race, rich in diversity, Peters is, one suspects, pressing a self-evident case too far. The doctor protests too much, and, in the process, lets in an arch tone of voice which offsets the genuine regret present in the poem's closing lines.

[32] *Ibid.* p. 101.     [33] *Ibid.*, p. 101.     [34] *Ibid.*, p. 129.

Much the same duplicity of feeling characterizes the hortative poem 'Tear Way (*sic*) the Façade' in which the poet addressed a symbolic member of the black ruling class in an attempt to point out the contradictions of his way of life.[35] The poem is a sermon from a preacher whose earnestness betrays his uneasy recognition that he is more than slightly besmirched by the sins he castigates. In an attempt to establish his case Peters indulges in a sentimental idealization of rural and traditional life very similar to that we noted before. Who one wonders are these 'great kings and queens / brutal and naked, without Ph.Ds', and in what sense is the mastery they represent superior to the advantages enjoyed by the subject of the sermon? In the context of the proffered argument 'brutal' too is an extremely inappropriate word, nor does it seem to connect with any detectable and coherent counterargument. True, Peters may be construed as addressing himself, in which case a certain amount of waywardness and backtracking might be expected, but again, one feels the element of self-revelation and confession is not systematically exploited in the poem in a way in which it is, for example, in the stronger pieces in *Katchikali*. This divisiveness of tone has much to tell us about the path of Peters's development since the previous volume. The commitment has hardened, but in such a way as to expose him to accusations of hypocrisy and intellectual double-think, the force of which he acknowledges, but which he has so far handled ineptly. The reason is hard to fathom, unless it originates in his feeling of an obligation towards certain polemical themes which do not come naturally to him. Certainly, the strongest pieces in the book, the self-analytical 'On This Public Day of Rest' (No. 79) and the affectionate portrait of the river Gambia printed as No. 75, are both about as far from the public stage as it is possible to go.

'On This Public Day of Rest' is interesting in that it is one of the few poems in Peters's output in which he broaches directly activity as a poet.[36] It is in at least one sense, like the other pieces from 'New Poems',[37] an admission of slavery, but this time to a jealous muse who will not leave him alone. It is also a poem which echoes T. S. Eliot's preoccupations in *The Four Quartets* with the poet's constant struggle with words which 'strain, / Crack and sometimes break, under the burden, / Under the tension, slip, slide, perish, / Decay with imprecision, will not stay in place, / Will not stay still.' The poet's calling is portrayed as a possessive mania, as demanding as a nagging wife, and

---

[35] *Ibid.*, p. 121.    [36] *Ibid.*, p. 109.    [37] *Ibid.*, pp. 00–00.

miserly with her rewards. The idea of maniacal possession is nicely portrayed in the lines:

> She throws you the hint of an idea
> Which when you are composed, has gone[38]

The lines are susceptible of two interpretations. 'When you are composed' means, on one level 'when you have completed the act of writing', thus conveying the idea of exhaustion of creative effort after the act of self-expression. It can also mean 'when you are devoid of emotion', thus conveying the conviction that poetic activity is impossible unless the writer is in a highly charged state. Both beliefs are part and parcel of the romantic view of the poetic vocation which Peters here shares. It is a pity that such convictions have to be expressed in the contexts of a group of poems in which the voltage of inspiration seems lower than in the previous books.

No such flagging of impetus, however, is discernible in the descriptive poem 'Sanguine river / Chaste River' / where all of Peters's old skill is evident. The Gambia is a long slow-moving river; the sloth of its advance and the life along its banks is here aptly conveyed by use of repetition, selective rhyme, and careful line movement. Look at the almost incantatory repetitions in the first stanza, dragging the slow 'o' vowel after them. Then examine the meticulous way in which the line-breaks in the second stanza are fixed so as to give us a sense of drugged indolent ease:

> the stealthy crocodile
> sliding between the
> veiled sun's transections,
> then motionless: and the Hippos'
> interminable yawn.[39]

The break after the long penultimate line leaves us staring right down the raised lethargic throat of the hippopotamus. There could be no clearer instance of the way in which a poet, using purely aural means, may convey an essentially visual sensation.

This piece serves to remind us that, apart from or perhaps despite the move towards a more committed stance evident during this phase of Peters's career, it is as a craftsman in sound that in the end he invites judgement. The best of his poetry shows an admirable

---

[38] *Ibid.*, p. 110.     [39] *Ibid.*, p. 105.

consistency in this regard. Even in the less accomplished, where errors of tone are detectable, he retains a fine sense of form. An analogy which may occur to the reader is that of music; and this is no accident, since Peters has long been a keen amateur musician, has a fine baritone voice, and is addicted to the interpretation of German *lieder*. At the time of the publication of his Mbari book in 1964 he had only recently resisted the temptation to abandon his medical career for an attempt on the operatic stage. That ambition may be a thing of the past, but it has paid metrical dividends. African poetry in English has arrived on the world scene in an age when the settled artistic forms, both musical and poetic, have broken down to be replaced by the improvisational versatility of the individual artist. Just as the composer has been set adrift on a sea of atonality, so the poet has had to do without the familiar landmarks of rhyme, regular metre, and recognizable stanzaic structure. It is to Peters's credit that, without the support of any of these conventional devices, he has managed so consistently to impress his readers with an instinctive, inbuilt sense of structure and formal decorum which, at his best, is invariably in strict accord with his subject matter. He has done this without forsaking the fluidity of free verse more than occasionally, guided only by his inner reflexes and sensitive ear. A crude estimate of Peters's contribution would be that what he has to say is often of less interest than the way he says it. It would be truer to state that, in his finest moments, theme and method come together in a way rare in the annals of contemporary poetry.

# CHAPTER 9

# The road to Idanre, 1959–67

For a long time I could not accept why Ogun, the Creator God, should also be the agency of death. Interpretation of his domain, the road, proved particularly depressing and symbolically vexed especially inasmuch as the road is so obviously part of this same cyclic order. I know of nothing more futile, more monotonous or boring than a circle.[1]

So, in 1965, wrote a thirty-one-year-old playwright at the foot of the typescript of his poem 'Idanre', written in Nigeria several months previously and performed that year at the Commonwealth Arts Festival. At the time Wole Soyinka's reputation rested primarily on his work as a dramatist. Though several of his poems had found their way into *The Horn*, *Black Orpheus* and other Nigerian periodicals, he was not to publish a full collection for another two years.

When in 1967 'Idanre' was published as the climactic piece in the volume which bears its name, rapid recognition followed, together with a spate of critical activity intent on asserting both the inner cohesion of the collection as a whole and its vital bearing on the adjacent world of the plays. Signs of internal organization were not hard to find. All of the poems, including the title work, dwelt on moments of transition: dawn, birth, death, the first pangs of war. The book was divided into sections which appeared to anticipate one another. In the opening piece, 'Dawn',[2] the figure of a palm tree is etched, 'lone intruder' against the flushed early morning skyline; the following section is called 'lone figure'. The concluding poem of this section, 'Easter',[3] closes on a memorable cameo of young children tenderly weaving palm crosses. The opening song of the next section proves to be a propitiation chant in which children sing the words 'Dolorous knot/Plead for me.'[4] This section ends with the poem 'Post Mortem', whose last verse paragraph reads:

---

[1] Soyinka's manuscript note to typescript, British Library Add. Ms 53785.
[2] Woke Soyinka, *Idanre and Other Poems* (London: Methuen, 1967), p. 9.
[3] *Ibid.*, p. 21.      [4] *Ibid.*, p. 23.

Let us love all things of grey; grey slabs
grey scalpel, one grey sleep and form,
grey images[5]

The next section but one is appropriately entitled 'grey seasons'. This is followed by a sequence of poems written in the months following the second Nigerian *coup d'état* of July 1966 and the ensuing fratricidal massacres, and hence serving as a fitting introduction to 'Idanre' itself at the climax of which Ogun, the Yoruba, god of war and of the forge, is described slaughtering his own people in the heat of battle.

So much attention was devoted then, as now, to such interconnections that it has seldom been noted that the poetry comprising the volume was composed over an eight-year period and under very diverse conditions. The neglect of this fact has led to two related critical failures: an assumption that the entire imaginative achievement had sprung fully armed from its originator's mind like Athena from the head of Zeus, and a consequent quest for symbolic patterns which would explain the meaning of the work as clearly as a cardiac pattern on a graph. Thus poems from different periods have been yoked by violence together and then forced into a bigamous union with plays which belonged to quite another date and marriage bed. The bastardly brood begotten of this spurious union has tended to drive out any legitimate consideration of the circumstances which, over a prolonged period of genesis, gave rise to so unique and interesting a volume.

At the time of Idanre's publication, Soyinka was director of the drama department at the University of Ibadan, fifty miles to the north east of his birthplace of Abeokuta, in the present Ogun state of Nigeria. While an undergraduate at the University of Leeds he had studied with the critic and Shakespearean scholar George Wilson Knight under whom he had taken a comprehensive two-year course of lectures on 'The Drama' stretching from the Athenian tragedians through the mediaeval morality, the Elizabethans and Jacobeans to the revolutionary European theatre of the closing years of the nineteenth century: Ibsen, Strindberg and Chekhov. Shortly after graduating he moved to London, where he joined a team of readers recruited by the impresario George Devine to assess submissions for the English Stage Company, the writers' theatre recently established at the Royal Court, Sloane Square. Devine's production policy included throwing

[5] *Ibid.*, p. 31.

the Court's tiny auditorium open to aspiring younger writers for one-off sessions on Sunday evenings. On 1 November 1959 the programme was advertised as an 'Evening of Poetry, Song and *The Invention*' by one Wole Soyinka.[6] In the following year, Soyinka returned to Nigeria, where a Research Fellowship at Ibadan enabled him to study traditional African drama and to cut his teeth as a playwright, poet and director.

Although Soyinka had written some verse while in Leeds, the earliest poetry collected in *Idanre and other Poems* belongs to the period immediately after his arrival in London. Both 'Abiku' and 'Deserted Markets' were composed early enough to be included alongside the apprentice poem 'Telephone Conversation' and several unpublished pieces in the Sunday evening performance at the Royal Court in 1959,[7] 'Death in the Dawn'. 'Season' and 'Night' were written in Nigeria and completed by 1961, when they appeared alongside 'Abiku' in Langston Hughes's influential *African Treasury*.[8] All had previously featured in small magazines: 'Death in the Dawn' and 'Season' in *The Horn*,[9] 'Abiku' in *Black Orpheus*.[10] All belong to the period of Soyinka's first emergence as a playwright. They draw on his experiences of making do in London, of footing it round the sleazier quarters of Paris, of early manhood, marriage and parenthood, aspects of which provide the substance of the first six sections of the book.

The title poem itself, on the other hand, poured forth in one day as the result of a transforming spiritual awakening, a coming together of many strands, early in 1965. Though later publicly recited in London, it was in no sense a commissioned piece, but rather the culmination of a process of fusion binding together particles in the poet's mental make-up which had, as his manuscript note to the typescript implies, until that time obstinately refused to cohere. Written the day after a nocturnal expedition to Molete, a hamlet sixteen miles from Abeokuta, it continually harks back to an earlier visit in 1962 to a range of hills in the vicinity of Old Idanre, which, almost 3,000 feet above sea

---

[6] Cf. James Gibbs, 'Comments on Some of Wole Soyinka's Early Verse', *The Literary Half-Yearly* XXII, 1, January 1981, pp. 47–63.　　[7] *Ibid.*, p. 50.
[8] *African Treasury* ed. Langston Hughes (New York: Pyramid Books, 1960), pp. 194-9.
[9] 'Death in the Dawn', *The Horn* 4, 6, 1962, pp. 2–3. 'Season', *The Horn* 4, 2, 1961, p. 2. 'Death in the Dawn' at the time suffered somewhat from over-exposure, appearing also in *Beacon* 1, 8, 1962, p. 48. It had already appeared in *Black Orpheus* 10 alongside 'Abiku', p. 8.　　[10] 'Abiku', *Black Orpheus* 10, 1961, p. 7.

level at their highest point, soar 2,000 feet above the valley formed by the confluence of the Apun Edun and Oto rivers, some 200 miles to the east.

Finally, the six poems which comprise the penultimate section 'October '66' refer to the catastrophic turn of events which in the aftermath of the first military intervention in Nigerian politics led inevitably to the outbreak of the Civil War in August 1967 – an eventuality which, when the volume went to press, was still some time in the future. Though placed before 'Idanre' in the running order they were all therefore written at least a year subsequently, a fact which any historical consideration of the volume's origins must take into account.

The source of the very earliest pieces in the immediacy of theatrical performance is manifest both in their cultivation of the inflections of either the singing or the speaking voice[11] and in their dramatic projection of the essentials of an attitude. Both 'Abiku' and the song 'Deserted Markets' express a certain asperity in the face of heart-rending circumstances: 'Abiku' of a stillborn child's disdain at its parents' futile grieving, and 'Deserted Markets' the desolation experienced during a liaison between a prostitute and her client in the Paris market district of Les Halles. Much of the strength of 'Abiku', derives from its loftiness of tone. Listen to the grandiose opening, dark with pure, lip-curling disdain:

> In vain your bangles cast
> Charmed circles at my feet
> I am Abiku, calling for the first
> And the repeated time.[12]

Dramatically rendered, the poem writhes with a kind of gloating mockery which at moments verges on the blacker extremities of farce. There is, for example, little affection in the words:

> Night, and Abiku sucks the oil
> From lamps. Mother! I'll be the
> Suppliant snake coiled on the doorstep
> Yours the killing cry.[13]

'Suppliant' here implies not deference but a devious lying in wait. And the stanza has a sting in its tail. The adjective 'killing' can only be

---

[11] Soyinka had learned to play the guitar while a student. 'Deserted Markets' is one of nine songs in which he accompanied himself in the Royal Court programme, though the only one included in *Idanre*.
[12] Soyinka, *Idanre*, p. 28. See especially, p. 96.  [13] *Ibid.*, p. 29.

taken to refer to the death of the snake if one assumes a fantastic syntactical contraction. The truer meaning is that the disguised Abiku is dying of laughter at its earthly mother's expense: 'I'll be back to torment you soon, and guess what shape I'll choose'. There is a species of cruelty in these lines which the critics, intent on anthropological readings but deaf to tone, have been slow to register, a callousness of feeling which the poem in its very wording courageously acknowledges.

It has also seldom been appreciated that this superciliousness of tone is shared by the more celebrated 'Death in the Dawn',[14] a poem whose understanding has sometimes been clouded by an overwillingness to press into service insights deriving from much later work. Goodwin, for instance, hijacks a remark from a much later lecture of Soyinka collected in *Myth, Literature and the African World* (1976) to explain the piece's ambivalent view of 'Progress',[15] and Gerald Moore connects the poem with the tragi-comedy *The Road* which, while possibly in gestation since the early sixties, was not completed until 1965.[16] The author's own prefatory note, however, refers us directly to an incident which occurred as early as 1960 when Soyinka, then a Research Fellow at the University of Ibadan, undertook to travel by landrover to Lagos several times a week to rehearse his play *A Dance of the Forests* for the national Independence celebrations. The old Lagos–Ibadan highway was notorious for its treacherous narrowness, its verges littered for miles with the abandoned hulks of burnt-out trucks. On the occasion described, Soyinka's windscreen was assaulted in the half-light of dawn by a stray cockerel some minutes before he encountered the sight, frequent in those days of unimproved roads, of a crushed foreshortened vehicle with the body of its dead driver freshly trapped within it. Soyinka had risen early from necessity, but at the beginning of the poem this obligation becomes an inner compulsion in which he involves the reader: 'Traveller, you must set out'; 'Traveller, you must set forth'. The poem's view of fate is Sophoclean: the reader is caught up despite himself in a headlong rush provoked partly by an inscrutable destiny and partly by his own inner restlessness. Goodwin plays etymology a poor trick here by interpreting the forward momentum of which the poet speaks as some-

---

[14] *Ibid.*, pp. 10–11.
[15] K. L. Goodwin, *Understanding African Poetry: A Study of Ten Poets* (London: Heinemann, 1982), p. 112.
[16] Wole Soyinka, *The Road*, produced by the Stage Sixty company at the Theatre Royal, Stratford East, London, September, 1965. The connection is discussed in Gerald Moore, *Wole Soyinka* (London: Evans; New York; Africana, 1971), pp. 91-2.

thing to do with 'Progress'. In fact the noun is 'Progression' and conveys less a divisive view of technology than an age-old instinct for movement of which the road and the hurtling car serve as extensions. It is this unremitting instinct which the cock's impalement on the windscreen questions by its ritualistic reminder that mankind's destiny is not subject to his own control, but rather prey to incomprehensible forces.

The poet's reaction to this reminder is torn between a chastened recognition of man's limitations and a haughty dismissal of all that these imply. It is noticeable, for instance, that Soyinka supplies no answer to the rhetorical question with which the poem ends. Most commentators have assumed that the implied answer is 'Yes', and that the poet therefore fully identifies with the dead driver. The truth is surely that the fraternal gesture involved in the salutatory 'Brother, silence by the hug of your invention' at line 32 is offset by a countervailing impulse of recoil. There is a part of the poet which is very unwilling to associate itself with this pathetic and comically grimacing hunk of meat whose expression of ridiculous surprise is 'mocked' not merely by the crushed cab in which it sits, but by the writer himself. Moreover, it is not merely the driver who is fooled by his own optimism but the reader and even Soyinka himself, both of whom are potential victims of the superficial nervous exhilaration earlier suggested by the phrase 'Racing joys and apprehensions for / A naked day'. The 'rite' of the cock's sacrifice is 'futile' because it fails effectively to remind us of our vulnerability, and 'perverse' because it underscores an ominous lesson which, despite the mother's spell weaved in lines 22–5, speaker and reader alike are slow to take to heart. The more fool me, says Soyinka, stepping on the accelerator and courting his own doom. We are all fools in the land of moral wisdom, and, though propitiation beckons and swerves before us, we will not hearken to it until we too rot amid a mass of rusting twisted metal by the roadside.

'Abiku' and 'Death in the Dawn' were printed in *Black Orpheus* as part of a set which also included 'Season' and 'Night'.[17] In *Idanre*, the last two of these pieces again stand side by side in the section 'Grey Seasons'. These are both descriptive pieces over which much irrelevant critical ink has been wasted. Eldred Jones, for instance, worried by the shift to the past tense at the end of the second stanza of

---

[17] *Black Orpheus* 10, 1961: 'Abiku', p. 7; 'Night', p. 9; 'Season', p. 9.; 'Death in the Dawn', p. 8.

'Season', converts the whole piece into an evocation of the life cycle.[18]
But read in the context of *Black Orpheus* where it first appeared, the
poem seems much closer to a straightforward harvest thanksgiving;
read in the context of 'Grey Seasons', it seems closer to an atmospheric
mood-poem. Philosophical extrapolation is only appropriate if we
take the poem's use of the first person plural to be authorial and fur-
ther interpret the word 'rust' as a spiritual symbol rather than, what it
patently is, a visual image of the sun-ripened corn. If we simply open
ourselves to the meaning of the text and resist the temptation to
impose extraneous significance, the poem makes perfect sense as a
dramatic piece in which the speakers are farmers, intent on the gather-
ing in of their crop, grateful for the recent promise of fields heaving
and tossing beneath the wind, but still apprehensive of what reaping
may reveal.

The tendency of the critics to make symbolic mincemeat out of
poetry characterized by tender lucidity reaches perverse proportions
when we approach the work contained in sections 3 and 4, which
deals with the private life of the emotions. The lovely birthday bene-
diction 'Dedication, for Moremi, 1963',[19] for example, has recently
been subjected to the gross distortions of an unwieldy post-
structuralist analysis by Sunday Anozie, who nonetheless persists in
misreading as a 'dirge' what is in essence a luminous act of blessing.[20]
Though the images at times lie a little thickly, the main drift is clear.
Like a planted yam, the child must grow gently by stages, cradled by
the beneficent earth. She must learn to achieve the goodness and use-
fulness of peat while remaining open to the lightness of the air and the
helpful influence of the seasons. She must be agile enough to take
advantage of such gifts as offer themselves on the tree of life, but
nimble enough to retreat when danger threatens. She should be a pru-
dent steward of nature's resources, yet not stint herself when confron-
ted with the fullness of joy. Only by living in thus open-hearted a
fashion will she fulfil herself and leave a permanent imprint on the
shores of eternity.

This mood of benediction is shared by 'For the Piper Daughters',[21]

---

[18] Eldred Durosimi Jones, *The Writing of Wole Soyinka* (London: Heinemann, 1973),
    p. 129.    [19] Soyinka, *Idanre*, p. 24.
[20] Sunday Anozie, 'Equivalent Structures in Soyinka's Poetry: Toward A Linguistic
    Methodology in African Poetry Criticism', *Research in African Literatures* 16, 1, Spring
    1985, pp. 20–37.    [21] Soyinka, *Idanre*, p. 27.

written three years earlier, the first of a series of the poems in the volume dedicated to friends and private individuals. It is a piece which leans a little heavily on W. B. Yeats's 'Prayer for My Daughter'[22] but manages nevertheless to achieve a personality all its own. In 1919 Yeats had prayed that his child be spared the conceit of beauty and the sort of strident 'intellectual hatred' whose divisive effect he had experienced all too clearly in his Irish homeland. Soyinka's poem adopts the protective pose, but bestows on Miss Piper less barbed a gift: eternal youth, and the sort of blemishless innocence associated with Shakespeare's more pallid heroines. Thus the poem forms an ideal bridge between these poems of mutual affection and avuncular concern, and a related sequence of personal pieces inscribed 'For women'.

Commentators have often complained that Soyinka's portrayal of the female sex, whether in drama or in verse, exemplifies all of the standard chauvinist vices, tending toward either canonization or degradation. It has less often been observed that in his more intimate poetry these attitudes are softened by a tenderness of concern and a sort of ardent compassion which appear to be the result of genuine empathy. 'Her Joy is Wild',[23] for example, is a poem which with great delicacy describes an act of love with a woman past her first youth who instinctually senses that this is her last chance of conception. It is an intuition shared by the speaker, and, in partaking of her vulnerability, his voice endows the poem with an unbridled generosity which sets the conventional half-rhymed stanzas aglow. In 'Psalm'[24] the poet speaks with the gratitude of a husband or lover, paying homage to the sacrifice all women must make for the privilege of creating new life: the loss of vitality and comeliness for which the miracle of childbirth is the only fit recompense. Once more the feminine half-rhymes, and the parallel phrasing reminiscent of the Hebraic psalmody which serves distantly as the poem's model set the sincerity of feeling within an elegant, aptly reverent frame.

The risk necessarily entailed in all loving is a theme running through many of these private pieces. At once the most personal and the most universal is 'By Little Loving',[25] an exercise explicitly written *'After Thomas Blackburn'*, the British poet of part-Mauritian parentage

---

[22] W. B. Yeats, 'A Prayer for my Daughter', *Collected Poems* (London: Macmillan, 2nd edition, 1950), p. 211.      [23] Soyinka, *Idanre*, p. 35.      [24] *Ibid.*, p. 34.
[25] *Ibid.*, p. 41.

whose work created a small stir in the early sixties with its courageous
baring of spiritual sores. Blackburn's father, a North-country parson
descended from generations of Anglican missionaries, had been so
terrified of his children lapsing into some abyss of equitorial depravity
that he had subjected the growing boy to a crippling régime of physi-
cal and emotional discipline. This background had spawned within
the poet's psyche a monster of guilt and a repressed sexuality which in
his poems he attempted to stalk through what he called the twisting
Cnossos of his heart. In the poem 'An Epitaph', on which Soyinka's is
based, he diagnoses in himself a tendency to take refuge from the Min-
otaur within by fleeing into the labyrinthine frivolities of social conver-
sation:

> By much speaking I fled from silence,
> To many friends from the one stranger,
> By food and drink I cheated hunger,
> And by meek words, abuse and violence.
>
> My loss increased as I grew richer,
> My load more great with lighter burden,
> With less guilt, more I sought pardon.
> As light flowered, I grew blinder.[26]

The tendencies which Soyinka detects in himself are almost the
polar opposite of Blackburn's: an unwonted, possibly arrogant re-
serve, a withholding of the self, a spurning of the common clay. It may
be argued that these are all ingredients present in the tone of voice to
be found in Soyinka's earliest poetry. Just as the speaker in 'Death in
the Dawn' turned in distaste from the spectacle of a dead lorry driver,
deigning only with reluctance to acknowledge his kinship with mortal
corruption, so the poet himself once fought shy of meaningful human
contact, a failing for which he now desires to make contrition. The
poem begins by comparing the barriers which the poet once construc-
ted around himself to a bank of sea shells scarcely containing the
pressures of a high tide:

> By little loving, once, I sought
> To conquer pain, a bank of bleached
> Shells kept floods at bay – once
> By little wisdoms, sought the welcome drought.

The poem's skill lies in a species of associative technique by which

[26] Thomas Blackburn, 'An Epitaph' in *A Smell of Burning* (London: Putnam, 1961), pp.
28–9.

one image is selected and promptly transformed into another sufficiently dissimilar to advance the argument by one step. The structure of the piece thus proceeds through a series of single, oblique steps, rather as a musical *motif* is systematically transformed during a Beethoven Symphony. In stanza 3, for example, the 'crypt' within which the poet has entombed himself against compromising human contact has become a chantry whose walls provide sanctuary for either haughtiness or timidity. By line 11 this has become clay ineptly thrown on the potter's wheel, collapsing inwards like the poet's mind. The idea of rotation is carried over to the next stanza, where, however, it is applied to a spool of thread gradually unwinding. Thus, as image steals into image, order and restraint give way to candour and flexibility, while the concluding image of a pheonix's delayed immolation brings together ideas of fire, deluge and burial with the very process of metamorphosis the poem's structure illustrates.

Though placed at the climactic point of the volume, there is little doubt that the title poem *Idanre* was conceived separately. Its relative length, and the rhetorical density of its language mark it out as a work devised on an epic scale. Though the autobiographical experiences evoked can have taken no longer than four or five hours, the scope of the imaginative enterprise reaches out to embrace the whole of cosmic history as embodied in Yoruba belief. The work runs on many levels and cuts across several dimensions: it is at once confession, autobiographical fragment, mythical enactment and declarative credo. Much comment has been passed by others on its cultural affinities and antecedents, and much explanation provided of the manner in which it illuminates the simultaneous achievement of the plays. Less light has so far been shed on its structure and the way that it holds together as a poetic artifact.

Soyinka's preamble, written in 1967 when the volume was in preparation, tells us all that we need to know about the personal circumstances which gave rise to the poem. At the turn of the rainy season in mid-1965 Soyinka was at work in his study when the first seasonal thunderstorm broke. Abandoning his writing, he made his way with a group of unidentified companions to the hamlet of Molete which lies sixteen miles above the poet's birthplace of Abeokuta. The terrain to the north-east of Abeokuta consists of rising ground about four hundred feet above sea level, covered by sparse shrubs and inter-spersed with patches of woodland. Despite the relative dissimilarity of the landscape, the nocturnal setting of the walk and the magnifi-cence of the drenched woods on the outskirts of the village were suf-ficient to recall another expedition, undertaken two years previously to the granite outcrop of Idanre which soars many hundreds of feet higher 200 miles to the east.

Sections I and II ('Deluge', 'And after') and Section VI ('Recessional') provide the outer narrative framework to the poem, the mythic core of which occupies Sections III to V. To segregate these strands com-pletely, however, is impossible. Section I, for instance, is an evocation of the full violence of the storm as it breaks around Soyinka's house. Yet this natural cataclysm is realized in terms of the legendary contest between Ogun, Yoruba, god of war, protector of orphans, and Ṣango, god of thunder, whose thunderbolts litter local grounds in the form of the prehistoric axeheads found all over this part of south-western Nigeria. Yoruba legend tells how Obatala, god of creation, was im-prisoned while visiting Ṣango's court, upon which Ogun wrought havoc among the thunderer's domains. As the poem opens, Ogun's horsemen have briefly withdrawn from the scene of pillage and stand poised for a fresh assault. After a renewed surge of violence, peace descends and the expectant earth prepares for the quickening of seeds which will bear fruit at the harvest. Though the poetic language of this section draws on the heroic strain of the European epic, there is also a delicacy of subdued shading, and the colour grey, familiar from the descriptive poetry in the section 'Grey Seasons' is prominent. The very ambivalence of grey – its tendency to veer toward intimations of either mortality or of glowing serenity – is viewed as an aspect of Ogun, destroyer and maker, as, for better or worse, he rallies his men for the last time. As Ogun throws one last assault at Ṣango's retreating army, Soyinka, safe still beneath the dry roof of his home, sends out a fraternal greeting, thus setting the seal on a personal allegiance which is to be one of the mainstays of the poem.

In Section II the poet emerges from his bungalow and, setting out across a countryside still electric with the after-throes of the storm, stops briefly to take refreshment before attempting the upward gra-dient. At this point the fusion between two different time levels which is so marked a feature of the poem's organization commences. What we are presented with is in fact less a literal account of the trip to Molete than an imaginary reconstruction of the earlier expedition to

Idanre shot through both with reminiscences of the Molete episode and with emanations from Yoruba mythology. The palm wine seller, for instance, is a memory from Soyinka's walk up Idanre. She is also Oya, Ogun's long-suffering wife, and her recalled presence on the later expeditions hence serves as an augury of the war god's blessing. The most awesome passages in this section are devoted to the strange after-effects of the tempest: the marriage of fire and steel which causes a corybantic dance amid the telegraph wires. Here Soyinka's vocabulary strains in two directions: toward a scientific terminology not always fully integrated into his lyric flow and a contrasting grace of phrase responsible for some of the poem's more memorable moments. 'Metagenesis', for example (l. 41), is a highly technical word employed in genetics to denote alternation in any one species between divergent modes of reproduction. It is used here to connote the incongruous yoking of heaven and earth which causes the electric storm. Such recondite usages are less evocative of true atmosphere than is this:

> Calm, beyond interpreting, she sat and in her grace
> Shared wine with us. The quiet of the night
> Shawled us together, secure she was in knowledge
> Of that night's benediction.[27]

The unpretentious verb 'shawled', bringing together in the mind's eye the girl's wrap and the healing canopy of night, is masterly in its inclusiveness. Similarly the simple sentence 'My skin/Grew light with eyes' tells us more about Soyinka's receptive state of mind on this occasion than does the blank verse satirical digression into 'looters and insurance men, litigant on/Spare part sales and terms of premium' (ll. 63–5). This uneasy blend of idiom is held in place by a loose five-line stanza, flexible enough to accommodate reverberations of the heroic line and echoes of Soyinka's own earlier verse. The line 'The road waits famished' (l. 59), for example, is a direct borrowing from the mother's spell in 'Death in the Dawn'. The allusion helps direct our thoughts towards an evolution within this poem of certain traits which had been latent in Soyinka's conceptual universe since early in the decade, and which only now attain complete expression.

It is often assumed that the metaphor of the road is entirely consistent within Soyinka's philosophy. In reality, it has always shifted to

[27] Soyinka, *Idanre*, p. 63.

meet his immediate requirements. In 'Death in the Dawn', the road approximates to an emblem of fate; in *Idanre* it comes to represent the frail causeway across the existential gulf along which passes the intermittent traffic between god and man. In the cosmography of Yoruba-belief there was one moment when this tentative link was ruptured. The legend of Atọọda is widespread throughout Yorubaland, but in Soyinka's work it partakes of a rather precise significance. Atọọda was slave to Orișa-nla, the original, comprehensive deity who contained within his person the totality of the divine pantheon. But, in a fit of rebelliousness Atọọda (the 'traitor' of Section III, l. 9) rolled down an immense boulder onto his recumbent master, thus fragmenting him into the plethora of deities, or *orișas*, worshipped by the Yoruba to this day. The same fracture also severed once and for all the connection between gods and men, until then in constant communion. In Soyinka's system Atọọda becomes the iconoclast of the universal, the patron saint of particularity who, despairing of uniformity, seeks to establish a world in which individuality reigns supreme. It is this state of affairs which Ogun seeks to reverse. The cosmic gap caused by Atọọda's affray is portrayed in Soyinka's vision of things as an ontological wound felt with especial keenness by Ogun in his gentler incarnation as protector of orphans, in this case orphaned mankind. By attempting to re-cross the yawning gulf which now separates the human from the divine sphere, Ogun plays havoc with the *status quo* and invites calamity.

Though firmly grounded in local folklore, Soyinka's realization of this network of intertwined legends also looks for support to other religious systems. The notion of an original fall from grace is, of course, a guiding tenet of Catholic theology. And in the person of Ogun, brooding in isolation, then prey to a sort of vatic euphoria, we have a glimmering both of Christ's sojourn in the wilderness and of Nietzsche's view of Dionysus as the vessel of divine frenzy. Throughout Ogun is also treated much like the protagonist of an Euripidean tragedy, one whose excess of zeal brings down doom on his own shoulders and on those who surround him. Even in Ogun's hour of greatest need and folly, Soyinka's personal identification with his god is nevertheless extreme. And, in contemplating both the enormity of his daring and the supreme necessity of the task which he has set himself, the poet's sense of empathy brings him close enough to the *orișa* to enable him to speak with his voice. At moments of greatest dedication, poet and god act and declaim as one:

> *This road have I trodden in a time beyond*
> *Memory of fallen leaves, beyond*
> *Thread of fossil on the slate, yet I must*
> *This way again.*[28]

In Soyinka's original typescript, now held in the British Library,[29] the opening lines of section IV have above them in long-hand the words 'Beginning of Accompaniment'. In the right-hand margin there then run intermittently to the end of the text a series of instructions to a musical ensemble including xylophone, two-tone hand bells, bass gong and metal bars. These directions represent Soyinka's require-ments for the percussive orchestra which accompanied his recitation of the poem at the Commonwealth Arts Festival in 1965. The delay of this aural contribution to the poem's texture until the inception of the fourth section would tend to suggest that in the poet's mind this point represents the entry of the protagonist into the tragic arena, the spring which activates the fatal mechanism – a supposition which the sec-tional heading 'The Beginning' would tend to endorse.

This then is the kernel of the work: the full-bodied enactment of Ogun's ill-fated quest of reconciliation, his journey from the dwelling place of the gods to the town of Ire, where, after several rebuttals he accepts the status of chief, only to bring the citizens to ruination. It is a journey which the poet symbolically repeats in reverse. There is ample precedent for such an enactment. The ritual of Ogun's passion is to this day celebrated annually in the Yoruba town of Ire Ekiti, where sacrifices, a procession and a set of symbolic skirmishes rep-resent the *oriṣa's* venture and its bloody sequel.[30] Soyinka's own account draws on Ire legend while tailoring it to his own purposes. In the original version, of which many variants exist, Ogun's journey was an endeavour to catch up with the people of the town, who had elected him their king and then, unbeknown to him, promptly up-rooted themselves in an effort to avoid an outbreak of pestilence. The sequel is told by R. I. Ibigbami:

The Onire and his people lived happily (at Igbo Irun) till after an outbreak of small-pox when they consulted the Ifa oracle, which instructed them to go

---

[28] *Ibid.*, p. 69.      [29] See note 1, above.

[30] Cf. Ulli Beier, *A Year of Sacred Festivals in One Yoruba Town* (Lagos: Nigeria Magazine, 3rd edition, 1959); also R. I. Ibigbami, 'Ogun Festival at Ire Ekiti', *Nigeria Magazine* 126–7, 1978, pp. 44–61.

further East for a better living. They then moved Eastwards for about five kilometres and settled in the present site of Ire-Ekiti.

The people of Ire had an annual festival which they celebrated in utter silence; 'ORIKI'. They had finished their wine and the empty kegs were standing around. Ogun had long been making a fruitless journey, looking for his people who had shifted from their old settlement. Hungry, thirsty and tired he suddenly walked into the midst of a silent group of people. The smell of wine that filled the air aggravated his thirst while the sight of the standing kegs made him anxious to drink. Since the people offered him neither wine nor salutations he bent down to serve himself; to his frustration he discovered that all the kegs were empty. He gave vent to his pent up indignation by drawing his sword and killing many of the people.[31]

In Soyinka's version, Ogun's acceptance of the crown is a gesture of reconciliation with man after the primordial rift, and his slaughter of his own subjects is a response both to his own drunkenness – in this case the kegs are full – and to the greater frustration of his existential alienation. The entire episode is evoked in the language of epic, reinforced by a crescendo of the percussive accompaniment from a single muted note on the hand-bell to a maestoso cadenza for xylophone during Ogun's instatement as chief. The elegy which opens Section v ('The Battle') is recited over a slow ostinato passage for solo xylophone. Then, after a sudden staccato note on the gong 'furious', pandemonium breaks loose. 'All metal' reads Soyinka's note opposite the massacre sequence, a cue for a fugal percussive fantasia. The first climax, in both the narrative and in the surrounding musical texture, arrives at the words:

> Lord of all witches, divine hunter
> Your men Ogun, your men!
> His sword an outer crescent of the sun
> No eye can follow it, no breath draws
> In wake of burning vapour. Still they cry
> Your men Ogun! Your men![32]

Soyinka's voice has now taken on the lineaments of an Aeschylean chorus attendant upon the tragic act. As his warnings to the blood-crazed god grow more insistent, so the furioso accompaniment grows ever more frenetic, until at the lines

> Murderer, stay your hand
> Your men lie slain – Cannibal![33]

---

[31] Ibigbami, 'Ogun Festival', pp. 44-5.    [32] Soyinka, *Idanre*, pp. 74-5.    [33] *Ibid.*, p. 76.

there is a sudden break in the sound as the awful reality of his outrage dawns on the *oriṣa*'s mind. When the music resumes Soyinka's choric discourse has become an ode contemplating the religious significance of the catastrophe, against which a 'piano' metallic continuo simmers ominously. At the point where the italicized elegy reappears with its image of a sacrificial ram (*'The rams / are gathered to the stream'*) the xylophone again makes a subdued entry 'pianissimo', tapering off at the re-introduction of the interrupted ode ('Let each seek wisdom where he can') to reappear in single, spiccato 'picked' notes towards the close.

With this the tragic action is complete. What follows is philosophical and personal elaboration both upon the dénouement and on the monumental incident of hubris it represents. In thus unravelling the inner meaning of a tragic mystery, Soyinka is again following classical precedent. His conclusions are also reminiscent of Euripides' intimation that rational management in human affairs is usually impossible and invariably dangerous. Ogun's *hamartia*, his tragic flaw, had been his desire to impose order on the flux of events by healing the breach in the cosmic fabric, an error of intent as presumptuous in its way as Pentheus' outlawing of the irrational cult of Dionysus in Euripides' *The Bacchae*, a play which Soyinka was later to adapt for Britain's National Theatre.[34] The danger is that the consequences of Ogun's failure will spill over to the human community which will then be caught up in an unending cycle of reparation and revenge. In order to prevent this happening, Soyinka is obliged to search for some kind of redemptive procedure which will contain the spreading stain of carnality and allow god and man to exist once more in a state of comparative equilibrium.

Soyinka's desire to absolve Ogun of his misdemeanour involves him in a sequence of theological and mathematical logic which not all readers will immediately follow. In most religious systems – the Hebraic; the Greek; by implication the Christian – there is a law according to which in the absence of absolution, justice must be measured out in exact proportion to the severity of any infringement. Unless Ogun's crime is absolved, the repercussions will be repeatedly visited upon history. The only hope for the future lies in a break in the retributive pattern, a moment of exemption from divine in-

---

[34] Wole Soyinka, *The Bacchae of Euripides*, produced at the National Theatre, August, 1974; published in *Collected Plays*, Vol. 1 (London: Oxford University Press, 1973).

exorability which might allow the healing powers of grace to flow, just as, in the closing section of the poem the harvest follows the first deluge of the West African rains. There is an analogous moment of respite at the very end of Aeschylus' *Oresteia* trilogy, when the Areopagus, the supreme Athenian court of justice, decrees that the stigma of Agamemnon's murder has exhausted itself in Orestes' vendetta, and that no further consequences need follow. In Soyinka's scheme of things, Ogun's outrage is absolved by a break in the wheel of justice, 'a possible centrifugal escape from the eternal cycle', which he compares to a mathematical figure.[35] In 1858 the German mathematician August Möbius (1790–1868) discovered a flat polyhedron, a continuous one-sided surface formed by connecting the ends of a rectangle after giving it a half-twist. Known to science as the Möbius strip, its value in Soyinka's thinking is that within a repetitive circular pattern it allows for a cork-screwing forward movement. It thus reconciles the idea of an endless circle, implicit within any pessimistic vision of history, with the more hopeful image of the road, representative of the 'Progression' of which the poem 'Death in the Dawn' spoke. 'I know of nothing more futile, more monotonous or repetitive than a circle', wrote Soyinka at the foot of his typescript. In experiencing the poem's definitive catharsis both writer and reader have now broken free of any such circular constraint.

The sections 'recessional' (VI) and 'harvest' (VII) are in effect postludes. Chastened by self-knowledge Ogun makes his saddened way down Idanre, and, shamed by his presence at his mentor's undoing, the poet follows him. The hymn to Atóòda which ensues is arguably the one ill-judged portion of the poem. The language fluctuates ponderously between the sub-Miltonic and the flagrantly ungrammatical. The passage from 'For who will stand' (l. 32) to 'the living and the dead' (l. 39) is especially opaque in its deployment of the archaic 'iterate' for 'iteration' and its uncomfortable image of the individual human soul as a particle floating in some gelatinous cosmic broth. The desired mood of serenity, all passion spent, is more successfully achieved in the subtle half-tints of the poet's word-painting of dawn:

> Ogun's mantle brushed the leaves, the phase of night
> Was mellow wine joined to a dirge
> Of shadows, the air withdrew to scything motions
> Of his dark-shod feet, seven-ply crossroads
> Hands of camwood, breath of indigo[36]

[35] Soyinka, *Idanre*, pp. 37–8.  [36] *Ibid.*, p. 83.

As the sun comes up over Idanre and, replete with promise, the harvest follows it, the musical accompaniment makes a brief reappearance in the background. 'Re-entry of xylos' is marked at line 16 of 'harvest' and 'sharp notes on the xylo' against the work's closing cadence, in which the successive images of the work resolve themselves into a unison.

The spontaneous creation of 'Idanre' by Soyinka's own admission enabled him to articulate strands of inspiration which, up until that moment, had existed as random elements within his mind. It is thus a fundamental critical error to attempt to impose the thought-structure of 'Idanre' on earlier material. The poems in the first six sections of *Idanre and Other Poems* can be seen from one vantage point as the raw material out of which the later poetry, starting with *Idanre*, was refined. From this point on Soyinka's work is distinguished less by a projection of a series of dramatic attitudes, the donning of many masks, than by a consistent, constantly evolving point of view. 'Idanre' was Soyinka's definitive philosophical and theological statement. The task which lay ahead consisted of the application of this viewpoint to a variety of fields, including, increasingly, politics.

Until 1966 Soyinka's poetry had been markedly less political and more private than his plays. The incident which galvanized his verse into a political instrument was the public turmoil which hit Nigeria in 1966, eventually giving rise to the Civil War. In *The Man Died*, his prison diary published in 1972 two years after the armistice, Soyinka spoke of 'the colossal moral failure within the nation, a failure that led to secession and war'.[37] The poems included in *Idanre* under the general heading 'October '66' deal with that failure, and more especially with the crisis which followed the massacre of Nigerians of eastern origin in the northern city of Kano on 29 September. For anyone who believed in the future of the nation, this was probably a greater setback than the military *coups* of January and July of the same year. The October massacres seemed to fly in the face of any constructive view of the possibilities of national unity, to contradict that pious longing

[37] Wole Soyinka, *The Man Died* (London: Rex Collings, 1972), p. 19.

for mutual tolerance and understanding which, towards the end of 'Idanre', Soyinka had adumbrated by the progressive figuration of the Möbius strip. In the very last movement of that poem Soyinka had portrayed a burgeoning harvest of confidence. Sadly, in the poem 'Harvest of hate', he converts the same image to raise again the spectre of an unending sequence of retribution:

> Now pay we forfeit on old abdications
> The child dares flames his father lit
> And in the briefness of too bright flares
> Shrivels a heritage of blighted futures.[38]

The imagery of this piece is so manifestly a blackened mirror image of the hopeful prognostications at the end of 'Idanre' – wine going stale in the pot, corn ears wilting on the stem – as to broach the question of a revision of Soyinka's philosophy of history. In his prefatory note to the earlier poem, written between October 1966 and the book's publication, Soyinka prefers to see the carnage of those bitter months as an eccentric excursion of the corkscrew, a replay of Ogun's instant of blind fury. He admits, however, that this time the lords of conflict would take longer to come to their senses, that the 'postscript image of dawn' must be almost indefinitely postponed.[39] As pogrom led to reprisal, the longed-for harvest home must have seemed further away than ever. And yet there is a sense in which the friction of the period, disastrous as it was for the commonweal, worked an amazing alchemy on Soyinka's verse. The Möbius strip is, after all, a passive figure, a mere shadowing forth of the unconscious reflexes of history. The effect of the internecine tension of late 1966 was to show Soyinka that history, abstractly considered, was powerless. There needed to be a human hand on the mechanism: destiny would get nowhere without deliberate effort. It is thus that for the first time in these miscellaneous pieces of the pre-war months we notice stirrings in his poetic work of genuine public commitment.

The development is clearest in 'Civilian and Soldier' where the poet, 'intent on my trade of living', meets an infantryman bristling with the weaponry of destruction.[40] This is among the most accomplished pieces in the collection. Its gentle, unaggressive command of irony, its unsentimental fraternity, its vexed but supremely confident teasing out of the mysteries of life and death – all evince a control of

---

[38] Soyinka, *Idanre*, p. 50.    [39] *Ibid.*, p. 58.    [40] *Ibid.*, p. 53.

theme and tone unusual in a volume where too often the voice falters in its anxiety to persuade or to impress. In its very emotional reserve, its avoidance of venom, this is a poem which does far more to convert the reader to Soyinka's side than the gratuitously malicious 'Malediction, for her who rejoiced' with which the section ends.[41] It also marks a considerable moral advance on 'Death in the Dawn' of six years previously, in which the poet's fraternal salutation to the dead driver is tinged with more than a glimmer of sarcasm. Here, on the other hand, though Soyinka's lips still tremble with amusement at the soldier's confusion, his closing 'do you friend, even now, know / What it is all about?' is patently and absolutely sincere. Once again, the surest strokes in this poem are the simplest and least insistent. The phrase 'death twitched me gently in the eye' and the mock-cornucopia of gifts with which the poet showers the perplexed infantryman are creations of a poet approaching the zenith of his skill.

The public emergency of October 1966 confronted Soyinka with a challenge which he would need every drop of his inner resources to meet. To proclaim a religion of wholeness in a time of peace and prosperity is one thing; to hold the banner steady when everything is breaking apart around you is quite another. It is scarcely surprising that Soyinka's art began to change direction in 1966. The Civil War affected not merely Nigerian, but West African, poetry in ways which proved both far-reaching and permanent. It is this sea-change in the literature of the late sixties, tangy with the salt of discord, which we must now examine.

[41] *Ibid.*, p. 55.

# CHAPTER 10

# The poet and war, 1966–70

And 'mid this tumult Kubla heard from far
Ancestral voices prophesying war!
Samuel Taylor Coleridge, 'Kubla Khan'

In the political and cultural evolution of West Africa the year 1966 was critical. At the end of 1965 the former colonial territories, both Anglophone and Francophone, seemed to be well advanced along the road of sovereignty and national progress. All of the former British possessions were now officially independent, and, although in 1958, all but one of the French territories had temporarily elected to stay within a loose economic community, the only absolute stranglehold which Europe retained in the area was in the still-enslaved Portuguese possessions of Guinea and Cape Verde, where wars of liberation still raged. By Christmas of that year, however, the horizon had assumed a louring aspect. In January 1966 a posse of army officers, led in the first instance by Major Emmanuel Ifeajuna, took over control in Nigeria, while in the following month President Kwame Nkrumah of Ghana was removed from power by a similar *coup* while absent on a state visit to China. In Lagos the dominating figure in the new military government soon emerged as Major-General J. T. U. Aguiyi-Ironsi who, when he announced plans to centralize the Federation by substituting 'provinces' for the existing semi-autonomous states, was himself ousted in a counter-*coup* on 29 July. Tensions between the various regions were already so severe that in August the Council of Regional Representatives advised military personnel to 'return to barracks within their respective regions of origin'.[1] There followed a pogrom against easterners resident in the Northern Region, which broke out in Kano on 29 September. The result was near-panic, and an insistent demand for an eastern secession. As 1967 opened, a last attempt to reconcile the competing factions was made when the leaders of each

---

[1] General Olusegun Obasanjo, *My Command, An Account of the Nigerian Civil War, 1967–70* (Nigeria: Heinemann, 1980), p. 7.

were invited to meet at Aburi in Ghana by General Ankrah, head of the new military junta in Accra. When the agreed compromise formula was emphatically rejected by the eastern leader Colonel Ojukwu, the secessionist republic of Biafra was established in May. As the first skirmish of the Nigerian Civil War occurred on 6 July, it seemed to many outside observers that independent Africa had forfeited an important kind of innocence.

For shrewder spirits, however, the trouble had been brewing for some time. Thus, when early in 1966, the civil administration of Sir Abubakar Tafawa Balewa collapsed, Christopher Okigbo sounded his sense of unease in his new sequence of poems, *Path of Thunder*:

> The smell of blood already floats in the lavender-mist of the afternoon.
> The death sentence lies in ambush along the corridors of power;
> And a great fearful thing already tugs at the cables of the open air,
> A nebula immense and immeasurable, a night of deep waters –
> An iron dream unnamed and unnameable, a path of stone.[2]

Not even C. P. Snow's hackneyed metaphor for bureaucratic evasiveness, combining so incongruously with a sharply realized image from the cable-ferries of the Nigerian creeks, can deflect the ominous majesty of these lines, which, though grounded in the events of the day, burgeons into a wider vision of sinister forces coming to light, the slow emergence of a carnal nightmare. The atmosphere of the sequence is heavy with premonition of developments which few, except the most acutely attuned of minds, could then foresee. It is the end of one phase of Okigbo's work and beginning of another, a closing cadence harsh with dread. For the long-sought embrace of his muse and mistress at the end of 'Distances', he has exchanged a remorseless tread along a narrowing pathway which leads nowhere but into the jaws of discord. Like the earlier sequences, 'Path of Thunder' is conceived in musical terms, but its tessitura is not the gentle register of a sighing flute, but the snarling insistence of scraping metal:

> FANFARE of drums, wooden bells: iron chapter;
> And our dividing airs are gathered home.
>
> This day belongs to a miracle of thunder;
> Iron has carried the forum

---

[2] Christopher Okigbo, *Labyrinths with Path of Thunder* (London: Heinemann, 1971), p. 66.

With token gestures. Thunder has spoken,
Left no signatures: broken

Barbicans alone tell one tale the winds scatter.[3]

This is verse designed to appeal to both eye and ear: notice the line break after the word 'broken' and the pun on 'airs'. There was one rare performance to percussive accompaniment in 1966 before the declaration of war sent Okigbo into the army. The poem gains much from an aural context of dissonance, of chafing, fragmented strains which lead to no resolution. Okigbo is marking more than the fall from grace of a government, more even than the impending dissolution of the Federation, sadly inevitable as he may have felt this to be; he is signalling the passing-away of one whole, temperate style of government – the democratic structure of conversation and consensus – and the frightful emergence of men who will listen to little except the shrill clash of steel and the most strident of certainties. It is this which is at stake as, hemmed in by events he cannot control, the majestic Tafawa Balewa, doomed prime minister of Nigeria, wheels and thrashes in a tightening circle of blood:

> WHATEVER happened to the elephant –
> Hurrah for thunder –
>
> The elephant, tetrarch of the jungle:
> With a wave of the hand
> He could pull four trees to the ground:
> His four mortar legs pounded the earth:
> Whatever they treaded,
> The grass was forbidden to be there.
>
> Alas! the elephant has fallen –
> Hurrah for thunder –[4]

Again, not even the intrusive phrase 'wave of the hand' can destroy the grandeur of the effect. The reiterated 'Hurrah for thunder' harks right back to the 'NO in thunder' from Melville's letter to Hawthorne quoted in 'Lament of the Silent Sisters'. Placed here it seems an oddly ambivalent cry, but there is little doubt that, despite his evident terror at the intransigence of events, Okigbo was also driven to exult at the sheer dynamic of history. These were heady days, all the headier for their very unpredictability. It is almost certain that, as the poet stormed the stage uttering his strange Cassandra-like warnings, he felt himself to be in the grip of a prophetic mania which would end by

[3] *Ibid.*, p. 63.    [4] *Ibid.*, p. 67.

destroying him:

> If I don't learn to shut my mouth I'll soon go to hell,
> I, Okigbo, town-cryer, with my iron bell.[5]

Despite his foreboding of disaster, or perhaps because of it, the poet dimly discerns himself as a force of destiny. Though deeply rooted in the developments of early 1966, 'Path of Thunder' is far from being an occasional sequence, a fact which ultimately sets it apart from other alarums sounded at the period. Its vision of history is violent and unrelenting, with none of the steady accretion and final serenity of the earlier pieces; yet it is grounded in the same mythology as *Labyrinths* and is entirely compatible in outlook. The elephant which expires in a trap of fire is from the same imaginative world as the 'beast / finishing her rest' by the sarcophagus in *Limits* v; and the robbers and eagles which 'come again' in 'Elegy for Alto' – a solitary cadenza for saxophone – are the same by means of which, in *Limits* VIII, Okigbo had uncannily predicted the first Federal bombing raids on the new Biafran capital of Enugu:

> Out of the solitude, the fleet,
> Out of the solitude,
> Intangible like silk thread of sunlight,
> The eagles ride low,
> Resplendent . . . resplendent;
> And small birds sing in shadows,
> Wobbling under the bones.[6]

It was just such a bombing raid in the rainy season of 1967 that saw one of the poignantly recorded partings of the war. As the country split into rival camps, Okigbo threw his hand in with the secessionist forces, and henceforth divided his time between duties at the front and unofficial moonlighting at the cramped offices of the Citadel Press, the small publishing concern which he and the novelist Chinua Achebe had formed in Enugu. One day in August, Achebe's apartment received a direct hit. One of the first on the scene was Captain Okigbo, dressed, as always when off-duty, in mufti:

I can see him clearly in his white 'gown' and cream trousers among the vast crowd milling around my bombed apartment, the first spectacle of its kind in the Biafran capital in the second month of the war. I doubt if we exchanged more than a sentence or two. There were scores of sympathizers pressing for-

---

[5] *Ibid.*    [6] *Ibid.*, p. 31.

ward to commiserate with me or praise God that my life and the lives of my wife and children had been spared. So I hardly caught more than a glimpse of him in that crowd and then he was gone, like a meteor, forever.[7]

The following month Achebe heard over his car radio that Okigbo was amongst those numbered dead in the battle for the university town of Nsukka. It was an occurrence from which Nigerian literary history seems never quite to have recovered. To some Okigbo remains a noble martyr to a nationalist cause; to others the quintessential poet *engagé*, to others still a traitor to the writer's obligation toward spiritual impartiality. The question as to whether, in laying down his life for a local conflict, he betrayed the larger responsibilities of his calling, is one of the great unresolved issues of modern African cultural history. It has been debated deftly and to great effect in Ali Mazrui's novel *The Trial of Christopher Okigbo* in which the soul of the dead poet is arraigned in the afterlife before a celestial Pan-African jury, who demand that he account for selling out to the compulsions of lesser men.[8] His passing gave rise to a whole flurry of tributes and elegies. Possibly the most insightful, Odia Ofeimun's 'For Christopher Okigbo', by a writer of a later generation that owes him much, comes close to defining the essence of Okigbo's tragedy when it sees him as an emblem of unrealized hopes, and of that sense of thwarted potential that occasionally afflicts all who aim for perfection of expression:

> And charged,
> beyond arms' reach
> beyond the power of our ululations to recall
> you brandish your unripened selves,
> riddles in the galloping peals
> of our derailed sun.[9]

The Enugu bombing raids were the first concerted attempt by Federal forces to strike at the Igbo heartland. They were coincidentally the means of alerting the outside world both to the vulnerability of the civilian population and to the beginnings of the slow strangulation of the Biafran people within their self-imposed fortress. The turmoil and confusion of the time were most vividly caught by Gabriel Okara, who

[7] *Don't Let Him Die, an Anthology of Memorial Poems for Christopher Okigbo*, eds. Chinua Achebe and Dubem Okafor (Enugu: Fourth Dimension Press, 1978), p. v.
[8] Ali Mazrui, *The Trial of Christopher Okigbo* (London: Heinemann, 1971).
[9] Odia Ofeimun, *The Poet Lied* (London: Longman, 1980), p. 17. *Don't Let Him Die*, p. 45.

like Okigbo had elected to support the secessionist cause, but who, being above military age, had to content himself with a desk job with the new Biafran administration. As a civilian Okara was perfectly placed to observe the havoc wreaked by these inexplicable assaults from the sky on a people unused to the rigours of modern technological war:

> Suddenly the air cracks
> with striking cracking rockets
> guffaws of bofors stuttering LMGs
> jets driving shooting glasses dropping
> breaking from lips people diving
> under beds nothing bullets flashing fire
> striking writhing bodies and walls –
>
> Suddenly there's silence –[10]

Suddenly too the whole pace of the poem changes. To this – perhaps the most effective purely descriptive piece written during the war – Okara has brought all of his extraordinary skill with modulating rhythms. One moment all is struggle and stress – topsy-turvy adjectives and the disdainful 'guffaw' of ammunition – and then, just as abruptly as the attack, a deceptive calm descends through which the poet causes us to see the delicate, acrid column of smoke that rises from the stricken town. The effect is a technical one, but in no sense unrelated to the poem's meaning, since Okara's business is with the inscrutability of war, the bewildering attrition which nobody can explain but which all, however guileless, must endure. Gradually the rhythms of normalcy revive and with them the familiar conviviality of speech: 'where's your bunker?' Then after another loud smash the verse again lurches into a dizzying impetus of confusion. Again much of the work is done by a combination of accumulated present participles and a scrupulous absence of punctuation:

> hugging gutters walls houses
> crumbling rumbling thunder
> bombs hearts thumping heads low
> under beds moving wordless lips –

How straightforward the near-oxymoron 'moving wordless lips', and yet, in context, how right! When at last the all-clear is given, the present participles recur, but this time with the lazy, swinging indulgence of an afternoon outing. War, after all, whatever else it may be, is

[10] Gabriel Okara, *The Fisherman's Invocation* (London: Heinemann, 1978), p. 37.

also an adventure:

> Things soon simmer to normal
> hum and rhythm as danger passes
> and the streets are peopled
> with strolling men and women
> boys and girls on various errands
> walking talking laughing smiling.

Conventionally we talk of a kettle simmering to boiling point. The image of the disrupted town simmering back to normal catches the resumption of tranquillity almost too well. Notice too the unemphatic precision of the word 'peopled' as once again the compounds, the zinc roofs and laterite thoroughfares assume a human scale. In its counterpoint of panic and calm, of movement and stasis, this is a poem which demands to be read aloud, and one which Okara himself reads well. Its significance – an overworked critical term, but one whose use seems here to creep like the children of Enugu from under the bed – lies in the very refusal of the writing itself to pass comment. Visualization is everything; it is more than enough.

The dominant quality wrung from Okara by these terrible months within the Biafran stronghold was a disinterested compassion at best latent within his other work. It is characteristic that his other well-known war piece 'Expendable name' is so broad in its range of sympathy as to transcend not only the agonies of the writer and his people, but the Nigerian struggle itself. War is no respecter of persons. Suffering is both universal and universally incomprehensible:

> I am only an episode
> in the morning papers
> which you put aside
> or throw into waste paper baskets
> and turn your bacon and egg
> and milk for your young
> while I whom you have
> drained of both flesh and blood
> tread with bare feet on thorns
> in bushes searching, searching
> for tiny snails and insects
> for my young with swollen feet.[11]

As the federal seige tightened its grip on the shrinking Biafran enclave the photographic image of a starving child, a signal of

---

[11] *Ibid.*, p. 39.

impending defeat in Port Harcourt, in Lagos a sting of reproach, became in the affluent world beyond Africa the commonplace of the tabloids and the glossy weekend colour supplements. Amongst the callous and ignorant it even became – shameful to recall – a kind of sick joke. Okara's poem points its finger at the reader, and, beyond him or her, the pitiless, gormandizing public gaze. Yet Okara's concern is with us almost as much as it is with the harassed mother in the picture. His sympathies are with her certainly, but his understanding embraces even the stupidity of our indifference. Indifference indeed is the real target of the poem, and the mesh of implied reference is wider than Africa. Though the original of the worn woman seen picking for crumbs amid the stubble and scrub in the Biafran countryside was certainly Nigerian, the decade of the sixties had already supped sufficiently of horrors to suggest a host of supplementary images from almost anywhere in the Third World – most pertinently from Vietnam. It is the very universality of Okara's concern that tempts us to apply to him, as to few other poets writing at the time, Wilfred Owen's words:

> I mean the truth untold,
> The pity of war, the pity war distilled. [12]

War works strange changes in poets. Some, such as Okigbo, it sends off in new, apparently unprecedented directions. From others like Okara it elicits unsuspected depths of humanity and calm. There are certain talents whom it appears to fit like a glove. If it was not for the outbreak of the Great War, Wilfred Owen might have died in old age, a minor undiscovered Georgian. For Pol Ndu, twenty-seven at the time of the secession, and like Okigbo inclined to the Biafran side, the Civil War seemed to work a similar magic. Over Ndu there hangs much the same fragrance of unrealized promise as permanently attaches to the name of Christopher Okigbo, since, though surviving the conflict, he was killed in a road accident in 1976 at the age of thirty-six. His early work has been compared to Okigbo's, but is in fact very different, at once less eclectic and more distilled. The best of it is like a kind of watercolour wash:

---

[12] Wilfred Owen, 'Strange Meeting' in *The Collected Poems of Wilfred Owen*, ed. Edmund Blunden (London: Chatto and Windus, 1931), p. 116.

Here again, Igwekala
I bend low and whisper:

when the rains went
and the sun over-spent
hours in violet eves;
old hoes hung low on eaves;

now pilgrim birds troop across the dimmed horizon,
and bereaved kites abandon smoky fields
for tunes of frustrated loneliness.

tell me, my true-god,
what holds back your hand?[13]

It was precisely this quality of graphic restraint, of light brush strokes evocative of fugitive atmospheres, that enabled Ndu to portray the ghastlier aspects of war in a way which few others matched. In general, the poetry produced by the Nigerian war was strong in declarative statement but weak in pictorial recall. 'Reburial of the Dead', certainly Ndu's finest piece, goes some way towards making up the deficiency:

Post home those heads severed in seven nights on seven stones
they are my heads
awaiting the planting season
resting on seven palms

They stamped the chests of the fallen
black-branding the alien,
falling pollen upon the dust of atom

And here,
where dying roses stink
crowned with daggers of diggers
we hear a far-away Ikora
rumbling its monotonous creed
to the black-maned lion
in the den.

where courage
brim-filled
shoots spade-fuls of *sal vitae*
to quicken the rot
of the many dead.[14]

The macabre irony of the opening, the pervasive sense of decay and putrefaction sweetened only by the poet's compassion, the eerie

[13] Pol Ndu, *Songs for Seers, Poems 1960–7* (New York: Nok Publications, 1974), p. 13.
[14] *Ibid.*, p. 30.

image of a ritual gong dinning senselessly in the distance: all evidence the very special talent that one associates with the drawings of war artists such as Henry Moore, a talent which war itself has focused.

But, if the war brought new talents to light, it did little for the cohesion of the literary establishment. In the September of 1967 Wole Soyinka was imprisoned, initially at Ibadan and Lagos, later at Kaduna, after an unsuccessful attempt to secure an impartial international arms embargo. Meanwhile John Pepper Clark had retired to Warri in the then mid-western state, from which he made infrequent sorties to lecture on the war to the concerned international community. Clark is the only Nigerian poet to have published a collection devoted exclusively to the ups and downs of the confrontation. *Casualties*, published a year after the cessation of hostilities, is a virtual verse diary of the seemingly unavoidable series of steps that led from the first military takeover of January 1966, through the declaration of war and the death of his friend Okigbo, to the eventual ceasefire and aftermath of bitterness. This journal, cloaked in the allegorical method of a Nigerian folk tale, is framed by a set of elegies which stand as prologue and postlude to the course of events described. The opening lament has a directness of feeling and an austere lyricism quite new in Clark's work:

SONG

I can look the sun in the face
But the friends that I have lost
I dare not look at any. Yet I have held
Them all in my arms, shared with them
The same bath and bed, often
Devouring the same dish, drunk as soon
On tea as on wine, at that time
When but to think of an ill, made
By God or man, was to find
The cure prophet and physician
Did not have. Yet to look
At them how I dare not,
Though I can look the sun in the face.[15]

[15] John Pepper Clark, *Casualties, Poems 1966–68* (London: Longman, 1970), p. 3. Collected in *A Decade of Tongues, Selected Poems, 1958–68* (London: Longman), p. 52.

This is Clark at his very best. Gone are the Hopkinsese, the oblique allusiveness, the tricks and turns of rhetoric that make some of the early work so unpalatable. Instead we have authentic feeling recalled in unselfconscious tranquillity. The constituent images are common-place, but their very ordinariness disarms criticism. The phrase 'bath and bed' has an affectionately tactile quality which is entirely unsenti-mental. The image of the sun has been used a thousand times; yet here with its implications of shearing away from memories too painful to face, it evinces that which, in his critical writing, Clark has always espoused: the example of Shakespeare.

The following piece, 'Skulls and Caps'.[16] amplifies the principal theme of the collection: the detrimental effect of war upon the infor-mal fabric of social life, particularly on long-established alliances and friendships. In Clark's eyes war is not, as it was pre-eminently for Okigbo, a mythic occurrence of cosmic proportions, nor yet what it was for Okara, a tragic diminution of human stature, but an imper-sonal mania which destroys the bonds that link one private individual with another. 'Skulls and Caps', for instance, exposes us to a surreal vision in which a field of battle – foremost, the field at Nsukka – is lit-tered with the indistinguishable remnants of the poet's friends. The poem is in the form of a dream conversation between the poet and an individual who shares his pain. The intimacy of the scale, the probing nature of the questions asked, and the affectionate style of address for persons both famous and less famous – 'Chris' (Okigbo); Sam (Agbam); Emman (Ifeajuna, instigator of the first *coup d'état*) – are typi-cal of the method in this collection. For Clark, historical events are meaningless unless personalized.

The scale of *Casualties* is thus far from epic. From these opening movements it proceeds naturally through a series of diary entries which document crucial turning points in the early phase of the con-flagration. There is little to dislike in this approach, and yet the treat-ment of events in individual poems remains disappointing. The principal reason for this is that the proximity of the episodes described to the time of writing has forced Clark into a discretion of statement typical of him but unhelpful to readers marginally involved in the cir-cumstances evoked. Thus, having bravely forsaken one kind of ob-scurity – the stylistic mannerism of the early work – Clark is obliged to take recourse in an obscurity of a different kind: the mazes of a some-

---

[16] Clark, *Casualties,* p. 4. (*A Decade of Tongues*, p. 53.)

times unwieldy allegory. As a result specific pieces gain in authorial detachment. Detachment, however, is not a perspective at which Clark excels. In a volume dedicated to the theme of friendship it is something of a handicap.

The point can most easily be illustrated by a comparison between poem 10 ('Leader of the Hunt') and poem 7 ('The Reign of the Crocodile'), each of which describes an incident in the period between the two military insurrections of January and July 1966. This was a period of great civil confusion when personalities and jockeying power groups changed position with bewildering rapidity. 'Leader of the Hunt'[17] describes an episode late in the life of Major Emmanuel Ifeajuna, a career army officer and acquaintance of Clark, who staged the first military takeover on 15 January only to see his efforts overridden by less scrupulous colleagues. When his personal star started to sink Ifeajuna fled to Ghana, whence he was escorted back to Nigeria by Clark and Okigbo working in tandem. Historically this was a swashbuckling episode with minor political repercussions. What redeems and humanizes the poem from the point of view of the reader is the poet's anguished sense of loyalty to a man whose best interests he fears he may have betrayed. At a slightly later stage in the war Ifeajuna was implicated in a failed attempt to return Biafra to the Federation, upon which he was executed behind the secessionist lines. The effect of his death on the poet has been to elicit an unpremeditated reflex of shame which blends well with the humility present in the collection as a whole. As a result the reprise of the preludial 'Song' at the end of this piece is both fitting and moving.

'The Reign of the Crocodile'[18] on the other hand describes the six-month reign of Major-General Aguiyi-Ironsi, the ill-fated head of the second military administration who, eclipsing the achievements of men like Ifeajuna, rode roughshod over the wishes of his subordinates, until his clumsy attempts at a reintegration of the union occasioned his own downfall. Ironsi was one of the more extravagant personalities to emerge during a period when much appeared larger than life; he was not, however, personally known to Clark, who is thus left with no alternative but to cast him in copper. Copper corrodes, however, and the allegorical treatment selected by Clark also fails on several counts. To begin with, the allegory itself is over-

[17] *Ibid.*, p. 4. (*A Decade of Tongues*, p. 63.)
[18] *Ibid.*, p. 9. (*A Decade of Tongues*, p. 58.)

Baroque; it continually shifts ground and, like the unfortunate General, swallows its own tail. We first meet Ironsi punting down the river Niger, floating with the tide of events. Then he has gathered a congress on its banks, and by stanza 3 he is a High Priest distributing benefits. The convolutedness of the symbolism is one thing; the uneasy confusion of sentiment quite another. Clark is half-impressed by Ironsi's strutting presence and half-appalled by his shifts and compromises. The tone of the poem hence vacillates improbably between the heroic and the satirical, leaving the reader to guess at Clark's real intentions. Implicitly he is working within a time-honoured convention; the celebration of men of destiny possesses a long pedigree. Andrew Marvell, whose allegiances during the English Civil War were similarly complicated, left a pattern which Clark would respect when he portrayed the doomed Charles I in lines which honour the victims of political insurrection even as they salute the energy of those who must supplant them:

> He nothing common did or mean
> Upon that memorable scene:
>   But with his keener eye
>   The axe's edge did try:
> Nor called the Gods with vulgar spight
> To vindicate his helpless right,
>   But bow'd his comely head
>   Down as upon a bed.[19]

Between this glimpse of Charles's dignity at his execution and Clark's sniping at Ironsi's administrative muddle lies one dividing quality: a magnanimity of spirit which is the equivalent of generosity in the public sphere, of forgiveness in the private. The absence of this quality in Clark's public pieces would explain why of the two sorts of poems present in *Casualties*, private and public, the public are invariably lesser things.

There follows a series of thumb-nail sketches of successive episodes in the war: the counter-*coup* ('July Wake');[20] the flights of the Igbos from the north ('Exodus');[21] the abortive Ghanaian peace conference

---

[19] 'An Horatian Ode upon Cromwel's Return from Ireland', in *The Poems and Letters of Andrew Marvell*, ed. H. M. Margoliouth Vol. 1 (Oxford University Press, 3rd edition, 1971), p. 93.

[20] Clark, *Casualties*, p. 23. (*A Decade of Tongues*, p. 70.)

[21] *Ibid.*, p. 25. (*A Decade of Tongues*, p. 72.)

('Aburi and After'),[22] Okigbo's demise ('Death of a Weaverbird'),[23] until in 'A Photograph in the *Observer*',[24] Clark accosts a theme which also had attracted Okara: the international reaction to the conflict. One Sunday in 1968 the colour supplement of the British *Observer* carried a front-page photograph depicting a phallanx of Biafran youths, their heads shaved, their torsos stripped, ready to pay the ultimate sacrifice at the front. By this time the Biafran population was already under growing pressure: supplies were limited, the secessionist stronghold had shrunk to a small enclave south of Onitsha. International opinion already sensed that the cause was doomed, yet looked on fascinated as the nascent republic was strangled at birth. The difference between Okara's and Clark's poems lies in this: whereas Okara's identification with the victims of atrocity is evident throughout, Clark starts with a dramatic journalistic gesture of documentary generalization ('Night falls over them') which he maintains until the very last line when he abruptly switches to an ungainly reflex of conciliatory inclusiveness ('Night falls over us'). The result is less to involve the readers in the fate of the soldiery than to surprise them by a trick of phrase which is too late to redeem what has gone before.

In poem 27, the eponymous 'Casualties', Clark reaches the nub of the matter. The real tragedy of the war does not lie in its cross-volley of accusation and counter-accusation, or even in the piled heaps of dead, but in a shrivelling of the spirit which has necessarily afflicted even the most generous-minded of participants. At last Clark can drop his mask of documentary observer and reveal his own face-wounds, the lacerations inflicted by a conflict in which to be entirely fair and impartial was always perhaps impossible. Again Clark attempts to modify his opening tone of generalized comment to one of private contrition, but this time the sequence of thought and continuity of feeling are so natural as to convince the reader entirely of the sincerity of his response:

> Caught in the clash of counter claims and charges
> When not in the niche others have left,
> We fall,
> All casualties of the war,
> Because we cannot hear each other speak,
> Because eyes have ceased to see the face from the crowd,
> Because whether we know or

22 *Ibid.*, p. 30. (*A Decade of Tongues*, p. 77.)
23 *Ibid.*, p. 32. (*A Decade of Tongues*, p. 79.)
24 *Ibid.*, p. 34. (*A Decade of Tongues*, p. 81.)

Do not know the extent of wrong on all sides,
We are characters now other than before . . .[25]


           ☽                  ☽                  ☽


Clark too had felt the lesion of once valued ties; one of the saddest con-
sequences of the three-year war was his own much-publicized quarrel
with the playwright and poet Wole Soyinka who had spent the dur-
ation of the war in detention and was not to be released until 1971. In
Appendix A of *The Man Died*, his prison diary of 1972, Soyinka accuses
Clark of complicity in the campaign of vilification mounted at his
expense by the Federal government.[26] The case is unproven, yet the
allegation acts as a sombre coda to a book whose principal theme is the
crucifixion of the artistic conscience by philistine authorities, them-
selves slaves to the will to power. Power, and the granite insensitivity
of power, are recurrent *motifs* throughout Soyinka's work, as witness
his slightly earlier 'Civilian and Soldier', in which the defenceless poet
encounters an infantryman intent on his trade of death soon after the
Kano massacres of October 1966.[27] For Soyinka power and death have
always been much the same thing, a conviction which lends sharp-
ness to his prose account of a two-year incarceration in which the slow
strangulation of the impulses, the systematic deprivation of all that
enhances living – daylight, conversation, books, sexual love –
becomes in itself a sort of gradual execution which the poet resists
with all the cunning, wit and resourcefulness at his disposal. Essential
for this regimen of survival was the daily outpouring of uncensored
thought in the margins and between the lines of the limited reading
material to which he had access: the Methuen edition of his own *Idanre*
and Paul Radin's *Primitive Religion* (1938). These scribbled jottings
were later exhumed to become in part the novel *Season of Anomy*,[28] the
play *Madmen and Specialists*[29] and the collection of lyrics *A Shuttle in the
Crypt*. Some of the poems had already been smuggled out of custody
during Soyinka's confinement and provisionally published in London

---

[25] *Ibid.*, p. 37. (*A Decade of Tongues*, p. 84).
[26] Wole Soyinka, *The Man Died* (London: Rex Collings, 1972).
[27] Wole Soyinka, *Idanre and Other Poems* (London: Methuen, 1967), p. 53. The final sec-
tion of this collection, 'October '66' gives us some shrewd Soyinkan side-glances at
the build-up to the war. For his reaction to the regional massacres, see especially,
'Massacre, October, '66' in *Ibid.*, pp. 51–2. See also chapter 9 of this study.
[28] Wole Soyinka, *Season of Anomy* (London: Rex Collings, 1973).
[29] Wole Soyinka, *Madmen and Specialists* (London: Methuen, 1973).

as *Poems from Prison*.[30] A selection of the more graphic, shorter pieces was also integrated into the text of *The Man Died*, where, read as soliloquies on Soyinka's evolving state of mind, they gain powerfully in significance.

What is remarkable in the longer poems that go to make up the earlier sections of *A Shuttle in the Crypt* is the way in which, from the very dregs and dross of his cell, the material substance of degradation, Soyinka was able to gather together the ingredients which sustain his lyrical complaint. The edge of the sky caught slant-wise through bars, the manic cackling of voices muffled through walls, the vermin and debris of the prison itself are transformed through a feat of intellectual heroism into a sort of inverted, cleansing sublime. Just as Keats on a summer's day took counsel of the nightingale, or Smart, in the less ample surroundings of eighteenth-century Bedlam, praised Geoffrey his cat, so Soyinka, caged far from the trappings of polite invocation, solemnly addresses a cockroach:

> Come out. Oh have you found me even here
> Cockroach? grimed in gloss connivance
> Carapaced in age, in cunning, oiled
> As darkness, eyed in decay rasps.
> Your subtle feelers probed prize chapters
> Drilled perforations on the magic words
> Our maps did not long survive your trails
> To mislead, false contours from secretions
> Of your poison ducts. Oh you have claws
> To leak the day of pity, skin the night
> Of love, pierce holes invisible
> Within the heart of nature for all
> Of good to seep through unnoticed and unmourned.[31]

Here, as so often in this collection, Soyinka seems to be concerned to turn the English romantic tradition on its head: rather than soar with Keats and his nightingale, Soyinka, an enforced earthling, grubs his way to a deeper solace. This is poetry of courageous immersion: it holds its nose, and diving down further than most of us have been, comes up brandishing an incongruous, scaly truth. Critics have often talked of Soyinka's being 'earthed'; this has washed itself in mud:

> Crow in white collar, legs
> Of toothpick dearth plunged
> Deep in a salvage morsel. Choirmaster

[30] Wole Soyinka, *Poems from Prison* (London: Rex Collings, 1969).
[31] Wole Soyinka, *A Shuttle in the Crypt* (London: Rex Collings and Methuen, 1972), p. 5.

When a hymn is called he conducts
Baton-breaking their massed discordance;
Invocation to the broken word
On broken voices

Air-tramp, black verger
Descend on dry prayers
To altars of evil
And a charity of victims[32]

Soyinka, mission-child, battered idealist, transforms the surround-ings of his own grim shelter into a sort of surrogate, clandestine cathedral to liberty. He has swapped his surplice for a plain cassock, but the canticles still beckon: he sends up his perverse morning prayer nonetheless:

Breath of the sun, crowned
In green crepes and amber beads
Children's voices at the door of the Orient

Raising eyelids on the sluggish earth
Dispersing sulphur fumes above the lake
Of awakening, you come hunting with the sun[33]

Throughout his incarceration in Kaduna gaol, to which he was transferred from Lagos early in 1968, Soyinka was kept in solitary con-finement, perhaps the most savage device yet conceived to prise the persecuted mind from its sanity. It is a form of punishment which holds especial terrors for the writer. The artist possesses two major re-sources: an alert sensibility and the cognitive mechanism through which he attempts to discipline it. Deprive him of control over his own life and his sensibility runs riot, while order stomps the corridor beyond his reach like a warder outside his cell. Hence:

Fragments
We cannot hold, linger
Parings of intuition
Footsteps
Passing and re-passing the door of recognition.[34]

Thus unleashed, the mind rages uselessly, rushing from image to image without the means or self-restraint to hold them together. In such circumstances, all the poet can do is long for a kind of lunar balm:

---

[32] *Ibid.*, p. 34.     [33] *Ibid.*, p. 37.
[34] 'Animistic Spells', poem 6 in *Ibid.*, p. 68. (*The Man Died*, p. 187.)

> Old moons
> Set your crescent eyes
> On bridges of my hands
> Comb out
> Manes of sea-wind on my tide-swept sands.[35]

In the second year of his confinement, the prison orderlies planted a cottage garden in the courtyard beyond Soyinka's bars. In its midst, just within the poet's reach, grew one solitary sunflower, whose graceful stem and searching petals recalled Blake's poem in which a 'sunflower weary of time', trapped in an impulse to freedom, yearns like a 'youth pined away in desire' for a land of uncluttered fulfilment.[36] Sacrificing its graceful form to his desire for sound, Soyinka uprooted the flower, from whose stalk he tried unsuccessfully to fashion a flute. 'My mind was like a compost heap',[37] he later wrote in his diary; the wasted sunflower thus became the stillborn impulse of self-expression which, uprooted, failed to make music:

> Notes immured
> In threadings of your stalk
> Haunt me still
>
> Dream of Pan hours
> In a silent wilderness[38]

There was something almost primeval about this flower-lust of Soyinka's. Confined in a cage of steel he experienced an urge toward the sun almost Incan. As an artist he was torn between a desire to put down roots and a contrary compulsion to break free and explore remote regions of consciousness. Only within the Yoruba mythology, with its twinning of contrary impulses, could these two desires perhaps be reconciled.

Deprived of all external contact, and unaware of the forces of protest gathering strength in the world outside, Soyinka at length elected for the prisoner's passive prerogative of hunger-strike. On the tenth day, made light-headed by abstinence, he experienced a sensation of detachment from the prison and its warders, and with it a renewed power of renunciation. '*I need nothing. I feel nothing. I desire nothing*', he

---

[35] 'Animistic Spells', poem 10 in *Ibid.*, p. 69. (*The Man Died*, p. 187.)
[36] Blake, *Complete Writings*, ed. Geoffrey Keynes (London: Oxford University Press, 1969), p. 215.
[37] Soyinka, *The Man Died*, p. 245.
[38] Soyinka, 'Flute Manqué' in *The Man Died*, p. 246.

wrote,[39] but out of this nirvana was born an enhanced conviction of justice. His voice, so far that of lonely frustration, became henceforth the chorus of all the oppressed:

> I anoint my voice
> And let it sound hereafter
> Or dissolve upon its lonely passage
> In your void. Voices new
> Shall rouse the echoes when
> Evil shall again arise.[40]

With this transition from private pain to unselfish indignation, it is possible to argue that a new genre was born in West African poetry, a genre I have later called the poetry of dissent. Despite their deep concern for the war and its victims, neither Okigbo nor Clark wrote what one would be justified in terming a political poetry, their work lacks both that edge and that sense of mission. Soyinka's verse, which retained a political potential from the earlier phase of *Idanre*, was galvanized by the war into an instrument of protest aimed less at his personal circumstances than against a deep, almost mystic source of injustice secreting its deadly juices into the body politic. The resultant writing was redeemed from partisanship by Soyinka's instinctual humanism. His work has never been political in the same sense as the propagandist's pamphlet. His concern was invariably to set immediate instances of oppression against a backdrop of comprehensive human evil. That against which he ultimately protested is something steely in the human heart, a capacity for boorishness and callous insensitivity as corrosive whether found in Franco's Spain, Gowon's Nigeria, or the Greece of the colonels.[41]

The intrinsic hostility of all such régimes to the life of the mind was illustrated by nothing as clearly as Soyinka's own experience. In a drastic attempt to reduce the country's leading writer to sullen silence, the authorities eventually deprived him of all writing materials: even a pen. He found his way back to articulacy through an uncanny accident. A moulting crow dropped one of its feathers on the ground near to the grill of his cell. Soyinka honed a quill from it with his pared-down thumbnail, with which he was able to write his final poetic protest against his confinement. In a bizarre compliment to Shelley's ode 'to a skylark' he offered up tribute to the hoarse rider of the skies

---

[39] *Ibid.*, p. 253.     [40] *Ibid.*, p. 19 (*The Man Died*, p. 253.)
[41] See Soyinka, 'A Letter to Compatriots' in *The Man Died*, pp. 11–16.

which had enabled his imagination to wing its way to freedom:

> He dropped
> His lone gift from the sky
> A rain of fiery coals – for he
> The lyric eye had scorned –
>
> And flew
> His raucous way. But newly
> Sounds the raw theme of your haloed throat –
> As trumpets at the lofty breach in walls
> Of immolation.[42]

Was this note of triumphant cajolery so new in the history of West African poetry? It may be objected, on the basis of earlier chapters in this study, that controversy and resistance had always been hallmarks of African poetry in the European languages. Yet, beginning in the period of the Nigerian Civil War, the discriminating reader began to notice a change in both the tone and the emphasis of West African verse. Up to 1966 the principal purpose of these poets had remained, what it still remained in Cape Verde and Guinea, the consolidation of national identity. Until the Civil War the opposition to this objective had always appeared resolutely *out there*, beyond the national boundaries: the alien, the unknown, the insatiably acquisitive. In the period of nationalist agitation the upholders of poetic resistance were careful not to break ranks, for their case depended, as it did most determinedly for the *négritude* poets of the forties, on the projection of an authentic and authenticated whole: the African personality, the validity of a local tradition. But then outside pressures formally receded, the informal cracks in the surface became visible: voices strove for individuality, sources of discontent were discovered nearer home. There are many who would claim that such instances of discord, and preeminently the Nigerian War itself, marked yet another phase in the manipulation of African life by outside interests; it is a point which we shall have reason to consider in the next chapter. Suffice it to say here that, if for commentators of one persuasion the transition from colonialism proper to neo-colonialism was no more than the replacing of

---

[42] *Ibid.*, p. 260

one façade by another, the effect in artistic terms was to make the cultural life of the countries concerned both more variegated and more interesting.

It was once fashionable to talk of the 'underdevelopment' of African society. In the sphere of literature, Nkrumah's phrase assumes a new meaning. A colonial culture is underdeveloped, not merely because all of its resources, physical and cultural, are diverted into extraneous channels, but, more crucially perhaps, because so much of its psychological energy is necessarily devoted to the removal of a single, seemingly impervious obstacle: the imperial power. There is a sense in which poetry trapped in the colonial stage can never be a mature poetry, however committed it may be to the constructive task of liberation. When a colonial poet sends out a cry for freedom, it is not only the freedom to vote that he seeks. He is also concerned with the liberty of the imagination to explore tracts and by-ways beyond the exigencies of purely political survival. The case can easily be substantiated by a brief look at Guinea and Cape Verde, where, during the years of the Nigerian Civil War, a war of liberation against the Portuguese was still in progress.

Nothing could more amply illustrate the differing consciousness produced by, on the one hand, a Civil War, and on the other, a War of Liberation, than the divergence at this point in time between Cape Verde literature and the work that was then emerging in Nigeria. Like the poetry produced by the sister struggles in Angola and Mozambique, the poetry of Guinea and Cape Verde, was at this time, simply and eloquently a relentless demand for the bare essentials of autonomy and self-respect. Here, for instance, is Guinea's Mindelense listening to the corpuscles of conflict seething through his own veins:

> The lights of the city glide within me
> but do not pierce through me with their glitter
> deep in me there still persists the black depths
> of the black history I hear singing . . .
>
> We here are the children of a dense night
> which is shattered in places by strange cries
> rages suppressed for many hundred years
> today are globules of our own red blood.
>
> Oh wonderful things, oh cities of light
> your lights do not keep company with me

within me there still remains the black base
of the black history I hear singing.[43]

Such verse has the elemental gravity of a *pietà* sculpted out of pure ebony. It inspires, but has the narrowness of range that goes with flexed muscles and clenched teeth. It desires to move on to another phase of self-expression if only history will let it. It is thus that, wearied by the pinched conditions which have reduced the poet's range to such a pitch, Onésima Silveira of Cape Verde registers his impatience for an opportunity to write a 'different poem':

> The people of the islands want a different poem
> For the people of these islands;
> A poem without exiles complaining
> In the calm of their existence;
> A poem without children nourished
> On the black milk of aborted time
> A poem without mothers gazing
> At the vision of their sons, motherless.
> The people of the islands want a different poem
> For the people of the islands;
> A poem without arms in need of work
> Nor mouths in need of bread.[44]

Would this longed for poem when it arrived possess any less a sense of disquiet than those which it had succeeded or than the impatient cries then being uttered by Nigerian poets? Perhaps not, but at least, like the Nigerian poetry of the post-war period, it would have moved on from mere indignation to a stage at which political criticism and self-scrutiny became one. Only with the arrival of this essential moment of transition could a true Poetry of Dissent be born.

[43] 'Attention' in *When Bullets Begin to Flower, Poems of Resistance from Angola, Mozambique and Guiné*. Selected and Translated by Margaret Dickinson (Nairobi: East African Publishing House, 1972), p. 62.
[44] 'A different poem' in *Ibid.*, p. 83.

# CHAPTER 11

# The poetry of dissent, 1970–80

For a continent increasingly inclined to criticize itself for its own fail-ings there was much, in the late 1960s and early 1970s about which to feel concern. The succession of *coups* which afflicted West African states in 1966 was far from the last. In Dahomey (Benin), there had been no fewer than five such insurrections by 1972. Meanwhile in Ghana a renewed attempt at democratic government in 1969 soon drove itself into the ground in a mire of corruption and usurped auth-ority. Early in 1972 another military cabal took over in Accra. The National Redemption Council under Colonel I. K. Acheampong was loud in its promises of a clean sweep of compromising interests, claims over which the population at large were already growing not a little cynical. Though the Nigerian Civil War ended with the absorp-tion of Biafra in 1970, the aftermath of bitterness and mistrust took many years to subside. No sooner was the Nigerian war at an end than unsavoury rumblings were heard from the desert state of Chad, which itself was soon embroiled in a civil conflict even costlier and more bloody. In Nigeria the promised return to civilian government was continually postponed, but after its arrival on 1 October 1979 almost as transient as in Ghana. By mid-decade Acheampong's government in Accra had bogged itself down in a quarry of venality and self-seeking. Though Lisbon had finally let go of her enslaved dominions, the failure to liberate South Africa and Rhodesia remained a constant source of self-reproach for many for whom emancipation was otherwise empty of significance.

It is against this background of frustrated hopes and growing dis-illusionment that the poetry of the 1970s has to be seen. The flounder-ing of the politicians imposed on writers a double burden. To a large extent, though differing in their orientation, in the fifties and early sixties politicians and writers had shared common ideals and a common vocabulary. By 1970, this common coin of moral and political idealism had become so debased through continual abuse that the

poet's classic obligation towards the regeneration of language itself –
the need, in Mallarmé's words, to 'purify the language of the tribe' –
had attained a new urgency. At the same time the failure of successive
governments to actualize the ideals of probity and justice which poets
and novelists still felt a duty to proclaim, begged both explanation and
redress. No longer would the facile dreams of 'progress' and 'develop-
ment' – the pimply optimism of the immediate post-colonial period –
pass muster in the face of such a welter of opportunism and apparent
incompetence.

The literature of the seventies was thus characterized by sporadic
attempts to refurbish the revolutionary vision accompanied by sim-
mering exasperation at the obduracy of history in refusing to live up to
its promises. To the writers of French-speaking West Africa, conscious
of the magnificence of the *négritude* inheritance, and yet anxious to
define themselves as against an elder generation of writer–politicians
who appeared to have betrayed the trust reposed in them, the prob-
lem presented itself as essentially one of the reinvigoration of poetic
diction. The founding fathers of *négritude* had exploited a vein of exal-
ted celebration which was now effectively exhausted. At the same
time the ideological pose of *négritude* seemed increasingly inadequate
in the face of the continuing political challenge.

One of the first attempts to confront these problems and to strike
out boldly towards an entirely new idiom originated in the sixties from
a country slightly beyond the bounds of West Africa. When, in 1962,
Tchikaya U'Tamsi's third volume of poetry *Epitomé* appeared in Tunis,
it was immediately claimed by Léopold Sédar Senghor as a further
achievement of the *négritude* movement. In fact, it was much more
than that, and already in two previous volumes (*Feu-de-brousse*,[1] 1958
and *À triche-coeur*,[2] 1960) U'Tamsi had proved himself to be one of the
few francophone poets since the 1940s capable of transcending *négri-
tude* towards a new language founded on a contradictory view of the
self. U'Tamsi was born in Mpile in the Moyen Congo (now Congo
Brazzaville) in 1931, but moved to Paris in 1946 when his father was
elected, alongside Senghor and Césaire, as a *deputé* in the newly recon-
stituted Assemblée Nationale. Educated in Orléans and then Paris,
U'Tamsi experienced something of the alienating force of the metro-
politan educational system, the worst strictures of which, however,
he managed to evade by refusing to matriculate at any university. His

---

[1] Tchikaya U'Tamsi, *Feu-de-brousse* (Paris: Caractères, 1957).
[2] Tchikaya U'Tamsi, *A triche-coeur* (Paris: Editions Hautefeuille, 1958).

more reflective earlier pieces appear to have been attempts to reconcile the various striving impulses in his being. At moments in *Epitomé*, he adopts the guise of a sort of refractory Narcissus, eternally gazing at himself in a pool which returns images ragged with the torsion of light. His talismen are a totem, a crucifix, a tree. To distinguish is impossible, since U'Tamsi reconciles his worlds by interlacing them:

> La mer s'en va, je viens;
> La mer vient, je m'en vais:
> ainsi nous dansâmes
>
> Cinq continents dérivent
> Un homme fuit son ombre
> La mer ouvre sa gueule d'eau
>
> son haleine pue la goémon de mon lit de verveine
> n'ai-je jamais fui mon ombre?
> Je dansais seulement
> la nuit mon deuil mon ombre
>
> L'eau pue la rose du désert
> quelle mer est plus riche en coraux que ma révolte?[3]

[The sea goes I come; / the sea comes I depart: / thus we dance together / Five continents float adrift / A man runs from his shadow / The sea opens its watery maw / its breath smells of the seaweed of my bed of laurel / have I never run from my own shadow? / I danced alone / the night my mourning my shadow / The water smells of the desert rose / What sea is richer in corals than my revolt?]

Imaginatively this 'syntax of juxtaposition' stood U'Tamsi in good stead when at the invitation of Thomas Kanza he was invited to work as chief editor of the daily newspaper *Le Congo* in Léopoldville during the crucial months of the Congolese Civil War in 1960. The violence U'Tamsi witnessed during those harrowing months wrung from him a mixture of anger, sorrow and pity which lend the central pieces in *Epitomé* a special brooding denseness:

> Christ je me ris de ta tendresse
> o mon doux Christ
> Epine pour épine
> nous avons commune couronne d'épines
> Je me convertirai puisque tu me tentes
> Joseph vient à moi.
> Je tète déjà le sein de la vierge de ta mère
> Je compte plus d'un judas sur mes doigts que toi

---

[3] Tchikaya U'Tamsi, *Epitomé: les mots de têtes pour le sommaire d'une passion* (Tunis: Oswald, 1962), pp. 87–8.

Mes yeux mentent à mon âme
où le monde est agneau ton agneau pascal-Christ
je valserai au son de ta tristesse lente[4]

[Christ I laugh at your sadness / oh my sweet Christ / Thorn for thorn / we
have a common crown of thorns / I will be converted because you tempt me /
Joseph comes to me / I suck already the breast of the virgin your mother / I
count more than your one Judas on my fingers / My eyes lie to my soul /
Where the world is a lamb your pascal lamb – Christ / I will waltz to the tune
of your slow sadness]

As U'Tamsi stands at the foot of the cross he feels the thorns biting
into his own flesh. The same tortured ingrowing devotion is visible in
his poems to St Anne, patron saint of the Congo, emblem of all suffer-
ing women, and, beyond that, of the suffering vigil of a continent.
Wherever the poet looks he sees evidence of his own complicated,
self-inflicted ordeal. Sub-titled 'Les Mots de têtes pour le sommaire
d'une passion' ('Headings for the Summary of a Passion'), *Epitomé*
gradually turns into an enactment of the poet's own crucifixion, the
*via dolorosa* of modern Africa.

The example of U'Tamsi had a tendency to suggest that the distinc-
tive francophone literature of the seventies would be a literature of
self-fracture, of warring selves struggling to be reconciled within the
singularity of the poetic voice. The object of such a literature would be
to pass beyond the false synthesis of Senghor, the Africanized galli-
cism of *négritude*, towards a more conclusive synthesis based on a
clash of opposing entities. In French West Africa itself, however, such
a synthesis at first obstinately refused to materialize. So daunting did
the personality of Senghor seem that his successors in Senegal de-
voted much of their energy to fretting endlessly against him in accents
scarcely distinguishable from his own. The result was a mood of
splenetic rejection founded as much on ideological scepticism as on a
recognition of *négritude*'s artistic limitations:

Vous me les brisez avec votre marxisme–léninisme
vous m'empêchez de réfléchir aves vos doctrines sacro-saintes
capitalo-socio-économico-communistes–bourgeois
j'en ai ma claque de votre négritude
        blanchitude

[4] *Epitomé*, p. 61.

jaunitude
rougitude[5]

[You destroy me with your marxist–leninism / You stultify my mind with your sacrosanct doctrines: / capitalo-socio-economico-bourgeois / I've had a belly-full of your negritude / blanchitude / jaunitude / rougitude]

Thus Senegal's Ibrahima Sall. As the shadow of *négritude* receded, Senegalese poetry returned to the sector of national life to which it had traditionally belonged: namely its womenfolk. A very high proportion of the new generation of poets which emerged in the seventies in Senegal were women. Though politically this represented an undeniable gain, few of the new poets proved themselves capable of devising a distinctive new language. In this Ibrahima Sall was not untypical. Where Senghor has his 'Femme nue / femme noire', her collection *La génération spontanée* has its 'Chante pour négresse'. Where Senghor has his 'Que m'accompangent trois koras et un balafong', she has her 'Solo de cora' her 'solo de tam-tam', her intriguing percussive instruction 'claquement des mains sur fond de balafon'. She too has her memories of village life, her habit of familiar invocation. Ideologically lucid, feminist in intent, Sall's work remains, nonetheless, *négritude* in skirts.

The crisis of poetic diction thus illustrated grew gradually more serious as the decade progressed. Many were the writers who conveyed their sense of unease, among them Senegal's Mbaye Kébé:

> Si nous nous abstenons, nous Afrique,
> Qui fortifiera la Parole?
> Qui purifiera l'Elan?
> Qui apprivoisera la Passion?[6]

[If we withhold ourselves, we of Africa, / Whoever will buttress the Word? / Who will sift the impulse / Winnow the Passion?]

However urgently the question posed itself, the answers seemed at first to be wanting. In the absence of any clear line of advance, the poetry of the immediate post-*négritude* phase tended to veer in one of two directions. First there was a marked tendency to repose tired limbs on the consoling downslopes of a winsome neo-romanticism. Despite academic developments elsewhere in Africa the literature

---

[5] Ibrahima Sall, *La Génération spontanée* (Dakar: Nouvelles Editions Africaines, 1975), p. 16.
[6] Mbaye Gana Kébé, *Ebeniques: poèmes* (Dakar: Nouvelles Editions Africaines, 1969), p. 18.

departments of the universities of Dakar and Abidjan were in the seventies as much devoted to a study of the French classics as were the equivalent departments in Tours or Montpellier. As a result, with no forward destination on offer, many poets continued to take their cue from French masters, tricking out their stanzas with local subject matter and a self-perpetuating nostalgia for *la brousse*. The consolations of the compound and of the extended family proved abiding themes. The Ivory Coast's Maurice Koné, for example, published three volumes of verse between 1969 and 1979,[7] and yet the channel through which his inspiration flowed was suggested more accurately by the title of his second collection *Poèmes verlainiens* than by any express commitment to authenticity. In *Argile du rêve*, beautifully produced with alternating woodcut illustrations by the firm of Nouvelles Editions Africaines in Dakar, his only real concession to plastic experience is an invocation to a 'Masque noire', which, however, has none of the scintillating power of Senghor's intercession in a famous earlier poem:

> Masque taillé dans le bois des forêts
> Sous les doigts habiles de l'artisan nègre
> J'aime te contempler accroché au mur
> Voir tes yeux qui semblent magiques
> O masque! Masque noir.[8]

[Mask hewn of the wood of the forests / Beneath the cunning hands of the carver, / How I dwell on your pendant presence, / Gaze at your magic-seeming eyes, / O mask! Black mask.]

This vein of wimpling, slightly maudlin sentimentality is common even among a number of poets who proclaimed their independence from the university mainstream. Both of Kiné Fall's volumes, *Les élans de grâce*[9] and *Chants de la rivière fraîche*[10], for example, bear titles which referred directly to her status as *ingénue*, yet her freedom from academic constraints has the effect less of liberating her from the influence of the *neuvième siècle* than of diluting it.

Where attempts were made to revitalize the poetic method towards something more dynamic, the result was often to ride too high and too

[7] Maurice Koné, *Poèmes* (Abidjan: Imp. Commerciale, 1969); *Poèmes verlainiens* (Millau, France: Imp. Maury, 1969); *Argile du rêve* (Dakar: Nouvelles Editions Africaines, 1979).
[8] Koné, *Argile du rêve*, p. 27.
[9] Kiné Kirama Fall, *Chants de la rivière fraîche* (Dakar: Nouvelles Editions Africaines, 1976).   [10] Kiné Kirama Fall, *Les Elans de grâce* (Yaounde: CLE, 1979).

fast. In Upper Volta, for example, Pacéré Tintinga produced three volumes of verse within a year.[11] Critics spoke of their raw, unaffected energy, and yet on second reading the short, jabbed lines, the arresting contrasts and monotonous pulse seem a disguise for an almost complete lack of content. Similarly Togo's Emmanuel Dogbé was loud in the announcement of a new African science of metre, and yet himself proved capable of little more than a rather slack *vers libre*.[12] In neighbouring Benin, Richard Dogbeh attempted to escape the stylistic stranglehold of *négritude* by expanding his lines until they sprawled over the page like giant anaconda, and yet, as his metrical ear failed to supply any real mechanism of control, the result is uncomfortably like the very convention he was so frantically attempting to escape. In the volume *Câp liberté*, for instance, he urges the denizens of Africa's shanty towns to rise and claim their inheritance, but in this attempt to play the demagogue, the only instrument of incitement at his disposal appears to be an echo of the depleted rhetoric of Senghor. In 'Salut Lagos', the long poem with which the volume begins, the rhythms and inflections of Senghor's 'A New-York' are only too apparent:

> Lagos
> Je me demande où dorment ces milliers d'hommes
> de femmes et d'enfants mal habillés impaludés
> qui circulent dans tes rues fourmis en processions interminables
> Pourquoi ces deux mères se tenaient-elles au bord
> du trottoir avec leur bébé au crâne rasé
> Pourquoi tant d'epáves humaines polluent les grandes avenues[13]

[Lagos / Where do they sleep, these teeming crowds of men women and children ragged feverous swarming your streets endless as ant-processions / Why do these two mothers loiter by the roadside clutching their shaven-headed infants / Why so many waifs polluting the great avenues?]

The technique of cumulative repetition, the tone of rapt supplication, the reiterated demands that the Lagosians, like Senghor's New Yorkers, remain true to their declared political principles: all proclaim a provenance which, despite his evident straining for originality, Dogbeh could never quite elude. A Beninois of Yoruba extraction, heir like Soyinka to the mythology of Ṣango and Ogun, Dogbeh made valiant efforts to invest his work with the vitality of realized myth, but

[11] Pacéré Tintinga, *Refrains sous le Sahel* (Paris: Oswald, 1976); *Ça tire sous le Sahel: satires nègres* (Paris: Oswald, 1976); *Quand s'envolent les grues couronnés* (Paris: Oswald, 1976).

[12] Yves-Emmanuel Dogbé, *Le Divin amour suivi de paix et bonheur* (Le Mée-sur-Seine, France: Akpagnon, 1979); *Flamme blême* (Le Mée-sur-Seine, France: Akpagnon, 1980).

[13] Richard Dogbeh, *Câp liberté* (Yaoundé: CLE, 1969), p. 8.

even when stretching out to salute the Congo, that most emblematic and archetypal of rivers, his muse could gather little of the dark, gloating, involuted power of U'Tamsi:

> Oho Congo fleuve de mon Afrique
> Image de la terre vaste
> Tes eaux poussent en bavant des séries innombrables de poutres
>   et de feuilles
> Congo, fleuve enragé d'Afrique
>   échappé au projet divin
> Il faut caresser tes eaux à contre-courant
>   puis se laisser porter par elles
> Ainsi l'Afrique
> Jamais de face
> Mais sur tes flancs
> Habile ouvrier du gouvernail
> Maître des eaux et des vents
> Et des hommes.[14]

[O Congo Congo river of my Africa / Mirror of the spreading earth / How your oozing streams thrust aside lattices of trunks and leaves / Congo, chaffing river of Africa, / adrift from your Destiny / Those who would swim against your tide / are carried by your impetus / Like Africa her very self / Swept helpless / Along your flanks / Mastered by you, piloted, / Lord of water and of wind / and of mankind.]

The other tendency apparent throughout much of the period was a tendency to retreat from the broad canvas of *négritude* towards a conception of tradition based more securely on an appreciation of distinctive local cultures. In Mauritania Oumar Ba devoted a life's work to the study of the oral resources of the Fulani people who stretch in a great band across the western Sudan from eastern Senegal through Mali and Niger to the northern-most districts of Nigeria. Ba has written in both Fulani (Peul) and French, and, beginning with *Poèmes peul modernes* in 1965 developed a way of drawing on the idiom of Fulani verse within a recognizable French poetic idiom.[15] Though few attained the depth and breadth of Ba's versions, the attractions of vernacular literature proved a welcome counterbalance to the bastard brood of the romantic movement and the dereliction of *négritude*. In Senegal in particular Mbaye Kébé sought to escape the impasse of

[14] *Ibid.*, p. 29.
[15] Oumar Ba, *Poèmes peul modernes* (Nouakchott: Imp. Mauritanienne, 1965); *Dialogue d'une rive à l'autre: poème* (Saint Louis: Senegal; IFAN, 1966); *Témoin à charge et à décharge: poèmes* (Dakar: Imp. Saint-Paul, nd); *Paroles plaisantes au coeur et à l'oreille* (Paris: La Pensée Universelle, 1977); *Odes sahéliennes* (Paris: La Pensée Universelle, 1978).

poetic language by going back to vernacular Wolof sources. Kébé works in a vein of panegyric very individual to Senegal. The best of his poems invites comparison with traditional Wolof and Serer praise songs. But Kébé is no mere archivist. For him the guardianship of the past is the essential prerequisite of the future; as he hymns the heroes and achievements of past ages, the prospect of a new exultant destiny seems to take wing, spurred on by the familiar strains of the kora:

> la parole du peuple debout n'est pas reste de râle
> D'un saxophone fatigué, d'un tambour troué dès
> Le début de la route dure,
> Sa parole aux allitérations fortes, sa parole tison.
> Sorciers et charlatans ont épuisé leurs interrogatoires
> Le bond solennel sourd dans les jarrets sous l'été des fronts.[16]

[the alert voice of a people: no flagging / death-rattling saxophone, no drum / Threadbare on its travail, / But a speech resolute and resonant / After the inquisition of sorciers and charlatans / hushed rippling of hamstrings beneath the summer of brows.]

Try as these poets would, however, the *cul de sac* of language proved largely insuperable. Forward impetus seemed to carry them inevitably in the direction of a négritudinous rhetoric, while the movement back in search of lost origins entailed a concomitant sentimentality which bogged down their inspiration as effectively as if it had stood still. To this general inertia and confusion there was, however, one glowing exception. The two volumes of verse published by Benin's Fernando d'Almeida in 1976 and 1980 demonstrated much of the alacrity, deftness and sheer verbal venom lacking elsewhere. His first collection *Au Seuil de l'exil* began by clearing the decks:

> Ils sont venus
> les bergers
> autochtones
> de l'insécurité
> ils sont venus
> les fils damnés
> de l'aurore
> indépendante
> ils sont venus
> aiguillonnés
> par la rhétorique
> verbale
> ils sont venus
> les cousins

[16] Kébé, *Ebéniques*, p. 30.

impolitiques
de la mendacité
sans force morale[17]

[They stepped / these herdsmen / aboriginal / out of chaos / they stepped / like sons spurned / from the dayspring / of freedom / they stepped / spurred on / by    soaring / rhetoric / they    stepped / these    impolitic / discredited / cousins / of the lie]

'La rhétorique / verbale'; 'La mendacité': these were the authentic war cries of the seventies, the castigation of moral and intellectual bankruptcy which, in the more vigorous of anglophone poets, we find sounded again and again. In this first book, written when still in his early twenties, Almeida's exasperation with the stalemate of language drove him toward experiments in automatic writing, alongside more conventional echoes of Saint-John Perse and a constant wrestling with the ghost of a quatrain still to be laid. There was a natural temptation to see the structures of corrupt power as themselves embedded in the structures of the language, as if by outraging the second the poet could somehow uproot the first. It was thus that at moments d'Almeida was forced to insist on his very artlessness:

je te prie de lire ce poème à la hâte qu'il est écrit
j'aime la vélocité de la déclamation
la transfiguration lyrique du poème brut
écoute derechef
j'ignore mon identité vraie
je me vêts d'un nom sans parenté ancestrale[18]

[I urge you, read this poem with the haste it was written / I adore the rush of declamation / listen anew / to its raw transmutation / assured of no identity / I come clothed in a nameless patrimony]

d'Almeida's name disguises a parentage half-Dahomean, half-Cameroonian. The severance of ancestral ties implied by so mixed an origin came to seem to him, in a manner not uncommon in his generation, an uncanny reflection both of a private rootlessness and a fracture of political trust. *Au Seuil de l'exil* was written on the brink of the poet's departure for France, and the prospect of exile enabled him to expand on the mythology of severance until it bore fruit in a metaphor of the river Jordan across which lay a land deceptive with milk and honey:

[17] Fernando d'Almeida, *Au Seuil de l'exil* (Paris: Jean Oswald, 1976), p. 11.
[18] *Ibid.*, p. 44.

je m'abreuve de creuses allocutions émaillées de citations latines
je porte en moi l'acculturation à nulle autre pareille
je suis baptisé dans le Jourdain de l'assimilation
je ne connais plus la langue de l'aïeule princesse
hurrah hurrah hurrah pour l'émancipation intellectuelle de mon peuple[19]

[sipping hollow pools of eloquence mantled by latin tags / my load of culture the like of no other / baptised in the Jordan of assimilation / I have lost the tongue of the ancestor princess / three cheers for the intellectual emancipation of my people.]

The condition of exile drew from d'Almeida no histrionic outburst, no fierce compensatory acclamation. The most honest of poets, he knows full well that physical separation from his fatherland is nothing but an attenuation of the process of alienation which has afflicted him since birth. It was this fragmentation of his essential being which in his second volume *Traduit du Je pluriel* drove him inevitably towards linguistic precision as the only possible means of integration in a floating, nebulous world. The effort towards reintegration of a split ego lends the book's title a peculiar poignancy. Victim of assimilation, dazed by exile, torn between two languages, the poet strives to reunite the portions of his being in a definitive act of imaginative assertion:

> Je ne suis sûr de rien
> j'ai voulu partager avec toi le poème de l'exil
> que la mer m'expédie comme une requête subversive
> j'ai voulu te parler de l'ambiguïté provocante du poème
> ayant longtemps vécu dans la contradiction
> j'en suis arrivé à m'adresser aux dieux.
> aux portes de la voyance et de la démesure
> je ne suis vraiment sûr de rien
> réduit à l'errance et à la mendicité quotidienne des mots[20]

[Finally I am certain of nothing / I had wished to share with you the poem of exile / which the sea washed up like a furtive request / wished to speak of the provocative ambiguity of the poem / having lived so long in a state of contradiction / I finished by beseeching the Gods themselves / at the gates of vision and of excess / I am truly certain of nothing / withered to vagary and a daily diet of lying.]

To knit up this nagging ambivalence, reach beyond negation, beyond even the 'provocative ambiguity' of his own speech,

[19] *Ibid.*, p. 46.
[20] Fernando d'Almeida, *Traduit du Je pluriel* (Dakar: Nouvelles Editions Africaines, 1980), p. 45.

d'Almeida longs for an ancient language based, however obscurely, on ancestral precedent. All that stands in his way is a French so brittle that, as Mallarmé warned, it seems constantly to come to pieces in the poet's hands, and a set of inner polarities which even his ache for wholeness, his 'sybilline' velocity of speech cannot resolve. He is stuck with the poem of interiority, the soul-baring of the endlessly displaced. Despite himself, he is still the poet of exile, an exile which stretches way inside him like an unrelenting metalled road he would be rid of:

> Je le sais Je parle toujours d'exil
> Pour voir grandir les lentes semailles de l'espérance
> Maintenant que je fais partie du symbole
> Pour payer ma facture au guichet de l'écriture
>
> L'Amante m'écrit qu'il faut réintégrer
> Ma ville atlantique où la révolution
> Donne semble-t-il un sens à l'action
> Brandissant haut la torche du salut
> Dans les entrepôts des mots d'ordre
>
> Je le sais Je dois un jour
> Connaître les limites du poème
> Parler à voix haute en m'engageunt dans la vie
> Quand l'exil ouvre ses parenthèses
> Pour me distraire du mal de vivre[21]

[I realize I harp on the subject of exile / Watching the seeds of hope ripen / Myself now part of that selfsame symbol / Paying my dues at the turnpike of literature / A loved one writes it is time I enlisted / This coastal town in the revolution / Lending our deeds some semblance of meaning / In this warehouse of decrees. / Some day I realize I will have to learn / The limits of pure poetry / Speak at full tilt, plunge into life / As the parentheses of exile divide / To coax me away from this living pain]

The problem is more than the insolvency of political promises in a tiny coastal state wracked by constant changes of régime, though that too is always at the back of d'Almeida's mind. More fundamentally it is a problem of self-description. d'Almeida can only speak of himself in the first person. His most ardent wish, however, is to dispose of this irritant 'I', this 'Je' that shadows his every step. How can he break through to a genuine plurality of voice, an authenticated 'nous' except through an eternal reduplication of the self, a 'Je pluriel' which stares back at him like a crowd of manic faces from the surface of a subjective

---

[21] *Ibid.*, p. 26.

mirror? To absolve himself of this multiplying individuality, this diffusion of self-love, he would sit humbly and learn from his own people. Yet here his dilemma repeats itself, since his people are split by divisive expectations which arise from the same polluted spring as his own inner discord:

> Ce soir j'ai dîné avec les chefs aînés de la rébellion
> J'ai prêté serment d'allégéance a mon peuple
> Je suis revenu fonder mon empire
> A l'endroit précis où gît le felspath de l'écriture
> Amoureux laboureur de la forme,
> J'appelle du geste la horde séditieuse des expectants
>
> Pour mieux dire
> J'ai trôné devant les hommes de beaucoup d'espoir
> J'ai interrogé les sources orales
> Pour me retrouver dans l'histoire vivante de mon ethnie
> Pour me reconnaître d'entre les inconnus
> Parce que je suis un homme acquis à la bipolarité[22]

[I dined tonight with the elders of insurrection / And swore an oath of allegiance to my people / Returning I planted an empire / On the buried quartz of literature / Tillman, besotted by form / I flannel to anxious restless hordes / To speak more plainly / Enthroned before the optimists / I interrogate the oral springs / To find my place in our living past / And discover myself amongst the unknown, man / Acquainted with ambivalence]

His people have raised on the slim foundations of their independence a 'grande cathédrale de l'Espérance' ('a vast cathedral of hope'). Is it the poet's fault if the transepts are sliding, the buttresses falling, the fabric patched and full of cracks? The poet may not blind himself to such evidence of decay, yet how may he make repair except through a thoroughly disruptive denunciation, an indictment of the peddlers of delusion which can only carry him still further from the soothing reintegration of which elsewhere he speaks? His demon is his conscience, a relentless self-knowledge which will not let him be:

> La parole m'a été léguée
> pour poser bas le masque du mensonge
> La parole m'a été donnée
> pour participer au rut de mon peuple
>
> Je suis dehors pour imposer aux distraits
> le discours inaugural de l'exigence

[22] *Ibid.*, p. 17.

285

Pour repasser mon enfance
comme un collégien qui repasse ses théories d'algèbre

Je commence – le temps aidant –
à comprendre pourquoi je n'ai cessé de plaider
De vouloir tout dire sous les pneus de l'écriture
je commence à me reconnaître d'entre les incertains.[23]

[The word was bequeathed to me / to tear down the mask of lies / The word was bestowed on me / To glory in my people's lust / I am set apart to lead the / Tormented into discipline / to repeat the steps of my childhood / like a school-boy repeating his theorems / Beginning – with time's assistance – / to grasp why I will not cease from / this special feather-bed pleading, / I acknowledge my brothers in doubt.]

Fernando d'Almeida was far from the only poet in the seventies who saw in exile an image of the tormented, broken self. The political conditions of the period were such as to set many writers at logger-heads with their governments, and thus to force them into an inner dialogue with their own idealism as well often as obliging them to for-sake their homeland in search of more tolerant pastures. A writer with whom d'Almeida has much in common is Syl Cheney-Coker of Sierra Leone, a writer whose two volumes published during this difficult decade – *Concerto for an Exile* (1973) and *The Graveyard Also Has Teeth* (1980) – proved him among the most energetic poets then writing in English-speaking Africa. For the larger part of the seventies a high proportion of Sierra Leonean intellectuals were driven into exile by the exigencies of a government which, though constitutionally formu-lated in 1971, became as the decade progressed increasingly intolerant of any comment which smacked of anything less than outright ob-sequiousness. Though Lenrie Peters, still working in a neighbouring Gambia, cannot be said to have felt the full force of these pressures, Yulisa Amadu Maddy, the playwright and novelist, and Coker him-self, were prominent among those who fell out of favour with Presi-dent Siaka Stevens's oligarchical administration. Though most eventually wound up in London, where a network of resistance was maintained through much of this period, there were those who strayed further afield. Coker's fluency in Spanish took him to the uni-versities of Oregon and Wisconsin where he cultivated a growing

[23] *Ibid.*, p. 9.

affinity for the literature of Latin America – principally the novels of Jorge Luis Borges, whose work he greatly admires, and the example of Chilean poet and diplomat Pablo Neruda, whose unfettered humanitarianism has done much to inspire him.

*Concerto for An Exile*, his first collection, published in London in 1973, read as a strenuous effort to make sense of his personal predicament by one, who though conscious of his Freetown creole inheritance, yet could not bring himself to be confined by it. Coker is acutely aware of a mixed inheritance. As a creole within Sierra Leone he belongs to a privileged group whose origins lie in a nineteenth century gesture of emancipation. Doubly estranged from parochial ties, first by enslavement, and then by an impulse of philanthropic resettlement, the creoles, whose mother tongue Krio blends an English lexis to a syntax part-Yoruba and part-Mende, are a group whose exact local allegiance has been smoothed over and obscured by history. There is thus a sense in Coker's collection in which the poet feels himself to be an exile even from his own passionate homesickness. Captive to a reluctant wanderlust, his anger, which is hard and keen, bites as often into his own befuddled being as into the political and moral forces ranged against him. There is in him a puzzlement, both at unassuaged drives in his own heart, and at the compromises and subterfuges of history:

> don't ask me
> why I look so sad
> I did not know my father
> only an apparition
> who said he was a phoenix
> my face is an apocalypse
> of my misery
> mind and body examined
> I stand a paradigm of sorrow[24]

The Christian religion, and especially the Protestant branch of it, has been especially important in the formation of the spiritual consciousness of the creole people. For Cheney-Coker, the image of the Christ, with which in his hounded isolation he is occasionally tempted to identify, becomes, in the context of the large-scale connivance in human misery by God's officers both in Africa and South America, a scorn and a reproach. Like Christ, the poet knows himself a man of

[24] Syl Cheney-Coker, *The Graveyard Also Has Teeth with Concerto for An Exile* (London: Heinemann, 1980), p. 18.

sorrow and acquainted with grief. And, like Christ too, his instinctive sympathies are for the outcast, the lost, the ravaged. Yet deeper than his sorrow runs his anger at a world which will take advantage of his charity even before he expresses it. And deeper still is the desolation of one who has seen Christ the scourged turn scourger. Wherever he looks, there is no redress:

> A protestant
> I swore I would be chaste
> to worship Mary the Virgin of saints.
> My sex is a sterile seed in the wind
> it has the sickness of my soul
> Christ I have your vanity in my head
> century to century summer to summer
> ocean to ocean continent to continent
> I carry the blessings of your rape
> I was a king before they nailed you on the cross
> converted I read ten lies in your silly commandments
> to honour you my Christ
> when you have deprived me of my race[25]

From Freetown to the Great Lakes, from Wisconsin to Buenos Aires, from Argentina to the Philippines, where in mid-decade he taught the literatures of Africa and Latin America, he carries his grief humped like a haversack on his back. And wherever he goes he leaves this trail of twining regret, a trickle of song unfurling in the wind. However loudly the big battalions may fume and stamp their feet, however oppressive the timpani and the braying brass, he will plough his lonely furrow. The violins dip and tackle, the celli rise and sway, but against the raucous *tutti* of the mighty, the soloist persists. His is an oboe concerto:

> Solitude of water and the silence of the eucalyptus
> of the moods man comes seeking that which was stolen
> from him by God who like the phoenix salts the pain grown enormous
> beaking sheets of water like the cancer of life
>
> solitude when the song escapes, the profusion of poetry
> dripping bit by bit from his perforated heart
> and solitude when the song returns to strip the heart
> of so much poetry; corrosive metalloid and bronze
> pitiable man like the crab lost from the sea
> following death at sunset, a pageant beloved death
> O pathetic, terra-cotta man suffering with me![26]

[25] *Ibid.*, p. 30.    [26] *Ibid.*, p. 99.

Coker is at his very best in such muted moods when, the tempest inside his breast subsiding, he sits in a pool of winnowed light making music to his own shadow. At his most enjoyable he abounds in half-shades, tired, autumnal, a little bitter to the taste. He is not what one might call a disciplined poet: his images are promiscuous rather than abundant, and he appears not to recognize the comma. But out of this very promiscuity and diffuseness he distils poetry like wine:

> Eyes of heavenly essence, o breasts of the purity of breasts
> Russian sapphire of the blue of your eyes
> O wine that mellows like the plenitude of Bach
> Sargassian sea that is the calm of your heart
> the patience of you loving my fragile soul
> the courage of you moulding my moody words
> I love you woman gentle in my memory![27]

The effect is sometimes not unlike reading a facsimile of a Shakespeare sonnet in which phrases yield alternative readings depending on the way in which they are grouped together within an elided syntax. However wide the resulting net of associations, Coker always seems to be just in control of the process. Finally the poem gives off an aroma which, analysed, it would be hard to reconstitute. For to pick a semi-precious stone, a draft of vintage and the curling counterpoint of a baroque *Kapellmeister*, to place all of them in the palm of one's hand, to toss them all in the becalmed reaches of the mid-Atlantic, and out of all of this, to raise up sirens singing: this argues a poet whose mastery of his medium has no need of rules. The lines are from a love poem, but in reality all of Coker's pieces are love poems, even when the love itself has fermented to vinegar. He is never more loving than, as when remembering Pablo Neruda on the Chilean master's death in 1973, his fury lashes and stings:

> Pablo America did not swallow you nor the generals
> who hunted you like guanaco over the Andes and across borders
> while miners and peasants kept you underground sharing
> their torn ponchos and bread and the fever exuding
> the nitrate and copper exploited over the centuries
> how generously you sang them in the *Canto General*
> the misery of a continent and people parcelled out
> like loaves by the generals and colonialists who dreamed
> of their banana republics peopled by serfs

[27] *Ibid.*, p. 110.

and they hounded you in Spain, in Argentina
they hounded you in Brazil and North America
with its chilling hypocrisy closed its doors
to you while proclaiming the freedom of the world
they shut you out they shut a poet out![28]

         ☽         ☽         ☽

Another poet for whom the example of Neruda was important was
Kofi Awoonor, who spent most of the late sixties and early seventies
in America where, after completing and publishing his academic re-
search into African traditions under the title *The Breast of the Earth*,[29] he
took up a position as professor of comparative literature at the State
University of New York at Stoney Brook, Long Island. Awoonor's
presence in America was partly to be explained by his association with
the politics of the Nkrumah government, under which he had served
as director of the national film corporation. The Ghana of the late
sixties, where overnight detestation of everything Nkrumaist had
suddenly become mandatory, was not a comfortable place for those
who remembered only too well how differently had stood the case
when Ghanaians were proud to recognize Nkrumah as the gleaming
hope of a continent. Though not an exile in the strict sense, there is
much in the poetry Awoonor wrote in these years to remind one of the
state of rootlessness in which so many of Africa's intellectuals
languished in the unsettled years when the first fruits of indepen-
dence ran so bitterly to seed.

*Ride Me, Memory* (1973), the volume which he published while in the
United States, contains a set of 'American Profiles' to balance the 'Afri-
can Memories' with which the book closes. Prospect of return there-
fore balances retrospect, and the biting edge of the collection falls
mid-way between the two. Awoonor was very far from the first West
African poet to give us his verse impressions of God's Own Country.
Both Okara and Clark had done the same during the sixties, and
Awoonor's countryman Kofi Anyidoho was to do so in *A Harvest of
Our Dreams*, his second volume published in London in 1984. But
Awoonor's case was exceptional because he was in possession of an

[28] *Ibid.*, p. 101.
[29] Kofi Awoonor, *The Breast of the Earth: A Survey of the History, Culture and Literature of Africa South of the Sahara* (New York: Anchor Doubleday, 1975).

especially portable talent. Though emphatically grounded in a local tradition, Awoonor appears to carry his Ewe soul around with him in his hand luggage. Here, for example, he extends the scope of the traditional Anlo insult poem or *halo* to lambast 'Stanislaus the Renegade' in the first of his 'Songs of Abuse':

> This is addressed to you, Stanislaus, wherever you are.
> Listen you punk, the last time we met you were selling faulty guns in Addis
> I heard you panting afterwards in a Cairo whorehouse
> Before I knew you split with my spring overcoat
> a cashmere job I danced for in a bar at Kabul.
> I heard you were peddling fake jewelry to Pueblo Indians
> and Washington hippies. The jail you occupied in Poonaville, Tennessee
> was burnt down after you escaped; they could not eradicate the smell.[30]

Awoonor's superbly flexible muse wafts him effortlessly through the airports of the world, yet he is always stubbornly his own man, a little arch, a little flippant, a little rueful, while, deep down beneath the inventive suaveté, an age-old pain lingers. His sense of ethnic and racial injustice did not spoil him for America, as it had done Clark, but rather opened up fresh perspectives which he colonized with his empathy and wit. In the poem entitled simply 'America' he coolly assesses Archibald Macleish's enfolding vision of a grandiose American destiny:

> Where did they bury Geronimo
> heroic chieftain, lonely horseman of this apocalypse
> who led his tribesmen across deserts of cholla
> and emerald hills
> in pursuit of despoilers,
> half-starved immigrants
> from a despoiled Europe?
> What happened to Archibald's
> soul's harvest on this raw earth
> of raw hates?
> To those that have none
> a festival is preparing at graves' ends
> where the mockingbird's hymn
> closes evening of prayers
> and supplication as
> new winds blow from graves
> flowered in multi-colored cemeteries even
> where they say the races are intact.[31]

[30] Kofi Awoonor, *Ride Me, Memory* (New York: Greenfield Review Press, 1973), p. 20.
[31] *Ibid.*, pp. 9–10.

The sense of Paradise destroyed which pervades these early sections of the book lends a peculiar urgency to the later poems in which Awoonor looks back to his childhood years in Eweland, drawing strength and consolation from a sense of shared sanctity and justice. In one of the most moving, a dream of family warmth and conviviality is suddenly rent by a nightmare in which the poet flees the compound pursued by his father whose features are suddenly distorted by anger. In another, he recalls a visit to his uncle, the diviner:

> You stood on the compound
> of our fallen homestead
> nodding. A divination procedes
> from the diviner's good stomach
> older memories and fire burning
> over the homesteads though fallen.
> I was the messenger of that fire
> the coming of that prophecy.[32]

Considering the intensity of the longing expressed in these lines, the actual circumstances of Awoonor's homecoming in 1974 contained a certain rueful irony. Appointed to a senior position at the University of Cape Coast, where he worked alongside the dramatists Martin Owusu and Ama Atta Aidoo, he was soon accused of collusion in a supposed Ewe-based counter-*coup*. Arrested in November 1975, his regional loyalties weighed against him and he was transferred to Ussher Fort where he spent the better part of the following year. After a brief court appearance on 21 October 1976, at which he was sentenced to another year's imprisonment, he was unaccountably released a few days later.[33] One of the few beneficial results of this incident was the publication, not long after his release of *The House by the Sea*, a volume which sets his prison experiences in the context of his developing political thoughts and aspirations. Perhaps his most impressive collection to date, *The House by the Sea* is a Mahlerian symphony to liberty in which Awoonor's lyrical gift seems to have reached an euphoric apotheosis.

Not surprisingly, considering the circumstances of its composition, when compiling the collection Awoonor chose to place close to its beginning two salutes to Pablo Neruda, who died shortly before Awoonor left the United States, and whose brand of fraternal comradeship is much after his heart. The twenty-six poems which make

---

[32] *Ibid.*, p. 40.     [33] *Index on Censorship* 2, 1976, p. 84; also 2, 1977.

up *Before the Journey*, the opening movement of the volume, are all set either in America or on the international circuit, and thus constitute both a preamble to the book's central event, the prison episode itself, and a kind of breezy harking back to the comparatively carefree world of *Ride Me, Memory*. From coast to coast, from Texas to Long Island, from Japan to India, Awoonor journeys across sights, smells, women. In Kalamazoo he sees two popinjays cavorting in a flawless blue sky, a sight which in those lonely, bitter months in the house by the sea would return to haunt him over and over again. Though composed for the most part before leaving Long Island, the poetry of this section seems with hindsight to have been deflected through the window of his prison cell, such are its lusciousness and its tender, heartfelt longing. This is some of the most delicate verse that Awoonor has written; the very imagery seems to curl round his finger ends like the tendrils within the open cup of a flower. The resulting purity and intensity, heightened by his subsequent desperation, is not unlike Japanese poetry or perhaps the French symbolists:

> My love, the naked mirrors
> of my soul, luminescent cancer
> and the adoration
> what profound mysteries these are
> in the curvature of the rose
> and the arc of the lonely autumn bee
> doomed to die
> as the earth dies.[34]

At first reading, and knowing the fate to which Awoonor was soon to return, one is at first inclined to approach these first poems as diversion or else simple *praeludium*; in fact they are an integral part of the structure of a book which is concerned throughout with the nagging, eternal problem of the nature of liberty. In the context of the massed enslavement of millions, Awoonor is asking, is the consciousness of the individual most truly free when lolling amid arcadian, summer-blest gardens, or else when chipping away at some unglamorous but necessary revolutionary task? It is a proposition which he puts to the ghost of Neruda in 'Requiem for Pablo', the second of his tributes, written, like Coker's elegy, shortly after the Chilean poet's death:

> Where are those who swear,
> poetry has nothing to do with it

[34] Kofi Awoonor, *The House by the Sea* (New York: Greenfield Review Press, 1978), p. 2.

'I don't want to be used for political causes'
they proclaim.
But the laugh is on them, hombre,
As they carry their inanities in man hats
envenoming themselves like our early serpents
for a battle that will be fought
on this earth, our earth.[35]

Later, in his cell in Ussher Fort, the house by the sea, he squats on his haunches debating the same question with the spectre of Ho Chi Minh who confirms that the real meaning of liberty is 'the possibility of being murdered in a dark cell'. The vision is a grim one, and the surrounding poetry almost equally so. The few verses which Awoonor managed to produce in the stifling régime of the gaol itself, with two exceptions, parade in prison fatigues or else Maoist pyjamas. As soon as the prison doors clang shut behind him, the lusciousness dies; what is left is concentrate: brittle, passionate, proud, the poetry of survival. It is a transition which we noted earlier in Soyinka's prison verse, but the defiant ebullience of the earlier phases of *A Shuttle in the Crypt* is a far cry from Awoonor's poetry, which picks its consolation like gruel from a mess tin:

The birds will fly back soon.
They remind me of leftovers
of rainy nights of insects
and the drum of rains
and the voices of 400 captives.[36]

The unceremonious numerals, the extreme concision are both in consonance with the gritty mood of the majority of these prison verses, which seem to take their cue from Chinese revolutionary poetry, and which occasionally remind one of the recent work of another former African detainee, Dennis Brutus.

Gradually, however, as Awoonor's reflexes adjust themselves, the lyrical juices begin to flow again. The collection ends with one of the strongest poems in the book, 'The Wayfarer Comes Home' which, though written in the poet's cell, seems to look forward to the world of his ultimate release. In it his characteristic starved, thwarted optimism bursts forth in a hymn of praise for all that, under the heel of autocracy, he has had to forgo for so many months: his land, his mother, the mother of his own children:

---

[35] *Ibid.*, p. 7.    [36] *Ibid.*, p. 46.

I sang on the sea of my love,
of you, home and invisible woman
whom I've known since conception
though you were lost once
among the high grass of infancy.
I searched for you in foreign lands
in the faces of strangers in the cities of Europe . . .

But you were another spirit
of another time and place
You were the tired salmon
after the torrent time of the river
 But like the spirit
  and the fish
You swam on upon your journey.[38]

The persecution or detention of writers was not, however, the only way in which the tensions of an increasingly fraught decade manifested themselves. By the mid-seventies, as the political currents of the region grew more embroiled, there was a growing tendency for the poet in West Africa to define himself through a state of permanent ostracism. From having viewed himself in the fifties and early sixties as the burning tip of the national advance, he had come twenty years later to identify himself solely through exclusion, as a lone voice crying in the wilderness. Increasingly too, he saw himself as the conscience or goad of the people, a view which the politicians resented but which their own opportunism did nothing to discourage.

The most sustained attempt to quicken the moral conscience of men of power was Wole Soyinka's masterpiece of Shelleyean exhortation *Ogun Abibiman*, written in 1976 in response to a decision by Mozambique's revolutionary leader Samora Machel, to align himself with those still fighting to secure majority rule within a Rhodesia dominated by the hegemony of Ian Smith. The Akan word 'Abibiman' implies that which pertains to the well-being and integrity of the black peoples. It is employed by Soyinka in his title because it asserts a firm recognition, within one of the more widespread of West Africa's languages, of an identity of interest and aspiration among those of negro inheritance surviving, and even disseminated by the diaspora of the last three centuries, a kinship of hope and consolation transcending the petty barriers which men set for themselves in defence of

[37] *Ibid.*, pp. 65–6.

295

smaller loyalties. It is thus of transparent relevance to Soyinka's attempt in this poem to combine a Pan-African vision with an act of renewed homage to Ogun, Yoruba god of iron, war and the hunt.

It was remarked earlier that there is in the best of Soyinka's work a double thrust: an immersion in the quick of locality, the *genius loci*, combined with a universality of human sympathy almost Voltairean. For Soyinka, to be truly Yoruba is by the same token to assert one's solidarity with all men; to pay homage at a village shrine to recognize one's membership of a wider religious community. In *Ogun Abibimañ* the supreme moment of revelation which surprised the poet on the summit of Idanre becomes the spark which kindles a seismic political event. As Ogun, god of the blacksmiths, flexes his arm, a whole continent waits breathless:

> Carillons in the distance. A festal
> Anvil wreathed in peals, split by the fervid
> Tongue of ore in whiteglow.
> The Blacksmith's forearm lifts,
> And dances. . . .
> Its swathes are not of peace.
>
> Who dare restrain this novel form, this dread
> Conversion of the slumbering ore, sealed
> So long in patience, new stressed
> To a keen emergence! – Witness –
> Midwives of fireadze, heartburn, soulsear
> Of rooting out, of rack and mindscrew – witness –
> Who dare intercede between
> Hammer and anvil
> In this fearsome weaning?[39]

The poem is one long crescendo from this hushed, expectant beginning – a vigilant landscape, bells over the bare hills – towards a fully orchestrated rhetorical peroration. Its texture abounds in rapid, and not always convincing connections, darting from allusion to allusion, place to place, paeon to paeon in a frantic endeavour to assert the unity of all life in the long search for fullness. The work is difficult to absorb outside of a deep conviction, which few readers share with Soyinka's intensity, of the interpenetration of all earthly substance, all forms, all manifestations. The ambitious scope of the poem, which switches from rural Yorubaland to the shanties of Sharpeville and on the nineteenth century Zululand of Shaka, is made feasible by the ele-

[38] Wole Soyinka, *Ogun Abibimañ* (London: Rex Collings, 1976), p. 3.

mental aspect of Yoruba religion itself: its identification of Ogun's hammer with all metal, whether cable, bell, sword or machine gun; its further association of the spark at the naked forge with all fire and hence with the conflagration which, in the wake of a conclusive call to liberation, might well engulf the whole land of Abibimañ. Once again the imagery of fire connects with the imagery of metal in the generative symbol of electricity. The whole poem is thus magnetic with the fusion of diverse elements into a single, glowing political instrument. Its accelerating pace, the urgency which sends phrase cascading over phrase in an onrush towards total definition, electrifies the imagination even as it disturbs the judgement:

> Though some have rooted out, set fire to,
> Denied the name, usurped the being of –
> These are the columns that have borne
> The weight of earth, quarrying wealth to fleck
> The greed-glow in the eyes of strangers,
> To shore the power-lust of kin renegades.
> Risen from fossils of that world's
> Shaming displacement, the earth's collapse,
> Their spine is one with the axis of the new
> Universe of being, in place of fallen
> Galaxies – say not the dead are dead! Heirs
> To the task's fruition, future world
> Upon whose brows the gods and the ancestors
> Crowd our powers – BAYETE![39]

We are very far from the tender lyrics of the opening pages of the *Idanre* volume, further still from the delicate mobiles of Soyinka's prison verse. This, detraction insists, is the Soyinka who assailed the complacency of London theatre-goers in the sixties with his anti-apartheid drama *The Experiment*,[40] or the Soyinka of the lecture podium, hammering his audience into stunned agreement with a *tour-de-force* of verbosity and cutting novelty. The multiple, hyphenated substantives – 'greed-glow' and, more conventionally, 'power lust' – the accumulation of redundant phrases, all argue a style of writing in which form is sacrificed to message, balance to immediacy.

And yet, critically examined, the poem yields a very respectable account of its form. The object of each of the three movements is to demonstrate the arrogating of one style of self-assertion over another: the concerted call to arms over the prevarications of moderate

---

[39] *Ibid.*, p. 17.      [40] Soyinka's polemical one-act play of 1959. See chap. 9, note 6.

discourse. The poem was written at the end of a period when several West African states – pre-eminently Houphouët-Boigny's Ivory Coast and Kofi Busia's Ghana – tired of a policy of economic and political attrition which seemed to have damaged black Africa rather than apartheid, had proposed an attempt at 'Dialogue', a two-way conversation between interlocutors so unevenly matched, as its opponents were not slow to point out, as to render the exercise meaningless. It therefore came as welcome news that the new Marxist government in Maputo had dedicated itself to the overthrow of Ian Smith's Rhodesia by military means. In support of this initiative Soyinka's poem urges the gathering momentum of righteous anger fused by the earth itself. Its opening section 'Steel usurps the forests, Silence dethrones Dialogue' is thus an account of the gradual swamping by the rhythms of conflict of the lusher, more timid modes of apathetic peace:

> NO longer are the forests green; storms
> Assail the palm, the egret and the snail.
> Bared, the dark heart of a hidden nursery
> Of embers flares aglow, a landmass writhes
> From end to end, bathed and steeped
> In stern tonalities.[41]

The section is entitled 'Induction', a pun implying both a 'leading into' the ranks of the committed and also the process of electrical induction whereby a piece of steel is magnetized. The metaphor is precise for a movement in which the magnificent god of iron emerges from his forest fastness to wrestle the whole of a continent to his sovereign will. In the next section 'Retrospect for Marchers: Shaka!', Ogun furthers his mission by going in search of the Zulu emperor in his savannah terrain to the south. The meeting is auspicious for several reasons, bringing together as it does patriarchs from two ends of the African continent and from two different historical strata. Yet Shaka and Ogun have more in common than their strength and representative quality. They also share a quality in which, for the purposes of this poem, Soyinka is more immediately interested, a tragic dimension issuing from moments of oversight or weakness. Ogun, so the Yoruba believe, once rounded on his own army and slaughtered them at the climax of battle. Shaka, once the terror of the central African plains, unaccountably lost faith in himself and his destiny towards the end of his life: a lapse for which he had to pay the penalty of forfeiting

[41] Soyinka, *Ogun Abibimañ*, p. 1.

his kingdom. Shaka then is not so much seen in this work as a hero for emulation as a personification of flawed greatness. One can reinforce this point by contrasting Soyinka's view of the Zulu emperor with that advanced in Senghor's dance-drama *Chaka*, in which a chorus leader encourages the people in homage to their doomed leader:

LE CORPYPHÉE [LEADER OF THE CHORUS]

Rosée ô Rosée qui réveilles les racines soudaines de mon peuple.

[Dew, o Dew awakening the sudden roots of my people]

LE CHOEUR [CHORUS]

*Bayêté Bâba! Bayêté ô Bayêté!*

LE CORYPHÉE [LEADER OF THE CHORUS]

Là-bas le Soleil au zénith sur tous les peuples de la terre.

[Down there the sun at the zenith over all the peoples of the earth.]

LE CHOEUR [CHORUS]

*Bayêté Bâba! Bayêté ô Bayêté!* [42]

In Soyinka's poem the same cries recur, but this time less in prostrate veneration than as encouragement to the flagging will of a king, who, conscious of having failed in an earlier hour of trial, now seeks a complement and mainstay in Ogun.

Hence the interpenetration of substance and symbol earlier noted has its equivalent on the historical plane in an interpenetration of time. Ogun and Shaka are held together in a sort of continuous, listless present. Such temporal transposition is not new in Soyinka's work. In 1960, at another moment of destiny, the official declaration of Nigeria's independence, his play *A Dance of the Forests* brought together a group of bewildered villagers and the inhabitants of one of the great pre-colonial Sahelian empires who were called upon to render an account of their custodianship of the past. Thus, in *Ogun Abibimañ*, Shaka is endowed with a modern revolutionary awareness and Pan-African commitment not typical of his earlier manifestation,

[42] Léopold Sédar Senghor, *Ethiopiques* (Paris: Editions du Seuil, 1956), p. 52.

just as earlier Ogun was entrusted with a will to change and a global perspective representing potentialities at best latent in his position within the Yoruba pantheon. And, at the apex of the second movement, Ogun and Shaka join hands in one heroic, irresistible pact:

> Memories of other times beset me yet –
> *Sigidi!* My sandals trampled the savannah
> Smooth as the splayed hide of the bull.
> Where I paused, Ogun, the bladegrass reddened.
> My impi gnawed the stubble of thornbushes,
> Left nothing for the rains to suckle after.
>      – Sigidi!
>      – Sigidi Baba! Bayete![43]

It has often been remarked that Soyinka's view of history is cyclical. This is emphatically true of his earlier poems and plays in which the individual human will seemed constantly to be battling within encroaching circles of retribution or revenge. The ideological jolt of the civil war, however, had by 1976 brought Soyinka to the point at which he wished to highlight two aspects of his earlier philosophy: to emphasize the potentiality for failure implicit within any credible account of history while, simultaneously to assert the possibility of change through responsible action. Both of these points are emphasized in *Sigidi!*, the poem's closing peroration. Though unremitting in its sequence of creation and destruction, history is seen to focus itself on certain memorable moments when, temporarily set free from the chains of guilt and recrimination, the collective mind is enabled to express itself in freedom. Action will gutter into futility, aftermaths must inevitably occur, but against his continuing recognition of the fallibility of all human aims and designs – the darkening vision of Yeats's 'Second Coming' – Soyinka is now able to incite one ardent instant of respite and of glory:

> Remember this. And remember Spain – Guernica
> Remember dreams that *will* go sour, ideals
> Afloat on the cesspools of time –
> Aborted foetuses – remember this. And remember
> Lidice – then Sharpeville too. Remember,
>
> When, safely distanced, throned in saintly
> Censure, the prophet's voice possesses you –
> *Mere anarchy is loosed upon the world* et cetera
> Remember too, the awesome beauty at the door of birth. [44]

[43] Soyinka, *Ogun Abibimañ*, p. 11.      [44] *Ibid.*, p. 21.

If Wole Soyinka felt able, at this relatively advanced stage in his career, to assert the possibility of purposeful escape from repetitive cycles of past failure, it was his earlier, bleaker vision of a dismal tread-mill of constant historical betrayal that proved more suggestive for other writers. Throughout the seventies, the tendency to ground inti-mations of the present in a fractious view of the past became ever more insistent in both verse and prose. There was a vogue for historical novels, Yambo Ouloguem's prize-winning *Le devoir de violence* (1968),[45] with its portrayal of pre-colonial Dogon society as a pit of lust and power-seeking, was followed by two works of harrowing beauty by the Ghanaian novelist Ayi Kwei Armah: *Two Thousand Seasons*[46] and *The Healers*[47] both of which recount the fragmentation of a cohesive African cosmology at an early period in Akan history. It is with a lengthy quotation from *Two Thousand Seasons* that the young Ewe poet Kofi Anyidoho chose to open the Greenfield Press edition of his first volume *Elegy for the Revolution*, published in New York in 1978:

This is life's race, but how should we remind a people hypnotized by death? We have been so long following the falling sun, flowing to the desert, moving to our burial...[48]

Much of the funereal gravity of Armah's vision of history finds its way into the inflections of Anyidoho's book. The 'Revolution' of the title was the overthrow in January 1972 of the democratically elected civilian government of Dr Kofi Busia by Colonel I. K. Acheampong, whose National Redemption Council had itself, six years later, lost every shred of the credibility with which the Ghanaian people had once endowed it. Already by 1978, the economy of the country was in dire straits, and all-too-familiar signs of corruption and venality had begun to make themselves apparent. To those who, like Anyidoho, could remember the high promises made by Acheampong and his henchmen in 1972, the irony was as cruel as it was absurd. Whatever

[45] Yambo Ouloguem, *Le Devoir de violence* (Paris: Editions du Seuil, 1968).
[46] Ayi Kwei Armah, *Two Thousand Seasons* (London: Heinemann, 1979).
[47] Ayi Kwei Armah, *The Healers* (London: Heinemann, 1978).
[48] *Two Thousand Seasons*, p. xi, quoted in Kofi Anyidoho, *Elegy for the Revolution* (New York: Greenfield Review Press, 1978), p. 1.

his failings, Acheampong was a man who knew how to twist the modern media of communication to his purpose. In January 1972 martial music and ghost-written speeches had thundered over the soundwaves of the Ghana Broadcasting Corporation to proclaim an end to corruption and bureaucratic delinquency. At public rallies from Black Star Square, Accra to Victoria Park, Cape Coast, a brand-new strategy of popular action had been declaimed through whispering microphones by men in khaki clothing. The 'Feed Yourself Campaign', a concerted policy of domestic cultivation was inaugurated as a weapon in the search for import substitution. It was in vain in such a Wordsworthian hour of rebirth that more cautious voices had warned that the new ideologues seemed not to know the difference between the popular will and the bayonet, or between a revolution and a mere revolt. Five years later, in his poem 'Radio Revolution', however, Anyidoho was able to display that vigilance over lexical truth which is a poet's prerogative:

> Again this dawn our Radio
> broke off the vital end of sleep
>
> Revolution! .... Devolution! .... Resolution!
>
> grab a razor-sharp machete
> and step onto the paths of war
>
> Across our yard I disturbed a courtship of
> the dogs. They barked and backed away
>
> through streets to all familiar walks
> through maze of slums to armed barracks
> of peace. Where? Where?
> old peasant with hoe in hand, I
> seek Revolution. Where is Revolution?
> young veteran with blood across blue eyes, I
> knew of no Revolution, but I
> met Revolt limping down this road
> chased by a howling herd of armed jackals
> down this road down this road
> to the market-square where an only
> pig searching for a morning meal
> took me for a moving lump of flesh
> and charged at me charged at me
> with fangs sharpened by hunger's despair
>
> I slashed her into two, wiped her
> blood upon
>       her head. . . .[49]

---

[49] Anyidoho, *Elegy*, p. 12. reprinted in Kofi Anyidoho, *A Harvest of Our Dreams with Elegy for the Revolution* (London: Heinemann, 1984), pp. 64–5.

The typographical highlighting of key phrases, the tone of curdled regret, the oblique use of autobiographical anecdote are all typical of the method of this first collection which shows Anyidoho, surely the brightest representative of his generation, still searching for an exact personal idiom in which to do lyrical justice to his sense of dereliction. In the meantime, the poem operates by brilliant flashes: the two dogs circling one another like politicians sniffing the rump of opportunity, the 'young veteran', already senile in hopeful scheming, and the pig which serves as a sardonic sacrifice to the doomed journey ahead. It is the 'old peasant hoe in hand', who has already lived through so many violent, remote changes and in whose name the insurrection has nominally been staged, however, who earths the poem. At the time of writing the poet was a mature student of linguistics at the University of Ghana, whence he had gone after several years of teaching Ewe and English. The pieces which eventually found their way into *Elegy for the Revolution*, published during the author's postgraduate studies in Indiana, are hence Accra poems invoking a ruined urban landscape. It is from Anyidoho's home district of Wheta in the Volta region, towards which his art would increasingly turn, however, from which these pieces derive their value system and their stubborn independence of thought.

Anyidoho possesses what can only be called a subversively provincial eye. At the very moment when the metropolitan demagogues are at their most deceptively strident, his attention will fix itself on the despised, silent northern servant as he reports for duty from his rudimentary backyard quarters in order to dance attendance on the argumentative employer who takes himself for the vanguard of the new revolutionary élite:

> a young revolutionary lays ambush in my thoughts
> firing sound bombs
> into colonial barricades
>
> my memory bumps
> into the silence of
> his 70-year-old
> HouseBoy
> he serves champagne in panelled living rooms
> retreats at night to a toy
> mud-hut with a bamboo bed
> swallows a glass of liquid flames
> turns his dreams loose
> upon his private agonies

> The dreams of Fanon's wretched of the earth
> condense into storms in our morning sky
> and
> The burden of our guilt
> hangs heavy upon our harvest joys[50]

'The dreams of Fanon' were substantially the dreams of Anyidoho's generation and of my own. Like all of his contemporaries Anyidoho grew to maturity against the distant rumblings of the Algerian War of Liberation and the independence struggles in Asia and Africa. By the age of twenty-nine, when the majority of these poems were written, he had already lived long enough to see most of these aspirations reduced to tatters. Under the first impact of disappointment, his early poetry veers between the satirical and elegiac in a way that is not always satisfactory. 'HouseBoy' gives us both styles in a nutshell. The unease with which the poet approaches the satirical vein is shown only too clearly in the inept punctuation and syntax of the second verse paragraph, and in his deafness to the intrusive double meaning present in the word 'sound' in line 2. But after a brief transition the poetry moves into the imagery of dirge and harvest which are the mainstay of Anyidoho's second collection *A Harvest of our Dreams* (1984). The regenerative possibilities of this second vein are manifested in the penultimate poem 'A Piece of Hope':

> The dolphins came riding the waves
> a mermaid on their shoulders
> She was casting your name upon the seas
> whispering your laughter to the winds
> They sat in the sand
> purged my heart with a dirge, gave me
> a piece of hope
>             They will send you back someday
>
> So now I search the waves at dawn
> for broken images of
> the world we built upon the shores
> with pools of troubled seas
> I would rebuild our laughter
> with echoes of the past
> dream at noon on forgotten shores
> think of
> souls asleep on moonbeams across my galaxy

[50] Anyidoho, *Elegy*, p. 16. (*Harvest* p. 67.)

I would search the skies for new Edens
reclaim your smile from rainbows in my soul[51]

This is one of the few poems in the collection actually written in the poet's hometown of Wheta. The line 'a piece of hope', which doubles as title, yields in reverse a punning second meaning, but the strength of this passage lies not in its cleverness, but in its beguiling undertow of sighing lament, like a nocturnal high tide tugging at the beeches of Eweland. We are reminded that the Atlantic Ocean both sustains the Anlo communities and erodes the very coastline on which they huddle. The sea, rife with possibilities both destructive and constructive, is not surprisingly central to the poetry both of Anyidoho and of his elder countryman Kofi Awoonor. The solemnity of Anyidoho's treatment here is offset both by the delighted playfulness of his imagery and by the life-enhancing kingdom of laughter he proposes to reconstruct. This is restorative poetry, and the writer's seriousness of purpose can too easily deafen us to the ripple of repressed mirth with which he invests the waves. Anyidoho's art is a sort of funereal keening, but its purpose is the resurrection of joy, and of an integrated world of 'image' and 'echo' within which the poet may work.

The poet's task was made no easier by the fact that, as the seventies drifted towards the eighties, the face of the region came more and more to be dominated by military governments. Further *coups* followed in Ghana, so that, by the beginning of the following decade, with the failure of Dr Limann's shortlived democratic administration, the rule of soldiers came to seem permanent. Meanwhile in Lagos, where military government had been unbroken since the end of the civil war, the date for the transfer to civilian authority was continually postponed. As the prospect of elections drifted further over the horizon, there were those who came to feel that the give-and-take of the parliamentary process was a memory which would never return. Among those who expressed the despair born of such a belief, none were more eloquent than the poet Odia Ofeimun.

Ofeimun worked in the office of a leading parliamentary candidate

---

[51] *Ibid.*, pp. 39–40. (*Harvest*, pp. 86–7.)

in the eventual election campaign of 1979, but the greater part of the
poems collected in *The Poet Lied* (1980), were written during the pre-
ceding period of frustrated political aspiration. On its appearance, the
title of the book was taken as a slighting reference to a literary col-
league, and, as a result of the ensuing fracas, the volume was tempor-
arily withdrawn. However, seen in a larger perspective the title of the
volume and the subsequent legal *débâcle* constitute no more than a
bizarre accident. The real worth of this collection lies in its dextrous
channelling of passions which had gradually built up in the Nigerian
consciousness since the civil war, until, in default of a satisfactory
settlement of the country's problems they had, by the closing years of
the decade, reached an almost uncontrollable pitch. Most of the pieces
date from 1967 to 1976, a nine-year period which takes us from the out-
break of the holocaust through a contentious peace settlement and on
to a time when, in the face of a growing demand for civilian insti-
tutions, the military government held firm, hoping to bolster its pre-
varication with talk of progress and action by consensus. In the face of
such wilful mendacity what more can the poet do than send up his in-
sistent call for truth – that, beyond any supposed biographical slur, is
the ultimate significance of the book's title. Like Anyidoho, with
whose earlier work many of these poems are contemporaneous, Ofei-
mun is concerned with the warping of veracity, a theme to which he
brings all the cauterizing power of a concentrated irony:

> in our model democracy
> the magic promises of yesterday
> lie cold like moulds of dead cattle
> along caravans that lead nowhere
>
> secular sermons wage war
> for souls denied the habit of thought:
> spewed from talking boxes
> divine falsehoods protect us from ourselves
>
> in our model democracy
> nothing is left of the old humour
> the sacked parliament of our collective desires
> appraise horizons burnt to dancing grey
> by tall threats, tall decrees, tall abominations[52]

Ofeimun is bemoaning the passing away of the 'old humour' associ-
ated with parliamentary government. More than that, however, he is
calling authority's bluff. There is in this poetry less concern with

[52] Odia Ofeimun, *The Poet Lied* (London: Longman, 1980), p. 4.

specific abuses – though the muzzling of the press, the state of the nation's markets and the turpitude of the bureaucracy all come in for side-blows – than with the sheer pomposity of power, its piping self-justification and refusal to hold itself accountable. The savour which lingers in Ofeimun's mouth is one of waste. Ofeimun's Nigeria is essentially the Nigeria of the oil boom, a country whose public coffers are bulging with revenues, but which chooses to spend these on limousines, plush carpets, and the acquisition of Swiss bank accounts while the demands of health, education and even main drainage go unmet. It is a granary bursting with wealth, while in the very shadow of plenty, thousands dwindle and starve. Little wonder then that Ofeimun's tone often verges on hoarseness. To call his poetry indignant is to understate it; it seethes rather with a black, almost jocund rage. It writhes and revels in the pure absurdity of injustice it knows itself powerless to redress. And, when vituperation fails, it falls back on its sharpest weapon, humour:

> The streets were clogged with garbage
> the rank smell of swollen gutters
> claimed the peace of our lives
>
> The streets were blessed with molehills
> of unwanted odds and bits
>
> Then, they brought in the bayonets,
> to define the horizons of our days
> to keep the streets clear
> they brought in the new brooms
>
>   To keep the streets clear
> they brought in the world-changers
> with corrective swagger-sticks
> they brought in the new brooms
> to sweep public scores away
>
> But today listen today
> if you ask why the wastebins are empty
> why refuse gluts the public places unswept
> they will enjoy you to HOLD IT:
> to have new brooms, that's something.[53]

At times like this Ofeimun seems like a macabre harlequin, dressed from head to foot in a kind of monochrome motley. The harlequin is only too aware that there are those who would bid him perform at the public feast. The temptations of compromise are always in the fore-

[53] *Ibid.*, p. 5

front of Ofeimun's mind. Poets too, as the title of the book cannily reminds us, are only too easily bought. A writer's salvation can only lie in a dogged adherence to the evidence of his senses. However far, in this new plutocratic Nigeria, words may wander at variance to the truth, however tight the blinkers others wear, the poet can do no other than point out discrepancies, again and again.

> I cannot blind myself
> to putrefying carcases in the market place
> pulling giant vultures
> from the sky
>
> Nor to these flywhisks:
> how can I escape these mind-ripping scorpion tails
> deployed in the dark
> with ignominious licence
> by those who should buttress faith
> in living, faith in lamplights?
>
> And how can I sing
> when they stuff cobwebs in my mouth
> spit the rheum of their blank sense
> of direction in my eyes
> – who will open the portals of
> My hope in this desultory walk?
>
> Yet I cannot blunt my feelers
> to cheapen my ingrained sorrow . . .[54]

Notice the image of cobwebs for a devalued language; also how much work is done by the unpretentious word 'cheapen'. Sorrow is the heart's purge; it is not for sale. And yet he inhabits a world where suddenly everything seems to be up for grabs: loyalty, love, words themselves. The very phrases in which he expresses his frustration have themselves been devalued by this systematic prostitution.

Through successive sections the volume charts the progression of despotism's grim cavalcade. After his opening refusal to keep silent ('How can I sing?'), Ofeimun proceeds to a caustic panorama of the Nigeria of the generals. There then follows a section entitled 'Where Bullets Have Spoken' which takes us back to the source of the problem, the Civil War, when truth first experienced a dressing down. After such debasement, the poet asks, how can anything ever again be held holy?:

[54] *Ibid.*, p. 1.

> And what prayers, pray, when bullets have spoken
> a plague rolled by madmen to feed eighty millions,
> what smile when dark craters have blighted
> a sun that we had despaired of holding[55]

And yet, the poet argues, it is at this very moment, when ideals have been degraded beyond recognition, that it is most necessary that the poet should send up his frail cry. For Ofeimun the art of writing is clearly two things: an act of inner cleansing, washing the mind of despair and hatred, and an assertion of some sort of primordial right, the relentless refusal of the human spirit to bow down before false idols:

> Sometimes, the urge to write
> juts out of the heart-mind, sears the flesh
> like a broken bone
>
> The inkling of an inner voice
> that you can hardly recognize as your own
> crashes with its wings of rotors
> against the petals of your indecision
>
> Locked within yourself
> a pain that is atrociously nuclear
> constrains your will;
> it is time for your tongue to flower,
> time to spirit yourself towards those you love.[56]

That image of the muse as some sort of obscene chopper landing on the unwilling heleport of the soul is something which, even if we had not already guessed it, marks Ofeimun out as a poet in a very rare and a very classical sense, as one who has no power to resist the clamouring of a talent which he resents even as he nurtures it. It is the secret of his mastery; but it is also the secret of his contempt. Charged himself with a voltage of extraordinary vision, he has nothing but scorn for those who settle for milder accommodations: the civil servant squatting 'on seat' at the Ministry; the student radicals with their facile, droning slogans, the Aladuras on the beach as they lose themselves in 'Christi'. Ofeimun's final section 'The Neophytes' is an amused portrayal of the new naïfs, those who come to the task of reconstruction with only banalities to offer, but, despite the contradictions in which the revolutionary will constantly entangles itself, the task is clear and the poet's voice in proclaiming it, triumphant:

[55] *Ibid.*, p. 21.    [56] *Ibid.*, p. 33.

> We will sing and dance
> because the garbage in the streets
> the false houses of prayer
> the gaudy sins of robber barons
> who licked their fat fingers
> at the market-place
> will be swept away
>
> We will sing and dance
> because our lives will come again to be written
> against happy prophecies
>
> No fire next time.[57]

   Not for Ofeimun the progressive, integrating message of James Baldwin, nor the petty readjustments of committee politics, nor even perhaps the radical vision of constructive destabilization. In fact, for all his articulate regret at the absence of parliamentary institutions, one comes away from Ofeimun's book with a feeling that, as poet rather than, say, citizen, he is less taken up with realizable solutions than with the imperatives of a sort of bardic possession. Ofeimun is the Jeremiah of modern Nigeria. His zestful warnings have all the impact of prophetic raillery. This is poetry which demands to be read aloud, or rather declaimed in a state of white heat. Ofeimun's voice is less that of the liberally educated man of letters than it is a vehicle for spiritual vision. Through him, as through many of his contemporaries, the oral poets of Africa's past seem to stir and sing again. But that, as we shall see in the next chapter, is another story.

[57] *Ibid.*, pp. 31–2.

# CHAPTER 12

# The return to orality

Early in the Second World War, a young Senegalese officer was sitting in a German prison camp listening to the expatiations of one of his captors, an Austrian who in civilian life was a linguist. The warder had just launched into a lecture on the significance of silence as a metrical ingredient in Austrian poetry when, like Archimedes of old, his interlocutor suddenly threw up his arms and shouted *Eureka!* How the Austrian reacted we do not know, but for the young Senegalese it was a moment of considerable clarification. What he had discovered was a formula which could explain the underlying order of West African, and more precisely Senegalese–Guinean, oral poetry. The discovery was important: the prisoner was a poet. He was also in search of a style.[1]

Thirty years later that Senegalese poet, now president of the Republic of Senegal, wrote up his conclusions in an essay entitled, in honour of a French writer he much admired, 'La Parole chez Paul Claudel et chez les négro-africains'. In this essay he tried to make his readers listen to traditional African poetry in a new way. So far, he believed, academic investigators into the structure of vernacular verse had lost themselves in a quagmire of irrelevance. The reason was that they had failed to take into account the pauses, or more strictly rests, in the extracts which they had so painstakingly transcribed:

The fact which misled researchers for a long time was that the lines they transcribed never seemed to possess the same number of syllables. Moreover, the syllables never seemed to account for the entire metrical structure of the line. To grasp such rhythms and fully appreciate them one must devote attention to the underlying silence: the master drum – masterful by virtue of its function – which pronounces the fundamental rhythm unwearyingly, like a metronome, while the other percussion instruments, if such there be, and supremely the poet, give full reign to their fantasy by besieging it with syncopation and counterpoint.[2]

[1] Léopold Sédar Senghor, *La Parole chez Paul Claudel et chez les négro-africains* (Dakar: Nouvelles Editions Africaines, 1973), pp. 50-1.    [2] *Ibid.*, pp. 50–1.

In that moment of oblique illumination in the prisoner of war camp so many years before, Senghor had happened upon something which might be called the principle of the gaps. According to him, previous researchers into African poetry had been so obsessed with the literal transcription of every syllable of the sung or spoken text, that they had ignored the essential element which bound it together: the regular pulse or *ictus* of the principal drum which, like a time-keeper, kept all else in place.

Forty years later, in the Ewe village of Wheta one hundred miles to the east of Accra, the young Ghanaian poet Kofi Anyidoho, on leave from his studies in the United States, was pursuing his field work into Anlo indigenous verse. Anyidoho was well qualified for his task. He came from a local family much involved in live recitation; both his mother Abla Adidi Anyidoho and his uncles Kwadzovi Anyidoho and Agbodzinshi Yortuwor were practising poets and composers. Several years previously Anyidoho himself had conducted a programme of re-search into the work of Henoga Domegbe, an elegist whose perform-ance style and songs belonged to the tradition inaugurated by Vinoko Akpalu, whose work we discussed in Chapter 1. Anyidoho thus already had firm ideas about the nature of the Anlo dirges, which had already been investigated amongst others by the Reverend A. M. Jones and Kofi Awoonor. But on this return visit Anyidoho's renewed acquaintance with the form caused him to see certain aspects of it in a new light.

Jones, whose contribution to the study of Ewe vernacular verse has already been discussed, had proposed in 1959 that the metrical foun-dation of Ewe verse lay in the simultaneity of 'two or more rhythms, each independent and complete in itself and yet linked intimately with the other'.[3] In the sixties Jones's suggestion had been taken up by the Ghanaian ethnomusicologist Kwabena Nketia, who had inferred that rhythmic stability within any composition was nevertheless maintained by what he termed the 'time line', a constant, regulated pulse heard throughout and, more often than not, stated by one of the percussion instruments. In turning his attention to the performances of his Wheta kinfolk it now appeared to Anyidoho that in most instances the essential rhythmic regulator was *gankogui*, the double hand-bell sometimes referred to familiarly as the 'gong-gong'. It fur-

---

[3] A. M. Jones, *Studies in African Music*, 2 Vols. (London: Oxford University Press, 1959), Vol. 1, p. 48.

ther seemed to him that there existed, in addition to this, a double-counterpoint between, on the one hand, the phrases articulated by the singer and the 'time span' indicated by the normative rhythm, and, on the other, between the time line and the dance movements and hand claps of the participants.[4]

The researches of Léopold Sédar Senghor and Kofi Awoonor were separated by 1,200 miles and almost half a century. Nevertheless both of them seem to be calling our attention to something which might tentatively be submitted as one tenet of an African poetic, namely that, within this network of traditions, *stresses or beats do not fall on the words of the text, but rather between them.* All other elements exist in counterpoise to one ordinal pulse which, whether audibly dictated or not, is throughout intimated by both singer and accompaniment as the basis of the compositional structure. The ramifications of this theory for any integrated theory of oral and written forms are far-reaching. It means that we must learn to regard the element of syncopation, which even in the Sprung Rhythm of Gerard Manley Hopkins was taken as an occasional effect, here to be all-embracing. Rather than the verbal text syncopating with itself, both words and music are in continuous syncopation with an intuitively discerned point of independent reference.

Senghor and Anyidoho are poets who are also theorists. Their agreement on certain points of prosodic analysis and their determination to apply their findings to their own written work bears witness to two facts: a potential cohesion within the universe of African poetry, and a common resolve, running through from the inter-war years to the present day, to reinvest the resources of traditional technique in what, in the etymologically just sense, is known as 'literature'. During our necessarily selective account of West African poetry in English and French we have come across a number of isolated attempts to honour these directives. Senghor's pieces for poet and *kora*, Okigbo's cadenzas for voice and wind, the percussive scoring for the London performance of Soyinka's *Idanre*: all bear witness to the same, unwavering desire. Despite such excursions into the field of declamation, however, it is fair to say that throughout the period in question there was an understandable tendency to regard public performance, whether solo or *avec ensemble*, as a preliminary to the definitive act of publication.

[4] Kofi Anyidoho, 'Oral Poetics and Traditions of Verbal Art in Africa', Ph.D. dissertation. University of Texas at Austin, 1983, chapter 9, p. 17 and *passim*.

Circumstances have changed. The economic recession which began to affect both Africa and Europe in the mid-1970s took its toll of publishing opportunities for poets everywhere, but especially in Africa where the local publishing industry was still in a nascent stage. In the years 1983–4 alone two major London houses connected in the minds of readers with the publication of books by African authors, felt the axe. The hiatus thus caused was severe, and in the meantime, while the indigenous publishing sector gathered strength, there was a growing tendency for African poets to reassess their priorities. Kofi Anyidoho alone had to wait for six years before his long-awaited second collection, *A Harvest of Our Dreams* saw the light of day. In such a climate, though newspapers, journals and other ephemera did something to fill the gap, it was not surprising that many contemporary writers chose to devote their energies to live performance. Schools, colleges, political rallies: all provided a temporary platform: informal groupings such as the Ghana Association of Writers and university literary societies also played a significant rôle. The positive result of these developments was that they thrust the oral transmission of verse, hitherto regarded chiefly as a standby, into the limelight, and hence procured a much needed rethinking of the way in which highbrow art could learn from the oral tradition. In many cases the consequence was a rediscovery of the immediacy of orality as a means of communication.

In considering this later period it is thus necessary to pay close attention to the ways in which the poets of West Africa came to regard the technique of indigenous verse and song. The proposals of Senghor and Anyidoho may serve as a useful starting point, if only because these two writers represent two widely spaced generations as also two divergent ethnic strands within the nexus of West African culture.

It will be convenient to begin with the Senegalese *poème gymnique* quoted by Senghor in his essay on Claudel and reproduced in part in chapter 2 of this study (p. 55). According to Senghor the rhythmic basis of this fragment, as projected by the *tam-tam majeur*, is a succession of dactylic tetrametres or, in musical terminology, a repeated four-bar phrase in triple time:

$$3 + 3 + 3 + 3$$

Against this the poet's voice insinuates a series of syncopating syllabic phrases, thus:

$$2 + 4 + 0 + 0$$
$$2 + 4 + 0 + 0$$
$$4 + 4 + 0 + 0$$
$$4 + 4 + 0 + 0^5$$

The blank measures in the voice part represent silences between lines through which the underlying rhythm is allowed to percolate. There are other, more narrowly stylistic aspects of Wolof poetic practice to which Senghor calls our attention: ritualistic repetition, the use of occult words or phrases, and the fullhearted audience refrains which, in a high proportion of cases, overcap the poet's own lines.

Anyidoho's analysis of Ewe dirge manifests several congruent features, though the involvement of a fully-fledged band of percussion instruments is apt to make the intercrossing of counterpoint rather more complicated. The syncopation, within a surrounding web of convoluted sound, between the dirge-singer and the 'time-line', here marshalled by the *atoke* drum, is suggested by figure 3, reproduced from Anyidoho's *Oral Poetics and the Traditions of Verbal Art in Africa.*[6] It may prove instructive to make comparison between this and Jones's scoring of an Akpalu dirge in figure 1 (see chapter 1).

A brief scrutiny will show how, against the foreground of voice and percussion, itself interleaved with the mesmeric dance and hand movements of the attendant performers, the time-keeper maintains his own constant, cantering pulse. Against this the cantor's text weaves its own filigree of sound, like a plant twining around delicate, but nonetheless solid lattice work. Meanwhile the two hand bells, here relegated to a supporting function, keep up syncopated rhythms of their own. Anyidoho further remarks that the momentum of the voice part is regularly interrupted by an elongation of the final syllable of individual lines so as to catch up with the time-keeper's slightly longer phrases, and by less frequent 'dramatic pauses' which are an occasion for a much needed intake of breath.[7]

The correspondences between Sengor's and Anyidoho's accounts of vernacular performance also embrace the following:

(a) Verbal repetition as a basis for incidental departure and variation;
(b) Gaps – 'dramatic pauses' Anyidoho calls them – between adjacent sections;

[5] Senghor, *La Parole*, p. 51.  [6] Anyidoho 'Oral Poetics', chapter 9, table 4, p. 22.
[7] *Ibid.*, chapter 9, p. 19.

Fig. 3

(c)  Audience participation and refrain;

(d)  Ritualistic incantation and expletive.

The adumbration of such an oracular terrain gives us some indication of the cultural and aural context within which contemporary poets, mindful of the backdrop of tradition and determined to learn from it, have chosen to work. To begin with, it is a context in which conventional critical language can lead us very far astray. Consider, for example, the simple idea of a refrain cited by both Senghor and Anyidoho. European poetry abounds in forms in which a sequence of lines, verses or stanzas is interspersed with a repeated set of words which set a symmetrical seal on its structure. The Renaissance rondel or rondeau is a clear case, an equivalent in the art of versification to the rondo form common in the concluding movements of instrumental music of the classical period. Traditional African verse, whether in translation or direct transliteration, is often set out in such a way as to appear to justify the application of related terminology. Yet there is a vital difference. The essence of the European rondel, at least since its adoption as a distinct literary mode in the sixteenth century, is that the refrain is articulated between stanzas. In African verse these two elements substantially overlap. The poet-cantor holds his own amid a canopy of interjection which lifts and supports him in his progress. The effect is strictly polyphonic. In Senghor's words:

> the wrestler-poet does not always
> wait until the crowd has finished before
> interjecting. It is thus that often, in our
> own poems, rhythmic counterpoint occurs.[8]

The nearest which European art approaches to this is the reiteration, within polyphonic settings of the Latin mass, of liturgical statements which are tossed from one voice to another amid a surge of swelling sound. Instead of the refrain model familiar from such nineteenth-century *memorabilia* as Tennyson's 'Mariana at the Moated Grange', we should perhaps be thinking more along the lines of the insertion of words 'In nomine domini' in the setting of the Benedictus in the mass 'Gloria Tibi Trinitas' by the Renaissance composer John Taverner (1495–1545) reproduced in figure 4.[9]

---

[8]  Senghor, *La Parole*, p. 52.

[9]  *Tudor Church Music*, eds. P. C. Buck, A. Ramsbotham, E. H. Fellowes, R. R. Terry and Sylvia Townsend Warner (London: Oxford University Press, 1923), Vol. 1, p. 126.

The relevance of such an analogy to instances of ritualistic incantation such as those discussed by Anyidoho does not need to be stressed. In each case a principal strand of melody (in the Taverner example the tenor, who carries the original Gregorian mode) weaves its way through a texture of repeated strains which clothe the central statement in an aura of sonorous mystery. No one voice appears to predominate, and yet the simultaneous articulation of commonly held sentiment offers up a declaration which is both personal and communal, both therapeutic and ceremonious.

The foundations of such art would seem to stem from a synthesis between individual expression and communal response, a synthesis which begs the further question of the oft-cited 'anonymity' of traditional African orature. It soon becomes evident to the dispassionate observer that, in the context of the traditions analysed by Senghor and Anyidoho such a notion has very little meaning. Speaking of the lyrics of Henoga Domegbe, Anyidoho asserts: 'Domegbe sings only of the sadness, the emptiness of life, his own life. His songs may record something of the anguish of his society, but they must be seen first as a creative expression of the agony of an individual soul: they are a legacy of a sad poet's attempt at defining his own funereal destiny.'[10] Elsewhere Anyidoho states that 'it is part of the Anlo practice to insert the name of the composer in the text'.[11] As further evidence of the very individuality of Ewe poetry we might press the frequency within the text of the first person singular, a frequency which at times is almost eclipsed by the incidence of the third person singular to refer to the poet as if from an additional external vantage point. In the following lament, translated by Anyidoho, Henoga Domegbe is both 'I' and 'he', both 'me' and 'Domegbe':

> A play-knife cut my finger in my room
> My destiny has tried and dragged me to the open
> I never aspired to take to song
> The misery that struck me in my room
> Domegbe says it was only that he tried to whisper
> to himself behind closed doors, and it's now a town affair.
> Domegbe says it was only that he tried to whisper
> to himself behind closed doors and it's now a town affair
> A play-knife cut my finger in my room

[10] 'Henoga Domegbe and His Songs of Sorrow', introductory notes and translations by Kofi Anyidoho, *The Greenfield Review*, No. 8 (1 and 2) (New York), 1979, p. 55.
[11] Anyidoho, 'Oral Poetics', chapter 6, p. 20.

Fig. 4

My destiny has tried and dragged me to the open
I never aspired to take to song
The misery that struck me in my room
Domegbe says it was only that he tried to whisper
to himself behind closed doors, and it's now a town affair.

> I say what am I to do
> Domegbe says what is he to do
> Song is dragging me to trial before the town
> Now fear has sunk into my flesh
> If I were thread tracing needle's footsteps
> It would be Awuno the Diviner
> Who would lead me on
> I say what am I to do
> Domegbe says what is he to do
> Song is dragging me to trial before the town
> Now fear has sunk into my flesh
> If I were thread tracing needle's footsteps
> It would be Awuno the Diviner
> who would lead me on.

A play-knife cut my finger in my room
My destiny has tried and dragged me to the open
I never aspired to take to song
The misery that struck me in my room
Domegbe says it was only that he tried to whisper
to himself behind closed doors, and it is now a town affair.[12]

In this poem or rather song (the Ewe term *ha* makes no distinction) several of the features common to Senghor's and Anyidoho's theories recur: the repetition of lines, the rests between sections, the implied audience intervention. But there are several more which are peculiar and unique. It will be noted that the compositional form is ternary. An opening section, called a *hadada* or 'mother song' expresses the cantor's predicament, which is emphasized through repetition. Then a middle section, called a *tatotro* or offshoot, introduces the image of the threaded needle as a symbol of Afa divination. Finally there is a brief reprise of the *hadada* closing on an identical note of private complaint. Yet the feelings contained in the text are far from exclusively personal. Domegbe starts by referring to his own distress, at which point he and the ensemble of which he forms part reinforce his sentiment by translating it into the third person: 'Domegbe says...' As the *hadada* progresses it becomes clear that the tension between pri-

---

[12] Anyidoho, 'Henoga Domegbe', pp. 58–9.

vate travail and communal concern is the real burden of the song; Domegbe is expressing his resentment at a society of busy-bodies who will not let him alone. The compulsion to sing of his misfortune itself becomes an imposition; he is weighed down by the cathartic responsibilities of his calling. If only he had entrusted his troubles to the keeper of the *Afa* oracle, father of secrets, his confidence would have been respected, but as a cantor he is driven to display his adversity on the public square for every passer-by to gape at. 'I never aspired to take to song' he declares, but sing he must though the lamentation does nothing to ease his pain.

The fluctuation between the first and third person gives the execution of such poetry a very singular flavour. Incongruously one is reminded of the choruses of Victorian operetta ('For I am a judge and a good judge too / For he is a judge and a good judge too'), but that would be to fly in the face of Senghor's remark about simultaneity of interjection. A closer analogy would be to the black Baptist Gospel music of the American South, a thin echo of which could be heard in the commercial 'soul music' of the sixties in which the blues-like sentiments of a solo singer were ratified by a trio of singers known collectively as the 'backing group'. But even this falls short of Ewe dirge in which the cantor or *heno* is seen to be enacting his tragedy for the public benefit, rather like the protagonist of a sacred opera or oratorio. Indeed in mood, though not in technique, the *genre* is similar to the representation, in the Bach passions, of the ordeals of the suffering Christ, with whom the chorus commiserates in interpretative chorales. The difference is that, in the Domegbe lament, the sufferer is playing himself.

◉          ◉          ◉

The challenge for West African writers of the 1970s and 1980s was to translate something of this wealth of language, association and meaning into written verse couched in another tongue, itself bearing alien associations, and without the accompanying benefits of music, dance or dramatic representation. Throughout the period covered by the earlier chapters of this book, this need was also felt. The trouble was that there existed as yet no adequate consensus as to how such a feat of cultural transposition might be achieved. As a result, two contrary impulses reigned: an impulse to straight ethnographic investigation on the one hand, and on the other, a simultaneous tendency to serve

*was it?*

up what could be gleaned from the oral tradition in a shape palatable to Western or *evolué* African readers.

The generation of West African intellectuals which passed through university in the fifties was not slow to pay academic tribute to indigenous literature when the occasion provided. The poet and critic Romanus Egudu and the academic Donatus Nwoga looked into the resources of Igbo praise poem and incantation, eventually publishing a collection of literally translated English versions.[13] Wole Soyinka translated Chief Fagunwa's Yoruba novel *Ogboju ode ninu igbo irunmale* into English under the title *The Forest of a Thousand Daemons*.[14] Most remarkably the poet John Pepper Clark devoted a ten-year period to the study and transmission of the *Ozidi* saga, an epic drama told over seven nights and days he had first heard as a child in the 1940s when a pupil at the Native Administration School at Okrika. Clark was convinced that the only way to convey the full range of expression contained in the saga was to record it in writing, in sound and on film. On his second visit to Orua in December 1963 with Doig Simmonds and the film-maker Frank Speed, he journeyed three hundred miles by road from the regional capital of Warri before finding himself and his crew waterlogged amid the flooding creeks.[15] By 1973, however, his researches were completed and he was able to publish a bilingual Ijọ and English text. The songs from the saga were issued on long-playing record[16] while a film of the entire saga was edited by Speed.[17] Most significantly for our purposes Clark had already reworked the existing material in an English language play for dramatic performance, *Ozidi*.[18]

In the play as opposed to the translated saga, rather than attempt to catch the immediacy of the original setting Clark opted for a free-verse rendition within a recognizably literary *genre*. The difference of approach may easily be illustrated by a brief extract from the first act of the play. The story tells of Ozidi, a hero among his people, who angers the city lords by his resentment at their election of his idiot

---

[13] *Poetic Heritage*, eds. Romanus N. Egudu and Donatus I. Nwoga (Enugu: Nwankwo–Ifejika, 1971), reissued as *Igbo Traditional Verse* (London: Heinemann, 1973).

[14] Wole Soyinka, *The Forest of a Thousand Daemons* (London: Nelson, 1968).

[15] John Pepper Clark, *The Ozidi Saga*, collected and translated from the Ijọ of Ọkabou Ojobolo (Ibadan: Ibadan University Press and London: Oxford University Press, 1977), p. xii.

[16] 'Songs from *The Ozidi Saga*' (EMI for the Institute of African Studies, University of Ibadan, Nigeria).

[17] *Tides of the Delta*, directed by John Pepper Clark and Frank Speed, distributed by Colour Film Services Ltd, 22 Portman Close, Baker Street, London W1.

[18] J. P. Clark, *Ozidi, a Play* (London: Oxford University Press, 1966).

brother Temugedege as king. Eventually the friction between Ozidi
and the war-lords grows so severe that they plan to ambush him
under cover of night. Suspecting the plot, Ozidi's wife pleads with
him not to step out of the house. Here is the parallel Ijǫ / English ver-
sion as given by Clark; there then follows the equivalent scene in
Clark's verse play:

> 'Iyei ya, emęnę mukumǫe.
> Emęnę a buru mukumǫe.
> Węridę, amęnę mu kǫnbo kǫn
> aki eni binaowei mę dǫbamǫ
> kpǫ ebimi ye.
> Emęnę mukumęe.'
> Ogdadę, omęnę kę mę ama
> olutu kęmę ka mukumǫǫ?
>
> Omęnę muumęnę ye.
> O 'erema gbadę
> 'Mukumǫe.'
> Mǫ gba tainbę omęnę bǫgha.

['My husband, you must not go. / Don't go to them. / Stay, it's right even if
they go alone / to bring your brother honour. / You yourself must not go.' /
Then he asked, whether it was he the hero of the state that should not go? /
Of course he had to go. / His wife pleaded / 'Do not go!' / But, although she
implored, he did not agree[19]]

OREA: Ozidi, do not go into the night.
OZIDI: It is not the night when you hold before me
    Your lamp.
OREA: I smell a foul wind blowing from the swamp that may
    Put out the light.
OZIDI: Then we will rekindle our lamp and carry
    On with the journey.
OREA: Ozidi, I still do not think
    You should go on today's raid.
OZIDI: Be not afraid my bride. The hawking-tray
    Roves and roves but it returns home all the same.
OREA: I have an evil vein tugging at my side; here,
    Come and feel it for yourself.[20]

Although the dramatic version has more variety of imagery than the
extract from the original saga, paradoxically it possesses less theatrical
impact. The reason is that Clark has felt the need to prettify it by the
importation of alien literary elements. A direct comparison of the two

[19] *The Ozidi Saga*, p. 6.    [20] Clark, *Ozidi*, p. 19.

passages shows that what lies behind Clark's free-verse reworking is less the Orua original than Act II Scene ii of Shakespeare's *Julius Caesar* where Calpurnia, Caesar's wife, suspecting the conspiracy of Brutus and Cassius, and cowed by dream portents, begs her lord and master not to go to the forum. From Shakespeare Clark has borrowed the idea of a portent, an element of blank verse rhythm ('Bē nŏt ăfraīd, mў brĭde, thĕ hāwkiňg trāy' is an almost perfect iambic pentameter), and the presence of a light ('Put out the light, and then put out the light'), *Othello*, Act V, Scene ii). The two traditions do not quite cohere.

The generation of the fifties, torn between allegiance to the oral tradition and an anxiety to score a literary effect, reacted to indigenous orature in one of two ways: either by preserving it in aspic or else as above by gentrifying it.

The tendency to rework oral echoes into an acceptably literary fabric became less predominant in the next generation, which, brought up with the beat poetry of the sixties and the general emphasis in that decade on poetry as a live medium, were anxious to search their own traditions for equivalent impulses. The poetry of Atukwai Okai was strongly instrumental in this process. Okai was exposed to a wider range of cultural and political influences than were most of his contempories. A Ga, born in Accra, he grew up during the Nkrumaist period, imbibing much of its perky optimism along with an enthusiasm for things slavonic partly to be explained by the gravitation of Ghanaian politics during that portion of its history towards the Soviet block. After leaving secondary school Okai went to Moscow where he graduated from the Gorky Literary Institute in 1967. On his return to Ghana, he found that the prevailing ideological climate had swung into reverse, and he was again obliged to leave the country this time for England to requalify at the then more acceptable University of London. It was a reverse of fortune which Okai took with all his characteristic wit and bonhomie, but his sardonic amazement at the zig-zagging political loyalties of his countryman never decreased. Whilst in London he published his first thin chapbook, *Flowerfall* (1968) and recited his work at the Camden Arts Festival. Finally returning to Ghana to a lectureship in Russian at Legon, he continued his active involvement in artistic administration, being elected president of the Ghana Association of Writers in 1971.

Some poets belong to an ambience of shelved books and the seclusion of a lamp-lit room. Okai belongs to a world of events. He is less concerned to list his publications than his readings, which I have shared, and which have always been packed and electrifying. He has more skill with purely rhythmic effects that any other living poet, except possibly Kofi Anyidoho. Indeed if one applies Anyidoho's own notion of a base rhythm suffusing all verbal declamation, much of Okai's work proves amenable to scansion. In figure 5,[21] for instance, he castigates the hypocrisy which, after the *coup d'état* of 1966, caused a large section of the Ghanaian intelligentsia to throw themselves off the cliffs of self-recrimination and wallow in a sea of bourgeois liberalism.

In these lines the metre reduces itself quite naturally to a triple measure trot with the strong beats of the intonation coinciding with

Fig. 5

[21] Atukwai Okai, *Lorgorligi Logarithms* (Accra: Ghana Publishing Corporation, 1974), p. 20. The rhythmic notation is my own.

the insistence of an implied percussive base. The resulting verbal rhythm is strongly dactylic. It may be appropriate to add that, in his essay on the metres of West African poetry, Senghor remarks that the most common 'foot' to be encountered in oral verse, is not, as in French or English poetry, the iamb, but the dactyl.[22]

In a not dissimilar mood in 1972 Okai sends out fraternal greeting and a gesture of solidarity to Wole Soyinka, newly released from prison. In this instance, it will be noted, the silences are as significant as the words (see figure 6[23]). Here the base rhythm is a sort of rampaging prowl, against which the voice syncopes its own staccato phrases.

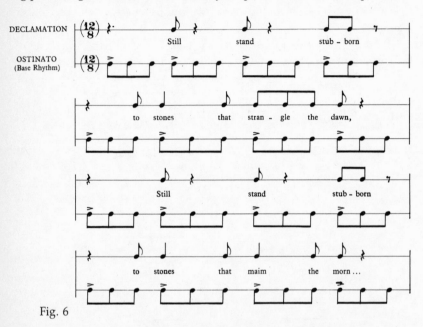

Fig. 6

As Okai's mood softens, his rhythms become more elusive and undulating. In 'Taflase' (Sorry), for example, he calls on all the great men of Africa's past, headed by the poet Raphael Armattoe, to bear witness to the contemporary desolation of Ghana, and more particularly, its capital city. He then opens out into a shaded street scene set in Nima, one of Accra's more disadvantaged residential areas (see figure 7).

The base pulse here is the sort of muffled hip-swinging shuffle associated with Afro-Cuban dances such as the Rumba. Experimentation with rumba rhythms as a metrical base for verse was frequent

---

[22] Senghor, *La Parole*, p. 53.  [23] Okai, *Lorgorligi Logarithms*, p. 113.

Fig. 7 [24]

amongst an earlier generation of Cuban poets such as Nicolás Guillén and Alejo Carpentier. The percussive effect Okai seems to have in mind is the stealthy, insinuating crunch of the gourd rattles found in many West African and Congolese orchestras, themselves probably ancestors of the Cuban Maracas. The blend of Latin American sultriness and dinginess of setting evokes perfectly the dust-infested torpor of afternoon in the backstreets of so many West African towns. The Ga question and answer with which the extract closes mean '"Have you heard how the world goes?" / "No, I haven't. Please relate it."' With its rapid transitions between languages this is a poetry of linguistic and musical fragments held together by a constantly running background pulse. Okai's oral recitation draws on Ga, Ewe, Twi and Hausa as well as a number of European and Slavonic languages. It is a polyglot form of orature which contrives to keep the listener alert by continual shifts of rhythm and linguistic register, a quasi-musical

[24] *Ibid.*, p. 22.

327

species of performance poetry which takes an almost impish delight in breaking its stride every few bars for the sake of aural and thematic variety.

Okai's themes draw on an international fraternity of literate aspiration very typical of the decade in which he grew to maturity, a decade serenaded by the syncopated pan-global duet of Yevgeny Yevtushenko and Allen Ginsberg. His responses are permanently conditioned by an ambiance of international brotherhood, forefingers flicking in greeting, the flash of a foreign phrase a seemingly instant passport to acceptance. Okai has little hauteur. His windows lie open, and between the panes drift love and lush vegetation. Poetry is what happens when the air-conditioning fails. Indolent ceiling fans nudge the air, the audience sways and cocks the ear. Meanwhile, tirelessly, the poet exults:

> Marcus garvey, ARE YOU THERE?!
> Malcolm x, WHERE ARE YOU?!
> angela davis, ARE YOU THERE?!
>
> SIMON KIMBUNGU, GRANT US THE SPIRIT . . .
> TOHOGU TOHAJIE, GRANT US THE SPIRIT . . .[25]

'Cape of Whose Hope', the fourth of his *Lorgorligi Logarithms*, starts like its companion pieces with a multiple invocation similar to those delivered at traditional Ghanaian libations. Okai's poetry often gives the impression of following a fixed traditional form, but can more properly be considered as an amalgam of several. 'Cape of Whose Hope', for instance, starts as invocation, proceeds through secular greeting (*agoo*) passes through an Ewe wake-keeping (*husago*), smacks its lips in post-prandial satisfaction (*pokunlenu*), issues a wayside threat (*kawo kudi*, Hausa for 'hand over the money'), raises a hue and cry ('flee *fiafito*') before closing on the cadences of a Christian, Anglican grace. In weaker poems, such eclecticism is apt to appear messy; in Okai's strongest it can be extremely moving.

Okai's formal experimentation is undoubtedly most successful when he grafts his diverse scion on to a single, rooted stock. The most impressive instance of such husbandry is 'Chain Gang – Soul Autopsy', the long elegy that he wrote for Kwame Nkrumah in 1972 when the former Ghanaian president was dying far from home in a Romanian hospital. Textually this poem is as varied as anything which Okai has written. It begins to the strains of the negro spiritual

---

[25] *Ibid.*, p. 35.

'Swing low, sweet chariot' before proceeding to evoke the lonely hospital bed on which Nkrumah lies, in a lumbering lilt strongly reminiscent of the Dylan Thomas of *Under Milk Wood*:

in a slow-rocking faraway sympathetic Rumanian hospital bed
a man in pain lies pining for his motherland and mother
and in his soul-suffocating dream, he finds himself in another country
called guinea–ghana guinea–ghana where the grass is gorgeously green.[26]

Throughout the slow opening section these rhythms of spiritual and lilting lullaby alternate before Okai sets off at a brisker pace for an animato interlude (see figure 8).

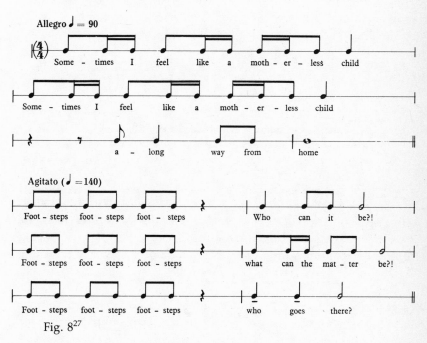

Fig. 8[27]

After a succession of guttering verbal fragments, the pace then slows down to the grave hymnody of Cardinal Newman's 'Lead, Kindly Light', against which Okai counterpoints the startled breathless cries of a child lost in the night-time forest (see figure 9).

Then the original lullaby metre is again heard in the distance as a preliminary to the full diapason entry of elephant-tusk horns in the traditional Ashanti lament for the dead:

[26] *Ibid.*, p. 63    [27] *Ibid.*, p. 65.

Fig. 9²⁸

damiri damiri damifira due due
damiri damiri damirifira due due
damifira due

Ecclesiastes' celebrated admonition to 'praise famous men' makes a fleeting, transformed appearance before the funeral horns again invite us to the final recessional in which Nkrumah's body is brought in imagination from exile to its chosen resting place in Nzimaland in the west of Ghana, like the body of a paramount chief being carried to its mausoleum on a river-bourne palanquin.

This entire afflatus of echoes, however, is securely earthed in an implied musical accompaniment which is unambiguously African. The writer's clear intention is an implied double orchestration alternating between the strains of the *mmenson*, the long arched elephant-tusk horns of the Akan people, and those of the *ntumpane*, the Ashanti timpani. The *ntumpane* consist of two cedar barrels, held in a common frame, over which are stretched membranes made from the dried skin of an elephant ear. The right hand or 'Male' drum is tuned to a pitch lower to that of the left hand or 'Female' drum, with the result that a tonal equivalent may be provided for Akan speech, itself intensely tonal. All Ashanti invocations may thus be drummed out: the incantation *damifira*, heard in Okai's elegy, for example, may be rendered by four quick, sharp strokes on the female drum.[29] In this way, Okai's poem blends the echoes of African music to the strains of negro spiritual, lullaby and Anglo-Catholic church music. Of all Okai's works, this comes closest to Anyidoho's description of oral verse as a species of musico-poetic 'composition'.

At its most incisive the musical structure is perfectly cognate with Okai's theme. 'Elavanyo Concerto', for example, describes the lonely battle cf the astronomer Galileo against the intransigent authorities of the Vatican with regard to his teachings on planetary motion. The concerto form has proved attractive to a number of contemporary poets as an analogy of the writer's lonely battle against the state.[30] It is an analogy too which has not been lost on musicians, America's Elliott Carter is one of a number of composers who have felt free to explore

---

[28] *Ibid.* The setting of 'Lead, Kindly Light' is that most usually heard in Ghanaian churches, J. B. Dykes's 'Lux Benigna', *The Hymnal Companion to the Book of Common Prayer* eds. Charles Vincent, D. J. Wood and Sir John Stainer (London: Longmans, 3rd edition, 1920), p. 14.

[29] For a fuller explanation of this effect, cf. R. S. Rattray, *Ashanti* (London: Oxford University Press, 1923), pp. 266–86.

[30] Syl Cheney-Coker, *Concerto for an Exile* (London: Heinemann, 1973).

the political ramifications of the concerto. The adoption of the concerto form then provides a rare opportunity for composer or poet, or composer–poet, to yoke meaning to structure.

The word 'Elavanyo' is an Ewe equivalent of Julian of Norwich's consoling 'All shall be well and all manner of thyng shall be well'. The poem contrasts the straining will of the beleaguered astronomer with the cries of his society, beneath which surges, like a restful undercurrent, the poet's own blessing and reassurance. It begins, however, like a French overture, with fourteen staccato hammer strokes, *Sturm und Drang*:

> Cross. Banner. Swastika. Sickle
> Dross. Hammer. Floodfire. Spittle.
> The sun is the centre of our system.
>
> The leaning tower. Two stones. Revolution.
> Summons to Rome. Burning stake. The Inquisition.
>
> The sun's not the centre of our system.[31]

We are then transported to a Spanish bullring. As the gates of his den swing open, Galileo bounds into the ring like a horned bull against a team of matadors:

> You still have things onto which you cling
> The bulls and bulls you kill in the ring
> Alone have no prospects of wearing a sling
> The bulls and bulls you kill in the ring.[32]

The bulls are papal bulls as much as the animal variety. So far, Okai's voice has fused with the shouts of the spectators, but at line 35 the astronomer's own voice, the voice of all suppressed thinkers, enters solo:

> Here evidence; the universe gives judgement.
> Place no mouldy margin upon what I
> Should imagine; and no single censor
> In hell or heaven shall tell me censor
> My sigh or sin.[33]

The word censor punningly merges the 'censer' to which wafts of obsequious incense are swung before the throne of authority, with the power of papal embargo, the Index. As the bull collapses in the bloody dust, the poet's voice, now entering as chorus, gives reassurance of

---

[31] Okai, *Lorgorligi Logarithms*, p. 114.     [32] *Ibid.*, p. 115.     [33] *Ibid.*

ultimate victory:

> O . . . Galileo Galilei . . . you fold
> your face like a praying mantis pawned for
> a pound of maize; and we erase all
> trace, taking no chances with cheating
> charcoal-sellers who hold the hand of hands
> over the hovering hawk hankering after
> human flesh[34]

As the body of the dead bull is carried in ceremony from the ring, the poem too fades away in one long seamless diminuendo and the poet's sobbing commiserations die *al niente*:

> O, Elavanyo . . . Galileo
> O, Elavanyo . . . Galilei.[35]

The achievement of Atukwei Okai manifests one way in which indigenous resources may be harnessed to the development of modern poetry without incongruity or strain. It also illustrates the assertive face of a tradition, in T. S. Eliot's sense, as a living, growing, diversifying thing.[36] The work of Kofi Anyidóho, a poet some ten years younger than Okai, exemplifies how all of these objectives may be realized, even intensified, within a narrower compass. The poetry published by Anyidoho under the title *A Harvest of Our Dreams* possesses as much commitment, dexterity and gravity as Okai's. Yet it remains resolutely Ewe. In so doing it bears witness to an alternative strategy. Although Ga allusions abound in Okai's work, there is no sense in which they can be taken as providing a foundation in which all other idioms are embedded. Rather they constitute in themselves one idiom among many, *primus inter pares*. But for Anyidoho, the art of the great dirge-singers of his people, his analytical accounts of which we have already discussed, forms the very bedrock of his poetic being.

When *A Harvest of our Dreams* was published in 1984 a reviewer in the journal *West Africa* wrote:

As the universe eaves-drops on Anyidoho it discovers at work an imagination of scope, subtlety and grace. His triumph is two-fold: to have learnt from the

---

[34] *Ibid.*, p. 116.     [35] *Ibid.*, p. 117.
[36] Cf. T. S. Eliot, 'Tradition and the Individual Talent' in *The Sacred Wood* (London: Methuen, 1920).

craft of the poet–cantors of his native Eweland, and also to have extended it in new thematic and linguistic directions. He is heir to a double tradition. Like his countryman Kofi Awoonor he has sat the feet of Akpalu and Ekpe, the great dirge-singers of his people. But he has also learned something from Awoonor himself of how to transmute this gold into the cold metal of printed English. And . . . he has gone further. The ancestral cantors of the Anlo communities lamented the severance of the dying from the bosom of the clan. In Anyidoho this full-throated threnody opens out into an elegy for the whole tormented history of present-day Ghana.[37]

The 'opening out' of a tradition is precisely what is at stake here, not the kind which dissolves the entity thus enlarged, but that observable in sea-anemones as, putting out feelers to absorb passing plankton, they nourish themselves while remaining resolutely fixed to the ocean bed. Anyidoho's verse has been fed by literary exposure, but it still exists recognizably within the Anlo dirge tradition, and Anyidoho himself is still recognizable a *heno* or cantor. The difference between him and his antecedents, besides their chosen language, consists principally in the fact that instead of bewailing the passing of a loved one, or the various ills which flesh is heir to, Anyidoho sees fit to lament the fate of his country:

> Do not search too hard
> for words to trap these thoughts
> the thoughts that bring the tears
> upon the harvest of our dreams
>
> They say our thoughts are threads, crossing
> and criss-crossing into new cobwebs of life
> And
> I shall spin a handful of hopes
> against this cutback in our dreams
> against this wild backlash of screams
> even against these lingering doubts
> at the testing time for our faith in Gods
>
> We load our voice with these burdens
> searching myths for miracle drugs
> distant cures for our sickness of the soul[38]

The 'testing-time' of which the cantor sings is the trial of a Ghana which even Jerry Rawling's first *coup* of 1979 had failed to salvage from bankruptcy. From its position in the early sixties as the world's

---

[37] *West Africa*, 4 March 1985.

[38] Kofi Anyidoho, *A Harvest of Our Dreams* with *Elegy for the Revolution* (London: Heinemann, 1984), p. 4.

leading exporter of cocoa, Ghana had slipped by the late seventies to
something like tenth in the world league; meanwhile the value of the
*cedi*, ever precarious, had sunk to a fifteenth of its value not five years
before. The timber and mining industries were also in a sorry plight,
and with yet another postponement of representative government,
morale was very low. All this the poet well knows, and his sense of
powerlessness is heightened by his absence from the scene in
America, where by April of 1979, Anyidoho had already embarked
upon his doctoral studies. The umbilical cord which attaches him to
Ghana, and more particularly the land of the Ewe, however, is still
strong. It is perhaps significant that Anyidoho published little work
recognizably within the dirge-tradition until he touched down on
American soil: there are few poems in his earlier collection *Elegy for the
Revolution* which can confidently be ascribed to it. It is as if, in the
United States, isolated from all familiar contact, he felt a need to
recreate the Volta Region inside his head, and these poems are one
result of such an undertaking.

A question which immediately arises in connection with the poetry
of *A Harvest of Our Dreams* is that begged by the Domegbe dirge dis-
cussed above (pp. 318-21), namely the identity of the speaker or
speakers. As in the Domegbe piece, there is a collation of the first and
third persons singular, to which, however, Anyidoho has added the
first person plural:

> We will not die the death of dreams
> We will not die the cruel death of dreams[39]

Like the Domegbe dirge, this piece clearly evisages an interchange be-
tween a soloist and an accompanying ensemble of performers which
in this case represents the nation. Again as in the Domegbe compo-
sition, the introspective angle of the cantor himself is supplemented
by the external, dramatising perspective of the crowd:

> There is no curse on us
> he sings
> There is no curse on us[40]

As was suggested in connection with Domegbe, the cantor here
appears to act as the protagonist in his own tragedy which is acted out
in the public gaze. In this instance, however, the drama is political,
and the cantor's *hamartia*, his flawed destiny, is also that of his people.

[39] *Ibid.*, p. 5.     [40] *Ibid.*

Throughout, the first person plural is used, not in accordance with the convention by which an author refers to himself as 'we', still less with the assumption of any kind of royal *fiat*, but as an expression of what I have elsewhere termed the 'plural sensibility',[41] the communal experience of all which pertains to the well being of each. The poet *is* his people, and they are he, which paradoxically in no way reduces his individuality. Across three thousand miles, from Wheta to Indiana, Anyidoho and his community call to one another in a sort of troubled transatlantic antiphony.

The element of antiphonal response between cantor and ensemble is perhaps seen most clearly in the contrastive rhythms of the verse. Anyidoho's rhythms are less emphatic than Okai's, and his manner of reading less strident; yet metrical variety is nevertheless an important ingredient in his work. In 'Seedtime', the title poem of the volume's opening section, the contrast is most clearly seen in the breathless, awestruck, slightly impetuous rhythm of the crowd with its accumulation of weak syllables leading up to a swell of collective amazement:

> Thĕre ĭs ño cūrse ŏn ŭs
> hĕ sĭñgs
> Thĕre ĭs nŏ cūrse ŏn ŭs.[42]

In contrast the cantor's lines have an amplitude, a measured, august tempo, which speaks of a bitter certainty of self-knowledge:

> Our orphan laid an egg across the backyard of the skies
> The rainstorm came and swept it all away
> Again he laid an egg across the backyard of the skies
> Again the rainstorm came and swept it all away
> Today he sows a seed in the bosom of whirlthoughts
> Our predator birds shall have to prey upon
> their own anger their own nightmares[43]

The 'orphan' is both the poet estranged from home and Ghana uprooted from her history. Thus, once more, private tribulation merges with national dispair. In *Oral Poetics and Traditions of Verbal Art in Africa* Anyidoho observes that the great Akpalu was orphaned at an early age,[44] as also was Henoga Domegbe. The *heno's* loss here mirrors the people's severance from its ancestors and from its faith in its own

---

[41] Cf. Robert Fraser, *The Novels of Ayi Kwei Armah: A Study in Polemical Fiction* (London: Heinemann, 1980), p. x. Also *Edward Brathwaite's Masks, A Critical View by Robert Fraser* (London: William Collins in association with the British Council, 2nd edition, 1985), pp. 20-1 and 39.     [42] Anyidoho, *Harvest*, p. 4.     [43] *Ibid.*, p. 5.
[44] Anyidoho, 'Oral Poetics', chapter 6, p. 3.

guiding tenets. The 'rainstorm' represents both the eruption of circumstance which has separated cantor from clan and the political eruptions which rock the ship of state. The 'predator birds' are the western commercial interests which first appropriated the country and then impoverished it.

Anyidoho's finest verse is a poetry of clashing voices, fugitive echoes (a word of which he is fond); a sort of gentle, muted dissonance like the distant crash of brass. In 'A Harvest of Our Dreams', the title poem of the collection, he seems to be listening to a collation of 'echoes' from the past, residues which his conscious mind struggles to assemble into a cognitive, applicable meaning. This temporal estrangement lends his geographical displacement a peculiar poignancy:

> There will be strange voices filling spaces
> In our mind, weaving murmurings upon
> the broken tails of songs abandoned once in playing fields
> Rumblings from our past are planting stakes
> across our new rainbows
> and in seasons of harvest dance
> there still will be a ghost
> on guard
> at Memory's door.[45]

This is a poetry, as he says, of 'Lost passwords' (1. 47), clues to a way of life irrevocably done. The shrewdest clue to the poet's own meaning is his music: he obliges us to listen. In so doing we notice how the metrical base of his verse is in a process of continual transition. Almost imperceptibly to the conscious, analytical mind, the verbal pulse shifts line by line (see figure 10).

'Pleasurable variation within the framework of cyclic stability' is how Anyidoho defines the essence of Ewe verse. Within the framework of this poem it is possible to catch three principal clusters of voices: the poet himself as, absent from his country, he struggles to reconcile himself to his position ('Our hive went up in flames. I was away', l.12); the dance group as they reiterate his sentiments ('We will hum a dirge for the burden of these winds', l.13) and, as in the extract immediately above, the voices of long-dead cantors, the voices, of tradition. Like Kofi Awoonor, Anyidoho has a marked tendency to approach the problem of identification by fastening on the continuities of the smallest ethnic denominator, the clan. At times, it is as if

---

[45] Anyidoho, *Harvest*, p. 6.

♩ = 100

Oot' - sa of the sea I am Oot - sa of the sea. / I

did not know it would be like this for me:

Yev - u's net has caught me with my dreams. / and

♩ = 60

now we tread by - ways / search- ing pass - ing fac - es / for

flee - ting im - age af - ter im - age

seek - ing kin - dred minds / for lost

pass - words in - to fi - es - tas of the soul

Fig. 10[46]

the concept of 'Ghana' were too wide for him; the only way in which
he can meaningfully relate to the nation is through utter immersion in
the culture of the Anlo, even the town of Wheta. The resulting per-
spective is very different from that possessed by a poet like Atukwei
Okai:

> Of course we are glad to be born to Universe.
> But we'd love to leave our home address somewhere
> specific directions about our house our home
> our little place in a monstrous world
> Yes we'd like to hang our own address
> Up at the crossroads of this earth
> lest the gods should one day
> come looking for us in wrong places[47]

For Anyidoho, it might almost be said, there *is* only one proper
place: the town square at Wheta. Yet even here, so the rigour of his
elegiac logic runs, the poet can never find peace. He stands with
Akpalu, with Domegbe, with Kofi Awoonor in prophetic isolation.

[46] *Ibid.*, p. 7. Once more, the rhythmic notion is my own.      [47] *Ibid.*, p. 28.

'Community' is a political idea, the acme of regionalism; for poets
there can perhaps be no such safe harbour. Much of Anyidoho's most
potent verse evokes this sense of isolation among kinfolk, the knowl-
edge that he will always bear the birthmark of a hounded destiny. In
an early poem, 'Dance of the Hunchback', he imagines himself as a
cripple stumbling on the very edges of the arena:

> Public squares broad highways
> and busy streets of town
> I leave them all to owners of our earth
> I crawl along quiet side-walks of life
> With the hedge-hog and the crab
> I carry a tedious destiny
>
> Mine is the dance of the hunchback
> In the valley behind my hill of shame
> I do my best to fall in step
> With the rhythms of grace and pomp
> But the eyes of the world
> see only a moving bundle of fun
> and upon my chest they heap
> a growing burden of scorn[48]

Already the poet knows himself as a man apart, despised by
'owners of the earth' whose revulsion he can never quite bring himself
to reciprocate. The sense of exclusion is strong, and in the poetry of *A
Harvest of Our Dreams*, threatens to succumb to the dictates of the dissi-
dent. But Anyidoho's poetry is only dissenting in the quite special
sense allotted to those who know that all human hopes and designs
are prey to inscrutable and divisive forces. In the strongest of his
pieces, the sensation of being set apart by a remorseless inner mania
nevertheless constantly seems to aspire toward definitive political
declaration. In 'The Diviner's Curse', the poet is seen as a prophet
without honour in his own country, while in 'The Hyena's Hymn' he
is a Christ rejected of men who in desperation turns to Pilate:

> I went into our parliament home
> seeking audience with Speaker's chair.
> They said I must have just returned from farm:
> Parliament had gone on sudden leave
> prior to retirement.

[48] *Ibid.*, p. 84.

339

They misdirected me to our Castle
where they gave me forms to fill
still standing at the gates.[49]

At such times Anyidoho's art teeters on the brink of self-directed comedy. As with Odia Ofeimun there is in his subtlest work a strong potential for compensatory hilarity, but it is always a hilarity shot through with a harrowing sadness. Whatever such poetry is, it is not mere satire, a measure perhaps of the extent to which Anyidoho has grown since the publication of his first collection.

For however severe the pressures building up in contemporary African societies to convert the writer into an instrument of state policy or else mere organ of sedition, there is an obstinate core in the makeup of most poets which will not be moved. The source of such resolve is less the liberal, sceptical tradition which reigns elsewhere, much as this may strike a sympathetic chord among certain individuals or academic institutions. Africa's poets by contrast take their stand less on a Rousseauistic ideal of personal prerogative, attractive as this may be, but essentially on their continuing conception of an ancient office. Poetry in Africa is as old as the sung or spoken word itself. As often as it has raised its voice, it has done so less in panegyric or diversion – though these too have had their hour – than in reverence to the demands of conscience and human wholeness. As long as this fragile cry is heard, and as long as there remain a few who will crouch in a corner and listen, so long will the song continue.

[49] *Ibid.*, p. 9.

# A guide to availability

The most compendious library of West African poetry in English remains the African Writers Series published by Heinemann Educational Books, 21–2 Bedford Square, London WC1B 3HH. Selected titles are also available in the Drumbeat Series published by Longman, Burnt Mill, Harlow, Essex CM20 2JE, and from The Greenfield Review Press RD1, Box 80, Greenfield Centre, New York 12833, USA, who over the last few years have done invaluable work familiarizing American audiences with African verse, as have Three Continents Press, Suite 224, 1346 NW Connecticut Avenue, Washington DC 20036, USA.

For African poetry in French there are two principal outlets: the Paris-based firm of Présence Africaine, 25 bis rue des Ecoles, 75005 Paris and on African soil the newer but no less reputable Nouvelles Editions Africaines, 10 rue Assane Ndoyo, BP 260, Dakar, Senegal. A certain number of lesser known francophone poets have also been issued in Cameroon by Editions CLE, BP 1501. Yaoundé.

A comprehensive bibliography of the field may be found in *A Reader's Guide to African Literature* (2nd Edition, completely revised), eds. Hans Zell, Carol Bundy and Virginia Coulon (London: Heinemann, 1983). The following is a selective list of current editions of poets discussed in this study, including translations and contributions to anthologies. The main anthologies cited are:

Awoonor, Kofi and G. Adali-Mortty (eds.), *Messages: Poems from Ghana* (London: Heinemann, 1970).
Moore, Gerald and Ulli Beier (eds.), *The Penguin Book of Modern African Poetry* (3rd Revised edition of *Modern African Poetry* (Harmondsworth: Penguin, 1984).
Nwoga, Donatus (ed.), *West African Verse* (London: Longman, 1966).
Reed, John and Clive Wake (eds.), *A New Book of African Verse* (London: Heinemann, revised edition, 1984).
Soyinka, Wole (ed.), *Poems of Black Africa* (London: Secker and Warburg, 1975; London: Heinemann, 1975; New York: Hill and Wang, 1975).

Adali-Mortty, Geormbeeyi. Selection in *Messages: Poems from Ghana*, and in *Poems of Black Africa*.
Akpalu, Vinoko. Selection in English translation in Kofi Awoonor, *Guardians of the Sacred Word: Ewe Poetry* (New York: Nok Publications, 1974).
d'Almeida, Fernando. *Au Seuil de l'exil* (Paris: Jean Oswald, 1976).

*Traduitdu Je pluriel* (Dakar: Nouvelles Editions Africaines, 1980).

*En attendant le verdict* (Paris: Silex, 1982).

*L'Espace de la Parole* (Paris: Silex, 1984).

Selection in English translation in *A New Book of African Verse*.

Anyidoho, Kofi. *Elegy for the Revolution* (New York: Greenfield Review Press, 1978).

*A Harvest of Our Dreams* with *Elegy for the Revolution* (London: Heinemann, 1984).

Selection in *The Penguin Book of Modern African Poetry*.

Armattoe, Raphael Grail Ernest. Selection in *West African Verse*.

Awoonor, Kofi. *Night of My Blood* (New York: Doubleday, 1971).

*Ride Me, Memory* (New York: Greenfield Review Press, 1973).

*The House by the Sea* (New York: Greenfield Review Press, 1978).

Selections in *Poems of Black Africa; The Penguine Book of Modern African Poetry; A New Book of African Verse;* and (as George Awoonor-Williams) in *West African Verse*.

Ba, Oumar. *Poèmes peul modernes* (Nouakchott: Imp. Mauritanienne, 1965).

*Dialogue d'une rive à l'autre: poèmes* (Saint Louis, Senegal: IFAN, 1966).

*Presque griffonnages ou la francophonie* (Saint Louis, Senegal: IFAN, 1966).

*Témoin à charge et à décharge: poème* (Dakar: Imp. Saint Paul, nd).

*Paroles plaisantes au coeur à l'oreille* (Paris: La Pensée Universelle, 1977).

*Odes sahéliennes* (Paris: La Pensée Universelle, 1978).

Selection in English translation in *The Penguin Book of Modern African Poetry*.

Casely-Hayford, Gladys. Selection in *West African Verse*.

Cheney-Coker, Syl, *The Graveyard Also has Teeth* with *Concerto for an Exile* (London: Heinemann, 1980).

Clark, John Pepper. *Ozidi, a Play* (London and New York: Oxford University Press, 1966).

*A Decade of Tongues* (London: Longman, 1981).

*The State of the Union* (London: Longman, 1984).

Selections in *Poems of Black Africa; The Penguin Book of Modern African Poetry; A New Book of African Verse,* and *West African Verse*.

Dadié, Bernard B. *Légendes et poèmes (Afrique debout!; Légendes africaines; Climbié; La ronde des jours)* (Paris: Séghers, 1966, reprinted 1973).

*Hommes de tous les continents* (Paris: Présence Africaine, 1967).

Selection in *West African Verse* and in *Poems of Black Africa*.

De Graft, Joe. *Beneath the Jazz and Brass* (London: Heinemann, 1975).

Selection in *Messages; Poems of Black Africa;* and *A New Book of African Verse*.

Dei-Anang, Michael and Warren Jaw, *Ghana Glory: Poems of Ghana and Ghanaian life* (London: Nelson, 1965).

and Kofi Dei-Anang, *Two Faces of Africa* (Accra: Waterville Publishing House; Buffalo, New York: Black Academy Press, 1965; 1972).

Selection in *West African Verse*.

Diop, Birago. *Leurres et lueurs* (Paris. Présence Africaine, 2nd edition, 1967).

Selections in *The Penguin Book of Modern African Poetry; West African Verse.* and *A New Book of African Verse*.

Diop, David. *Coups de pilon* (Paris: Présence Africaine, revised edition, 1973).

*Hammer Blows and Other Writings* (bilingual edition) trans. and ed. Simon Mpondo and Frank Jones (Bloomington: Indiana University Press, 1973), issued as *Hammer Blows* (London: Heinemann, 1975).

Selections in *The Penguin Book of Modern African Poetry; West African Verse,* and *A New Book of African Verse.*

Dogbé, Yves-Emmanuel. *Le Divin amour suivi de paix et bonheur* (Le Mée-sur-Seine, France: Akpagnon, 1979).

*Flamme blême* (Le Mée-sur-Seine, France: Akpagnon, 1980).

Dogbeh, Richard, *Les Eaux du mono* (Vire, France: Lec-Vire, 1963), reprinted in *African Poems in French* (Nendeln, Liechtenstein: Kraus Reprint, 1970).

*Rives mortelles* (Porto Novo, Benin: Silva, 1964), reprinted in *African Poems in French. Câp liberté* (Yaoundé: CLE, 1969).

Fall, Kiné Kirama, *Chants de la rivière frâiche* (Dakar: Nouvelles Editions Africaines, 1976).

*Les Elans de Grâce* (Yaoundé: CLE, 1979).

Kébé, Mbaye. *Ebéniques* (Dakar: Nouvelles Editions Africaines, 1969; reissued 1975).

*Guirlande* (Paris: Editions Saint-Germain-des-Prés, 1978).

Koné, Maurice. *la Guirlande de verbes* (Paris: Grassin, 1961), reprinted in *African Poems in French.*

*Au Bout de petit matin* (Bordeaux, France: Jean-German, 1962).

*Au Seuil de créspuscule* (Rodes, France: Subervie, 1965).

*Poèmes* (Abidjan: Imp. Commerciale, 1969).

*Poemès verlainiens* (Millau, France: Imp. Maury, 1969).

*Argile du rêve* (Dakar: Nouvelles Editions Africaines, 1979).

Mindelense. Selection in *When the Bullets Begin to Flower*, ed. Margaret Dickinson (Nairobi: East African Publishing House, 1972); and *Poems of Black Africa.*

Ndu, Pol. *Golgotha* (Ile-Ife, Nigeria: Pan-African, Pocket Poets 4, 1971).

*Songs for Seers, Poems 1960–7* (New York: Nok Publications, 1974).

Selection in *The Penguin Book of Modern African Poetry.*

Ofeimun, Odia. *The Poet Lied* (London: Longman, 1981).

Selection in *The Penguin Book of Modern African Poetry.*

Okai, Atukwei. *Oath of the Fontomfrom* (New York: Simon and Shuster, 1971).

*Lorgorligi Logarithms* (Accra: Ghana Publishing Corporation, 1974).

Selection in *Poems of Black Africa* and *The Penguin Book of Modern African Poetry.*

Okara, Gabriel. *The Fisherman's Invocation* (London: Heinemann, 1978).

Selections in *Poems of Black Africa; The Penguin Book of Modern African Poetry; A New Book of African Verse;* and *West African Verse.*

Okigbo, Christopher, *Labyrinths with Path of Thunder* (London: Heinemann, 1971).

*The Collected Poems of Christopher Okigbo*, ed. Adiwale Pearce, intro. Paul Theroux (London: Heinemann, 1986).

Selections in *Poems of Black Africa; The Penguin Book of Modern African Poetry A New Book of African Verse* and *West African Verse.*

Osadebay, Dennis. Selection in *West African Verse.*

Peters, Lenrie. *Satellites* (London: Heinemann, 1967).
  *Selected Poetry* (London: Heinemann, 1981).
  Selections in *Poems of Black Africa; The Penguin Book of Modern African Poetry* and *West African Verse* and *A New Book of African Verse*.
Rabéarivelo, Jean-Joseph. *Vieilles chansons du pays Imerina* (Tananarive: Editions madprint, 1980). (In English Translation) *Translations from the Night*, trans. and eds. John Reed and Clive Wake (London: Heinemann, 1975).
  Selection in *The Penguin Book of Modern African Poetry*, and *Poems of Black Africa*.
Sall, Ibrahima, *La Génération spontanée* (Dakar: Nouvelles Editions Africaines, 1975).
  *Crépuscules invraisemblables* (Dakar: Nouvelles Editions Africaines, 1977).
  *Le choix de madoir* (Dakar: Nouvelles Editions Africaines, 1981).
Sekyi, Kobina. *The Blinkards* (London: Rex Collings, 1974; London: Heinemann, 1974; Washington: Three Continents Press, 1974).
Senghor, Léopold Sédar, *Poèmes* (Paris: Seuil, Dakar: Nouvelles Editions Africaines, 1974), contains all of the work discussed in this study.
  *Elégies majeures suivi de dialogue sur la poésie francophone* (Paris: Seuil, 1979).
  *Selected Poems of Léopold Sédar Senghor*, ed. Abiola Irele (Cambridge: Cambridge University Press, 1977).
  Selected Editions in English: *Selected Poems*, trans. and eds. John Reed and Clive Wake (London; Oxford University Press, 1964; New York: Atheneum, 1964).
  *Prose and Poetry*, trans. and eds. John Reed and Clive Wake (London: Oxford University Press, 1965; London: Heinemann, 1976).
  *Nocturnes: Love Poems*, trans. John Reed and Clive Wake (London: Heinemann, 1969; New York: The Third Press, 1971).
  *Selected Poems*, trans. Craig Williamson (London: Rex Collings, 1976).
  Selections in *Poems of Black Africa; The Penguin Book of Modern African Poetry; The New Book of African Verse*; and *West African Verse*.
Silveira, Onésimo. Selections in *When the Bullets Begin to Flower; The Penguin Book of Modern African Poetry*; and *Poem of Black Africa*.
Soyinka, Wole. *Idanre and Other Poems* (London: Methuen, 1967; New York: Hill and Wang, 1968).
  *Poems from Prison* (London: Rex Collings, 1969).
  *A Shuttle in the Crypt* (London: Rex Collings, 1971; New York: Hill and Wang, 1972).
  *Ogun Abibimañ* (London: Rex Collings, 1976; Washington: Three Continents Press, 1976).
  Selections in *Poems of Black Africa; The Penguin Book of Modern African Poetry; A New Book of African Verse* and *West African Verse*.
Sutherland, Efua. Selection in *Messages*.
U'Tamsi, Tchikaya. *Arc Musical precédé de Epitomé* (Paris: Jean Oswald, 1970. Distributed by Harmattan, Paris).
  *la Veste d'intérieur suivi de Notes de veille* (Paris: Nubia, 1977).
  *Le Mauvais sang suivi de Feu de brousse et A Triche-Coeur* (Paris: Harmattan,

1978).

*Le Ventre suivi de le pain ou la cendre* (Paris: Présence Africaine, 1978).

Selections in *Poems of Black Africa; The Penguin Book of Modern African Poetry;* and *A New Book of African Verse.*

Wheatley, Phillis. *The Poems of Phillis Wheatley*, ed. Julian D. Mason, Jr (Chapel Hill, NC: University of North Carolina Press, 1966).

Extracts quoted in Richmond, Merle. *Bid the Vassal Soar: Interpretative Essays on the Life and Poetry of Phillis Wheatley, ca. 1753–1784, and George Moses Horton, ca. 1797–1883* (Washington D.C.: Howard University Press, 1974) and in Robinson, William, *Phillis Wheatley and Her Writings* (New York, London: Garland, 1984).

# Index